D0628704

Global Restructuring,
Employment, and Social Inequality
in Urban Latin America

Global Restructuring, Employment, and Social Inequality in Urban Latin America

Edited by

Richard Tardanico and Rafael Menjívar Larín

North·South Center Press
UNIVERSITY OF MIAMI

The publisher of this book is the North-South Center Press at the University of Miami.

The mission of the North-South Center is to promote better relations and serve as a catalyst for change among the United States, Canada, and the nations of Latin America and the Caribbean by advancing knowledge and understanding of the major political, social, economic, and cultural issues affecting the nations and peoples of the Western Hemisphere.

© 1997 North-South Center Press at the University of Miami.

 Published by the North-South Center Press at the University of Miami and distributed by Lynne Rienner Publishers, Inc., 1800 30th Street, Suite 314, Boulder, CO 80301-1026. All rights reserved under International and Pan-American Conventions. No portion of the contents may be reproduced or transmitted in any form, or by any means, including photocopying, recording, or any information storage retrieval system, without prior permission in writing from the North-South Center Press.

All copyright inquiries should be addressed to the publisher: North-South Center Press, 1500 Monza Avenue, Coral Gables, Florida 33146-3027, U.S.A., phone 305-284-8914, fax 305-284-5089, or e-mail mvega@nsc.msmail.miami.edu.

To order or to return books, contact Lynne Rienner Publishers, Inc., 1800 30th Street, Suite 314, Boulder, CO 80301-1026, 303-444-6684, fax 303-444-0824.

Cover photo of São Paulo © D. Donne Bryant Stock Photography, Michael Everett, photographer.

Library of Congress Cataloging-in-Publication Data

Global restructuring, employment, and social inequality in urban Latin America/edited by Richard Tardanico and Rafael Menjívar Larín.
    p. cm.
    Includes bibliographical references and index.
    ISBN 1-57454-019-X (alk. paper: pbk.)
    1. Labor supply — Latin America. 2. Structural adjustment (Economic policy) — Latin America. 3. Latin America — Economic policy. I Tardanico, Richard. II. Menjívar Larín, Rafael.
    HD5730.5.A6G56   1997
    338.98—dc21   97-30442
                                        CIP

Printed in the United States of America: EB/NC

02 01 00 99 98 97   6 5 4 3 2 1

Contents

Preface and Acknowledgments

Questions of geographic variability have risen to the fore of the burgeoning academic literature on the contemporary restructuring of the world economy. In contrast to the sweeping generalizations and economic reductionism of much of the early writings on this topic, recent perspectives tend to emphasize the mediation of world-scale shifts by variable local patterns of society, culture, and politics and increasingly by variable geostrategic relations as well. For the most part, though, this literature has been written from the standpoint of Europe, the United States, and Japan/East Asia, and thus it has said relatively little about the range of late twentieth-century transformations across the less-developed areas of the world. Its detailed empirical attention to the less-developed areas commonly has focused on their most advanced, "semiperipheral" cases, such as Brazil and Mexico, which sometimes are presented erroneously as more or less representative of less-developed countries at large. When poorer countries are mentioned, it often has been in terms of the very same style of sweeping generalizations and economic reductionism that used to characterize this body of writings on the whole. To be sure, rigorous scholarship has indeed come to examine key aspects of restructuring across Latin America, Asia, and Africa. This scholarship has tended to focus on the dynamics of state policy and on specific sectoral and social topics, such as export-assembly manufacturing, nontraditional agricultural production, the informal economy, and gendered employment. In the stage of infancy is the incorporation of such research into systematic comparisons of the features of socioeconomic restructuring that are taking shape in Latin America, Africa, and Asia.

In the case of Latin America, such comparisons assume importance in identifying the unfolding regional gamut of national, subnational, and transnational conditions, prospects, and options during an era of wrenching change. This project was conceptualized and carried out as a contribution to this intellectual, political, and policy process in Latin America, as well as to its counterpart processes in Africa and Asia and on a global scale.

As the project's co-directors, we thank the North-South Center at the University of Miami for having funded the project and enabled publication of this book in both English- and Spanish-language editions (the latter being published through the Facultad Latinoamericana de Ciencias Sociales [FLACSO]-Costa Rica). In particular, we thank Senior Editor Jayne Weisblatt for copy editing, Editorial Assistant Mary D'León for proofreading and composing the first draft of the index, Associate Publications Director Susan Kay Holler for creating the index and all the tables and sharing the formatting, Publications Director Mary Mapes for designing the cover and formatting the book, and Editorial Director Kathleen Hamman for overseeing the editorial side of our mini-transnational enterprise. We also thank FLACSO-Costa Rica and Florida International University's Latin American and Caribbean Center and Department of Sociology and Anthropology for having provided various essential forms of direct and indirect support. And, of course, we thank the contributing authors for having greatly enriched the project during its very slow evolution over the course of six years, as well as for having put up with the trials and tribulations of seemingly endless rounds of comment, revision, translation, and editing. We should mention that, with the principal exceptions of one early discussion/planning session involving most of the project's participants (at Florida International University, Spring 1992) and one mid-point paper-presenting session involving another, smaller set of participants (at the conference of the Latin American Studies Association, Washington, D.C., Fall 1995), this project was largely coordinated by means of sporadic, international communication. If there's one thing our group of editors and authors has firmly established, it's that the futurists need to beam down from cyberspace: a globalized culture of (very) long-distance communication will never rival face-to-face contact — especially over good food and drink — for sparking lively debate, hammering out ideas, and solidifying professional and personal bonds. On that note, we propose that — someday, somehow — our group reconvene on another balmy evening at the News Cafe in Miami Beach, where, to bring the project to a fitting, tropical close, one of our most esteemed members will again read our palms.

Richard Tardanico
Miami, Florida, USA

Rafael Menjívar Larín
San José, Costa Rica

Chapter 1

From Crisis to Restructuring: Latin American Transformations and Urban Employment in World Perspective[1]

Richard Tardanico

As the "lost decade" of the Latin American economy in the 1980s has yielded to tenuous, uneven reactivation in the 1990s, the interplay of growth and equity commands increasing attention in debates over the reshaping of national and regional development policies (Bulmer-Thomas 1996; Carnoy et al. 1993; ECLAC 1994b and 1994c; Ellison 1996; Korzeniewicz and Smith 1997; Lustig 1995; Morley 1995; Ramos 1995; Stewart 1995; Teitel 1992). National versus international, public versus private, centralized versus decentralized, and equitability versus accumulation are among the polarities that crisscross the political, economic, and social terrains of debate. What is arguably most novel about the discourse of the 1990s is the extent to which such polarities are dissolving into hybrid ideas that are generating more fluid, pragmatic approaches to addressing the contemporary manifestations of Latin America's long-term structural problems (for example, Davis 1992; Godio 1993; ILO 1991; Mesa-Lago 1994; PREALC 1991; Sheahan 1992; Stallings 1995; Sunkel 1995).

Coupled with the demise of military dictatorships, this trend toward more pragmatic approaches has fostered a certain optimism about the direction of Latin American development policy, above all in the neoliberal circles of government policymaking, international business, and multilateral agencies[2] (see Hayward 1995 and Smith, Acuña, and Gamarra 1994a). Yet the onset of severe financial crisis in Mexico in 1994-1995, the deepening of its austerity measures, and the contraction of the Mexican economy underscored the speculative and fragile basis of much of Latin America's recent economic growth. The combination of long-standing, fundamental problems of Latin American development, the contemporary politics of foreign debt and neoliberal policy, and the geographic reconfiguration of international investment, aid, and trade implies increased

Richard Tardanico is associate professor of sociology at Florida International University.

vulnerabilities for Latin American societies in the world economy[3] (Adelman 1995; Bulmer-Thomas 1996; Carnoy et al. 1993; Ellison 1996; Korzeniewicz and Smith 1997; Roberts 1995; Stallings 1995; Walton and Seddon 1994).

Underlying this view are the growing transnational mobility of capital and the declining importance of primary products and mid- to low-technology manufactured goods in a world economy whose most dynamic branches are based on advanced research and development, microchip technology, producer services, and finance capital. As Saskia Sassen (1994, 4) observes, under these circumstances "a vast territory...has become increasingly peripheral, increasingly excluded from the major economic processes that fuel economic growth in the new global economy." Latin America's leading national economies — or, more precisely, its most infrastructurally developed and strategically located subnational areas and economic subsectors — have the potential to make significant strides, though these seem more likely to widen the gap with the rest of the region than to reduce the gap with the world's most advanced zones (see Gereffi 1995 and Gereffi and Korzeniewicz 1994). Some areas ranked at the intermediate to lower echelons in economic infrastructure, diversity, and location stand to make strides as well, based on activities such as nontraditional agriculture and manufacturing, artisan production and tourism, and complementary services. Their gains will tend to be greatest where such activities intersect with socioterritorial structures and state policies that foster widespread local economic linkages and relative social equity. In contrast, those industries and localities that compete mainly on the bases of low cost and docile labor forces face the threat of not only intensified exploitation but also displacement from national and world circuits of accumulation (Amin 1994; Amsden and van der Hoeven 1996; Arrighi 1996; Fajnzylber 1990; Gereffi 1995; PREALC 1991; Roberts 1995; Sassen 1994; Stallings 1995; Wallerstein 1995).

Across this panorama cuts the matter of Latin American social inequality and poverty. By no means is this problem absent in the region's zones of greatest economic dynamism. Rather, its aggregate dimensions and compositional forms are likely to vary geographically in two ways: first, *among* the most advanced, the intermediate, and the most backward national and subnational locales; and second, *within* each of these tiers according to the interrelations of local matrices of state, society, and economy with global trends of market and geopolitics(see Bulmer-Thomas 1996; Díaz 1997; Evans 1995; Gereffi 1995; Gilbert 1994; McMichael 1994; Morley 1995; Portes 1989; Roberts 1995; Stewart 1995). In the more backward cases, it is likely that inequality and poverty impose especially severe limits on the nexus between transnational linkages and local development. Such limits may cause stagnation or regression in economic and social standards through what has become even more feared and resented than direct exploitation: withdrawal or neglect by local and foreign capital (Arrighi 1994, epilogue, and 1996; Carnoy et al. 1993; Grugel and Payne 1996; Roberts 1995; Sheahan 1992; Stallings 1995; Wallerstein 1995).

The threat of continued weakening of their position in the global division of labor extends to all Latin American countries but to widely varying degrees. It lies at the core of the increased salience of trade policy throughout the region, including the scramble to gain entry into a U.S.-based regional bloc of investment, production, and trade and also to strengthen such ties with East Asia.[4] Yet simultaneous recognition of cross-Latin American differences in the consequences of economic transnationalization for social inequality and poverty is sparking heightened awareness that, whether stressing liberalization or strategic protectionism, reforms of trade policy are just one part of the contemporary development equation.

Comparative historical evidence indicates that the long-range impact of increased international trade on local development may be positive, negative, or neutral, depending mainly on domestic institutional patterns and state policies, together with geopolitical relations (for example, Arrighi 1994; Cardoso and Faletto 1979; Evans 1995; Freeman 1994; Noponen, Graham, and Markusen 1993; Sanderson 1992; Sassen 1994; Sheahan 1992; Stallings 1995; Stewart 1995; Wallerstein 1979 and 1995). According to the evidence, then, trade policy by itself is rarely an effective agent of development. Essential to the possibility of its success are complementary macroeconomic and social policies that foster local infrastructural and socioeconomic gains, thereby enhancing local value-added, linkages, and equity.

To be sure, the implementation of such a policy formula is no mere matter of technical tinkering; it is powerfully bound up both with baseline development conditions and with vectors of national and transnational power that vary considerably across Latin America and across the less-developed world as a whole. At the same time, no policy formula can ensure that a given local, national, or regional economy will climb upward into more strategic positions in the transnational hierarchy of technology, capital, skill, and markets. This is particularly true under today's conditions of accelerating change, as the technology, capital, and skill components of global commodity chains experience constant and intense upward revision.[5] A consequence is that even during periods of local prosperity, economic actors and geographic areas may find themselves losing ground to more dynamic actors and areas — or, at least, to those whose geostrategic positions are more advantageous — elsewhere in the world division of labor (Arrighi 1994, epilogue; Gereffi and Korzeniewicz 1994; Stallings 1995; Wallerstein 1995).

Integration into a hemispheric economic bloc could neutralize or minimize relative displacement for Latin America, perhaps even activating some of its more stagnant territorial zones. On more circumscribed geographic and economic scales, the same could be true of commercial pacts that link particular Latin American countries and intraregional blocs to the European Community, East Asia, the wider Pacific Basin, and North American Free Trade Agreement (NAFTA) member countries; and of those intraregional blocs, such as the Southern Cone Common Market (MERCOSUR — Mercado Común del Cono Sur), that combine substantial economic size, diversity, and strength. Yet the benefits of such integration schemes are likely to accrue overwhelmingly to those subnational, national, and transnational areas of Latin America that are most competitive in state capacity, economic infrastructure, labor skills and productivity, and location, as well as that enjoy the greatest breadth and density of local socioeconomic linkages in finance, production, and commerce. Even in such cases, the degree of long-range development will be restricted greatly by their current worldwide ranking along these lines (Conroy and Glasmeier 1992-1993; Gereffi and Korzeniewicz 1994; Roberts 1995; Sheahan 1992; Varas 1995).

In the mid-1990s, the growth-inducing aspects of neoliberal reform in Latin America — market opening, privatization, and nontraditional exports — appear to have entered a phase of sharply decelerating returns or sheer exhaustion (Díaz 1997). Complicating this apparent phase are emergent twists, turns, and transformations. One example in contrast to the 1970s "early neoliberalism" of military-authoritarian Chile and Argentina is the seemingly distinctive political, social, and economic traits of the "late neoliberalism" of civilian democratic regimes in Brazil and Venezuela in the mid-1990s. Another example is the incipient "post-neoliberalism" of Chile.[6] Given the ambiguous and uncertain conditions of the late twentieth century, this discussion of baseline inequalities points to the worsening of inequality at several levels: between Latin America in general and the North American-Western European-East Asian axis of the world economy, between Latin America's more-developed and less-developed national and subnational areas, and between Latin America's wealthier and poorer social groups. This scenario calls not for continued neoliberal policies of austerity, reduced state protections for economy and society, and large-scale privatization but for innovative policies of agile, targeted state intervention, including supranationally orchestrated development initiatives.[7] For Latin America (as well as the underdeveloped world at large), the objective of such policies would be the bolstering of socioeconomic infrastructure, value-added, linkages, and social welfare on the widest territorial scale possible. In the absence of substantial progress along this path, significant social and geographic segments of Latin America will face long-run marginality in the world economy and exacerbated poverty, the implications of which are troubling for the prospects of authentic democratization[8] (see Bulmer-Thomas 1996; Korzeniewicz and Smith 1997; Roberts 1995 and 1996; Sunkel 1995; Varas 1995).

Transnational Restructuring, Urban Employment, and Social Inequality: Comparative Hypotheses

In reaction to the economism of neoliberal theory and policy is a resurgence of international scholarship on the economy's embeddedness in social institutions, ranging from households to the state (see Block 1989; Sayer and Walker 1992; Smelser and Swedberg 1994). Integral both to this scholarly current and to debate on the future of Latin American development is a comparative understanding of contemporary transformations of the region's employment structures. Employment simultaneously stands at the crossroads of Latin American and global patterns of restructuring and at the crossroads of Latin American patterns of state, economy, class, gender, and community. In short, the comparative analysis of late twentieth-century changes in Latin American employment structures is vital to a conceptualization of development policies that — especially in this age of intensified worldwide transformations — underscores the interdependence of economic growth, productivity, social and territorial equity, and political democracy across the region's diverse national and local settings.[9]

What, from this standpoint, are the key dimensions of contemporary employment restructuring? A starting point is recognition of the heuristic nature of the concept of "restructuring," as commonly used in the burgeoning literature on the reordering of the world economy during the late twentieth century (for example, Borocz and Smith 1995; Dicken 1992; Fainstein and Fainstein 1989; Gereffi 1995; McMichael 1994; Mittelman 1996; Noponen, Graham, and Markusen 1993; Palat 1996a and 1996b; Thurow 1996; Sassen 1994; Sayer and Walker 1992; Smith and Feagin 1987; Walton and Seddon 1994). The concept refers to basic, more-or-less-rapid change in the technical, social, political, and territorial organization of investment, production, trade, and aid. Among the shifts most typically identified are the transnationalization of communication, commerce, production, ownership, consumption, sociocultural reproduction, and politics; the increased segmentation and volatility of market demand; the organizational decentralization of firms and the enhanced flexibility of production; the strategic ascendance of finance capital and specialized services relative to manufacturing; the transfer of public resources to private hands; the proportional relocation of manufacturing activity from the United States and Western Europe to East Asia as well as poorer geographic areas; and deterioration in the average pay, stability, and other conditions of employment.

Four problems of the literature on global restructuring increasingly are recognized: It tends to 1) overgeneralize about the extent of restructuring across economic sectors, geographic areas, and social groups; 2) overemphasize contemporary discontinuities with past conditions of world capitalism, including a neglect of the possibility of the reversal of some contemporary shifts; 3) underplay the roles of culture and domestic and international politics in shaping the paths of local, national, and regional change; and 4) underestimate the continued importance of domestic market demand by governments, producers, and consumers (for example, Arrighi 1994 and 1996; Benería 1989; Block 1989; Borocz and Smith 1995; Chase-Dunn 1989; Fainstein and Fainstein 1989; Freeman 1994; Gilbert 1994; Glyn 1995; Kyle 1995; Logan and Swanstrom 1990; McMichael 1994; Mittelman 1996; Noponen, Graham, and Markusen 1993; Palat 1996a and 1996b; Pérez Sáinz 1994 and 1996; Piven 1995; Smith and Tardanico 1987; Stallings 1995; Wilson 1995). Some of these analytical problems are especially germane to Latin America, as well as to Africa and Asia. In this respect, perhaps most misleading is the literature's tendency to compress the diverse conditions of the countries and subnational zones of the underdeveloped world into a simplistic image of "the global assembly line" and derivative political regimes. To a considerable degree, this image reflects the literature's emphasis on the world's dominant and most innovative industry branches and geographic sites. Whatever the roots, it provides little insight into territorial and temporal variation across subordinate regions and countries regarding obstacles to development as well as potential resources and strategies for confronting such obstacles.[10]

From this perspective, a major part of the Latin American research and policy agenda seeks to disentangle the cyclical features of the economic downturn of the 1980s from the secular features of change in the region's linkages with a restructuring world economy. Among the components of this agenda are comparative and longitudinal studies both across Latin American cases and between cases in Latin America and other parts of the world, above all East Asia (Bulmer-Thomas 1996; Evans 1995; Fajnzylber 1990; Gereffi 1995; Gilbert 1994; Horton, Kanbur, and Mazumdar 1994; Marshall 1994; McMichael 1994; Palat 1996a and 1996b; Pérez Sáinz and Menjívar Larín 1991; Portes, Itzigsohn, and Dore-Cabral 1994; Roberts 1995; Stallings 1995).

Based on these concerns, this volume analyzes comparative trends in Latin America's contemporary urban restructuring in the context of world-scale transformations. It does so by focusing on national cases of change in urban employment and their nexus with emerging patterns of social inequality. The emphasis on *urban* Latin America reflects the fact that, as the primary winner in import-substitution development during the mid-twentieth century, urban Latin America has been the focal point of the process's institutional unraveling since the 1980s (Gilbert 1994; Portes 1989; Roberts 1995; Stewart 1995; Walton and Seddon 1994). Within this framework, the volume examines comparative Latin American change in urban employment and social inequality in terms of a series of hypotheses on labor markets drawn from the larger body of research on global restructuring. These labor market hypotheses involve the themes of sectoral recomposition, expansion of precarious and informal activities, gender recomposition, and territorial redistribution.

In worldwide perspective, the most basic prediction is that as a result of transnationalization, austerity, and privatization, employment conditions have become degraded for an enlarged portion of the labor force[11] (Aronowitz and DiFazio 1994; Arrighi 1996; Córdova 1996; Elson 1995; Gilbert 1994; ILO 1996; Kapstein 1996; McMichael 1994; Portes, Castells, and Benton 1989; PREALC 1991 and 1994; Roberts 1995; Sassen 1994; Standing and Tokman 1991; Sunkel 1995; Thurow 1996). Key questions for Latin America concern the validity of this prediction for the many economic and social divisions of its labor force within and across national boundaries. Equally important are ramifications for the region's current development patterns; for its everyday practices, alignments, and sociopolitical movements of class, ethnicity, gender, and community; for its state-society and state-state relations; for its emerging gamut of local relations with nongovernmental and suprastatal entities; and for the possibilities of defining and establishing alternative national and transnational development policies in the interests of equity and democracy.

Sectoral Recomposition

The point of departure for hypotheses on the sectoral recomposition of employment is that against the backdrop of the heightened transnational mobility and bargaining leverage of capital, state policies of austerity and privatization — as, so far, have been most zealously promulgated through the complex of ideology and institutions that Barbara Stallings and Wolfgang Streeck (1995) call the "Anglo-American model of capitalism"[12] — redistribute the socioeconomic burdens and benefits of fiscal policy (Bulmer-Thomas 1996; Elson 1995; Przeworski 1992; Smith, Acuña, and Gamarra 1994a and 1994b; Stewart 1995; Walton and Seddon 1994). A vital part of this redistribution is the reconfiguration of social access to public sector employment and its impact on the composition of employment overall. Worldwide, the massive creation of public sector employment during the early to late phases of the twentieth century was essential in broadening social access to stable, legally regulated jobs; in stimulating national economic transformations and the expansion of labor unions; and thus in improving labor's skills and living standards as well as securing its political commitment to the authority of national states. This was certainly true of Latin America under the mid-twentieth century's policies of state building and import-substitution industrialization[13] (Collier and Collier 1991; Infante and Klein 1991; Oliveira and Roberts 1994; PREALC 1991; Roberts 1995). It is therefore likely that the region's recent government policies of austerity and privatization have restricted access, particularly for semiskilled and unskilled workers, pushing an increased percentage of the labor force into insecure, unstable, and often informal employment and reducing the social welfare of workers and their households. The implications for social inequalities, development capacity, sociopolitical movements, and regime structures are major concerns (Arrighi 1996; Ellison 1996; Evans 1995; Gilbert 1994; ILO 1991 and 1996; Jelin 1997; Marshall 1994; PREALC 1991 and 1994; Roberts 1995 and 1996; Roxborough 1997; Smith, Acuña, and Gamarra 1994a; Walton and Seddon 1994).

For Latin America, then, a recent decline is hypothesized in the relative weight of employment in the public versus the private sector, through either contraction or slower growth.[14] According to the literature on restructuring, the impact of this decline on the industry structure of employment will be the continuation of the post-Second World War trend of fastest growth in tertiary jobs[15] (see Infante and Klein 1991 and PREALC 1991 and 1994). The main difference is that the new growth will be tied primarily to the damage inflicted by economic globalization and policies of austerity, privatization, and trade liberalization on locally oriented manufacturing and agricultural producers, rather than to the expansion of the state and of capital-intensive manufacturing production.

The argument begins by anticipating that economic transnationalization and neoliberal policies foster employment declines in import-substitution manufacturing and agricultural output for the domestic market, accelerating the long-term rise in the percentage of employment in tertiary activities. This is predicted to occur notwithstanding some job creation in manufacturing and agricultural production for export markets, possible job-making or job-conserving linkages with national import-substitution manufacturing,[16] new or continued availability of jobs in manufacturing for local niche markets under novel production arrangements, and decreased service jobs in the state sector. The argument goes on to anticipate an emergence or hastening of other changes as well: decline in the weight of government and social services relative to producer services, to modern and luxury consumer services (tourism, upscale and chain restaurants and shopping malls, supermarkets), and to petty commerce in the composition of tertiary employment and decline in the weight of unionized labor relative to nonunion labor. These processes can be expected to worsen the composition of tertiary employment in terms of earnings equality, job stability, and other conditions. The emerging socioeconomic structure of employment in producer services and luxury-consumer services is likely to promote the same trend (as discussed below under precarious and informal activities). Given the state-mediated interplay of shifts in the organization of production and the gendered features of households, labor conditions stand to become more differentiated and polarized within and across agriculture, manufacturing, and services (Amsden and van der Hoeven 1996; Carter, Barham, and Mesbah 1996; FitzGerald 1996; Gereffi 1995; ILO 1996; Lavinas and Nabuco 1995; McMichael 1994; Pérez Sáinz 1994 and 1996; Portes, Castells, and Benton 1989; Roberts 1995; Sassen 1994; Sunkel 1995; Thomas 1996; Weeks 1996).

Research on global restructuring does not predict the disappearance of the relatively advanced branches of manufacturing production across Latin American countries. It recognizes that depending on local economic composition, structures of state and social class, state policies and capacities, infrastructural conditions, and geopolitical and geomarket relations, some import-substitution manufacturing may make a successful transition to, or be replaced by, new transnationalized forms of advanced production. An alternative is that more advanced forms of export-oriented manufacturing may be introduced in certain places and will represent not only new activities but also substantial upgrades of the local economy's technology. Whatever the path, transitions are likely to incorporate some significant portion of labor whose skill and pay represent equivalence or gain for the workers, industry, and place (Gilbert 1994; Infante and Klein 1991; Lavinas and Nabuco 1995; Pérez Sáinz 1994 and 1996; Portes and Schauffler 1993; Roberts 1995). More generally, though, the research predicts that even as commerce and services come to command an enlarged share of total employment, a fast-growing part of many job markets has been manufacturing that is geared to low-wage flexible production, primarily for export. As the analysis of gender recomposition will explain, low-wage manufacturing has tended to be a site of job displacement for men but job growth for women. It also can be anticipated that in tandem with the privatization of public sector employment and the tertiarization of employment on the whole, the replacement of significant portions of import-substitution manufacturing by more fluid forms of manufacturing for export and local markets has tremendously weakened traditional urban-based labor unions.[17] The intersection of this pattern with tertiarization raises fundamental questions about the new kinds of labor and community organizations that eventually may crystallize in their place (Amsden and van der Hoeven 1996; Arrighi 1996; Carr 1996; Córdova 1996; Díaz 1997; Godio 1993; Hays-Mitchell 1995; Jelin 1997; *Latin American Labor News* 1995; Roberts 1996; Roxborough 1997; Schoepfle and Pérez-López 1993; Standing and Tokman 1991; Weeks 1996).

Hence, the restructuring literature anticipates a trend of differentiation and polarization in the skill, work conditions, and income of Latin America's labor force, juxtaposing general deterioration with significant social and geographic instances of successful adaptation and upgrading. It expects such uneven change to occur across industries, including in agriculture, where it predicts that investment in the production of nontraditional exports will displace many small landholders, pushing most of the displaced into insecure employment in rural and urban areas at home or abroad[18] (Carter, Barham, and Mesbah 1996; McMichael 1994; Roberts 1995; Thrupp 1995; Weeks 1995).

With respect to the industry composition of urban employment, studies on restructuring suggest three basic hypotheses: Tertiary employment has increased its share of total jobs; export employment has increased its share of total jobs in manufacturing;[19] and although some layers of the workforce have managed to protect or improve their conditions, low-wage employment has increased its share of jobs in all sectors.

Precarious and Informal Employment

Studies on restructuring stress the reorganization and downgrading of employment conditions worldwide. They emphasize that for a growing percentage of the labor force, employment is becoming more precarious — that is, less stable, less remunerative, less regulated by government authority, and in other ways less amenable to collective and individual control by workers. A central task of this volume is to contribute to research on how dimensions of reorganization and downgrading may vary not just between but within the hierarchical zones of the world economy. In any event, this process of change tends to begin as enterprises, responding to conditions of growing national and international competition, seek to undercut the leverage of states and organized labor in order to make production cheaper and more flexible. Political impetus, generated by the interaction of domestic and foreign capital, foreign agencies and states, and national state managers, is also integrated into the process, as governments alter their policies to foster export competitiveness. Change continues as the supply of labor force participants expands in response to decreased real earnings by household members, reduced government welfare subsidies, transnationalized consumerism, and shifting gender alignments in households and society at large. This particularly includes the expansion of the female labor force[20] (Arrighi 1996; Deyo 1989; Gilbert 1994; ILO 1996; Infante and Klein 1991; Marshall 1994; Oliveira and Roberts 1994; Pérez Sáinz and Menjívar Larín 1991; Portes, Castells, and Benton 1989; PREALC 1994; Standing and Tokman 1991; Thomas 1996; see also Blank 1994, Kapstein 1996, Thurow 1996, and Walters 1996).

The literature provides evidence that economic informalization — that is, the state's deregulation of existing economic activities as well as the growth of new activities beyond the bounds of state regulation — is not the only means of employment downgrading. Indeed, labor's losses also occur through deteriorating terms of formal employment and may occur primarily or exclusively through this channel. Because job earnings and conditions are heterogeneous in both the formal and informal economies, many entrepreneurs and brokers as well as mainstream workers prefer the informal economy because it provides advantages of pay, autonomy, and flexibility. In this respect, at the core of the emerging research and policy agenda is the concept of "neoinformality," which underscores that under certain structural conditions, informal economic activities may involve modalities of improved employment for some social groups, industries, and locales[21] (Despres 1991; Infante and Klein 1991; Itzigsohn 1996; Pérez Sáinz 1994 and 1996; Pérez Sáinz and Menjívar Larín 1991; Portes, Dore, and Landolt 1997; Rakowski 1994; Roberts 1995). Attached to this concept is the possibility that inasmuch as employment conditions become more fluid, differentiated, and unequal within the formal and informal economies alike, the controversial analytic distinction between the two spheres may, in some geographic places, be of diminishing relevance. This possibility — which includes less job stability and security for the middle classes in both wage and nonwage employment — points in the direction of placing less emphasis on change in the balance of formal versus informal labor and more emphasis on change in the social, industrial, occupational, and territorial dimensions of employment insecurity and instability.[22] Moreover, to the extent that many of the standard measurement proxies for formal versus informal employment (for example, wage versus nonwage, large firm versus small firm, full time versus part time) decreasingly capture variation in the severity and conditions of precariousness, researchers confront the methodological challenge of devising new indicators that better correspond to the more fluid and ambiguous realities of turn-of-the-century capitalism[23] (see Bodson, Cordero, and Pérez Sáinz 1995; Bromley and Birkbeck 1988; Díaz 1997; Tilly 1996; Walters 1996).

Clearly, then, the use of standard national data sources to analyze change in precarious and informal activities during the contemporary era — which is virtually unavoidable in a comparative-national project like this — grafts a new layer of methodological limitations onto those that other analysts have stressed (for example, Benería 1992; Elson 1995; Palat 1996a). Cognizant of such limitations, it is hypothesized that to the degree that precarious and informal activities have grown as a percentage of all urban employment in Latin American countries, studies will find increased rates of unemployment and increased proportions of employment in unregistered, nonwage, small-firm, contingent, part-time, and subminimum-wage jobs (see Berry 1994; Bromley and Birkbeck 1988; Córdova 1996; Ellison 1996; Gilbert 1994; Humphrey 1994; Pérez Sáinz and Menjívar Larín 1991; Portes, Castells, and Benton 1989; PREALC 1991 and 1994; Rakowski 1994; Roberts 1995; Schoepfle and Pérez-López 1993; Standing and Tokman 1991).

A related hypothesis stems from research on employment tertiarization and on employment restructuring. While the former predicts that manufacturing upgrades conditions, the latter predicts that over the last couple of decades this trend has been reversed (Amsden and van der Hoeven 1996; Despres 1991; Lawson 1995; Standing and Tokman 1991). Thus, if the tertiarization studies are correct, Latin America's indicators of precarious and informal employment should show manufacturing to be the industry of either greatest improvement or least deterioration.

Research on global restructuring leads one to expect diversification and polarization of employment conditions, with implications for interoccupational inequalities. For underdeveloped countries in particular, comparative research points out that employers tend to be the highest earners in both the formal and informal economies. It also demonstrates that whereas the self-employed who work in the informal economy as job brokers often earn more than wage workers in the formal as well as informal economies, a large portion of the self-employed engages in subsistence activities. For urban Latin America, therefore, it is anticipated that over the period of study the average earnings of employers were higher than those of wage workers and the self-employed, that the average earnings of wage workers were higher than those of the self-employed, and that as a reflection of economic restructuring, the earnings advantage of employers over the other occupational categories increased (Benería and Roldán 1987; Pérez Sáinz 1994; Pérez Sáinz and Menjívar Larín 1991; Portes, Dore, and Landolt 1997; Portes and Schauffler 1993; Roberts 1993).

These interoccupational patterns may be at odds, of course, with intraoccupational shifts. In fact, the comparative literature leads to the hypothesis that, even where average earnings by occupational category have risen, a worsening of intraoccupational inequalities is connected to the polarizing dimension of economic restructuring (Benería and Roldán 1987; Pérez Sáinz 1994; Portes and Schauffler 1993; Roberts 1993 and 1995; Standing and Tokman 1991; Ward 1990). Hence, based on shifts in the organization of production and markets across industries, it can be predicted that the category of employers became increasingly divided between relatively high-earning formal and informal layers, which tend to be overwhelmingly male, and low-earning informal layers, which tend to have a disproportionate percentage of females. Among wage workers, males and females alike probably became more stratified by income not only within firms but across firms according to their size, technology, organization, strategic importance and market share of production, foreign or domestic ownership, degree of incorporation into global markets, and formal or informal status. The self-employed, too, probably became more stratified by income. It can be expected that this involved relative gains by formal sector professionals and technicians, skilled craftspersons, and informal sector job brokers, combined with relative losses by informal sector petty merchants, service providers, and — insofar as they are officially classified as self-employed — domestic outworkers. A crucial question is under what conditions informal enterprises and jobs enable poor families and communities to achieve some degree of upward socioeconomic mobility[24] (Gilbert 1994; Pérez Sáinz 1994 and 1996; Pérez Sáinz and Menjívar Larín 1991; Portes, Dore, and Landolt 1997; Rakowski 1994; Roberts 1995).

Gender Recomposition

A principal theme of research on global restructuring is change in the gender balance of the labor market and its interrelations with the nonmarket dynamics of households (Benería 1989 and 1992; Boris and Prugl 1996; Elson 1995; Fernández Kelly 1994; Haddad et al. 1995; Menjívar Larín and Pérez Sáinz 1993; Safa 1995; Standing and Tokman 1991; Tiano 1994; Ward 1990; Wolf 1992; *World Development* 1995). The sources of change in these interrelations range from the secular (advances in technology, gains in women's rights and educational achievement, declines in fertility, changes in the structure of households, the spread and deepening of consumerism) to the cyclical (the economy's ups and downs, short-term socioeconomic impacts of state policies).

Most basically, this research predicts intensified growth in women's share of the officially measured labor force,[25] but it also predicts specific linkages of gender realignment with sectoral recomposition and the disproportionate expansion of low-skilled, low-paid, unstable, and legally unregulated jobs. The impact of austerity and privatization on the gender pattern of jobs in the public sector is critical, given its important role in the past in Latin American women's access to decent employment (see Infante and Klein 1991). After gauging this impact, analysis can turn to the consequences of austerity and privatization for the gender distribution of jobs across industries. Here, again, there is some divergence in hypotheses from studies on tertiarization and on restructuring. The former predict that even if female jobs in the public sector are reduced, employment growth for women will remain fastest in services and commerce (Infante and Klein 1991). The latter predict that countries experiencing major expansion of export-assembly production will see the fastest overall job growth for women in downgraded manufacturing sectors, and within those sectors growth in jobs for women will outpace that for men (Safa 1995; Standing and Tokman 1991; Ward 1990; Wolf 1992). Complicating the matter is an incipient shift, often connected to the upgrading of the technical content of jobs in export-assembly firms, whereby young men are sometimes gaining jobs formerly held by women, and thus may be redefining aspects of the gendered boundaries of employment (Lawson 1995; Pérez Sáinz 1994; Sklair 1993).

Concerning precarious and informal jobs, much of the literature on gender and labor markets claims that the downgrading of employment is virtually tantamount to growth in the labor force's percentage of female participants because women are disproportionately allocated into low-end jobs (see the discussions of this argument in Elson 1995; Gilbert 1994; Haddad et al. 1995; Lantican, Gladwin, and Seale, Jr. 1996; Rubery 1988; *World Development* 1995). For Latin America, this perspective leads to several more hypotheses: 1) Female employment grew fastest in precarious and informal jobs; 2) growth was faster for women than men in such jobs; 3) growth was slower for women than men in more desirable jobs; and 4) the gender distribution of earnings became more unfavorable to women. How these and other possible gender trends overlap with the previously raised issues of sociospatial patterns of subsistence and accumulation is central to the emerging agenda of development studies and policy.

Territorial Redistribution

The nature of change in the sociospatial organization of production and labor markets, not only transnationally but nationally across urban and rural locales, lies at the heart of research on world-scale restructuring. Such research emphasizes the contemporary organizational and geographic decentralization of some branches of production, especially at the middle to lower levels of manufacturing and services, as opposed to the continued or strengthened centralization of the most advanced services (Arrighi 1996; Dicken 1992; Gereffi 1995; Noponen, Graham, and Markusen 1993; Sassen 1991 and 1994). It can be expected that this global process has fostered a territorial dispersion of production and employment across urban Latin America, thereby reducing some aspects of the economic preeminence and dominance of the uppermost tier of metropolitan areas (Gereffi 1995; Gilbert 1990; Portes 1989; Roberts 1995; Sassen 1994).

Relevant to this is evidence that in contrast to an import-substitution era trend toward occupational uniformity across urban Latin America, the occupational profiles of the region's urban areas are now diversifying (Roberts 1995). One reason is that given transnationalization and the Latin American debt crisis, economic competition among firms, nations, and subnational localities has intensified on the basis of variable combinations of cheap labor, state subsidy, advanced technology, and market access. Another reason stems from the import-substitution era's state-led improvement in the economic infrastructure of intermediate urban areas and growth of their population relative to the dominant metropolises. The infrastructure and workforces of intermediate and even lower-tier urban areas therefore have become capable of sustaining export manufacturing. Furthermore, organized labor has been less influential in intermediate and smaller urban areas, and firms commonly have enjoyed more secure access to cheap, flexible labor in such areas than in the largest cities. Simultaneously or alternatively, new geographic patterns of agriculture and tourism may generate notable local offerings in regional services and craft industries.

Intersecting with these factors are others such as the transnationalization of communities and the production and trafficking of narcotics (Despres 1991; Gereffi 1995; Gilbert 1990; Kyle 1995; Maingot 1991; Pérez Sáinz 1994 and 1996; Portes 1989; Portes, Itzigsohn, and Dore-Cabral 1994; Roberts 1995; Sassen 1988 and 1994; Spener 1996).

The development prospects of localities depend, therefore, on their sociopolitical abilities not only to translate particular advantages into strategic niches in the national and world economies but also to find new, upwardly mobile niches in the face of accelerating market flux and transformations. This situation is fostering widened disparities in economic composition, employment structures, and development prospects between nations as well as between subnational zones. The character of such change depends on the relations of a country or geographic zone with emerging transnational circuits of investment, loans, aid, production, trade, and migration, as mediated by local conditions of state, economy, class, and culture.

Insofar as Latin American countries have conformed to this configuration, it is hypothesized that their labor markets have undergone territorial decentralization. This process could be led by a centrifugal push involving the rapid growth of export manufacturing. It could also include geographic redistribution in commerce and services that complements the provincial expansion of nontraditional agricultural exports and tourism. In many cases, new geographic patterns of migration and remittance may likewise be important, as at times may be the provincial expansion of narcotics production and trade. One consequence is likely to be greater diversity in occupational and class structure across localities. To the degree that export manufacturing and other decentralizing activities primarily employ women, then the territorial shifts are likely to promote gender realignments as well.

The Case Studies: An Orientation

Informed by this set of comparative hypotheses, the contributors to the volume examine contemporary urban patterns of employment restructuring and social inequality in the Dominican Republic, Guatemala, Costa Rica, Venezuela, Chile, Argentina, and Mexico. These cases provide substantial coverage from the lower to higher end of Latin American countries in economic size, population size and urbanization, industrialization, foreign investment, and export composition and dependency[26] (Table 3). In light of the period's continuing transition from military authoritarianism to formal democracy in Argentina, Chile, and Guatemala, the range in political regimes among the volume's case studies became more homogeneous by the mid-1980s to early 1990s, as the principal variation began to be defined by Mexico's outlying civilian-authoritarian state as well as by the marked differences in state-class relations, civil-military balance, and other state organizational traits that characterize the region's countries (Table 1; Cook, Middlebrook, and Molinar Horcasitas 1994; Nelson 1990; Smith, Acuña, and Gamarra 1994a and 1994b; Stallings and Kaufman 1989). Finally, pronounced contrast is the rule with respect to geostrategic location. On the one extreme, adjacency or proximity to the United States has been a powerful force in shaping the political economies and policy options of the Caribbean Basin countries of Mexico, the Dominican Republic, Guatemala, Costa Rica, and Venezuela, though not to be underestimated is the extent of difference in the manifestation of this force across these national cases. On the other extreme, the location of Argentina and Chile far away from the United States in the Southern Cone has shaped their distinctive geopolitical optics, which in turn carry implications for the past and present characteristics of their domestic political economies. Nonetheless, examples such as the U.S. government's roles in Chile's collapse of democracy in the early 1970s, the course of Chilean and Argentine policies of austerity and deregulation, Argentina's transition in the 1980s from military to civilian rule, the role of U.S. capital in the privatization of state enterprises in the Southern Cone in the 1990s, and the continued possibility of North American-South American economic integration underline the significance of U.S. geopolitical and economic influence in the southernmost tier of the Americas (Díaz 1997; Grugel and Payne 1996; Nelson 1990; Smith, Acuña, and Gamarra 1994a and 1994b; Stallings 1995; Stallings and Kaufman 1989)

It is helpful to review briefly the experiences of these countries with economic crisis and structural adjustment since the 1970s (see Tables 1 through 3). Latin America's economic crisis of the 1980s was rooted in the structural weaknesses of the import-substitution development model, together with a surge in government borrowing of petrodollars from foreign

Table 1.
Regime Types

Established Electoral-Democratic
Costa Rica
Dominican Republic
Venezuela
From Military-Authoritarian to Transitional Electoral-Democratic
Argentina
Chile
Guatemala
Civilian-Authoritarian
Mexico

Sources: Kauffman and Stallings 1989; Nelson 1990; Smith, Acuña, and Gamarra 1994a and 1994b; Portes, Itzigsohn, and Dore-Cabral 1994.

Table 2.
Latin American Labor-Market Trends

Average Real Wages (1990=100)

	1980	1985	1988	1989	1991	1992	1993	1994	1995[a]
Argentina	130.0	135.7	118.0	95.5	101.3	102.7	101.0	102.0	100.9
Bolivia	—	64.9	92.4	97.6	93.4	97.1	103.6	112.8	115.2
Brazil									
Rio de Janeiro	94.0	96.2	109.8	111.9	79.3	79.5	85.7	87.1	87.9
São Paulo	88.6	93.8	108.0	111.7	88.3	85.3	94.6	98.0	98.2
Chile	95.4	89.3	96.3	98.2	104.9	109.6	113.5	118.8	123.3
Colombia	85.0	97.4	100.0	101.3	97.4	98.6	103.2	104.1	104.2
Costa Rica	115.8	106.8	97.8	98.4	95.4	99.3	109.6	113.8	111.5
Ecuador	—	135.2	110.8	99.3	104.6	112.8	122.1	132.9	—
Guatemala	122.5	121.6	117.8	122.2	93.6	107.6	115.2	122.9	—
Mexico	128.3	97.4	92.1	96.5	106.5	114.3	124.5	129.1	112.0
Nicaragua	477.6	262.5	37.3	61.9	103.2	123.0	118.8	121.4	—
Panama	96.2	103.4	99.1	106.6	103.8	106.2	106.1	—	—
Paraguay	102.1	90.1	104.8	108.9	104.7	103.6	104.5	106.1	—
Peru	309.3	250.2	208.6	114.5	115.2	111.1	110.2	127.4	122.6
Uruguay	108.5	95.5	108.3	107.9	103.8	106.1	111.2	112.2	109.1
Venezuela	—	184.5	144.5	105.9	89.5	98.7	75.3	—	—

Urban Real Minimum Wages (1990=100)

	1980	1985	1988	1989	1991	1992	1993	1994[a]
Argentina	465.9	541.5	442.2	323.5	259.1	203.7	263.7	363.9
Bolivia	—	185.5	131.1	117.2	165.6	164.8	181.2	199.9
Brazil	138.4	135.0	129.9	133.1	112.8	102.5	113.0	107.4
Chile	114.4	87.3	84.5	91.3	109.3	114.3	120.0	124.4
Colombia	93.1	101.4	101.9	102.7	96.7	95.0	97.6	96.0
Costa Rica	82.7	93.5	95.1	99.1	92.8	92.5	92.7	93.6
Dominican Republic	153.3	122.9	133.9	119.2	101.6	123.7	117.6	125.0
Ecuador	288.3	203.6	140.5	110.2	87.0	87.1	100.0	115.9

Continued on next page

Table 2—*Continued*

Urban Real Minimum Wages (1990=100) (Continued)

	1980	1985	1988	1989	1991	1992	1993	1994[a]
El Salvador	287.2	190.1	125.2	106.3	97.8	101.0	97.8	99.8
Guatemala	207.5	195.0	157.5	141.3	80.7	72.5	62.8	—
Haiti	136.2	124.4	129.1	120.3	84.6	71.7	60.3	44.3
Honduras	118.0	105.1	94.1	85.7	100.1	113.4	115.5	94.8
Mexico	252.9	181.2	136.4	111.4	95.8	90.9	89.4	89.6
Panama	100.8	101.8	100.5	100.7	98.9	97.4	108.8	107.3
Paraguay	76.4	75.6	102.7	104.5	95.6	87.1	83.8	86.0
Peru	428.0	232.8	222.4	107.3	68.0	68.0	47.8	61.9
Uruguay	145.0	134.8	122.2	112.8	89.6	87.4	75.8	67.3
Venezuela	171.4	165.5	163.3	126.1	86.9	123.6	106.3	116.7

Urban Open Unemployment (Average annual rates)

	1987	1988	1989	1990	1991	1992	1993	1994	1995[a]
Argentina	5.9	6.3	7.6	7.5	6.5	7.0	9.6	11.5	18.6
Bolivia	7.2	11.6	10.2	9.5	7.3	5.8	5.4	5.8	—
Brazil	3.7	3.8	3.4	4.3	4.8	5.8	5.4	5.1	4.7
Chile	11.9	10.2	7.2	6.5	7.3	5.0	4.1	6.3	5.6
Colombia	11.8	11.3	10.0	10.5	10.2	10.2	8.6	8.9	8.6
Costa Rica	5.9	6.3	3.7	5.4	6.0	4.3	4.0	4.3	—
Ecuador	7.2	7.4	7.9	6.1	8.5	8.9	8.9	7.8	8.4
El Salvador	—	9.4	8.4	10.0	7.5	7.9	8.1	7.2	7.5
Guatemala	11.4	8.8	6.1	6.5	6.4	5.7	5.5	5.2	4.3
Honduras	11.4	8.7	7.2	6.9	7.1	5.1	5.9	6.3	4.5
Mexico	3.9	3.5	2.9	2.7	2.7	2.8	3.4	3.7	6.4
Nicaragua	5.8	6.0	8.4	11.1	14.2	17.8	21.8	20.7	20.2
Panama	14.1	21.1	20.4	20.0	19.3	17.5	15.5	15.8	14.3
Paraguay	5.5	4.7	6.1	6.6	5.1	5.3	5.1	4.6	4.8
Peru	4.8	7.1	7.9	8.3	5.9	9.4	9.9	8.8	8.2
Uruguay	9.3	9.1	8.6	9.3	8.9	9.0	8.4	9.1	10.7
Venezuela	9.9	7.9	9.7	11.0	10.1	8.1	6.8	8.7	10.3

Sources: CEPAL 1995; ECLAC 1995a and 1996.
a = Preliminary figures.

Table 3.
Macroeconomic and Social Data[a]

Dominican Republic

	1980	1992	Net Growth Rate
Population	5,697[b]	7,471[b]	31.1%
GDP	6,438[c]	8,314[c]	29.1%
GDP per Capita	1,130	1,113	-1.5%
Agriculture/GDP	20.2%	17.9%	
Manufacturing/GDP	15.3%	14.1%	
Exports/GDP	14.9%	9.0%	
Imports/GDP	23.6%	23.6%	
Manufactured Exports/ Total Exports	N.A.	N.A.	
Gross Fixed Investment/GDP	23.4%	22.2%	
Trade Balance	-647	-582	
Balance on Current Accounts	-725	-478	
Debt Interest Due/Total Exports	18.0%[d]	12.1%	
% Urban Population	50.5%	60.4%[e]	
Infant Mortality Rate	74.5%[f]	56.5%[g]	
Illiteracy Rate	31.4%	16.7%[h]	
% Poor Urban Households	N.A.	N.A.	
Income of Top 10%: Bottom 40% Urban Households	N.A.	N.A.	

Sources: ECLAC 1993, 1994a, and 1995b; World Bank 1994.
a = Countries listed in order of chapter presentation
b = Thousands of persons
c = Millions of dollars, 1980 prices
d = 1979-1981
e = 1990
f = 1980-1985
g = 1990-1995
h = Estimate for 1990

Continued on next page

Table 3—*Continued*

Guatemala

	1980	1992	Net Growth Rate
Population	6,917[a]	9,744[a]	40.9%
GDP	7,801[b]	9,206[b]	18.0%
GDP per Capita	1,128	945	-16.2%
Agriculture/GDP	27.1%	27.7%	
Manufacturing/GDP	17.6%	15.5%	
Exports/GDP	19.5%	16.4%	
Imports/GDP	18.9%	24.5%	
Manufactured Exports/ Total Exports	24.4%	29.9%	
Gross Fixed Investment/GDP	15.7%	13.6%	
Trade Balance	-228	-955	
Balance on Current Accounts	-165	-758	
Debt Interest Due/Total Exports	5.3%[c]	8.8%	
% Urban Population	38.5%	42.0%[d]	
Infant Mortality Rate	70.4%[e]	48.5%[f]	
Illiteracy Rate	44.2%	44.9%[g]	
% Poor Urban Households	41.0%	54.0%[h]	
Income of Top 10%: Bottom 40% Urban Households	11.6[h]	12.5[i]	

Sources: ECLAC 1993, 1994a, and 1995b; World Bank 1994.
a = Thousands of persons
b = Millions of dollars, 1980 prices
c = 1979-1981
d = 1990
e = 1980-1985
f = 1990-1995
g = Estimate for 1990
h = 1986
i = 1989

Continued on next page

Table 3—*Continued*

Costa Rica

	1980	1992	Net Growth Rate
Population	2,284[a]	3,191[a]	39.7%
GDP	3,545[b]	4,839[b]	36.5%
GDP per Capita	1,552	1,516	-2.3%
Agriculture/GDP	17.8%	19.4%	
Manufacturing/GDP	18.6%	19.1%	
Exports/GDP	28.2%	46.6%	
Imports/GDP	38.8%	41.0%	
Manufactured Exports/ Total Exports	29.8%	24.5%[c]	
Gross Fixed Investment/GDP	23.9%	22.7%	
Trade Balance	-460	-323	
Balance on Current Accounts	-659	-446	
Debt Interest Due/Total Exports	19.7%[d]	8.5%	
% Urban Population	46.0%	53.6%[e]	
Infant Mortality Rate	19.2%[f]	13.7%[g]	
Illiteracy Rate	7.4%	7.2%[h]	
% Poor Urban Households	16.0%[i]	25.0%	
Income of Top 10%: Bottom 40% Urban Households	4.9[i]	6.4	

Sources: ECLAC 1993, 1994a, and 1995b; World Bank 1994.
a = Thousands of persons
b = Millions of dollars, 1980 prices
c = 1991
d = 1979-1981
e = 1990
f = 1980-1985
g = 1990-1995
h = Estimate for 1990
i = 1981

Continued on next page

Table 3—*Continued*

Venezuela

	1980	1992	Net Growth Rate
Population	15,024[a]	20,187[a]	34.4%
GDP	61,597[b]	74,983[b]	21.7%
GDP per Capita	4,100	3,714	-9.4%
Agriculture/GDP	4.2%	4.4%	
Manufacturing/GDP	18.8%	19.7%	
Exports/GDP	30.9%	32.0%	
Imports/GDP	17.7%	16.3%	
Manufactured Exports/ Total Exports	1.5%	11.0%	
Gross Fixed Investment/GDP	29.0%	21.3%	
Trade Balance	4,838	-1,290	
Balance on Current Accounts	4,749	-3,356	
Debt Interest Due/Total Exports	9.5%[c]	17.4%	
% Urban Population	83.3%	90.5%[d]	
Infant Mortality Rate	38.7%[e]	33.7%[f]	
Illiteracy Rate	15.3%	11.9%[g]	
% Poor Urban Households	18.0%[h]	32.0%	
Income of Top 10%: Bottom 40% Urban Households	4.3[h]	6.8	

Sources: ECLAC 1993, 1994a, and 1995a; World Bank 1994.
a = Thousands of persons
b = Millions of dollars, 1980 prices
c = 1979-1981
d = 1990
e = 1980-1985
f = 1990-1995
g = Estimate for 1990
h = 1981

Continued on next page

Table 3—*Continued*

Chile

	1980	**1992**	**Net Growth Rate**
Population	11,145[a]	13,599[a]	22.0%
GDP	25,296[b]	37,723[b]	49.1%
GDP per Capita	2,270	2,774	22.2%
Agriculture/GDP	7.0%	8.7%	
Manufacturing/GDP	15.1%	15.3%	
Exports/GDP	18.6%	29.9%	
Imports/GDP	21.6%	23.3%	
Manufactured Exports/ Total Exports	11.3%	13.2%	
Gross Fixed Investment/GDP	16.6%	20.6%	
Trade Balance	-1,055	886	
Balance on Current Accounts	-2,020	-940	
Debt Interest Due/Total Exports	24.7%[c]	11.2%	
% Urban Population	81.1%	85.6%[d]	
Infant Mortality Rate	23.7%[e]	16.9%[f]	
Illiteracy Rate	8.9%	6.6%[g]	
% Poor Urban Households	38.0%[h]	28.0%	
Income of Top 10%: Bottom 40% Urban Households	12.6[h]	11.9	

Sources: ECLAC 1993, 1994a, and 1995b; World Bank 1994.
a = Thousands of persons
b = Millions of dollars, 1980 prices
c = 1979-1981
d = 1990
e = 1980-1985
f = 1990-1995
g = Estimate for 1990
h = 1987

Continued on next page

Table 3—*Continued*

Argentina

	1980	1992	Net Growth Rate
Population	28,237[a]	33,101[a]	17.2%
GDP	116,067[b]	125,348[b]	8.0%
GDP per Capita	4,110	3,787	-7.9%
Agriculture/GDP	6.3%	7.1%	
Manufacturing/GDP	29.3%	28.3%	
Exports/GDP	6.9%	12.7%	
Imports/GDP	8.1%	8.2%	
Manufactured Exports/ Total Exports	23.1%	26.3%	
Gross Fixed Investment/GDP	25.1%	18.5%	
Trade Balance	-3,188	-3,565	
Balance on Current Accounts	-4,774	-8,361	
Debt Interest Due/Total Exports	24.1%[c]	28.5%	
% Urban Population	82.7%	86.2%[d]	
Infant Mortality Rate	36.0%[e]	28.8%[f]	
Illiteracy Rate	6.1%	4.7%[g]	
% Poor Urban Households	5.0%[h]	10.0%[h]	
Income of Top 10%: Bottom 40% Urban Households	6.7	8.3	

Sources: ECLAC 1993, 1994a, and 1995b; World Bank 1994.
a = Thousands of persons
b = Millions of dollars, 1980 prices
c = 1979-1981
d = 1990
e = 1980-1985
f = 1990-1995
g = Estimate for 1990
h = Buenos Aires

Continued on next page

Table 3—*Concluded*

Mexico

	1980	1992	Net Growth Rate
Population	67,046[a]	88,153[a]	31.5%
GDP	175,918[b]	221,014[b]	25.6%
GDP per Capita	2,624	2,507	-4.5%
Agriculture/GDP	8.2%	7.3%	
Manufacturing/GDP	22.1%	22.8%	
Exports/GDP	8.8%	18.0%	
Imports/GDP	10.7%	19.9%	
Manufactured Exports/ Total Exports	12.1%	52.3%[c]	
Gross Fixed Investment/GDP	24.8%	21.1%	
Trade Balance	-4,365	-18,318	
Balance on Current Accounts	-10,789	-22,924	
Debt Interest Due/Total Exports	31.8%[d]	18.9%	
% Urban Population	66.4%	72.6%[e]	
Infant Mortality Rate	48.8%[f]	35.2%[g]	
Illiteracy Rate	16.0%	12.4%[h]	
% Poor Urban Households	28.0%[i]	30.0%	
Income of Top 10%: Bottom 40% Urban Households	5.1[i]	8.4	

Sources: ECLAC 1993, 1994a, and 1995b; World Bank 1994.
a = Thousands of persons
b = Millions of dollars, 1980 prices
c = Preliminary figure
d = 1979-1981
e = 1990
f = 1980-1985
g = 1990-1995
h = Estimate for 1990
i = 1984

banks, the onset of First World recession, the escalation of international interest rates, a plunge in regional terms of trade, and the withdrawal of private foreign lending (see Arrighi 1994, 302-324, 331; Stewart 1995, Chapter 7; Suter 1992). Guatemala, which was simultaneously engulfed by extreme sociopolitical violence, emerged with the greatest percentage of net loss in domestic product per capita among the entire group of countries between 1980 and 1992 (Table 3). Contributing to this and other forms of severe socioeconomic loss in Guatemala was the failure of the feebly constructed, post-military government that began in 1986 successfully to implement a Christian-Democratic brand of structural adjustment (Pérez Sáinz this volume, Chapter 3; Trudeau 1993). In the Dominican Republic, the government's response to economic downturn mirrored the country's own variant of polarized as well as fragmented domestic conditions when it slashed both the average pay of workers and the nation's flimsy welfare safety net (Espinal 1995; Itzigsohn this volume, Chapter 2; Nelson 1990). In both countries, though, the value of nontraditional exports has risen sharply since the 1980s, even as the overall value of their exports as a percentage of gross domestic product (GDP) has declined (Table 3; Itzigsohn this volume, Chapter 2; Pérez Sáinz this volume, Chapter 3).

In Costa Rica, whose economy in size and composition is similar to the Guatemalan and Dominican economies, the politics of adjustment has diverged strikingly from theirs in that its measures of social welfare rank in the upper echelon of Latin American countries (ECLAC 1995b; World Bank 1995). Costa Rica seriously lost ground in domestic product per capita, the average pay of workers, and other indicators of living standards during the early 1980s. Yet its economy gathered considerable momentum thereafter, as many of the country's economic and social indicators recovered completely or substantially. The reason was the juxtaposition of the social-democratic structure, stability, and other organizational traits of the Costa Rican state with a class structure whose conflicts had been diffused rather than polarized and with the geopolitics of U.S. intervention and aid in response to revolution and warfare elsewhere in Central America. Compared with Guatemala and the Dominican Republic, therefore, Costa Rica's leadership could mobilize sufficient domestic consensus and foreign aid to maintain a high degree of continuity with its post-Second World War model of social-democratic development, even as it undertook to dismantle much of the country's import-substitution apparatus. In doing so, leadership boosted Costa Rica into the upper tier of the Caribbean Basin in the growth of nontraditional agricultural and assembled exports as well as international tourism (Table 3; Dunkerley 1988; Nelson 1990; Pérez Sáinz 1994 and 1996; Tardanico and Lungo this volume, Chapter 4).

With respect to the group of larger national economies,[27] the cases of Argentina and Chile demand a broadening of attention to the 1970s, when their democracies collapsed, their states became militarized, and their economies contracted. In Argentina, military repression and the local brand of sociopolitical polarization and fragmentation played a key role in perpetuating that country's macroeconomic crisis and in worsening poverty while weakening its statist and nationalist orientation. In Chile, the unity of the governing coalition and the disunity of its opposition enabled the military government's leadership to use official violence and neoliberal orthodoxy to tear down state-centered development institutions in favor of a privatized, denationalized model (Acuña 1994; Petras and Leyva 1994).

In Argentina, humiliating defeat in the Malvinas War plus continued economic crisis and state terrorism fostered both the unification of opposition groups and rifts within the military government, eventuating in the latter's demise in the early 1980s. Consistent with a domestic political context of disarray, the economy's performance remained erratic under the subsequent succession of heterodox and orthodox adjustment policies, whose impact included hyperinflation and a plunge in living standards for much of the population. With the end of hyperinflation in 1991-1992, Latin America's most sweeping program of neoliberal reform and privatization attracted a massive injection of foreign investment and triggered rapid aggregate economic expansion. The basis of Argentina's upswing was speculative, however. Even as demand from its MERCOSUR partners (primarily Brazil) provided a major boost to the country's export performance, the economy's job-producing capacity remained flat, and social and regional inequalities worsened. Argentina's vulnerabilities were more clearly exposed in 1995-1996 as its macroeconomic and social indicators took a dive as part of the regional fallout from Mexico's financial crisis (Acuña 1994; Canitrot 1994; CEPAL 1995; Cortés this volume, Chapter 7; ECLAC 1996; Ellison 1996).

The transition from military to civilian government began later in Chile than Argentina, with the unification of opposition groups occurring not under economic regression and hyperinflation but during a region-leading surge in prosperity premised on a combination of abundant local natural resources; advanced production technologies in mining, agriculture, forestry, and agroindustrial processing; and burgeoning world-market demand (Díaz this volume, Chapter 6; Table 3; see Collins and Lear 1995). This export-based prosperity has endured during the post-military years of the 1990s. Yet, given the continued political leverage of the military and its rightist allies, the trend toward more complicated alignments of social class, a widespread sociopolitical stake in not jeopardizing the economy's robustness, and a technocratic slant in post-military governance, the civilian-implemented changes in Chilean adjustment policy have been modest on the whole. Post-authoritarian social policies and economic growth have sharply reduced the percentage of Chileans living in official poverty but without seriously redressing the twenty-year trajectory of greatly worsening income inequality. Although social indicators still place Chile in Latin America's top tier along with Argentina, Uruguay, and Costa Rica,[28] its income distribution remains second to Brazil's as the region's most unequal. Against this backdrop, Chile's economic, political, and social conditions encompass a complex mix of profound and intriguing structural change, including sharply divided access to the fruits of macroeconomic prosperity and emerging sociopolitical pressures toward a post-neoliberal order (Díaz this volume, Chapter 6; Collins and Lear 1995; Garretón 1994; Petras and Leyva 1994; Vergara 1994).

In Mexico, a highly centralized, civilian-authoritarian state and pronounced sociopolitical disunity among actual and potential opposition across the class spectrum enabled government leadership to orchestrate a largely orthodox policy response to economic downturn. These conditions also protected the monopoly of the governing Institutional Revolutionary Party (Partido Revolucionario Institucional — PRI) in the face of acute socioeconomic repercussions and widespread predictions of the demise of the state's one-party structure. With the continuation of the largely orthodox approach, the market, migratory, and political advantages of adjacency to the United States facilitated a modest, sectorally and socially uneven recovery into the mid-1990s (Cook, Middlebrook, and Molinar Horcasitas 1994; Oliveira and García this volume, Chapter 8). Mexico and Chile rank as the major Latin American economies having undergone the most thorough recent export-based transformations[29] (Díaz this volume, Chapter 6; Varas 1995, 287-289, 300- 308). In this setting, Mexico has experienced the politics of NAFTA, the exacerbation of long-standing rifts within the PRI, agrarian rebellion in the southern periphery, the assassination of the PRI's candidate for the presidency, and increasingly common PRI election losses. Definitively undercutting the credibility of international and official Mexican optimism about the course of structural adjustment — including sanguine predictions about the rapidity and scope of NAFTA-based gains — was the precipitate fall in the value of the peso in 1994-1995. This led to economic contraction, a massive new injection of foreign loans, the implementation of yet another stage of painful austerity measures, deepened problems of social inequality and poverty, and intensified pressures for the dissolution of one-party governance (Oliveira and García this volume, Chapter 8).

Finally, economic crisis during the 1980s cut deep into the neopopulist appendages of the Venezuelan state's elitist and ossified two-party system, thereby rupturing the socioeconomic and, eventually, political tendons of the country's "exceptionalism." By the late 1980s, the crisis led to a government program of radical orthodoxy that neither operated through the established institutional channels of state-society relations nor attempted to forge new ones. There ensued several years of rapid but structurally unsustainable and sectorally jagged economic growth. In the absence of government initiatives to either buttress the traditional political edifice or build modified structures, the harsh social impact of the orthodox program and its pattern of economic growth generated violent mass protest, military revolt, fissures within the party system, and other dimensions of governmental instability.[30] These problems have since been compounded by the economy's marked per-capita decline and by ambiguous, contradictory state policies veering between neopopulist and neoliberal (Fajardo Cortez and Lacabana this volume, Chapter 5; Goodman et al. 1995; McCoy et al. 1995). The intersection of the renewed commitment of civilian-democratic state leadership to market-oriented reform with highly mobilized domestic political resistance has made Venezuela — along with Brazil under the presidency of Fernando Henrique Cardoso — a prime example of "late neoliberalism."

Against the background of global restructuring, these national trajectories provide the context for this volume's assessment of comparative Latin
American paths of contemporary transformation in urban employment and
socioeconomic inequality. There are several limitations, however. First,
pronounced differences in the availability and quality of data across the
national cases restrict the comparative analysis to approximations. Second,
the data do not always permit the disentangling of cyclical and secular
features of change. And third, the data go just minimally beyond structural
trends of socioeconomic inequality, thereby leaving largely unexamined
the fundamental role of human agency in shaping the gender, household,
community, class, state, and ideological dimensions of both restructuring
and the quest for alternatives (Bergquist 1986; Buchanan 1995; Collier and
Collier 1991; Eckstein 1990; Evans 1995; Hays-Mitchell 1995; Jelin 1997;
Roxborough 1997; Smith and Tardanico 1987; Walton and Seddon 1994).[31]
Nonetheless, the case studies permit rich exploratory analysis of urban Latin
America's variation in the socioeconomic aspects of restructuring, a
necessary step in identifying changes in macro-micro linkages and in
making appropriate policies toward the objectives of equity, productivity,
sustainability, and democracy.

This chapter's discussion of country comparisons has introduced the
basic approach of the case-study authors: José Itzigsohn on the Dominican
Republic, Juan Pablo Pérez Sáinz on Guatemala, Richard Tardanico and
Mario Lungo on Costa Rica, Víctor Fajardo Cortez and Miguel Lacabana on
Venezuela, Alvaro Díaz on Chile, Rosalía Cortés on Argentina, and
Orlandina de Oliveira and Brígida García on Mexico. This approach
considers, at least in broad terms, the state organization, economic
composition, social and territorial structures, and external economic and
geopolitical relations of each country. In this setting, it examines the
contours of each country's recent experience with economic crisis and
structural adjustment. It then devotes the bulk of analysis to documenting
urban patterns of employment restructuring and social inequality within the
framework of the comparative hypotheses presented in this chapter. The
concluding chapter, by Tardanico and Rafael Menjívar Larín, compares the
national cases of urban restructuring and social inequality and lays the
groundwork not only for further research on these cases but also for
comparison with other cases in Latin America and beyond.

Notes

1.   My thanks to Rafael Menjívar Larín, the co-director of the research project upon which this book is based, and to the project's participants for many of the ideas expressed in this chapter; to Diane Leiva and Craig Wrathell for research assistance; and to Walter Goldfrank for his helpful comments on an earlier draft. Whatever is wrong with the chapter is my fault alone.

2.   On both the fundamental ideas and the national and temporal variants of neoliberalism as an ostensibly laissez-faire approach to politico-economic reform, see Arrighi 1994; Díaz 1997; Elson 1995; Korzeniewicz and Smith 1997; Przeworski 1992; Roberts 1995; Smith, Acuña, and Gamarra 1994a and 1994b; Stallings 1995; Stallings and Kaufman 1989; Wallerstein 1995; and Walton and Seddon 1994. These writings indicate that without denying the importance of national and temporal variation, neoliberal reforms are not weakening the Latin American state's role across the board, as the proponents of such reforms claim. Rather, they are strengthening the state's role at some levels (for example, regulating financial markets, coordinating international investment and trade, promoting technological and organizational innovation, neutralizing or repressing oppositional groups) while weakening it at others (such as the establishment and protection of national industries, the creation of employment, the protection of labor rights, the provision of social welfare). This pattern amounts to a reconfiguration of the social and territorial beneficiaries of state protections and subsidies.

3.   See Agnew and Colbridge 1995; Amin 1994; Grugel and Payne 1996; Palat 1996a and 1996b; Roberts 1995; Sassen 1994; Stallings 1995; and Wallerstein 1995 on the ramifications of geopolitical and geoeconomic attachments in shaping the comparative economic prospects of regions and countries across the less-developed world.

4.   Ravi Arvind Palat (1996a, 295-296) observes that as part of "the creation of new regional designations" under worldwide restructuring, it also involves the fact that "...Latin American countries — even Brazil which fronts the Atlantic — attempting to attract investments from the 'miracle' economies of East Asia are seeking to be included in a 'Pacific' region..."

5.   "Commodity chain" refers to the series of stages involved in the production, distribution, and sale of a final product, which increasingly binds together geographic sites on a global scale (see Gereffi and Korzeniewicz 1994; Wallerstein 1979).

6.   Exemplifying "early neoliberalism" was the injection of market reforms into Chile and Argentina — especially the former — during the 1970s as part of a massive wave of repression by military-authoritarian regimes before the onset of Latin America's debt crisis and during the Cold War. Exemplifying "late neoliberalism" are Venezuela during the late 1980s and the 1990s and Brazil during the 1990s, where such reforms have been introduced by civilian-democratic regimes that face, on the

one side, more effective domestic social and political resistance to the new policies, and on the other, the hugely reconfigured world terrain of the debt crisis and the post-Cold War epoch. I thank Alvaro Díaz for bringing these ideas to my attention.

7.   In this hopeful scenario, the actual and potential roles of civil society's subaltern groups are a fundamental issue within the framework of the changing contours of citizenship, including its nascent transnational dimensions (see, for example, Arrighi 1996; Jelin 1997; Roberts 1996; Roxborough 1997; and Walton and Seddon 1994). Throughout this volume, the argument is not that neoliberal policy is solely responsible for Latin America's current configuration of external vulnerabilities and internal inequalities but that it ignores and exacerbates the region's fundamental structural problems.

8.   In considering the long-range prospects of authentic democratization, not to be overlooked is the role of the current phase of Latin America's post-authoritarian transitions and its decentralizing organizational reforms in legitimating painful slashes in state protections and subsidies while weakening and repressing oppositional forces (see Díaz 1997; Jelin 1997; Korzeniewicz and Smith 1997; Petras and Leyva 1994; Roberts 1995; Roxborough 1997; and Walton and Seddon 1994).

9.   On this matter in comparative-international and historical perspective, see Granovetter and Tilly 1988 and Tilly and Tilly 1994.

10.   On variation in pertinent dimensions of contemporary change across the world's most advanced national economies and in their corresponding international policies, see Agnew and Colbridge 1995; Block 1989; Freeman 1994; Noponen, Graham, and Markusen 1993; and Stallings 1995.

11.   Stanley Aronowitz and William DiFazio (1994, 303), who focus on the United States and other advanced economies, succinctly put the overriding question as follows: "What are the implications of technological change — not merely the introduction of new machinery into the workplace but also sweeping organizational changes — for the quantity and quality of paid work?" (see ILO 1996). As specialists in Latin America, the contributors to this volume would add another crucial consideration: the implications of reconfigured state policies across both the national and the world-regional levels (see Stallings and Streeck 1995 and note 12 on the Anglo-American, continental-Western European, and Japanese "models of capitalism"). The contributors would also add consideration of the consequences for the gamut of unpaid labor and for gendered social relations in households, communities, and labor markets.

12.   Barbara Stallings and Wolfgang Streeck (1995) contrast the "Anglo-American" model with the "continental-Western European" and the "Japanese" models, taking into consideration the heterogeneous and malleable features of each (see Agnew and Colbridge 1995 and Grugel and Payne 1996). For discussions of consequences of these models for employment structures and dynamics, see Aronowitz and DiFazio 1994; Blank 1994; Castro, Méhaut, and Rubery 1992; Cheng and Gereffi 1994; Freeman 1994; Locke and Thelen 1995; Marshall 1994; Pérez Sáinz 1994; and Sabel 1995.

13.   In myriad direct and indirect ways, the creation — or elimination — of employment in the "public sector" spills beyond the centralized and decentralized entities of government into the labor market of the "private sector." That is, while convenient as well as arguably valid in certain respects, this conceptual dualism tends to obfuscate the fact that the economic and labor market structures of these

two institutional spheres have never been more than *partially* autonomous from each other (see, for example, Arrighi 1994; Evans 1995; Granovetter and Tilly 1988; Sayer and Walker 1992; Smelser and Swedberg 1994; Tilly and Tilly 1994; Wallerstein 1979 and 1995; and Walters 1996). Essentially the same issues pertain to the conceptual division between the "public" spheres of economy and state and the "private" spheres of households (see, for example, Elson 1995; Korzeniewicz and Smith 1997; Sayer and Walker 1992; Smelser and Swedberg 1994; and Walton and Seddon 1994). Within and beyond Latin America, the comparative and historical modalities of these interdependencies are a fertile field of research.

14. This trend probably includes reductions in employment as well as pay and benefits within the civilian and military wings of the state's organizational machinery (see Acuña and Smith 1995). Of related concern is the impact of such a trend on employment within the gamut of businesses that directly and indirectly supply the various needs of the state's machinery. This includes the impact of austerity, democratization, and post-Cold War geopolitics on the range of military-linked employment across Latin American countries and the geographic variation in that impact within countries and its ramifications for political change. In turn, these Latin American patterns should be compared to "post-fordist" and post-Cold War transformations in the rest of the world (Acuña and Smith 1995; Aronowitz and DiFazio 1994; Block 1989; Noponen, Graham, and Markusen 1993; Sassen 1994).

Relevant to this and the other hypotheses that guide the case studies are PREALC's aggregate data on change in the structure of nonagricultural employment in Argentina, Brazil, Chile, Colombia, Costa Rica, Mexico, and Venezuela from 1980 to 1992 (cited in Thomas 1996, 88). According to these data, the portion of formal sector jobs decreased, based on declines in the shares of employment in the public sector (from 15.7 percent to 14.9 percent) and in large private firms (from 44.1 percent to 30.8 percent). The portion of informal sector jobs reportedly increased, based on growth in the shares of own-account workers (from 19.2 percent to 25.0 percent), domestic-service workers (from 6.4 percent to 6.9 percent), and small-firm workers (from 14.6 percent to 22.5 percent). Ricardo Infante and Emilio Klein (1991, 127) write that according to aggregate data for the 1980s based on Brazil, Chile, Colombia, Costa Rica, Mexico, Uruguay, and Venezuela, women's portion of the labor force rose from 32 percent to 38 percent. In these and other data sets, of course, matters of conceptual definition and measurement — most basically with respect to the gendered categories of "active/inactive" and "employed/unemployed" — are crucial in generating particular findings (see, for example, Benería 1992; Elson 1995; and Walters 1996).

15. The contributors to this volume are cognizant of the methodological problems inherent in using the categories of primary, secondary, and tertiary employment (see, for example, Sayer and Walker 1992).

16. Technological and organizational innovations are gearing the world's most advanced national economies to more dynamic, newly defined segments of transnational commodity chains. In this setting, the conservation and creation of jobs in import-substitution manufacturing through linkages with export-oriented activities may be most common in those import-substitution branches that have become relocated to less advanced zones of the global economy. Consequently, it can be anticipated that these branches tend to face reduced, minimal, or no competition from the most advanced national economies. This could be so to the extent that distance impedes the supply of manufactured inputs from more advanced econo-

mies and that the local economy is developed sufficiently not only to house such branches but also to integrate them with the sites of export-oriented manufacturing. The same considerations pertain to producer services. For example, adjacency to and close integration with the U.S. economy has impeded the development of local manufacturing and service linkages in northern Mexico's *maquiladora* zones (Roberts and Tardanico 1997; Sklair 1993; Spener 1996; Wilson 1992). Conversely, such linkages have been an important part of Chile's recent economic prosperity and transformation, in no small part owing to its location (Díaz 1997 and this volume, Chapter 6; see Gereffi 1995 and Stallings 1995 on this issue in East Asian perspective). An important question is how such production and employment linkages are connecting Latin America's more-developed and less-developed zones, as in Chile's emerging economic relations with areas of the Southern Cone.

17. This is not to say that labor unions have suffered sociopolitical losses uniformly. It should be remembered that the maneuverability and leverage of the region's labor unions have always been circumscribed by the limited size and socioeconomic representation of their memberships, by inter- and intra-union factionalism and personalism, and by the highly subordinate terms of their incorporation into state structures (Bergquist 1986; Buchanan 1995; Collier and Collier 1991; Cook, Middlebrook, and Molinar Horcasitas 1994). As with other recent and emerging aspects of employment, the standing of labor unions is likely to become more differentiated and unequal within nations and across the region. For instance, unions in such strategic economic sectors as mining and petroleum may be most capable of defending themselves against anti-labor state policies (see Johnson 1996).

With respect to the future of the world labor movement, Giovanni Arrighi (1996) predicts that it will be anchored in East Asia, will become more centered on concerns of gender and race, and will be less oriented to statist and nationalist issues — but not necessarily more oriented to internationalist objectives and goals.

18. See Infante and Klein (1991, 131-133) for a discussion of why employment deterioration was less severe in rural than in urban Latin America during the 1980s. They conclude, however, that agricultural entrepreneurs and peasant producers did far better than agricultural wage-workers, especially as the emergence of nontraditional production led to growing use of temporary agricultural wage-labor (see Carter, Barham, and Mesbah 1996; McMichael 1994; Thrupp 1995).

19. The studies also suggest two other hypotheses: first, that an increased percentage of service jobs will become linked to international activities; and second, that innovative forms of flexible-specialization organization and employment are increasingly common in the more advanced branches of Latin American manufacturing and in certain branches of services (including the public sector's subcontracted activities). Given the sparseness of national data, however, this volume's case-study chapters say little about these matters (see Díaz 1997; Pérez Sáinz 1994; Sassen 1994; and Wilson 1992). Regarding flexible specialization, of importance would be a Latin American version of Charles Sabel's (1995) analysis of the structural obstacles to the adoption of such innovative kinds of production and employment in the United States and Europe, as well as an analysis of the sociopolitical and economic ramifications of adoption patterns (see also Aronowitz and DiFazio 1994; Block 1989; Locke and Thelen 1995; and Walters 1996).

20. In some national or local cases, it likewise could include significant expansion of the number of children in the labor force. The virtually exclusive reliance of this volume's country chapters on official employment-census data, which typically report on labor force participants no younger than 12-16 years of age and which otherwise undercount youths in the labor force, minimizes or precludes attention to this important topic. For comparative perspectives on the topic, see *Labour, Capital & Society* 1994; Morley 1995, 63-66; PARLACEN, PREALC/OIT, UNICEF 1994; Roberts 1995, 153-154 and Chapter 7; and *World of Work* 1996.

21. Vital to this discussion — as well as to discussions of global restructuring and local transformations in general — is awareness of the increasing role of immigration and transnational communities in linking the economies and labor markets of the developed and the less-developed worlds (Itzigsohn 1995; Kyle 1995; Maingot 1991; Portes, Dore, and Landolt 1997; Sassen 1988; Spener 1996).

22. This emphasis must include the "nonmarket" dimensions of precarious employment, which revolve around gendered and generational relations within households and communities (see Benería and Roldán 1987 and Elson 1995).

23. The case studies in this volume are organized within the "traditional" conceptual and methodological framework, in no small part because official data sources are so organized. Delineating how this framework yields or restricts insight into emerging socioeconomic complexities is a vital part of the research agenda on contemporary restructuring.

24. With or without regard to the concept of "informality," an emerging conclusion of the international literature on contemporary economic transformation — including for the advanced economies of Western Europe, North America, and East Asia — is that patterns of inequality and mobility under conditions of global restructuring are more territorially and socially fluid, complex, and variable than previously recognized (see Cheng and Gereffi 1994; Esping-Andersen 1993; Freeman 1994; Gilbert 1994; Hamnett 1994; Portes 1989; Rakowski 1994; Roberts 1995; and Stallings 1995).

25. Feminist scholars have demonstrated the methodological limitations of most labor market data with respect to the participation of women, as well as youths and the elderly in general (Benería 1992; Boris and Prugl 1996; Elson 1995; Ward 1990; and *World Development* 1995). They convincingly show how such limitations pertain to both past eras and the emerging new era of production and employment.

26. On the logic of comparison across a small number of cases, see Portes 1989 and Portes, Itzigsohn, and Dore-Cabral 1994. Ideally, this volume would have included the case of Brazil (see Lavinas and Nabuco 1995 and Melo 1995) in order to strengthen the breadth of comparison for the largest countries in terms of population and economy; at least one other case of intermediate size, such as Colombia or Peru; and at least one South American case of small size, such as Bolivia, Ecuador, Paraguay, or Uruguay.

27. This group encompasses a wide range of cases in terms of GDP (see Table 3). Mexico clearly leads the way within the group, followed by Argentina, though in 1993 Mexico's GDP was just 54 percent and Argentina's just 42 percent of the level of Latin America's largest national economy, Brazil. By this standard Venezuela ranks fourth in the region, with Chile ranking sixth, behind Colombia and ahead of Peru (World Bank 1995, 33).

28. Of course, these indicators tend not to have recovered to their pre-crisis levels (Bulmer-Thomas 1996; CEPAL 1995; ECLAC 1995a, 1995b, and 1996; Korzeniwicz and Smith 1997).

29. Argentina's political program of privatization and neoliberal reform was the most severe, but export-based economic transformation has been greatest in Chile and Mexico among the major economies (Acuña 1994; Cortés this volume, Chapter 7; Díaz 1997 and this volume, Chapter 6; Oliveira and García this volume, Chapter 8; Varas 1995). With regard to the programmatic aspects of neoliberal change, it should be remembered, however, that state-owned copper production in Chile and state-owned petroleum production in Mexico remain vital to the financial positions and policy options of their state machinery.

30. Writing on political realignments and protest in contemporary Venezuela, Daniel Levine and Brian Crisp (1995, 245-246) add a cautionary note that may well apply to other cases: that economic crisis and structural adjustment are not, strictly speaking, the causes of discontent but rather are conditions that greatly exacerbate longer-standing political and social divisions.

31. Although addressing the broad features of neoliberal policy in each country, the country chapters are, for the most part, limited in their ability to discuss specific features of change in state labor-market policies (see, for example, Blank 1994; Córdova 1996; Godio 1993; Granovetter and Tilly 1988; *International Labour Review* 1995; Locke and Thelen 1995; Marinakis 1995; Marshall 1994; Schoepfle and Pérez-López 1993; Turnham, Foy, and Larraín 1995; and Walters 1996). Furthermore, the country chapters vary widely in their degrees of attention to specific features of labor process, that is, to specific features of "how labor is used in the production of goods and services" (Granovetter and Tilly 1988, 177). The topics of state labor-market policy and labor process merit in-depth attention that goes beyond the possibilities in this book.

References

Acuña, Carlos H. 1994. "Politics and Economics in the Argentina of the Nineties (Or, Why the Future No Longer Is What It Used to Be)." In *Democracy, Markets, and Structural Reform in Latin America*, eds. William C. Smith, Carlos H. Acuña, and Eduardo A. Gamarra. Coral Gables, Fla.: North-South Center at the University of Miami.

Acuña, Carlos H., and William C. Smith. 1995. "The Politics of 'Military Economics' in the Southern Cone: Comparative Perspectives on Democracy and Arms Production in Argentina, Brazil, and Chile." *Political Power and Social Theory* 9:121-157.

Adelman, Jerry. 1995. "The Money Store." *Hemisphere: A Magazine of the Americas* 7(1):30- 33.

Agnew, John, and Stuart Colbridge. 1995. *Mastering Space: Hegemony, Territory and International Political Economy*. London: Routledge.

Amin, Samir. 1994."The Future of Global Polarization." *Review: Fernand Braudel Center* 17(3):337-346.

Amsden, Alice H., and Rolph van der Hoeven. 1996. "Manufacturing Output, Employment and Real Wages in the 1980s: Labour's Loss Until the Century's End." *Journal of Development Studies* 32(4):506-530.

Aronowitz, Stanley, and William DiFazio. 1994. *The Jobless Future: Sci-Tech and the Dogma of Work*. Minneapolis: University of Minnesota Press.

Arrighi, Giovanni. 1994. *The Long Twentieth Century: Money, Power and the Origins of Our Times*. London: Verso.

Arrighi, Giovanni. 1996. "Workers of the World at Century's End." *Review: Fernand Braudel Center* 19(3):335-351.

Benería, Lourdes. 1989. "Gender and the Global Economy." In *Instability and Change in the World Economy*, eds. Arthur MacEwan and William K. Tabb. New York: Monthly Review Press.

Benería, Lourdes. 1992. "Accounting for Women's Work: The Progress of Two Decades." *World Development* 20(11):1547-1560.

Benería, Lourdes, and Martha Roldán. 1987. *The Crossroads of Class and Gender: Industrial Homework, Subcontracting, and Household Dynamics in Mexico City*. Chicago: University of Chicago Press.

Bergquist, Charles. 1986. *Labor in Latin America: Comparative Essays on Chile, Argentina, Venezuela, and Colombia*. Stanford, Calif.: Stanford University Press.

Berry, Albert. 1994. "Practice Round." *Hemisfile* 5(6):4-5.

Blank, Rebecca. 1994. "Does a Larger Social Safety Net Mean Less Economic Flexibility?" In *Working Under Different Rules*, ed. Richard B. Freeman. New York: Russell Sage Foundation.

Block, Fred. 1989. *Postindustrial Possibilities*. Berkeley: University of California Press.

Bodson, Paul, Allen Cordero, and Juan Pablo Pérez Sáinz. 1995. *Las nuevas caras del empleo*. San José, Costa Rica: FLACSO.

Boris, Eileen, and Elisabeth Prugl, eds. 1996. *Homeworkers in Global Perspective: Invisible No More*. New York: Routledge.

Borocz, Jozsef, and David A. Smith, eds. 1995. *A New World Order? Global Transformations in the Late Twentieth Century*. Westport, Conn.: Greenwood Press.

Bromley, Ray, and Chris Birkbeck. 1988. "Urban Economy and Employment." In *The Geography of the Third World*, ed. Michael Pacione. London: Routledge.

Buchanan, Paul G. 1995. *State, Labor, Capital: Democratizing Class Relations in the Southern Cone*. Pittsburgh, Pa.: University of Pittsburgh Press.

Bulmer-Thomas, Victor, ed. 1996. *The New Economic Model in Latin America and Its Impact on Income Distribution and Poverty*. New York: St. Martin's Press.

Canitrot, Adolfo. 1994. "Crisis and Transformation of the Argentine State (1978-1992)." In *Democracy, Markets, and Structural Reform in Latin America*, eds. William C. Smith, Carlos H. Acuña, and Eduardo A. Gamarra. Coral Gables, Fla.: North-South Center at the University of Miami.

Cardoso, Fernando Henrique, and Enzo Faletto. 1979. *Dependency and Development in Latin America*. Berkeley: University of California Press.

Carnoy, Martin, Manuel Castells, Stephen S. Cohen, and Fernando Henrique Cardoso. 1993. *The New Global Economy in the Information Age*. University Park, Pa.: The Pennsylvania State University Press.

Carr, Barry. 1996. "Crossing Borders: Labor Internationalism in the Era of NAFTA." In *Neoliberalism Revisited: Economic Restructuring and Mexico's Political Future*, ed. Gerardo Otero. Boulder, Colo.: Westview Press.

Carter, Michael R., Bradford L. Barham, and Dina Mesbah. 1996. "Agricultural Export Booms and the Rural Poor in Chile, Guatemala, and Paraguay." *Latin American Research Review* 31(1):33-66.

Castro, Alberto, Philippe Méhaut, and Jill Rubery, eds. 1992. *International Integration and Labour Market Organization*. London: Academic Press.

CEPAL (Comisión Económica para América Latina y el Caribe). 1995. "Balance preliminar de la economía de América Latina y el Caribe 1995." *Notas sobre la economía y el desarrollo*, no. 585/586 (December). Santiago, Chile.

Chase-Dunn, Christopher. 1989. *Global Formation*. Cambridge, Mass.: Blackwell.

Cheng, Lu-Lim, and Gary Gereffi. 1994. "The Informal Economy in East Asian Development." *International Journal of Urban and Regional Research* 18(2):194-219.

Collier, Ruth Berins, and David Collier. 1991. *Shaping the Political Arena: Critical Junctures, the Labor Movement, and Regime Dynamics in Latin America*. Princeton, N.J.: Princeton University Press.

Collins, Joseph, and John Lear. 1995. *Chile's Free-Market Miracle: A Second Look*. Oakland, Calif.: Food First.

Conroy, Michael E., and Amy Glasmeier. 1992-1993. "Unprecedented Disparities, Unparalleled Adjustment Needs: Winners and Losers on the NAFTA Fast Track." *Journal of Interamerican Studies and World Affairs* 34(4):1-37.

Cook, María Lorena, Kevin J. Middlebrook, and Juan Molinar Horcasitas, eds. 1994. *The Politics of Economic Restructuring: State-Society Relations and Regime Change in Mexico.* La Jolla, Calif.: Center for U.S.-Mexican Studies, University of California at San Diego.

Córdova, Efrén. 1996. "The Challenge of Flexibility in Latin America." *Comparative Labor Law Review* 17(2):314-337.

Davis, Diane E. 1992. "Unlearning Languages of Development: From Rhetoric to Realism in Recent Studies of Latin America." *Latin American Research Review* 27(1):151-168.

Despres, Leo A. 1991. *Manaus: Social Life and Work in Brazil's Free Trade Zone.* Albany: State University of New York Press.

Deyo, Frederic C. 1989. *Beneath the Miracle: Labor and the New Asian Industrialism.* Berkeley: University of California Press.

Díaz, Alvaro. 1997. "New Developments in Social and Economic Restructuring in Latin America." In *Politics, Social Change, and Economic Restructuring in Latin America,* eds. William C. Smith and Roberto Patricio Korzeniewicz. Coral Gables, Fla.: North-South Center Press at the University of Miami.

Dicken, Peter. 1992. *Global Shift.* New York: The Guilford Press.

Dunkerley, James. 1988. *Power in the Isthmus: A Political History of Modern Central America.* London: Verso.

ECLAC (Economic Commission for Latin America and the Caribbean). 1988. *Economic Survey of Latin America and the Caribbean 1988.* Santiago, Chile: ECLAC.

ECLAC. 1993. *Statistical Yearbook on Latin America and the Caribbean.* Santiago, Chile: ECLAC.

ECLAC. 1994a. *Statistical Yearbook on Latin America and the Caribbean.* Santiago, Chile: ECLAC.

ECLAC. 1994b. *Open Regionalism in Latin America and the Caribbean: Economic Integration as a Contribution to Changing Production Patterns with Social Equity.* Santiago, Chile: ECLAC.

ECLAC. 1994c. *Latin America and the Caribbean: Policies to Improve Linkages with the Global Economy.* Santiago, Chile: ECLAC.

ECLAC. 1995a. *Economic Survey of Latin America and the Caribbean 1994-95.* Santiago, Chile: ECLAC.

ECLAC. 1995b. *Social Panorama of Latin America 1995.* Santiago, Chile: ECLAC.

ECLAC. 1996. *Cepal News* 16(7). Santiago, Chile: ECLAC.

Eckstein, Susan. 1990. "Poor People Versus the State and Capital: Anatomy of a Successful Mobilization for Housing in Mexico City." *International Journal of Urban and Regional Research* 14(2):274-296.

Ellison, Katherine. 1996. "Latin Economies Leaner, Also Meaner." *The Miami Herald.* September 15: 1A, 18A.

Elson, Diane, ed. 1995. *Male Bias in the Development Process.* 2nd ed. Manchester: Manchester University Press.

Espinal, Rosario. 1995. "Economic Restructuring, Social Protest, and Democratization in the Dominican Republic." *Latin American Perspectives* 22(3):63-79.

Esping-Andersen, Gosta, ed. 1993. *Changing Classes: Stratification and Mobility in Post- Industrial Societies.* London: Sage.

Evans, Peter B. 1995. *Embedded Autonomy: States and Industrial Transformations.* Princeton, N.J.: Princeton University Press.

Fainstein, Susan, and Norman I. Fainstein. 1989. "Technology, the New International Division of Labor, and Location: Continuities and Discontinuities." In *Economic Restructuring and Political Response*, ed. Robert A. Beauregard. Newbury Park, Calif.: Sage.

Fajnzylber, Fernando. 1990. *Unavoidable Industrial Restructuring in Latin America.* Durham, N.C.: Duke University Press.

Fernández Kelly, M. Patricia. 1994. "Broadening the Scope: Gender and the Study of International Development." In *Comparative National Development: Society and Economy in the New Global Order*, eds. A. Douglas Kincaid and Alejandro Portes. Chapel Hill: University of North Carolina Press.

FitzGerald, E.V.K. 1996. "The New Trade Regime, Macroeconomic Behaviour and Income Distribution in Latin America." In *The New Economic Model in Latin America and Its Impact on Income Distribution and Poverty*, ed. Victor Bulmer-Thomas. New York: St. Martin's Press.

Freeman, Richard B., ed. 1994. *Working Under Different Rules.* New York: Russell Sage Foundation.

Garretón, Manuel Antonio. 1994. "The Political Dimension of Processes of Transformation in Chile." In *Democracy, Markets, and Structural Reform in Latin America*, eds. William C. Smith, Carlos H. Acuña, and Eduardo A. Gamarra. Coral Gables, Fla.: North-South Center at the University of Miami.

Gereffi, Gary. 1995. "Global Production Systems and Third World Development." In *Global Change, Regional Response: The New International Context of Development*, ed. Barbara Stallings. Cambridge: Cambridge University Press.

Gereffi, Gary, and Miguel Korzeniewicz, eds. 1994. *Commodity Chains and Global Capitalism.* Westport, Conn.: Praeger.

Gilbert, Alan. 1990. "Urbanization at the Periphery: Reflections on Changing Dynamics of Housing and Employment in Latin American Cities." In *Economic Growth and Urbanization in Development Areas*, ed. D.W. Drakakis-Smith. London: Routledge.

Gilbert, Alan. 1994. "Third World Cities: Poverty, Employment, Gender Roles and the Environment during a Time of Restructuring." *Urban Studies* 31(4-5):605-633.

Glyn, Andrew. 1995. "Social Democracy and Full Employment." *New Left Review* 211(May/June):33-55.

Godio, Julio. 1993. *Los sindicatos en las economías de mercado en América Latina.* Bogotá: Fundación Friedrich Ebert de Colombia.

Goodman, Louis W., Johanna Mendelson Forman, Moisés Naim, Joseph S. Tulchin, and Gary Bland, eds. 1995. *Lessons of the Venezuelan Experience.* Washington, D.C.: The Woodrow Wilson Center Press; Baltimore: Johns Hopkins University Press.

Granovetter, Mark, and Charles Tilly. 1988. "Inequality and Labor Processes." In *Handbook of Sociology*, ed. Neil J. Smelser. Newbury Park, Calif.: Sage.

Grugel, Jean, and Anthony Payne. 1996. "A Matter of Deconstruction." *Hemisphere: A Magazine of the Americas* 7(2):6-8.

Haddad, Lawrence, Lynn R. Brown, Andrea Richeter, and Lisa Smith. 1995. "The Gender Dimensions of Economic Adjustment Policies: Potential Interactions and Evidence to Date." *World Development* 23(6):881-896.

Hamnett, Chris. 1994. "Social Polarisation in Global Cities: Theory and Evidence." *Urban Studies* 31(3):401-424.

Hays-Mitchell, Maureen. 1995. "Voices and Vision from the Streets: Gender Interests and Political Participation Among Women Informal Traders in Latin America." *Environment and Planning D: Society and Space* 13(4):445-469.

Hayward, Susana. 1995. "Mexico Faces Precarious New Year." *The Miami Herald*, January 1.

Horton, Susan, Ravi Kanbur, and Dipak Mazumdar, eds. 1994. *Labor Markets in an Era of Adjustment*, 2 vols. Washington, D.C.: The World Bank.

Humphrey, John. 1994. "Are the Unemployed Part of the Urban Poverty Problem in Latin America?" *Journal of Latin American Studies* 26(3):713-736.

Infante, Ricardo, and Emilio Klein. 1991. "The Latin American Labour Market, 1950-1990." *Cepal Review* 45 (December):121-135.

ILO (International Labour Office). 1991. *Políticas de empleo en la reestructuración económica en América Latina y el Caribe*. Geneva: ILO.

ILO. 1996. *World Employment 1996/97: National Policies in a Global Context*. Geneva: ILO.

International Labour Review. 1995. Issue on Employment Policy in the Global Economy. 134(4-5).

Itzigsohn, José. 1995. "Migrant Remittances, Labor Markets, and Household Strategies: A Comparative Analysis of Low-Income Household Strategies in the Caribbean Basin." *Social Forces* 74(2):633-655.

Itzigsohn, José. 1996. "Globalization, the State, and the Informal Economy: The Articulations of Informal and Formal Economic Activities and the Limits to Proletarianization in the Periphery." In *Latin America in the World-Economy*, eds. Roberto Patricio Korzeniewicz and William C. Smith. Westport, Conn.: Praeger.

Jelin, Elizabeth. 1997. "Emergent Citizenship or Exclusion? Social Movements and Non-Governmental Organizations in the 1990s." In *Politics, Social Change, and Economic Restructuring in Latin America*, eds. William C. Smith and Roberto Patricio Korzeniewicz. Coral Gables, Fla.: North-South Center Press at the University of Miami.

Johnson, Tim. 1996. "Latin Trade Unions Losing Power as Economic Changes Continue." *The Miami Herald*. September 15:18A.

Kapstein, Ethan B. 1996. "Workers and the World Economy." *Foreign Affairs* (May/June):16-37.

Korzeniewicz, Roberto Patricio, and William C. Smith, eds. 1997. *Latin America in the World-Economy*. Westport, Conn.: Praeger.

Kyle, David J. 1995. "The Transnational Peasant: The Social Construction of International Economic Migration and Transcommunities from the Ecuadoran Andes." Unpublished Ph.D. dissertation, Department of Sociology, The Johns Hopkins University.

Labour, Capital & Society. 1994. Issue on Child Labour within the Globalizing Economy. 27(2).

Lantican, Clarita P., Christina H. Gladwin, and James L. Seale, Jr. 1996. "Income and Gender Inequalities in Asia: Testing Alternative Theories." *Economic Development and Cultural Change* 44(2):235-264.

Latin American Labor News. 1995. Issue on Labor and Free Trade in the Americas. 12/13. Miami: Center for Labor Research and Studies, Florida International University.

Latin American Weekly Report. 1995. "Mexico Heralds, Not Another 1992 Debt Crisis, Just a Different One." January 12.

Lavinas, Lena, and María Regina Nabuco. 1995. "Economic Crisis and Tertiarization in Brazil's Metropolitan Labour Market." *International Journal of Urban and Regional Research* 19(3):358-368.

Lawson, Victoria. 1995. "Beyond the Firm: Restructuring Gender Divisions in Quito's Garment Industry under Austerity." *Environment and Planning D: Society and Space* 13(4):415-444.

Levine, Daniel H., and Brian F. Crisp. 1995. "Legitimacy, Governability, and Reform in Venezuela." In *Lessons of the Venezuelan Experience*, eds. Louis W. Goodman, Johanna Mendelson Forman, Moisés Naim, Joseph S. Tulchin, and Gary Bland. Washington, D.C.: The Woodrow Wilson Center Press; Baltimore: Johns Hopkins University Press.

Locke, Richard M., and Kathleen Thelen. 1995. "Apples and Oranges: Contextualized Comparisons and the Study of Comparative Labor Politics." *Politics & Society* 23(3):337-367.

Logan, John R., and Todd Swanstrom, eds. 1990. *Beyond the City Limits: Urban Policy and Economic Restructuring in Comparative Perspective.* Philadelphia: Temple University Press.

Lustig, Nora, ed. 1995. *Coping with Austerity: Poverty and Inequality in Latin America.* Washington, D.C.: The Brookings Institution.

Maingot, Anthony P., ed. 1991. *Small Country Development and International Labor Flows.* Boulder, Colo.: Westview Press.

Marinakis, Andrés. 1995. "New Trends in Wage Policies." *Cepal Review* 57(December):75-84.

Marshall, Adriana. 1994. "Economic Consequences of Labour Protection Regimes in Latin America." *International Labour Review* 133(1):55-73.

McCoy, Jennifer L., Andrés Serbín, William C. Smith, and Andrés Stambouli, eds. 1995. *Venezuelan Democracy under Stress.* Coral Gables, Fla.: North-South Center at the University of Miami.

McMichael, Philip, ed. 1994. *The Global Restructuring of Agro-Food Systems.* Ithaca, N.Y.: Cornell University Press.

Melo, Marcus C. 1995. "State Retreat, Governance and Metropolitan Restructuring in Brazil." *International Journal of Urban and Regional Research* 19(3):342-357.

Menjívar Larín, Rafael, and Juan Pablo Pérez Sáinz, eds. 1993. *Ni héroes ni villanas: género e informalidad urbana en Centroamérica.* San José, Costa Rica: FLACSO.

Mesa-Lago, Carmelo. 1994. *Changing Social Security in Latin America: Toward Alleviating the Social Costs of Economic Reform.* Boulder, Colo.: Lynne Rienner Publishers.

Mittelman, James H., ed. 1996. *Globalization: Critical Reflections.* Boulder, Colo.: Lynne Rienner Publishers.

Morley, Samuel A. 1995. *Poverty and Inequality in Latin America: The Impact of Adjustment and Recovery in the 1980s.* Baltimore: Johns Hopkins University Press.

Nelson, Joan M., ed. 1990. *Economic Crisis and Policy Choice: The Politics of Adjustment in the Third World.* Princeton, N.J.: Princeton University Press.

Noponen, Helzi, Julie Graham, and Ann R. Markusen, eds. 1993. *Trading Industries, Trading Regions: International Trade, American Industry, and Regional Economic Development.* New York: The Guilford Press.

Oliveira, Orlandina de, and Bryan Roberts. 1994. "Urban Growth and Urban Social Structure in Latin America, 1930-1990." In *The Cambridge History of Latin America,* ed. Leslie Bethell, vol. VI, pt. 1. Cambridge: Cambridge University Press.

Palat, Ravi Arvind. 1996a. "Fragmented Visions: Excavating the Future of Area Studies in a Post-American World." *Review: Fernand Braudel Center* 19(3):269-315.

Palat, Ravi Arvind. 1996b. "Pacific Century: Myth or Reality?" *Theory & Society* 25(3):303-347.

PARLACEN, PREALC/OIT, UNICEF. 1994. "Los niños trabajadores en Centroamérica." *Cuadernos de Ciencias Sociales,* no. 66. San José, Costa Rica: FLACSO.

Pérez Sáinz, Juan Pablo, ed. 1994. *Globalización y fuerza laboral en Centroamérica.* San José, Costa Rica: FLACSO.

Pérez Sáinz, Juan Pablo. 1996. *De la finca a la maquila.* San José, Costa Rica: FLACSO.

Pérez Sáinz, Juan Pablo, and Rafael Menjívar Larín, eds. 1991. *Informalidad urbana en Centroamérica: entre la acumulación y la subsistencia.* Caracas: FLASCO/Nueva Sociedad.

Petras, James, and Fernando Ignacio Leyva. 1994. *Democracy and Party in Chile: The Limits to Electoral Politics.* Boulder, Colo.: Westview Press.

Piven, Frances Fox. 1995. "Is it Global Economics or Neo-Laissez Faire?" *New Left Review* 213(September/October):107-114.

Portes, Alejandro. 1989. "Urbanization during the Years of the Crisis." *Latin American Research Review* 24(3):7-44.

Portes, Alejandro, Manuel Castells, and Lauren A. Benton, eds. 1989. *The Informal Economy: Studies in Advanced and Less Developed Countries.* Baltimore: Johns Hopkins University Press.

Portes, Alejandro, Carlos Dore, and Patricia Landolt, eds. 1996. *Caribbean Cities on the Threshold of a New Century.* Baltimore: Johns Hopkins University Press.

Portes, Alejandro, José Itzigsohn, and Carlos Dore-Cabral. 1994. "Urbanization in the Caribbean Basin: Social Change during the Years of the Crisis." *Latin American Research Review* 29(2):3-37.

Portes, Alejandro, and Richard Schauffler. 1993. "Competing Perspectives on the Latin American Informal Sector." *Population and Development Review* 19(1):33-60.

PREALC (Programa Regional del Empleo para América Latina y el Caribe). 1991. *Empleo y equidad: el desafío de los 90.* Santiago, Chile: PREALC.

PREALC. 1994. *Empleo precario en América Latina.* Santiago, Chile: PREALC.

Przeworski, Adam. 1992. "The Neoliberal Fallacy." *Journal of Democracy* 3(3):45-59.

Rakowski, Cathy A., ed. 1994. *Contrapunto: The Informal Sector Debate in Latin America.* Albany: State University of New York Press.

Ramos, Joseph. 1995. "Can Growth and Equity Go Hand in Hand?" *Cepal Review* 56(August):13-24.

Roberts, Bryan. 1993. "The Dynamics of Informal Employment in Mexico." In *Work Without Protections: Case Studies of the Informal Sector in Developing Countries*, eds. Gregory K. Schoepfle and Jorge F. Pérez-López. Washington, D.C.: U.S. Department of Labor, Bureau of International Labor Affairs.

Roberts, Bryan. 1995. *The Making of Citizens: Cities of Peasants Revisited.* London: Arnold.

Roberts, Bryan. 1996. "The Social Context of Citizenship in Latin America." *International Journal of Urban and Regional Research* 20(1):38-65.

Roberts, Bryan, and Richard Tardanico. 1997. "Employment Transformations in U.S. and Mexican Gulf Cities." *LACC Occasional Paper Series.* Miami: Latin American and Caribbean Center, Florida International University.

Roxborough, Ian. 1997. "Citizenship and Social Movements under Neoliberalism." In *Politics, Social Change, and Economic Restructuring in Latin America*, eds. William C. Smith and Roberto Patricio Korzeniewicz. Coral Gables, Fla.: North-South Center Press at the University of Miami.

Rubery, Cheryl, ed. 1988. *Women and Recession.* London: Routledge.

Sabel, Charles F. 1995. "Bootstrapping Reform, Rebuilding Firms, the Welfare State, and Unions." *Politics & Society* 23(1):5-48.

Safa, Helen I. 1995. "Economic Restructuring and Gender Subordination." *Latin American Perspectives* 22(2):32-50.

Sanderson, Steven E. 1992. *The Politics of Trade in Latin American Development.* Stanford, Calif.: Stanford University Press.

Sassen, Saskia. 1988. *The Mobility of Labor and Capital.* Cambridge: Cambridge University Press.

Sassen, Saskia. 1991. *The Global City: New York, London, Tokyo.* Princeton, N.J.: Princeton University Press.

Sassen, Saskia. 1994. *Cities in a World Economy.* Thousand Oaks, Calif.: Pine Forge Press.

Sayer, Andrew, and Richard Walker. 1992. *The New Social Economy: Reworking the Division of Labor.* Oxford: Blackwell.

Schoepfle, Gregory K., and Jorge F. Pérez-López, eds. 1993. *Work Without Protections: Case Studies of the informal Sector in Developing Countries.* Washington, D.C.: U.S. Department of Labor, Bureau of International Labor Affairs.

Sheahan, John. 1992. "Development Dichotomies and Economic Strategy." In *Towards a New Development Strategy for Latin America: Pathways from Hirschman's Thought,* ed. Simón Teitel. Washington, D.C.: Inter-American Development Bank.

Sklair, Leslie. 1993. *Assembling for Development: The Maquila Industry in Mexico and the United States.* La Jolla, Calif.: Center for U.S.-Mexican Studies, University of California at San Diego.

Smelser, Neil J., and Richard Swedberg, eds. 1994. *The Handbook of Economic Sociology.* Princeton, N.J.: Princeton University Press; New York: Russell Sage Foundation.

Smith, Michael Peter, and Joe R. Feagin, eds. 1987. *The Capitalist City: Global Restructuring and Community Politics.* Oxford: Blackwell.

Smith, Michael Peter, and Richard Tardanico. 1987. "Urban Theory Revisited: Production, Reproduction and Collective Action." In *The Capitalist City: Global Restructuring and Community Politics,* eds. Michael Peter Smith and Joe R. Feagin. Oxford: Blackwell.

Smith, William C., Carlos H. Acuña, and Eduardo A. Gamarra, eds. 1994a. *Latin American Political Economy in the Age of Neoliberal Reform.* Coral Gables, Fla.: North-South Center at the University of Miami.

Smith, William C., Carlos H. Acuña, and Eduardo A. Gamarra, eds. 1994b. *Democracy, Markets, and Structural Reform in Latin America.* Coral Gables, Fla.: North-South Center at the University of Miami.

Spener, David. 1996. "Small Firms, Commodity Chains, and Free Trade: The Transformation of the Texas-Mexico Border Region." In *Latin America in the World-Economy,* eds. Roberto Patricio Korzeniewicz and William C. Smith. Westport, Conn.: Praeger.

Stallings, Barbara, ed. 1995. *Global Change, Regional Response: The New International Context of Development.* Cambridge: Cambridge University Press.

Stallings, Barbara, and Robert Kaufman, eds. 1989. *Debt and Democracy in Latin America.* Boulder, Colo.: Westview Press.

Stallings, Barbara, and Wolfgang Streeck. 1995. "Capitalisms in Conflict: The United States, Europe, and Japan in the Post-Cold War World." In *Global Change, Regional Response: The New International Context of Development,* ed. Barbara Stallings. Cambridge: Cambridge University Press.

Standing, Guy, and Victor E. Tokman, eds. 1991. *Towards Social Adjustment: Labour Market Issues in Structural Adjustment.* Geneva: International Labour Organization.

Stewart, Frances. 1995. *Adjustment and Poverty: Options and Choices.* New York: Routledge.

Sunkel, Osvaldo. 1995. "Economic Reform and Democratic Viability." In *The Consolidation of Democracy in Latin America,* ed. Joseph S. Tulchin. Boulder, Colo.: Lynne Rienner Publishers.

Suter, Christian. 1992. *Debt Cycles in the World-Economy.* Boulder, Colo.: Westview Press.

Teitel, Simón, ed. 1992. *Towards a New Development Strategy for Latin America: Pathways from Hirschman's Thought.* Washington, D.C.: Inter-American Development Bank.

Thomas, Jim. 1996. "The New Economic Model and Labour Markets in Latin America." In *The New Economic Model in Latin America and Its Impact on Income Distribution and Poverty*, ed. Victor Bulmer-Thomas. New York: St. Martin's Press.

Thrupp, Lori Ann, with Gerard Bergeron and W.F. Waters. 1995. *Bittersweet Harvests for Global Supermarkets: Challenges in Latin America's Agricultural Export Boom.* Washington, D.C.: World Resources Institute.

Thurow, Lester C. 1996. *The Future of Capitalism.* New York: Morrow.

Tiano, Susan. 1994. *Patriarchy on the Line: Labor, Gender, and Ideology in the Mexican Maquila Industry.* Philadelphia: Temple University Press.

Tilly, Chris. 1996. *Half a Job: Bad and Good Part-time Jobs in a Changing Labor Market.* Philadelphia: Temple University Press.

Tilly, Chris, and Charles Tilly. 1994. "Capitalist Work and Labor Markets." In *The Handbook of Economic Sociology*, eds. Neil J. Smelser and Richard Swedberg. Princeton, N.J.: Princeton University Press; New York: Russell Sage Foundation.

Trudeau, Robert H. 1993. *Guatemalan Politics: The Popular Struggle for Democracy.* Boulder, Colo.: Lynne Rienner Publishers.

Turnham, David, Colin Foy, and Guillermo Larraín, eds. 1995. *Social Tension, Job Creation and Economic Policy in Latin America.* Paris: Organization for Economic Cooperation and Development.

Varas, Augusto. 1995. "Latin America: Toward a New Reliance on the Market." In *Global Change, Regional Response: The New International Context of Development*, ed. Barbara Stallings. Cambridge: Cambridge University Press.

Vergara, Pilar. 1994. "Market Economy, Social Welfare, and Democratic Consolidation in Chile." In *Democracy, Markets, and Structural Reform in Latin America*, eds. William C. Smith, Carlos H. Acuña, and Eduardo A. Gamarra. Coral Gables, Fla.: North-South Center at the University of Miami.

Wallerstein, Immanuel. 1979. *The Capitalist World-Economy.* Cambridge: Cambridge University Press.

Wallerstein, Immanuel. 1995. *After Liberalism.* New York: The New Press.

Walters, William. 1996. "The Demise of Unemployment?" *Politics & Society* 24(3):197-219.

Walton, John, and David Seddon. 1994. *Free Markets and Food Riots.* Oxford: Blackwell.

Ward, Kathryn B., ed. 1990. *Women Workers and Global Restructuring.* Ithaca, N.Y.: ILR Press.

Weeks, John, ed. 1995. *Structural Adjustment and the Agricultural Sector in Latin America and the Caribbean.* New York: St. Martin's Press.

Weeks, John. 1996. "The Manufacturing Sector in Latin America and the New Economic Model." In *The New Economic Model in Latin America and Its Impact on Income Distribution and Poverty*, ed. Victor Bulmer-Thomas. New York: St. Martin's Press.

Wilson, Patricia A. 1992. *Exports and Local Development: Mexico's New Maquiladoras.* Austin: University of Texas Press.

Wilson, Patricia A. 1995. "Embracing Locality in Local Economic Development." *Urban Studies* 32(4-5):645-658.

Wolf, Diane L. 1992. *Factory Daughters: Gender, Household Dynamics, and Rural Industrialization in Java.* Berkeley: University of California Press.

World Bank. 1994. *World Tables.* Washington, D.C.

World Bank. 1995. *World Development Report.* Washington, D.C.

World Development. 1995. Issue on Gender, Adjustment, and Macroeconomics. 23(11).

World of Work. 1996. "Child Labour: Targeting the Intolerable." Geneva: International Labour Office. No. 18(December):6-9.

Chapter 2

The Dominican Republic: Politico-Economic Transformation, Employment, and Poverty

José Itzigsohn

After a profound crisis and the implementation of neoliberal adjustment policies in the 1980s, the national economies of Latin America and the Caribbean have assumed a path of renewed but uncertain growth. The structural transformations of the 1980s brought about or consolidated a new mode of insertion in the world economy. Barriers to trade have been greatly reduced, and the privatization of state-owned enterprises has been widespread, as the previous inward-oriented policies are being supplanted by an emphasis on exports and open economies (see Chapter 1, this volume; Gereffi and Fonda 1992). What are the social dynamics and contours that labor markets assume under the new model? That is, what types of jobs are being created? And what are the consequent prospects for the reduction of poverty and inequality in the long term?

This chapter focuses on the Dominican Republic, which, in terms of assembly-manufacturing and service exports, has gone the furthest of any Caribbean country in linking itself with the world economy. Does this new economic model promise to improve or worsen working conditions and living standards for the majority of the population in the Dominican Republic? Given that neoliberal export-oriented policies rely on the comparative advantage of cheap labor, the latter outcome is likely. Yet, alternatively, because those policies revolve around labor-intensive technologies, they could lead conceivably to rapid labor absorption, the reduction of underemployment, and a general increase in labor remuneration. To examine this question, the chapter analyzes changes in the urban labor market between 1980 and 1991 that are linked to the Dominican Republic's transition from an inward-oriented to outward-oriented economy. It evaluates the consequences of the transition for employment conditions and the long-term prospects of the new model for social welfare and social inequality.[1]

José Itzigsohn is assistant professor of sociology at Brown University.

The findings suggest that as nontraditional exports and employment boomed in the Dominican Republic, job growth was greatest not in the internationalized activities but in locally oriented, low-wage tertiary activities. Against the backdrop of a precipitous weakening of the state's social safety net and a modest drop in the public sector's share of employment, the overall process of change was marked by worsening labor-market conditions, involving the persistence of a very high reported rate of open unemployment as well as the spread of insecure and informal employment. Intertwined with this pattern was the continued feminization of the labor force, characterized by high levels of female unemployment and low-wage and informal employment, in spite of significant gains in female representation in professional and technical occupations. And although there occurred some geographic decentralization of employment, this tended to bypass the country's poorest areas and to generate low-end jobs in secondary cities.

Industrialization and Labor Markets in the Dominican Republic: An Overview

Industrialization in the Dominican Republic took place under the political leadership of President Joaquín Balaguer (1966-1978, 1986-1996). The Balaguer government emerged out of the U.S. invasion of the country in 1965 and was the result of a compromise between the traditional agrarian and commercial elites, the rising urban middle classes, and the military (Lozano 1985). Balaguer's political effectiveness was based on his ability as president to play the different support and opposition groups against each other and on the backing of the U.S. government, which guaranteed the regime's stability.

The Balaguer regime was initially authoritarian but evolved into a political system that can be described as a "neo-patrimonial democracy" (Hartlyn 1994).[2] Balaguer implemented import-substitution industrialization policies that led the country along a path of economic growth and social transformation. The Dominican Republic became an urban society with significant urban middle and working classes. Under Balaguer, however, the Dominican state sought to guarantee capital accumulation through the politico-economic subordination of the working class and thus through the provision of cheap labor, which was facilitated by ample access to Haitian migrant workers (Ceara Hatton 1993; Lozano and Duarte 1992).

The transformation of the Dominican labor market during the import-substitution period revolved around urbanization and the creation of an urban workforce anchored in formal (that is, state-regulated) wage relations (see Table 1). From 1960 to 1980, the urban share of the country's economically active population grew from 33.2 percent to 58.6 percent. Over the same period, formal urban employment grew from 57.5 percent of total urban employment to 72.7 percent.

Table 1.
Profile of the Urban Labor Market in the Dominican
Republic under Import-Substitution Industrialization
percentages

	1960	1970	1980
Urban EAP[a]	33.2	45.6	58.6
Formal employment	57.5	66.0	72.7
Unwaged EAP in manufacturing	34.8	30.2	—
Unwaged EAP in commerce	62.0	63.2	—
Urban unemployment	—	24.0[b]	19.2[b]

Sources: IEPD (1991, Tables 4.8, 4.9, 4.10); Lozano (1987, Tables 1, 4); García and Tokman (1984, Table 4).
a = Economically active population.
b = See the discussion on reported levels of unemployment in note 3.

Nevertheless, unwaged labor in manufacturing was only marginally reduced, and unwaged labor in commerce slightly increased. The growth of the formal economy over this period may indeed be overstated. In 1980, "underemployment" (full-time subminimum wage earners and part-time workers seeking full-time jobs) reached 43.4 percent of the total urban economically active population and 38.7 percent of the urban wage workers (Lozano 1987). Urban unemployment was reportedly very high as well (19.2 percent).[3]

The Dominican Republic, therefore, experienced both rapid industrialization and elevated rates of both unemployment and underemployment. The small size of the internal market, a problem exacerbated by an official policy of low urban wages, hampered the dynamism of manufacturing growth and labor absorption. Furthermore, a policy of keeping food prices low to subsidize the costs of the urban labor force combined with the state's neglect of rural economy and society and the agricultural employment of cheap Haitian labor to fuel large rural-urban migrations. Wilfredo Lozano (1987) asserts that the swollen unemployed and underemployed population served as a labor reserve for the modern sector during the import-substitution period. In times of growth, the formal sector absorbed labor from this reserve; in times of recession, formal workers were forced to join its ranks. The urban unemployed and underemployed labor pools were constantly nourished both by migrations from rural areas and by the internal growth of the urban economically active population. Most of the rural-urban migration was directed toward Santo Domingo, the capital city, which experienced annual average rates of population growth of 5 to 6 percent during the 1960s and 1970s.

The Dominican state's managers never attempted to develop an effective welfare net for the underemployed and unemployed. In addition, the objective of labor and social laws legislated since 1966 has been to limit or erase those worker rights and benefits that had been previously granted, at least in the letter of the law (Hernández Rueda 1989; Lozano 1985). In practice, workers were granted few protections in terms of job security and working conditions, and protections were seldom effectively enforced (Murphy 1990).

Toward the end of the 1970s, the import-substitution model was reaching exhaustion. The immediate causes of the economic crisis in the Dominican Republic were reductions in the demand for and the prices of traditional exports and a rise in the price of oil imports. These trends exacerbated the chronic trade deficit that characterized the import-substitution period. An upswing in interest rates on the country's external debt then triggered the debt crisis of the 1980s.

These conditions led the state's managers and segments of the business class to adopt a new mode of insertion into the world economy that transformed the country into an exporter of services, low-wage products, and labor itself. Tourism, export-assembly manufacturing, and agroindustry became the new growth sectors. To these should be added remittances from Dominican migrants in the United States, who became a crucial source of foreign exchange.[4]

Among the countries of the Caribbean, the Dominican Republic has advanced the farthest in the application of export-oriented policies. This advance is the result of state policies that allowed the country to capitalize on the opportunities offered by the Caribbean Basin Initiative (CBI) launched by the U.S. government under the Reagan administration in the 1980s. The Dominican state legislated strong incentives for the development of export manufacturing zones, tourism, and agroindustry.[5] Yet the policy instrument most responsible for the success of the export policies has been the successive devaluations of the currency since 1984, which have made Dominican labor among the cheapest in the Caribbean Basin.[6] This fact, together with relative political stability and the state-led improvement of infrastructure for export-assembly manufacturing and tourism, turned the Dominican Republic into an attractive site for investors and visitors alike (Abreu et al. 1989; Lozano and Duarte 1992).

It is important to recognize that the Dominican Republic's switch to export-oriented policies during the 1980s was not accompanied by a sustained commitment to policies of fiscal austerity and market liberalization. In the early to mid-1980s, the administration of Salvador Jorge Blanco[7] (1982-1986) did implement the standard package of International Monetary Fund (IMF) stabilization measures, but Balaguer's return to power in 1986 was connected to the popular rejection of those measures. After his return, Balaguer carried out expansionary fiscal policies based on public expenditures in the construction sector. Not until 1991 was a new agreement with the IMF reached and a series of neoliberal reforms of state institutions and trade regime agreed upon (Ceara Hatton 1993). So far, they have been inconsistently applied. And while by indicators such as aggregate growth the economy has not done badly, by others — such as the widespread bankruptcy of state-owned enterprises, the frequent inability to pay the salaries of public sector employees, and worsened income inequality — it has deteriorated (Castro 1996; ECLAC 1996). This pattern is likely to have reinforced the main labor-market trends documented in this chapter.

Export-oriented Transformation and Sectoral Recomposition

Export-oriented policies in the Dominican Republic have focused on the promotion of export-assembly manufacturing, tourism, and agroindustry (FUNDAPEC 1992). What occurred, then, with respect to employment in import-substitution manufacturing and in the public sector, the most important generators of employment under the previous inward-oriented development model?

During the 1980s, there was a clear trend downward, both absolute and relative, in employment in manufacturing for the domestic market (see Table 2). Employment in the public sector did not change in absolute terms but declined in relative terms. In sharp contrast, the volume of employment in export-assembly manufacturing multiplied seven times, its share of the employed labor force swelling from 1.1 percent to 5.8 percent. Export-assembly employment alone accounted for 17 percent of total job growth during the period.

Table 2.
National Employment in Selected Sectors
numbers in parentheses are percentages

	EAP[a]	Employed	Domestic manufac- turing	Govern- ment[b]	Export manufac- turing zones
1980	2,111,500	1,642,700 (100)	156,365 (9.5)	187,212 (11.4)	18,338 (1.1)
1991	3,036,837	2,310,715 (100)	145,100 (6.2)	186,998 (8.1)	134,998 (5.8)
Growth	925,337	668,015	-11,265	-214	116,559

Source: FUNDAPEC (1992, Table 1.11).
a = Economically active population
b = Does not include employment in state-owned enterprises.

Job growth in tourism and agroindustry has not been as rapid. The number of jobs in tourism increased by a net 13.8 percent during the 1980s. Agroindustry was already an important employer during the import-substitution era. During the 1980s, however, state policy attempted to direct agroindustry's production toward exports. Although agricultural exports grew considerably during the decade, employment in agroindustry rose only by 3.7 percent.[8] Yet, overall, jobs in export-assembly manufacturing, tourism, and agroindustry increased substantially as a portion of total nationwide employment, from 8.9 percent in 1980 to 12.3 percent in 1991. This increase points to a significant internationalization of the production of goods and services.

What was the pattern of remuneration in these internationalized sectors? Under the shift to an export-oriented economy, a rise in the share of low-wage employment is expected, as discussed in Chapter 1. Of those Dominicans who worked at least 44 hours a week (the legal full-time working week) in 1991, roughly 19 to 26 percent earned less than the legal minimum wage in the private sector.[9] According to estimates, the private sector minimum wage provided only 47.5 percent of the amount needed for a worker to live above the poverty line (CIECA 1993a). Table 3 shows that 65 percent of the workers in the internationalized activities had earnings below the poverty line.

In view of the long-range earnings trend, these wage data seem to confirm the expected increase in the prevalence of low-wage jobs. Indeed, as a result of government policies of promoting capital accumulation

Table 3.
Distribution of Earnings of Workers Employed 44 or More Hours per Week in Export Manufacturing Zones, Agroindustry, and Tourism, 1991
percentages

Monthly Wages (in RD$)	Export Manufacturing Zones	Agroindustry	Tourism
<1,200[a]	18.9	20.6	25.5
1,200-1,500	22.5	21.8	25.9
1,501-2,000	20.5	27.0	13.7
2,001-3,000	19.9	18.9	18.3
3,000+	18.2	11.6	16.5
Average Wage	2,201.3	1,910.1	2,148.6

Source: CIECA (1993a, Table 2.27)
a = Minimum wage in the private sector at the time of the survey.

through cheap labor, the Dominican economy has experienced a decline in average wages since the early 1970s — much before the economy's shift toward exports. The real minimum wage in the private sector in 1992 was 58 percent of its 1970 level, and in the public sector it was only 32 percent (CIECA 1993b). Hence, low wages in the nontraditional growth sectors are part of a broader trend of diminishing pay, and the average earnings of workers in export-manufacturing zones, tourism, and agroindustry are actually higher on average than those in the public sector and agriculture (CIECA 1993a; IED 1992).

How are these findings explained? Balaguer's policy during his 1986-1990 administration was to expand public expenditures, particularly in construction. In this way, he fostered job growth while confronting deficitary pressures on the government budget through a heavy reduction of public employees' salaries. Balaguer even justified this policy by claiming that public employees supplement their salaries by accepting bribes (Ceara Hatton 1993). Migrants from Haiti facilitated the lowering of wages in agriculture during the import-substitution era. The slightly higher wages in the internationalized activities were supposed to pull labor from the declining traditional activities.[10] Following Gary Fields (1990), it could be claimed that wages in the public sector are repressed, whereas in the internationalized sectors wages are market-determined. The next section, though, will show that wages in the new growth sectors are below market-clearing levels (see note 10), pushing many workers from the public sector and from import-substitution manufacturing into the informal economy.

So far, the data show a fall in the percentage of total jobs in government and in domestically oriented manufacturing, a rise in the percentage of total jobs in export manufacturing and tourism, and falling average pay across the economy. Yet, in spite of their rapid ascent, the internationalized spheres of the economy do not account for the majority of employment growth. Tertiary activities (that is, commerce and services in general) have absorbed most new entrants into the labor market. According to Table 4, locally based commerce, services, and transport represented a greater share of the urban economically active population in 1991 than in 1980 — notwithstanding the fast growth of export-assembly jobs.[11] This apparent pattern contrasts with the case of Costa Rica, where the share of urban employment in manufacturing increased, based on expanded export production (Tardanico and Lungo this volume, Chapter 4).

In Latin America and the Caribbean, the recent expansion of tertiary employment is associated substantially with the growth of the informal economy (see, for example, Portes, Itzigsohn, and Dore-Cabral 1994). Under the new, internationalized model, the growth of tourism provides a source of formal sector tertiary employment. The main contribution of tourism to the new internationalized model, however, is not job creation but the provision of hard currency. In addition, expanded tertiary formal sector employment in tourism is likely to be offset by decreased formal employ-

Table 4.
Distribution of the Urban Economically Active
Population by Industry
percentages

	1980[a]	1991[a]
Agriculture	6.9	5.4
Manufacturing	18.9	16.5
Construction	6.1	3.9
Commerce	21.0	25.2
Services	35.0	39.1
Transportation	3.9	4.9
Other	7.2	5.2

Source: Ramírez (1993, Graph 3.1).
a = Does not equal 100 percent due to rounding.

ment and by deteriorating job conditions in general in the public and private sectors. The bulk of tertiary employment is therefore likely to be created in the informal economy, particularly in the form of low-skilled, low-paid jobs.

Informalization and Casualization

As mentioned above, neoliberal export policies appear to be accelerating the informalization and casualization (that is, rise in the share of temporary and unprotected employment) of labor relations in Latin America and the Caribbean. On the one hand, formal firms may informalize part of their production processes, mainly through subcontracting, to reduce labor costs and enhance flexibility. On the other hand, workers expelled from the shrinking formal firms or from the public sector may enter into informal activities, especially when pay and conditions in newly created formal jobs do not prove attractive. The decreased income of household heads may induce other household members into the labor market, during a time of a steep rise in the hiring of contingent workers, which amounts to a de facto deregulation of labor markets (ILO 1991). Thus, in the urban Dominican Republic, informal and casual jobs are expected to grow as a percentage of all employment.

During the 1980s, urban areas of the Dominican Republic apparently underwent a rise in the percentage of self-employment and a reduction in the percentages of employers and wage workers (see Table 5). For Santo Domingo, the capital and principal city, part of the large increase in the percentage of self-employment may be the result of the methodological inclusion of casual workers (that is, people doing occasional self-employed work, called *chiriperos* in the Dominican Republic) under this category. The data do not distinguish between wage workers in large firms (with 50 or more workers), medium-sized firms (five to 49 workers), and microenterprises (less than five workers), making it impossible to see if there were changes in the employment of wage workers in the formal and informal sectors.

There is one major difference between the trends for Santo Domingo and for the country's other urban zones. The proportion of owners decreased in the capital, while experiencing a sizable increase elsewhere. Unpaid family work grew during the peak of the economic crisis and then

Table 5.
The Labor Market by Occupational Sector in the Urban Dominican Republic and in Santo Domingo
percentages

	1980	1991[a]
Urban Dominican Republic		
Employers	2.1	3.8
Self-employed	25.1	27.9
Wage workers	70.5	62.2
Unpaid family workers	2.3	4.6
Santo Domingo		
Employers[b]	5.1	2.9
Self-employed[b]	14.5	25.2
Wage workers[b]	73.5	70.0
Unpaid family workers[b]	1.2	1.9
Casual workers[b]	5.7	—
Unemployment[c]	21.4	21.9[d]

Sources: Ramírez (1993, Graph 3.3); Duarte (1986, Table 4 [Chapter 3]); Lozano (1987, Table 1); CED (Centro de Estudios Dominicanos) and Central Bank of the Dominican Republic (statistical information compiled by the author).

a = The percentages for the urban Dominican Republic for 1991 sum only to 98.5 percent. The other 1.5 percent are classified as "other."

b = The figures for 1980 are from Duarte (1986, Table 4 in Chapter 3). The figures for 1991 are from CED, information compiled by the author.

c = The figures for 1980 are from Lozano (1987). The figure for 1980 was calculated by the author based on data obtained from the Central Bank of the Dominican Republic. See note 3.

d = Figure for March 1990.

decreased, but its reported 1991 level was still higher than in 1981. Open unemployment reportedly remained constant and very high during the decade, at 21 to 22 percent of the labor force (see note 3).

The rise in the percentage of self-employment does not mean necessarily that jobs grew disproportionately at the bottom end of income and working conditions. Anthropologist Martin Murphy (1990) reports that almost all of the *lechugueros*[12] that he interviewed in Santo Domingo prefer their occupation to a minimum-wage job in the formal economy, in spite of the fringe benefits attached to the latter. The reason, explains Murphy, is that their income is consistently higher than that of minimum-wage workers. Similar responses were found in a study of the informal economy in Santo Domingo (Itzigsohn 1994). A high proportion of the labor force involved in informal activities is male and in its mature years — including microentrepreneurs, the self-employed, and wage workers in microenterprises — who can be expected to form the core of the working class. They choose to work in the informal economy because of its higher pay or better working conditions. This preference for informal over formal employment is connected to the declining formal sector wages and increasingly precarious formal sector labor conditions. In other words, the border between the formal and informal economies has become increasingly blurred.[13]

In order to capture the changing scope of precarious work, two indicators are examined: the percentage of workers who are paid below the legal minimum wage, or "invisible underemployment," and the percentage of workers unprotected by social security. These indicators were selected for their universality — most countries have regulations regarding these two issues — and for their importance in the reproduction of the labor force (that is, the daily replenishment of labor's capacity to work).

A large layer of underemployed workers has been a constant element of the urban labor market in the Dominican Republic since the beginning of industrialization. A survey conducted in Santo Domingo in 1980 found that 38.7 percent of wage workers and 56.1 percent of the self-employed earned less than the legal minimum wage (Lozano 1987). A survey of manufacturing and construction workers conducted in Santo Domingo in 1981 found that 7 percent of workers in the import-substitution industries, 30.2 percent of construction workers, and 12 percent of the export-zone workers were paid less than the minimum wage (Duarte 1986).

This chapter does not have comparable data for the beginning of the 1990s, but other studies have reported high percentages of workers earning less than the minimum wage in the export zones, tourism, and agroindustry (see Table 3; FUNDAPEC 1992; CIECA 1993c). A 1992-1993 survey of medium-sized firms (with five to 49 workers) and microenterprises (with less than five workers), which are major sites of employment growth, reports that 56.3 percent of workers in the surveyed firms earned less than the minimum wage (Cabal 1993). The underemployed encompassed 42.5 percent of those working in manufacturing, 62 percent in retail, and 63.8 percent in services. This research concludes that the larger the firm, the fewer the number of underemployed workers. In firms with four to 10 workers, the number of workers earning less than the minimum wage was 27.1 percent, while in firms employing 11 to 50 workers, it was only 7 percent.

This profile points to two tendencies in the Dominican labor market. First, precarious work not only is quite pervasive but has expanded as a share of overall employment in the growing segments of the formal economy, which are export-processing zones, tourism, and agroindustry. Second, informal work is most widespread throughout the economy in firms with less than 10 workers. The data seem to confirm the expectation that labor's position has become more insecure under a neoliberal regime of export-oriented growth. Parallel tendencies are reported throughout this volume.

Concerning the extent of worker coverage by social security — another key indicator of precarious employment — there are no definitive numbers. Against prediction, though, there is evidence that social security coverage of the economically active population increased from 8.5 percent in 1985 to 13.9 percent in 1991.

This growth of social security coverage suggests an extension of formal labor relations in the Dominican Republic during the 1980s. These figures, however, mask some countervailing trends. First, violations of the social security law are widespread in export-assembly manufacturing, tourism, and agroindustry. In these leading growth sectors, supposedly the state-regulated arenas of the new development model, social security coverage encompasses just 75 percent of workers in the export-processing zones and 72 percent in tourism and agroindustry. In violation of the law, then, one-quarter of the labor force in these internationalized sectors is informal (CIECA 1993c).

Second, the quality of social security services has deteriorated, a sign that the state is retreating from whatever meager commitment it previously had to guarantee labor reproduction. The extension of coverage was accompanied by an abrupt drop in social security expenditures. Moreover, a study of demand for health services in Santo Domingo found that, among the people who consulted a physician in 1987, only one-half of those insured under the IDSS (Instituto Dominicano de Seguro Social — Dominican Social security Institute) used its medical facilities, and one-third turned to private health services (Gómez, Bitran, and Zschock 1988).

Large formal businesses have begun to offer workers affiliation with private health organizations. Most of the people who enjoy health insurance are members of private health organizations, and about one-third of the people who contribute to the IDSS are also covered by private health insurance (CNHE 1992). Thus, despite expansion of the share of the population covered by social security, its provisions are becoming less important for the reproduction of the labor force. That is, the reproduction of the working population of Santo Domingo is carried out decreasingly by state programs and increasingly by private means.

To summarize, the data suggest a general informalization and casualization of labor relations in the Dominican Republic that accelerated under the export-oriented policies of the 1980s. Employment became more insecure and informal while the state's welfare institutions played a diminishing role in the reproduction of the labor force. There is also evidence that in the early 1990s precarious employment was widespread in the internationalized spheres of export-assembly manufacturing, tourism, and agroindustry. The main urban occupational responses to the new export policies were a substantial rise in self-employment and a small rise in unpaid family labor as percentages of the workforce. Thus, the boundaries between the formal and informal economies in the Dominican Republic became blurred by both the economic crisis of the 1980s and the state-orchestrated shift in development models (Itzigsohn 1994).

Exports, Informalization, and Gendered Employment

The deterioration of real income and the informalization of labor relations in the Dominican Republic were accompanied by a massive growth of the labor force. For the working-age population, the rate of labor-force participation grew from 46.8 percent in 1981 to 54.7 percent in 1990 (Baez 1992). The changes in occupational structure described above altered the gender composition of both specific occupations and the labor market in general. This is likely to have occurred for two reasons. On the supply side, falling household income caused more women to enter the labor market to maintain the living standards of households. In this regard, the Dominican Republic's economic crisis of the 1980s imposed additional pressures on many households, boosting the number of female-headed households and transforming many women into the primary household earners (Safa and Antrobus 1992). On the demand side, the wage gap between women and men signals that as firms compete in the market by reducing labor costs, they increasingly recruit women.

Two hypotheses merit testing. The first is that as household income deteriorates, more women enter the labor market. The second is that women enter the labor market mainly in low-wage, export-assembly manufacturing and in informal occupations.

Industrialization in Santo Domingo was characterized by growing rates of women's labor-market participation even before the transition from inward-oriented to outward-oriented development models. For the whole country, men's rate of participation dropped from 75.9 percent in 1960 to 68.2 percent in 1981, while women's rate ballooned from 9.3 percent to 27.1 percent. In the urban areas in 1981, the level of women's participation was reportedly even higher, 32.7 percent (Ariza et al. 1991; Baez 1992).

The expansion of women's share of the labor force continued during the 1980s, when the nationwide rate of participation rose for both genders but much more so for women. For every 100 men in the labor force, there were 40.7 women in 1981 but 55.1 women in 1990 (Baez 1992). Major increases in women's share of the labor force are documented throughout this volume.

The nationwide rise in participation rate was steepest for 15- to 24-year-old women, followed by 25- to 39-year-old women, 15- to 24-year-old men, and 25- to 49-year-old men. It contracted sharply for early adolescent females and males, and it contracted for women 45 and older but generally

Table 6.
Labor-Force Participation Rates by Gender and Age
percentages

	Male			Female		
Age	1981[a]	1990[a]	1991[b]	1981[a]	1990[a]	1991[b]
10-14	21.8	5.4	22.6	13.8	8.8	25.9
15-19	44.9	56.4	75.3	22.0	37.0	62.2
20-24	72.3	93.7	86.5	35.0	58.9	78.9
25-29	84.7	95.2	93.7	40.5	57.7	79.8
30-34	87.7	98.4	95.4	39.5	51.6	78.6
35-39	88.5	98.7	93.9	35.2	56.4	77.4
40-44	88.5	99.3	96.4	36.0	42.4	71.1
45-49	88.3	98.9	92.6	34.1	32.4	65.6
50-54	87.0	94.5	94.1	31.1	22.0	47.7
55-59	85.6	85.4	80.9	30.0	25.3	41.0
60-64	83.9	88.0	79.3	29.1	11.7	29.8
65+	74.5	50.0	42.9	28.1	9.1	16.9
Total	68.2	72.2	78.9	27.1	38.0	60.0

Sources: Baez (1992, Table 2); Ramírez (1993, Table 2.2).
a = Nationwide participation rates (Baez 1992, Table 2).
b = Urban participation rates (Ramírez 1993, Table 2.2).

rose at a moderate pace for men (see the chapters on Costa Rica [4] and Guatemala [3]). The nationwide data indicate, in sum, a vigorous influx of younger women into the labor market and a withdrawal of women 45 and older, together with a more moderate influx of young men and a more even age distribution of growth in men's rate of participation.[14] Put simply, women and mid-teenage to middle-age adults in general became more preponderant in the labor force.

Strikingly, the officially measured rise in women's participation was primarily based on women's entry into the ranks of the unemployed (see Table 7). Apparently, the proportion of unemployed women rose substantially between 1981 and 1990. A dramatic change, moreover, seems to have occurred in the composition of female unemployment. According to the data, the number of formerly employed women looking for jobs dropped, while the number of female first-time job seekers grew elevenfold. Reportedly, then, about two-thirds of the women who entered the labor

Table 7.
Women's Labor-Force Participation and Unemployment

	1981		1990	
	N	**%**	**N**	**%**
Female EAP[a]	554,279		1,099,420	
Employed	444,146	80.1	713,457	64.9
Unemployed[b]	110,113	19.9	385,945	35.1
Formerly employed	75,340	68.4	12,556	3.3
First-time job seekers	34,793	31.6	373,389	96.7

Source: Baez (1992, Table 1).
a = Economically active population.
b = See note 3.

force during the decade did so as previously unemployed. In other words, for every woman who found a job, two others tried but seemingly failed (see note 3).

So, regarding the hypothesis that falling household income accelerates the incorporation of women into the labor market, the data appear to reveal three trends: first, an increase in women's and men's rates of labor-force participation; second, greater increase for women than men, based on the robust upswing for young and early-mature women; and third, an apparent lack of jobs for most of the labor force's new female participants.

Next consider the hypothesis that female employment grew mainly in low-wage manufacturing and informal occupations. Export zones, whose comparative advantage is based mainly on their ability to recruit cheap labor, absorb high levels of female labor. Indeed, in 1992, 60.5 percent of the 141,054 employees in the export-assembly zones were women.[15] The number of women working in these zones in 1980 is not known, but the total number of export-assembly-zone workers — female and male — was 18,000. Thus, even if all the employees in those zones in 1980 were women (which, of course, they were not), the numbers for 1992 indicate a faster absorption of female than male labor in export manufacturing.

Two-thirds of the female employment in the export-assembly zones is concentrated among unskilled workers and office employees, who rank among the zones' lower earners. In contrast, male workers have greater representation among the skilled workers, supervisors, and administrative personnel, who rank higher on the earnings scale (CIECA 1993a; FUNDAPEC 1992). Some 89 percent of export-zone workers are between 20 and 40 years old. This fact partially explains the Dominican Republic's vigorous rise in female labor-force participation within this age span (FUNDAPEC 1992).

To reiterate, wages in the export-processing zones are not the lowest in the Dominican urban labor market. There is evidence that many women working in the export zones are new entrants into the labor market from rural areas near cities where the export zones are located (FUNDAPEC 1992; Santana 1993). For these women, work in the export zones is a mixed situation. Working conditions are very bad, and the women are exploited severely. Yet the jobs give women access to economic resources that they otherwise would not have and that may improve their bargaining position within households.

Manufacturing, in general, has been a site of expanded female employment. It represented 15.1 percent of the country's female employment in 1981 and 17 percent in 1990. Nonetheless, nationwide job growth for women has been fastest in tertiary activities, which grew from 72.5 percent to 79.9 percent of the Dominican Republic's total female employment. Female tertiary employment rose fastest in the category of "commerce, restaurants, and hotels," from 15.8 percent of the nation's total female employment in 1980 to 24.5 percent in 1990. Social and personal services employed the most sizable share of women in 1980, 53.8 percent of all employed women, but by 1990 this had shrunk to 45.8 percent. Nevertheless, the absolute number of employed women grew, and social and personal services still concentrate the greatest portion of female employment (Baez 1992).

The rise in female tertiary employment may be an indicator of the expanded insertion of women in the informal economy. In particular, the major expansion of employment in commerce may signal that informal activities are the primary vehicle of female entry into the labor market. In 1990, 22.3 percent of the urban women with jobs were self-employed. Furthermore, some research reports that women came to own a disproportionate fraction of the country's informal enterprises and to represent one-third of the workforce in those enterprises (Cabal 1992; FUNDAPEC 1992).

Women's employment in low-wage manufacturing rose as a result of the expansion of export industries that compete on the basis of cheap labor; indeed, women have constituted the majority of the labor force in export-assembly manufacturing. The principal area of expanded women's employment, though, was service and commerce occupations that can be considered part of the informal economy. It is not clear whether women became the predominant labor force in those occupations, but, considering the gamut of data, it can be surmised that their share grew.

Reflecting the special vulnerability of female workers, most of the women entering the labor market did so through unemployment. Nevertheless, in a country where income levels are so low and have declined so much, and where there is virtually no government safety net, it is doubtful that many people who express their desire to work are truly unemployed. It is more likely that they are engaged in unrecorded gainful activities of different kinds, such as doing occasional work, organizing *sanes*,[16] or even selling clandestine lotteries. Yet, since these activities are not reported as work, the true extent of people's participation in them is not known.

Finally, a contrasting trend is a marked upturn in the portion of women working in professional and technical occupations (as is also documented in other chapters in this volume). These occupations rose from 10.6 percent of female employment in 1981 to 17 percent in 1990. The upturn is a consequence of more women having technical and higher education, which is also associated with decreased rates of unemployment (Baez 1992).

Exports and the Labor Markets of Secondary Cities

What have been the effects of the Dominican Republic's shift to nontraditional exports on the spatial concentration of urban work? Across Latin America and the Caribbean, the import-substitution model tended to concentrate industry and population in one or two major cities. This occurred because industrialization was linked to the internal market and the larger internal markets were concentrated in those major cities. Industries established themselves in the main urban centers, thereby attracting even more people to them. In the Dominican Republic, the core site of manufacturing growth was the capital city, Santo Domingo.

In contrast, the export-oriented model is not linked to the internal market and does not necessarily lead to spatial concentration. Tourist activities are often located away from the main urban center. Export-assembly firms need access to transportation by air or sea, industrial infrastructure, and access to cheap labor. While access to transportation and industrial infrastructure is usually easier near the principal city, cheaper labor is not necessarily found there because the principal city usually has some political tradition of labor organization. Moreover, if state leadership seeks industrial decentralization, it may implement policy enabling the construction of appropriate infrastructure in locations outside the main urban center. It can be said, therefore, that the export-oriented model has the potential to foster industrial decentralization. Whether or not this will happen depends on the political and economic configurations of each country (Portes, Itzigsohn, and Dore-Cabral 1994).

In the Dominican case, export-oriented policies appear to have indeed led to a measure of economic decentralization, although there are no data adequate for longitudinal comparison. Most of the employment in tourism has been located outside of Santo Domingo, especially in the Central Cibao region, where Santiago de los Caballeros is located. A secondary concentration in tourism employment has been the Valdesia region, where Santo Domingo is located, and most of those jobs are probably located in the capital city. The location of some of the larger hotels and the country's main airport in Santo Domingo or its vicinity explains this pattern in the Valdesia region (see Lozano and Duarte 1992).

The geography of export-assembly activities is related to efforts by the state's leadership to develop areas of the country outside Santo Domingo. The Dominican state took upon itself the building of infrastructure for export zones in secondary cities. As a result, the growth in assembly manufacturing employment took place mainly in the secondary cities of Santiago de los Caballeros, La Romana, and San Pedro de Macorís. In 1992, out of a national total of 142,000 persons employed in export-processing zones, those three cities concentrated 81,000 jobs, while the export zones of Santo Domingo and its neighboring areas employed around 11,000 people (calculated on the basis of information compiled by the author at the Consejo Nacional de Zonas Francas de Exportación [National Council of Free Export Zones]).

Thus, export-assembly manufacturing apparently brought about fastest growth of employment in areas other than the capital city. Wilfredo Lozano and Isis Duarte (1992) remark, though, that the growth of such employment has taken place predominately in cities that were already important components of the urban system under the import-substitution model. Employment growth has not reached the more backward areas of the country, which are outside of the principal transportation arteries that connect the secondary cities with Santo Domingo. As a consequence, export-assembly manufacturing has slightly changed the population ratio between Santo Domingo and the main secondary cities, but it has not altered the basic pattern of population concentration in a few urban centers and relative neglect of the rest of the country. This contrasts with the trend found in Guatemala and Costa Rica toward the expansion of the primary city and the inclusion of its adjacent urban centers within a larger metropolitan area without significant growth in secondary cities (Pérez Sáinz, [Chapter 3] and Tardanico and Lungo [Chapter 4], this volume).

To be sure, export-assembly jobs were created in Santo Domingo, while much of the administrative infrastructure for the functioning of the zones is located in the capital. It is probable that Santo Domingo's share of jobs indirectly related to the export zones is greater than the city's share of directly related jobs. In any case, the scale of the Dominican Republic's overall employment shift has not jeopardized Santo Domingo's status as the primary city.

A related issue is that the development impact of the export zones in the regional economies has been very weak (Lozano and Duarte 1992). That is, the creation of the export zones promotes regional employment, but because of the absence of local economic linkages, it has not promoted regional development. The findings of Julio Santana's (1993) study on the effects of the Santiago export-processing zone on the regional economy parallel this chapter's findings on the national urban economy. In the Cibao Central, Santana finds an increase in labor-force participation by men and women as well as an increase in unemployment. He also finds that the export zone generates mainly female employment, above all for new entrants into the labor market. Perhaps most significant, Santana concludes that the primary multiplier effect of export-zone employment is the creation of a market for informally produced goods and services. That is, the expansion of export-assembly manufacturing has tended to promote low-skill, low-paid informal activities that provide basic consumer goods and services to the low-wage workers of the export zones.

The data, in short, give apparent support to the following conclusions on geographic patterns. First, the export-oriented model has accelerated employment growth in secondary cities relative to Santo Domingo. Second, this acceleration has yet to challenge the position of Santo Domingo as the dominant city, in both demographic and socioeconomic terms. And third, the growth of export zones in secondary cities reproduces at the regional level the labor-market trends found for the country as a whole.

Conclusions

At the beginning of the 1980s, the import-substitution model was in crisis, and the Dominican Republic needed desperately to increase its foreign currency earnings. In response, the country's government leaderships adopted export-oriented policies. What were the consequences of these export-oriented policies and economic change for the urban labor market, social welfare, and social inequality? The following summarizes the findings of this chapter concerning sectoral recomposition, the informal economy, gendered participation, and spatial change.

The export campaign focused on assembly manufacturing, international tourism, and agroindustry. Wages in these sectors are not the lowest in the national labor market and are significantly higher than wages in the public sector, where jobs fell in relative but not absolute terms, and in agriculture. In this context, jobs grew quite rapidly in assembly manufacturing and substantially in tourism but only slightly in agroindustry. Yet, the fastest growing sectors of employment seemingly were not in the export economy but in the locally oriented branches of tertiary activity. This apparent trend was tied to the heightened precariousness and informalization of labor conditions at large.

Indeed, heightened precariousness and informalization are the most evident labor-market consequences of the country's export-oriented policies and economic change. This overriding trend was interlaced with a notable decline in the role of the state's welfare institutions in the reproduction of the labor force. The period's rise in the informal economy's share of total employment was primarily expressed in a considerable increase in the percentage of self-employment. Above all, employment became more insecure — including in the new internationalized growth sectors — substantially as a result of weakened enforcement of labor law and the deterioration of social security services.

During the 1980s, social security coverage of the labor force expanded in Santo Domingo. Yet, countering this apparent "formalization" of the economy was a pronounced worsening of social security services. As a result, the reproduction of the labor force became increasingly privatized for all segments of society: for the more protected sectors among formal workers who, through contractual agreements in firms, obtain access to private health care and private pension funds; and for the other workers who are compelled to find the means for socioeconomic reproduction through household-based means or other private strategies. Hence, the demarcation between the formal and informal economies in the labor force's reproduction became much more ambiguous.[17]

The period's drop in average real household income hastened the entry of women into the labor market, thereby reinforcing its longer-term feminization. Women tended to enter the labor force in low-wage and informal occupations. The main form of women's incorporation, however, was reportedly through the status of unemployment. Since there is essentially no government safety net in the Dominican Republic, it stands that many so-called unemployed women are in fact engaged in informal economic activities. Going against informalization, though, was the smaller-scale trend of female incorporation into professional and managerial activities.

Geographically, there occurred a dispersion of employment, reversing the import-substitution tendency toward the concentration of employment in Santo Domingo. This reversal brought about the growth of the already established secondary cities, bypassing the most backward and neglected areas of the country. Yet, rather than seeing significant development gains, the expanding secondary cities experienced growth in low-wage manufacturing and the low-wage informal economy. In any case, the territorial dispersion of employment was not strong enough to threaten the standing of Santo Domingo as the principal city of the country's urban system.

Thus, the new policy of emphasizing internationalized economic activities — based on the comparative advantage of cheap labor — has contributed to widening inequalities and deterioration of social welfare. An important question, though, concerns the labor market's long-term prospects: Is the deterioration in labor conditions a permanent or temporary trend? In conditions of excess labor supply, such as in the Dominican Republic, it is possible that the growth of labor-intensive manufacturing and services will eventually have the positive consequences of increasing labor absorption and reducing underemployment and unemployment. Ostensibly, in turn, these consequences could lead to a rise in average real earnings and a reduction in earnings inequality.

Unfortunately, the evidence presented in this chapter provides little hope for a turn toward a higher-wage economy. The growth of low-wage employment has not generated a significant expansion of desirable categories of employment. To the contrary, it has provoked a considerable reactive expansion of the economically active population and of underemployment, while by no means alleviating the chronic problem of high levels of open unemployment. So, instead of absorbing the excess labor supply, the neoliberal export-oriented policies have exacerbated the problems that characterized the import-substitution era. It is important to recognize that these processes unfolded in spite of widened emigration to the United States during the 1980s. Notwithstanding the abundance of cheap local labor and the outlet of international migration, the Dominican Republic's version of export-oriented growth and economic internationalization has not provided any solution to the problems of labor absorption in the cities of the Dominican Republic.

It is interesting to note some similarities and differences between the case of the Dominican Republic and the cases of Costa Rica since the 1980s and Chile in the 1990s (see Díaz [Chapter 6] and Tardanico and Lungo [Chapter 4], this volume). Labor conditions have worsened in all three countries. Compared with the Dominican Republic, though, Costa Rica and Chile have witnessed much less expansion of the informal economy and much lower levels of unemployment. Moreover, the increased insecurity of formal employment in Costa Rica and Chile has been tempered by state policies designed to protect the weakest strata of workers. In particular, the conditions of public sector employment in Costa Rica and Chile have not deteriorated as much as in the Dominican Republic. These labor-market differences can be substantially attributed to differences in state structure and policy among these countries (Díaz this volume, Chapter 6; Itzigsohn 1994; Tardanico and Lungo this volume, Chapter 4).

The labor-market processes described in this chapter have important implications for social policy. With the exception of successful microentrepreneurs and artisans, the upward mobility of labor and households under import-substitution development was tied to entry into formal wage relations. In recent years, however, this situation may have been reversed. In labor markets shaped by economic globalization and neoliberal policies, both resistance to downward mobility and the incidence of upward mobility often appear tied to the resourceful use of opportunities created through the informal economy (see Itzigsohn 1994 and Chapter 3 in this volume by Pérez Sáinz). For a growing share of people, this trend involves the widened and deepened risks inherent in the drastic weakening of the state's role in market regulation. The findings of this chapter suggest that labor-market deregulation is not the solution to the employment problems of the region. They point, therefore, to the need for a renewal of state activism — in some form that corresponds to the globalization of the contemporary world — in the upgrading of employment conditions in underdeveloped countries.

Notes

1.   This chapter is based on the analysis of secondary sources, published and unpublished, from the Dominican Republic. The most important ones are Encuesta Demográfica y de Salud 1991 (Endesa-91) (IEPD 1991) and Encuesta Nacional de Mano de Obra (ENMO '91) (FUNDAPEC 1992). The analysis of diverse secondary sources confronts the analyst with two basic problems. First, the last national census was conducted in 1981. This means that research for the 1990s consists of various surveys that differ in sampling methodologies and in the questions asked. As a result, the surveys are not strictly comparable. Nevertheless, combined with other studies on changes in the political economy of the Dominican Republic, the data provide a reasonably coherent picture of the period's labor-market transitions. Second, the data often do not distinguish between urban and rural employment. Since much of the data, however, are on manufacturing and other, mostly urban occupations, it can be assumed with a high degree of certainty that they primarily represent trends in urban employment.

2.   The key elements of neo-patrimonialism are "...a centralization of power in the hands of the ruler...and a blurring of public and private purposes within the administration" (Hartlyn 1994, 94). Neo-patrimonialist regimes combine elements of democracy and authoritarianism.

3.   Low rates of open unemployment are typically reported for countries that fall within or below the Dominican Republic's range of pronounced economic underdevelopment. A common observation is that, due to the virtual absence of a government safety net, unemployment tends to be an unaffordable luxury for the impoverished masses in such countries and that low rates of open unemployment are offset by high rates of low-wage, often informal, employment (see, for example, Chapter 3 on Guatemala). In the case of the Dominican Republic, there are very high rates of reported unemployment and low-wage and informal employment. In comparative perspective, it should be kept in mind that many people who are officially classified as unemployed in the Dominican Republic are probably in fact engaged in informal labor activities and that the very high rate of unemployment is probably, to some extent, an artifact of survey methodology. At the same time, there is ample evidence that both general and particular features of the state policies and socioeconomic sweep of agricultural and manufacturing transformation in the Dominican Republic, as well as the large and long-standing presence of Haitians in its agricultural economy, have indeed created severe unemployment problems (Ferrán and Pessar 1991; Grasmuck 1982; Lozano 1987; Lozano and Duarte 1992; on the case of Jamaica, which has also long reported very high rates of unemployment, see Henry 1991 and Portes, Itzigsohn, and Dore-Cabral 1994).

4.   Revenues from tourism represented 8.6 percent of exports of goods and services in 1977 and 30.4 percent in 1986. During the same years, remittances grew from 12.6 percent to 14.5 percent of hard currency revenues, and income from export-processing zones grew from 2.5 percent to 5.3 percent of those revenues. Meanwhile, earnings from traditional exports decreased from 51.9 percent of hard

currency revenues in 1977 to 22.8 percent in 1986. In 1990, sugar exports provided only 8 percent of export revenues, while tourism provided 40 percent (Ceara Hatton 1991; Fundación Economía y Desarrollo 1989).

5.   Most of the incentives and protections that fueled the growth of tourism and agroindustry were abolished during a sweeping economic reform in 1991.

6.   In 1983, the hourly cost of labor in the Dominican Republic's export-processing zones was US$0.85, higher than in Costa Rica, Honduras, and Colombia. In 1988, after four years of currency devaluation policies, the hourly cost was $0.60, equal to that in Honduras and higher only than that in Jamaica, Haiti, and Guatemala among the countries of the Caribbean Basin (Abreu et al. 1989).

7.   Salvador Jorge Blanco headed the second and last administration of the Partido Revolucionario Dominicano (Dominican Revolutionary Party — PRD), which held office from 1978 to 1986, a brief interlude in the many years of Balaguer hegemony.

8.   As of 1991, employment in tourism was 27,268, compared with 124,196 in agroindustry and 134,998 in export-assembly zone employment.

9.   At the time of the survey, the minimum wage in the private sector stood at RD$1200, the equivalent of US$100.

10.   The higher wages in the growing sectors correspond nicely to the "old" W. Arthur Lewis (1954) model of industrialization with unlimited supplies of labor. Lewis asserted that in a context of labor surplus, a wage slightly above the prevalent subsistence level will prompt the move of the labor force from the "traditional" toward the "modern" sector. This chapter shows that the overall consequences for the labor market in the Dominican Republic have been very different from those envisioned by Lewis.

11.   A similar trend, not shown in the table, characterizes the rural economically active population, where commerce and services have increased their share of employment at the expense of agriculture.

12.   *Lechugueros* are mobile retail vendors who sell vegetables and fruits from their tricycles, essentially push carts mounted on bicycle frames. They are representative of Santo Domingo's informal self-employed workers.

13.   On the connections of the country's urban informal enterprises with emigration to and remittances from the United States, see Portes and Guarnizo 1991.

14.   The rates of participation for urban areas are higher than for the country as a whole. This is in part because, at least for women, rates of labor-force participation are higher in urban than rural areas (IEPD 1991). It is also the result of an atypical feature of the survey methodology that disproportionately affects the reported level of women's participation rate. The survey from which the data are taken includes in the economically active population those people who expressed a desire for work even though they did not search for a job. Thus, the rate of participation and, particularly, the rate of unemployment are higher than those obtained with traditional methodologies. Most surveys include as "unemployed" only those people who have been searching for a job within a determined period of time. When excluding those who express a desire for work, the survey reports men's urban rate of participation at 72 percent (down from 78.9 percent) and women's at 35.5 percent (down from 60 percent), much closer to the national level.

15. This information was provided to the author by the Consejo Nacional de Zonas Francas de Exportación. It contradicts the results reported by ENMO'91 (FUNDAPEC 1992), which puts the proportion of the female labor force at 48.2 percent. But, since the data provided by the Consejo represent the sum of the information provided by the employers rather than a result of a survey, I am confident that they are accurate.

16. *Sanes* are rotative saving schemes, which are very common among the working class and the poor in the Dominican Republic.

17. Ironically, the deregulation of labor relations was accompanied in the Dominican Republic by congressional legislation of a new labor code that extended worker rights. For example, the new law guarantees legal protection for union members against arbitrary dismissal, a guarantee that did not exist formerly. There is a growing gap, however, between labor laws and actual employment practices in the Dominican Republic.

References

Abreu, Alfonso, Manuel Cocco, Carlos Despradel, Eduardo García Michel, and Arturo Peguero. 1989. *Las zonas francas industriales*. Santo Domingo: Centro de Orientación Económica.

Ariza, Marina, Isis Duarte, Carmen Julia Gómez, and Wilfredo Lozano. 1991. *Población, migraciones internas y desarrollo en la República Dominicana 1950-1981*. Santo Domingo: Instituto de Estudios de Población y Desarrollo.

Baez, Clara. 1992. "Mujeres: fuerza laboral y sector informal." *Estudios Sociales* 88: 99-116.

Cabal, Miguel. 1992. *Microempresas y pequeñas empresas en la República Dominicana*. Santo Domingo: FONDOMICRO.

Cabal, Miguel. 1993. *Evolución de las microempresas y pequeñas empresas en la República Dominicana: 1992-1993*. Santo Domingo: FONDOMICRO.

Ceara Hatton, Miguel. 1993. "De reactivación desordenada hacia el ajuste con liberalización y apertura." Unpublished manuscript. Santo Domingo: Centro de Investigación Económica para el Caribe (CIECA).

Ceara Hatton, Miguel. 1991. "La economía dominicana 1980-1990." Paper prepared for the Third Conference of Caribbean Economists, Santo Domingo, July 16-20.

Castro, Max. 1996. "The Long Transition: Dilemmas of Democracy and Development." *North-South Focus* 5:2. Coral Gables, Fla.: North-South Center at the University of Miami.

CIECA (Centro de Investigación Económica para el Caribe). 1993a. *Impacto del ajuste y las reformas estructurales en la pobreza y el desarrollo humano en la República Dominicana*. Santo Domingo: CIECA.

CIECA. 1993b. "El comportamiento del salario." *Notas de Coyuntura* 23(May).

CIECA. 1993c. "La distribución del ingreso en 1991." *Notas de Coyuntura* 22(February).

CIECA. 1992. *El gasto público social de República Dominicana en la década de los ochenta*. Santo Domingo: CIECA/UNICEF.

CNHE (Consejo Nacional de Hombres de Empresa). 1992. "Diagnóstico financiero-actuarial y costo de factibilidad de la ampliación de cobertura sin modificar el modelo de prestación del IDSS." Report to the CNHE, Santo Domingo.

Duarte, Isis. 1986. *Trabajadores urbanos*. Santo Domingo: UASD.

ECLAC (Economic Commission for Latin America and the Caribbean). 1989. *The Evolution of the Latin American Economy in 1987*. Santiago, Chile: ECLAC.

ECLAC. 1996. *Economic Survey of Latin America and the Caribbean 1995-1996*. Santiago, Chile: ECLAC.

Ferrán, Fernando I., and Patricia R. Pessar. 1991. "Dominican Agriculture and the Effect of International Migration." In *Small Country Development and International Labor Flows*, ed. Anthony P. Maingot. Boulder, Colo.: Westview Press.

Fields, Gary S. 1990. "Labor Standards, Economic Development, and International Trade." In *Labor Standards and Development in the Global Economy*, eds. S. Herzenberg and Jorge F. Pérez-López. Washington, D.C.: U.S. Department of Labor.

FUNDAPEC (Fundación APEC). 1992. *Encuesta nacional de mano de obra*. Santo Domingo: Fundación APEC.

Fundación Economía y Desarrollo. 1989. *Impacto del sector privado en la economía dominicana*. Santo Domingo: Acción Empresarial.

García, Norberto. 1991. "Ajuste estructural y mercados de trabajo." *Crítica & Comunicación* (1).

García, Norberto, and Victor E. Tokman. 1984. "Changes in Employment and the Crisis." *CEPAL Review* (December).

Gereffi, Gary, and Stephanie Fonda. 1992. "Regional Paths of Development." *Annual Review of Sociology* 18:419-448.

Gómez, Luis Carlos, Ricardo Bitrán, and Dieter Zschock. 1988. "La demanda de servicios de salud en el Distrito Nacional." *Población y Desarrollo* 24(October-December).

Grasmuck, Sherri. 1982. "Migration within the Periphery: Haitian Labor in the Dominican Sugar and Coffee Industries." *International Migration Review* 16(2):365-372.

Henry, Ralph M. 1991. "A Reinterpretation of Labor Services in the Commonwealth Caribbean." In *Small Country Development and International Labor Flows*, ed. Anthony P. Maingot. Boulder, Colo.: Westview Press.

Hernández Rueda, Lupo. 1989. *Manual de derecho del trabajo*. 2 vols. Santo Domingo: Editorial Tiempo.

Hartlyn, Jonathan. 1994. "Crisis Ridden Elections (Again) in the Dominican Republic: Neopatrimonialism, Presidentialism, and Weak Electoral Oversight." *Journal of Interamerican Studies and World Affairs* 36:91-144.

IED (Instituto de Estudios Dominicanos). 1992. *Carta de información sobre empleo, sector informal y microempresas* 29(May).

IEPD (Instituto de Estudios de Población y Desarrollo). 1991. *Población, migraciones internas y desarrollo 1950-1981*. Santo Domingo: Profamilia.

ILO (International Labor Organization). 1991. "Politicas de empleo en la restructuración económica en América Latina y el Caribe." WEP 1-4-07(Doc. 1). Geneva.

Itzigsohn, José. 1994. "The State, the Informal Economy, and the Reproduction of the Labor Force: A Comparative Analysis of the Informal Economy in Santo Domingo and San José." Ph.D. dissertation, Department of Sociology, The Johns Hopkins University.

Katzman, Reuben. 1984. "Sectoral Transformations in Employment in Latin America." *CEPAL Review* (December).

Lewis, W. Arthur. 1954. "Economic Development with Unlimited Supplies of Labour." *The Manchester School of Economic and Social Studies* 22(May): 139-191.

Lizardo Espinal, Magdalena. 1989. *Cambios en la economía mundial y sus repercusiones sobre el sector externo dominicano.* Santo Domingo: Fundación Friedrich Ebert.

Lozano, Wilfredo. 1985. *El reformismo dependiente.* Santo Domingo: Editora Taller.

Lozano, Wilfredo. 1987. "Desempleo estructural, dinámica económica y fragmentación de los mercados de trabajo urbanos: el caso dominicano." *Ciencia y Sociedad* 12(3):360-388.

Lozano, Wilfredo, and Isis Duarte. 1992. "Proceso de urbanización, modelos de desarrollo y clases sociales en la República Dominicana 1960-1990." In *Urbanización en el Caribe,* eds. Alejandro Portes and Mario Lungo. San José, Costa Rica: FLACSO.

Murphy, Martin. 1990. "The Need for a Re-evaluation of the Concept of 'Informal Sector': The Dominican Case." In *Perspectives in Economic Anthropology,* ed. Mary E. Smith. Lanham, Md.: University Press of America.

ONE (Oficina Nacional de Estadísticas). 1990. *República Dominicana en cifras.* Santo Domingo: ONE.

Pineda, Magaly. 1990. "*...la vida mía no es fácil." La otra cara de la zona franca.* Santo Domingo: CIPAF.

Portes, Alejandro, José Itzigsohn, and Carlos Dore-Cabral. 1994. "Urbanization in the Caribbean Basin: Social Change during the Years of the Crisis." *Latin American Research Review* 29(2):3- 38.

Portes, Alejandro, and Luis Guarnizo. 1991. "Tropical Capitalists: U.S.-Bound Immigration and Small-Enterprise Development in the Dominican Republic." In *Migration, Remittances, and Small Business Development in Mexico and the Caribbean Basin,* eds. Sergio Díaz-Briquets and Sidney Weintraub. Boulder, Colo.: Westview Press.

Ramírez, Nelson. 1993. *La Fuerza de trabajo en la República Dominicana.* Institute of Population and Development Studies Monograph Series, no. 3.

Ramos, Joseph. 1984. "Urbanization and the Labor Market." *CEPAL Review* (December).

Safa, Helen, and Peggy Antrobus. 1992. "Women and the Economic Crisis in the Caribbean." In *Unequal Burden: Economic Crises, Persistent Poverty and Women's Work,* eds. Lourdes Benería and Shelley Feldman. Boulder, Colo.: Westview Press.

Santana, Julio. 1993. "Reestructuración neoliberal, zonas francas y proceso de urbanización en la Región del Cibao: el caso de Santiago, República Dominicana." Unpublished manuscript. Santo Domingo: FLACSO.

World Bank. 1993. *World Tables.* Baltimore: The Johns Hopkins University Press.

Chapter 3

Crisis, Restructuring, and Employment in Guatemala

Juan Pablo Pérez Sáinz

During the 1980s, Guatemala, like other Latin American countries, suffered a severe economic crisis. It also embarked upon a process of economic restructuring aimed at establishing a new, transnationalized model of accumulation. Crisis and restructuring have aggravated Guatemala's profound social inequalities, the historical roots of which run deep: More than three-fourths of the population now lives in poverty and more than one-half lives in extreme poverty. Exacerbating Guatemala's socioeconomic plight is its persistent crisis of governability, although the brutality of Guatemala's military regime and civil war gave way to democratic opening in the mid-1980s and to the signing of United Nations-mediated peace accords between the government and guerrilla forces in late 1996.

This chapter begins with a brief analysis of the course of Guatemala's economic crisis and structural adjustment during the 1980s, and then, from the perspective of the hypotheses that underlie this volume's comparative agenda, it examines the period's changes in the structure of employment and social inequality. The reader should be forewarned that the data for Guatemala are far less abundant than for most other countries included in this volume. Consequently, this chapter emphasizes only the broadest features of transformation in employment and social inequality.

By the end of the 1980s, labor conditions in Guatemala were even more insecure than before. The expansion of informal, subsistence activities as a share of total employment was manifested in increases in subsistence employment in agriculture and urban informal commerce, along with an initial phase of growth in low-wage, export-platform manufacturing. In this setting, the basic form of labor-market adjustment was a precipitous rise in employment paying less than the legal minimum wage rather than growth of open unemployment. Employment diminished in agriculture relative to commerce/services and manufacturing and in the public sector relative to the private sector. As the female portion of jobs expanded, the degradation of employment conditions was more uniform for women than men. Thus, women's employment became much more informalized and much more

Juan Pablo Pérez Sáinz is senior researcher at FLACSO-Costa Rica. Translated by Richard Tardanico.

centered on subsistence activities, as its industry share of jobs rose most in agriculture followed by manufacturing and commerce. Yet, while men's employment became somewhat more formalized, men's informal employment became, like women's, much more weighted toward the subsistence economy. Employment for women and men seems to have become more differentiated and unequal within the formal and informal economies alike.

The most vulnerable to the polarizing impact of economic crisis and adjustment were indigenous groups, women, the least-educated, and non-heads of households. A noteworthy departure from this rule were gains by the most educated women in the middle and upper tiers of the urban occupational structure. At the same time, transnational restructuring seems to have been associated with some amount of socioeconomic gain in certain localities, as in the case of San Pedro Sacatepéquez, an indigenous community located in the vicinity of Guatemala City, which appears to have parlayed the economy's nascent upturn in export-platform manufacturing into some capacity for local accumulation.

Economic Crisis and Structural Adjustment

As elsewhere in Central America and Latin America during the 1980s, economic crisis in Guatemala was related to the exhaustion of the import-substitution model of development, including, in the case of Guatemala, the unraveling of the model's Central American underpinnings of regional economic integration. Guatemala's aggregate prosperity of the 1970s — average annual growth of 5.7 percent in gross domestic product (GDP) — came to a halt (see Table 1). During the 1980s, the economy experienced five years of stagnation punctuated by a period of contraction, followed by nascent recovery. In the early 1990s, however, a surge in inflation and currency devaluation raised troubling questions about the depth and stability of recovery.

The economic crisis hit bottom in 1982-1983, the moment of greatest intensity in Guatemala's socially polarized, bloody civil war.[1] A military coup in March 1982 — promoted by young officers critical of the course of the war and the military's corruption — put an end to the electoral fraud by which the army had maintained its hold on the reins of government since the previous decade. Another military coup in August 1983 made the army more disposed to political reform. A process of democratic opening led to non-fraudulent elections in 1985, a rarity for Guatemala. Emerging victorious was a civilian, the Christian Democrat Vinicio Cerezo, who began his six-year term as president the following year.

Guatemala's economic deceleration during the early 1980s stemmed most basically from declines in the market value of the country's traditional exports (primary products such as coffee, cotton, and sugar and Central American-oriented manufactured products such as processed food and textiles) and in the volume of private investment (Table 1). The latter decline was a consequence of both Guatemalan and Central American political volatility and the regional economic crisis. Guatemalan industrialization had

Table 1.
Economic Indicators
Five-Year Averages in 1980 Dollars

	1980-1984	1985-1989
GDP[a]	0.1	2.2
GDP per capita[a]	-4.0	-0.9
Gross fixed capital formation[a]	-6.7	-5.3
Exports[a]	-1.7	2.2
External public debt service[b]	16.8	40.8
Consumption per capita[c]	899.4	798.8

Source: Pérez Sáinz 1994, Table 1.
a = Average annual rate of growth.
b = As percentage of exports.
c = Average annual total.

grown during the 1960s within the framework of Central American market integration. Then during the early 1980s, the economic contraction in the rest of the region, which was more abrupt even than in Guatemala, plunged the country's manufacturing sector into recession. Simultaneously, drought and flooding eroded agricultural exports.

Compounding these problems was an upturn in world petroleum prices, which increased the cost of imports. The negative impact on the country's trade balance led, as elsewhere in Central America and Latin America, to a severe balance-of-payments crisis. Then came capital flight, reflecting not only a steep increase in U.S. interest rates but, in view of the mounting trade deficit and political uncertainty, national expectations of a currency devaluation (Bulmer-Thomas 1989, 317-319).

Capital flight had major ramifications for capital accumulation (see Table 1), as disinvestment continued throughout the decade. Initially, public sector investment compensated for the drop in private investment, with government spending generating the largest share of domestic demand in 1979-1981. Government spending instigated, however, a spiral of foreign indebtedness. At the beginning of the 1980s, debt-service payments stood at just 3 percent of exports; by the end of the decade, they stood at 41.7 percent.

Economic recovery took hold during the second half of the 1980s, coinciding with the installation of a democratically elected, civilian government. Three elements fostered the recovery. First, foreign exchange became more available because export prices improved, political stability lured capital back to the country, the government deployed national monetary reserves, and the International Monetary Fund provided credits. Second, the civilian government implemented a policy of increased real wages, thereby bolstering private consumption to regenerate domestic demand. And third, the rate of gross fixed capital formation rose, particularly as flight capital returned to Guatemala.

The Christian Democratic administration of Vinicio Cerezo (1986-1992) managed to stabilize the economy by strengthening the quetzal and controlling inflation as part of its recovery program, Short-term Plan for Socio-Economic Reorganization (Plan de Reordenamiento Económico Social de Corto Plazo — PRES).[2] The administration's success contrasted with the unsuccessful attempts at economic stabilization by the preceding military governments, most notably the effort by President Efraín Ríos Montt in 1982-1983, which ultimately contributed to his overthrow in a military coup. In addition to PRES, the Cerezo government formulated two other strategic plans: Guatemala Plan 2000 (Plan Guatemala 2000) sought to foster economic restructuring, including the growth of nontraditional exports, while the National Reorganization Program (Programa de Reorganización Nacional — PRON) sought to offset the country's deteriorating standard of social welfare. Plan Guatemala 2000 may have been successful. PRON, however, failed to survive the opposition of powerful business groups to tax reform proposed to fund the program. By the end of the 1980s, economic uncertainty loomed again. In 1990, inflation reached historic levels, and the quetzal was devalued by more than one-half; since then, Guatemalans have faced ongoing economic as well as political uncertainty, albeit including the optimism surrounding the peace accords of 1996 (see, for example, ECLAC 1995a; FLACSO/SEGEPLAN/UNICEF 1992).

In regard to structural adjustment, the Cerezo government's performance was contradictory. On the one side, through the Law for the Promotion and Development of Export and Maquila Activities (Ley de Fomento y Desarrollo de la Actividad Exportadora y de Maquila) and other measures, it made important strides toward the restructuring of domestic production to meet the demands of the globalizing world economy. Nevertheless, dominant business groups militantly opposed the proposed tax reform, thereby undercutting a potential pillar of support. The government's erratic, uncoordinated implementation of economic measures left its programs all the more vulnerable to the political opposition (FLACSO/SEGEPLAN/UNICEF 1992, 41-50). Hence, the second stage of adjustment, restructuring, began without the full achievement of the first stage, stabilization.

The social costs of crisis and adjustment were high (see the last two indicators in Table 1). The magnitude of the contraction in per capita GDP underscores the severity of the social impact, especially during the early 1980s. The decade-long drop in per capita consumption was even steeper, signaling that the social impact of the economy's problems of the 1980s was comparable to what had occurred in the 1930s (Bulmer-Thomas 1989, 334). It is the increase in poverty, though, that most accurately captures the deterioration in social conditions during the 1980s. The incidence of poverty rose from 63.4 percent of the population in 1981 to 79.9 percent in 1989. Even more dramatic was the rise in extreme poverty, from 31.6 percent of the population to 59.3 percent (INE 1991; Ruiz 1990).

The period's changes in the labor market are closely intertwined with the spread and deepening of poverty (see Chapter 1). The data for 1989 indicate that two labor-market measures, open unemployment and working fewer hours than desired, are not linked to poverty (Table 2). In other words, being unemployed or "visibly underemployed" does not appear to have a notable effect on the likelihood of being poor. Perhaps because open unemployment and visible underemployment are, in the absence of a government safety net, veritable luxuries for poor households, these rates were very low in Guatemala. Conversely, what bears the strongest connection to poverty is working more than 40 hours per week for less than the legal minimum wage — that is, jobs with low productivity, prolonged work shifts, and low pay (so-called "invisible underemployment").

Employment in the 1980s

What changes took place in Guatemala's structure of employment during the 1980s?[3] Rates of labor force participation and employment rose during the early 1980s, while the rate of open unemployment remained low. Instead of shrinking toward its previous level during the subsequent nascent recovery, labor force participation remained at the newly elevated level. Apparently economic crisis forced households to send more members into the labor market to offset decreases in household income, yet the incipient macroeconomic upturn did not reverse this trend.

Consideration of gender and age allows one to address the social contours of Guatemala's employment recomposition. With respect to gender, the expansion of the labor force was due largely to the incorporation of more women. Their rates of participation and employment doubled,

Table 2.
National Labor Profile of the Poor and Non-Poor
1989

Rates	Indigent	Non-Indigent	Total Poor	Non-Poor	Grand Total
Participation[a]	44.7	53.1	47.1	58.7	49.7
Unemployment	1.7	3.0	2.1	1.8	2.0
Employment	44.0	51.5	46.1	57.7	48.7
Visible under-employment	10.1	11.1	10.4	10.7	10.5
Invisible under-employment	72.8	41.4	62.8	24.2	52.5

Source: INE 1991.
a = Refers to total population.

Table 3.
National Labor Profile of Population by Gender and Age

	Population 10+Years	Rates		
		Participa-tion	Employ-ment	Unemploy-ment
1981				
Men	2,024,311	71.6	70.4	1.7
Women	2,070,842	12.0	11.7	1.7
10 to 20 years		23.0	22.4	2.8
20 to 39 years		52.1	51.2	1.7
40 years and over		49.4	48.9	1.0
Total	**4,095,153**	**41.4**	**40.7**	**1.7**
1986-1987				
Men	2,670,744	77.5	75.3	2.8
Women	2,801,330	24.0	22.6	5.7
10 to 20 years		32.3	30.6	5.2
20 to 39 years		62.1	59.5	4.2
40 years and over		55.7	55.1	0.6
Total	**5,472,074**	**50.1**	**48.3**	**3.5**
1989				
Men	2,806,429	76.9	75.3	1.6
Women	3,023,801	24.5	23.7	3.2
10 to 20 years		31.5	30.6	2.8
20 to 39 years		61.7	60.2	2.4
40 years and over		56.7	56.3	0.8
Total	**5,830,230**	**49.7**	**48.7**	**2.0**

Source: INE 1985, Table 16; 1987, Table I.1; 1990, Table I.1.

while those of men rose only slightly (see Table 4). Evidently, the entry of women into the labor force was a principal response of households to economic crisis and structural adjustment.[4] The case of Guatemala, then, is consistent with the broad findings on gender presented throughout this volume. Turning to age, the net rate of increase in participation and employment was greatest by far for the youngest group (under 20 years of age) followed by the middle-aged group (20-39 years of age), although the data do not disaggregate this trend by gender. Thus, the entry into the labor pool of not only women but also female and male youths was a key reaction of households to worsening economic hardship.

What can be discerned about changes in the distribution of employment across occupational categories? In 1981, the two principal categories, private sector wage workers and the self-employed, had nearly identical shares, 39 and 40.9 percent, respectively, of total employment (see Table 4). By 1986-1987, the share of private sector wage workers had risen to 41.2 percent, while that of the self-employed had dropped substantially to 33.4 percent. This pattern of change does not imply, however, that economic crisis induced a major shift to wage employment: When public sector employees are added, wage workers made up 47.2 percent of total employment in 1981 and 48.6 percent in 1986-1987 (see Table 4). Hence, the decline in self-employment was more than offset by a startling growth in unpaid family labor, which jumped from 6.8 to 16.6 percent of total employment.[5] This is a notable occupational recomposition of informal employment in the direction of subsistence activities. This altered composition remained intact during the decade's subsequent years of aggregate economic improvement.[6]

Thus, a fundamental response of households to crisis and adjustment appears to have been a striking expansion of home-based economic activities. This suggests that the labor force's growth did not always translate into new sources of income, even though the greater deployment of labor in family-based economic initiatives may have led to some increase in, or less acute decrease of, household income.

In regard to gender, women's share of employment increased in every occupational category, most rapidly during the years of economic downturn. Their greatest decade-long proportional increases were in the nonwage categories of self-employment (220.3 percent) and unpaid family employment (182.9 percent) (see Table 4).[7] The broader evidence on occupational structure reveals a gendered pattern of change. Among men, the crisis led to an expanded significance of private sector wage labor, together with change in the structure of nonwage labor. Wage work in private sector firms rose from 36.7 percent of all male jobs in 1981 to 40.9 percent in 1989. Self-employment's portion of all male jobs dropped from 44.2 to 33.3 percent, but the portion of unpaid family labor more than doubled, from 7.4 to 17.3 percent. That is, nonwage jobs dropped from 51.6 to 50.6 percent of overall male employment, but the percentage of males working as unpaid family labor leaped. Combined with the relative expansion of private sector wage work, there emerges a picture of further differentiation and polarization of

Table 4.
Employed Population by Occupational Category and Industry[a]
in percentages

	1981		1986-1987		1989	
	Men	Women	Men	Women	Men	Women
Occupational Category						
Employers	1.7	1.3	2.8	1.7	1.6	1.1
Public wage employees	7.4	12.8	6.2	7.7	6.9	8.8
Private wage employees	36.7	52.5	42.5	41.5	40.9	42.5
Self-employed	44.2	21.7	31.4	34.1	33.3	33.5
Unpaid family workers	7.4	3.5	17.1	15.0	17.3	14.1
Unknown	2.6	8.2				
	100	**100**	**100**	**100**	**100**	**100**
Industry						
Agriculture	61.2	9.3	63.5	15.2	61.3	16.0
Manufacturing	9.3	18.1	10.6	19.2	10.4	23.2
Commerce	6.8	21.0	7.8	32.6	8.0	28.7
Personal, social, and community services	7.9	43.4	9.0	31.4	9.7	29.4
Other	14.8	8.2	9.1	1.6	10.6	2.7
	100	**100**	**100**	**100**	**100**	**100**

Source: Calculations based on INE (1985, 1987, 1990).
a = For each year, each category represents the percentage of total occupational employment and total industry employment for men and the percentage of total occupational employment and total industry employment for women.

men's occupational structure. This included a pronounced occupational restructuring of men's informal employment toward subsistence activities.

For women, the worsening of occupational composition was even clearer. The exception was the most highly educated women, whose share of jobs expanded in the middle and upper echelons of the urban occupational hierarchy (according to data not presented here; see this volume for Itzigsohn on the Dominican Republic [Chapter 2] and Tardanico and Lungo on Costa Rica [Chapter 4]). Their gains, though, exemplified the differentiation and polarization of female employment. On balance, the portion of women engaged in private sector wage jobs plunged, from 52.5 percent of all female employment in 1981 to 42.5 percent in 1989. Hence, the expansion of women's employment centered on nonwage labor, which nearly doubled, from 25.2 to 47.6 percent of all women's jobs. One reason for this increase is that nonwage economic activity eases the entry of women into the labor force. By allowing more flexible control over the schedule and place of work, it is easier than wage employment to combine with family responsibilities. Not to be overlooked, however, is that as the percentage of women in formal employment dropped, this category appears to have been reorganized occupationally as well, but in the direction of improved rather than worsened composition.

The data suggest, then, that open unemployment was not Guatemala's core mechanism of labor-market adjustment. Neither was the growth of public sector employment, whose share of all jobs fell slightly (from 8.2 to 7.4 percent). The other chapters of this volume show that open unemployment and public sector employment played larger roles in Latin America's more developed countries during the 1980s' economic crisis. In the case of Guatemala, the evidence indicates that a massive expansion of women's self-employment and unpaid household employment and a reproportioning of men's nonwage work toward unpaid household employment were the focal points of labor-market adjustment.[8]

So, within a framework of increased differentiation and inequality, informal employment among both women and men centered increasingly on subsistence activities. Formal employment, particularly for women, likewise became more differential and unequal.

The agricultural sector's position as the country's largest employer is indicative of Guatemala's severe economic underdevelopment, although its share of total national employment reportedly declined (from 54 percent in 1981 to 49.9 percent in 1989). Each of the other sectors gained in national employment share. Commerce made the largest gain (from 8.7 to 13.2 percent) followed by manufacturing (from 10.5 to 13.7 percent) and services (from 12.8 to 14.7 percent).[9] At the end of the decade, however, job growth was fastest in manufacturing for men as well as women.[10]

With respect to urban versus rural activities, crisis and adjustment do not appear to have accelerated the migratory flow from countryside to city, especially to Guatemala City.[11] In fact, countervailing transformations have been taking place in Guatemalan agriculture, particularly in the western region (see Negreros 1989b). In the coastal areas of traditional export-oriented agriculture, regional population growth, the subdivision of small landholdings, and mechanization have fostered a more wage-based labor force. This has reduced the local demand for seasonal migratory labor. In the highlands, moreover, improved productivity (in both export and subsistence production), diversification toward livestock and toward nonagricultural activities, such as handicrafts and commerce, and international migration and remittances have reduced the dependence of the region's permanent and temporary wage workers on urban employment (Baumeister 1991).

Considering both the urban and rural economies, between 1981 and 1989, employment in commerce became predominately female, growing from 33.5 to 54.9 percent of the sector's total. Women's portion of service employment expanded from 47.4 to 50.5 percent. Nonetheless, the most rapid decade-long growth in women's share of intra-industry employment was in agriculture (237.5 percent versus 79.5 percent in manufacturing and 63.9 percent in commerce).[12] Between 1986 and 1989, however, the feminization of manufacturing outpaced all other sectors, even as it became the point of fastest job growth for men as well as women. This shift in industry distribution of job growth likely reflects the expansion of export-assembly manufacturing (see this volume's chapters on the Dominican Republic [2], Costa Rica [4], and Mexico [8]).

A comparison of data for 1981 and 1989 supports this project's comparative hypothesis predicting growth in the employment share of tertiary activities (see Tables 3 and 4). From 1981 to 1989, tertiary activities grew from 21.5 to 27.9 percent of total employment, as male but not female employment became more tertiarized (see note 12). The bulk of this trend took shape during the early part of the decade, when the economic crisis fueled a massive expansion of low-end employment in commerce. Subsequently, it was manufacturing — probably export-assembly production in particular — that generated the fastest job expansion (see Table 4). The reduction of employment in agriculture was not tantamount to significant de-ruralization of Guatemala's labor market, since much of the shift involved the countryside's economic diversification from agriculture into handicraft production and commerce.

Another hypothesis predicts increased feminization of the workforce. The data tend to confirm this given that the greater female than male upturn in participation during the years of economic crisis did not reverse during the macroeconomic recovery. So far, then, the enhanced feminization of Guatemala's workforce during the period of economic downswing in the early 1980s appears to be an enduring trend.

The data also indicate that, as anticipated, women's portion of jobs rose most in the nonwage occupational categories of self-employment and unpaid family employment. Evidently, then, women, even more than men, took on insecure labor activities. Nevertheless, women also showed advances in professional and technical jobs. While tertiary employment became predominately female, women's intra-industry portion of jobs climbed fastest in agriculture, followed by manufacturing and commerce.[13]

Given that, as expected, public sector employment diminished as a percentage of all jobs, the low rate of open unemployment throughout the 1980s points to underemployment as the main form of labor-market adjustment. The slight proportional growth of self-employment and unpaid family employment (from 47.7 to 49.9 percent of all jobs) — which reflected intense nonwage occupational growth and recomposition for women together with nonwage occupational recomposition for men — bolsters this conclusion. This pattern of change confirms the hypothesis that precarious and informal employment would become more prevalent.

This volume's most basic hypothesis — that degraded employment became more prevalent — can be explored further from the standpoints of visible underemployment (working fewer hours than desired) and invisible underemployment (working more than 40 hours weekly and for less than the legal minimum wage). The available data refer only to the recovery years of 1986-1987 and 1989. Across this period, the rate of visible underemployment remained virtually constant (from 10.8 to 10.5 percent), while that of invisible underemployment rose (from 47.7 to 52.5 percent) (INE 1991). Clearly, invisible underemployment — a prime measure of precarious and informal labor activity — solidified its standing as the most prominent feature of Guatemala's employment structure.

The sociodemographic and occupational profile of unemployment and underemployment for 1989 reveals that the rate of unemployment for women was twice that of men but that the absolute levels for both groups were very low (Table 5). The most glaring gender difference is in visible underemployment. The much higher rate of female than male visible unemployment reflects women's traditional family responsibilities, which preclude many women from working as many hours as men.

Two dimensions stand out regarding the impact of education (Table 5). The rate of unemployment was highest among persons with high school education, as is generally the case across Latin America (ECLAC 1995b, 184). Furthermore, the lower the level of education, the higher the rate of invisible underemployment. That is, the terms of employment were by far worst for the least educated.

Concerning ethnicity, the social correlates of invisible underemployment are clear: Indigenous groups are the most vulnerable to precarious employment (Table 5). One study of indigenous workers in Guatemala City (Pérez Sáinz, Camus, and Bastos 1992) argues that this group is caught up in a vicious cycle, whereby low-wage employment compels indigenous families to push as many members as possible into the labor force, including women and children. This limits educational opportunities, which in turn consigns indigenous groups to the lowest-paid jobs. In short, lack of educational capital condemns the indigenous population of Guatemala City to the most insecure kinds of employment.

Table 5.
Socio-Occupational Profile of Rates of Underemployment
and Unemployment, 1989[a]
in percentages

	Visible Under-employment	Invisible Under-employment	Open Unem-ployment
Men	7.6	53.1	1.6
Women	18.9	50.8	3.2
No education	9.8	68.3	0.7
Primary education	10.1	52.4	1.8
Secondary education	12.9	21.4	6.1
Tertiary education	13.7	6.0	2.1
Indigenous	8.3	71.7	0.5
Non-indigenous	11.7	41.7	2.9
Public employees	12.0	8.7	0.5
Private employees	9.2	42.7	1.3
Self-employed	12.3	59.4	3.3
Unpaid family workers	10.1	88.6	0.0
Agriculture	7.3	69.3	0.5
Manufacturing	15.3	36.5	2.4
Commerce	13.2	49.9	2.1
Personal, social, and community services	17.0	32.7	3.0
Other	10.5	52.5	2.0

Source: INE 1990, Tables I.1, I.3, I.7, II.1, and II.2.
a = The data for occupational category and industry do not include first-time job seekers.

In occupational categories, there is an anticipated pattern: The incidence of invisible underemployment was lowest in the public sector and highest among unpaid family workers (Table 5). Also as expected, regarding industries, measures of degraded employment were highest outside manufacturing. The rate of visible underemployment was highest in services, presumably personal services; the rate of invisible underemployment was highest in agriculture; and the rate of unemployment was highest in construction (6.9 percent) (Table 5).

The range of data imply an informalization of urban employment. It must be kept in mind, however, that most of this chapter's data do not distinguish between urban and rural locations. Two studies on informal employment in Guatemala City allow for a better approximation. The first study (PREALC 1986) estimates that in 1981 informal employment accounted for 30 percent of the city's total employment; the second study (Pérez Sáinz 1991) estimates that in 1989 informal employment was 33 percent of the total. Acknowledging the lack of strict comparability between them, the two studies suggest that urban informal employment became more common.

A comparison of Guatemala City's informal and formal sectors in 1989 with regard to labor supply and labor demand[14] shows that the percentage of female employment was higher in the informal sector (see Table 6).[15] The difference in average worker age between the informal and formal sectors is much less important than the fact that workers of mature age predominate in both. Nonetheless, disaggregating the age data reveals some interesting patterns (see Pérez Sáinz 1991, 48-50). There is no difference between the informal and formal sectors in the percentage of workers younger than 20 years of age. This finding suggests that the sectors play comparable roles as paths of entry into the labor market for the youngest segment of the labor force. Conversely, a substantial difference characterizes workers older than 64 years of age: Twice as many are employed in the informal sector as in the formal sector. In large part, this difference corresponds to the magnitude of micro-entrepreneurs and the self-employed in the informal sector. It appears, therefore, that the informal sector provides a crucial place for the elderly to continue being employed if they manage to gain access to means of production (Pérez Sáinz 1991, 48-50).[16]

Education plays a key role in allocating workers to either the formal or the informal sector (Table 6; see also Table 5). In 1989, Guatemalan workers with advanced education had easy access to the formal sector, whereas those with little or no schooling were relegated to the informal sector.[17] With regard to another demographic trait, it may be surprising at first glance that household heads in Guatemala City comprised virtually equal percentages of employment in the formal and informal sectors (Table 6). It appears that informality was not exclusively a refuge for the so-called secondary workers of households but that it was by far the more accessible sector for indigenous labor.

Table 6.
Profile of Formal and Informal Employment
in Guatemala City
1989

	Formal Sector	Informal Sector	Total
Average age	35.9	40.1	36.0
% Women	30.3	41.7	37.0
% without education	3.6	15.3	8.3
% with higher education	21.2	0.2	14.6
% Household head	50.2	51.3	48.8[a]
% Indigenous	6.8	18.1	11.3
% Employed in services	35.0	39.6	32.9[b]
% Social security coverage	73.6	4.8	46.5
Average hours per week	42.7	48.6	44.7
Average monthly income (quetzals)	506.3	348.8	438.2

Source: Pérez Sáinz 1991, Tables 1-8.
a = The total presented for this category is less than the figures presented for the formal and informal sectors because domestic service employees, who are exclusively household dependents rather than heads, are not included in the data for either the formal or the informal sector.
b = The total presented for this category is less than the figures presented for the formal and informal sectors because domestic services are not included.

What can be said about the characteristics of workplaces? A profile of workplaces in Guatemala City shows that service activities accounted for the largest share of workplaces in the formal sector (see bottom of Table 6). This is no surprise given the dominant administrative role of the capital city and its large share of public sector employment relative to the rest of the country. In the informal sector, commerce represented the largest share of workplaces.

The length of the work week also differed between the formal and informal sectors (Table 6). The work week in the formal sector conformed to what is considered the full-time standard (40-44 hours). A longer work week in the informal sector suggests a greater incidence of marginally paid work. This emerges strikingly from the difference in average monthly income between the two sectors. In terms of long-range income, the prevalence of marginally paid work also emerges from the data on social security coverage (Table 6).

The data, in sum, uncover multiple differences between the formal and informal sectors in Guatemala City, particularly regarding gender, education, ethnicity, industry composition, and precarious conditions. The informal sector was marked by higher percentages of female and indigenous labor, much lower levels of schooling, and a greater focus on commerce. Moreover, its employment conditions were much worse in terms of its minimal degree of state regulation, its marginal average pay, and its longer work week.

By no means, however, is the informal sector homogeneous. For instance, data for Guatemala City based on the categories defined by the Regional Program for Employment in Latin America and the Caribbean (Programa Regional del Empleo para América Latina y el Caribe — PREALC) yield pronounced variation within the informal sector between micro-entrepreneurs and the self-employed. Typical of micro-entrepreneurs is a proclivity to pursue business strategies that enable their establishments to prosper and grow; typical of the self-employed is a strategy of mere subsistence. Variation within the informal sector is also evident in that its opportunities for accumulation are more restricted in commerce than in services (Pérez Sáinz 1991).

Bastos and Camus (1993) provide an in-depth analysis of heterogeneity within the informal sector in a sample of lower-class zones of Guatemala City. They find that just 7.3 percent of all informal businesses could be considered "dynamic"; in other words, a minute share are driven by strategies of "entrepreneurial rationality" and accumulation. Their findings anticipate that in areas whose residents tend to be quite poor, "subsistence informality" is likely to predominate. This brand of informality severely restricts the prospects for upward socioeconomic mobility. Bastos and Camus conclude that, compared with subsistence informality, dynamic informal businesses tend to be newer, more diversified beyond commerce to other economic activities, and more likely to be located outside the home, to employ a higher number of paid workers, and to employ fewer women or family members.

Consequently, this project's hypothesis on the informal economy must be qualified to take into account the sector's considerable heterogeneity. In short, informality assumes a wide variety of conditions, logics, and prospects.

Conclusions

Increased open unemployment does not appear to have characterized labor-market adjustment in Guatemala in the 1980s. In late-modernizing societies such as Guatemala — where a public social safety net is notoriously absent — open unemployment tends to bring unbearable social costs to lower-class households. Moreover, public sector employment is much less prevalent in Guatemala than elsewhere in Latin America. This is because, with the obvious exception of the armed forces, the Guatemalan state has historically been weak due to the economic and political dominance of the oligarchy, which has always regarded the state as a mere instrument for fulfilling its own interests. In this institutional setting, increased employment in subsistence agriculture and in the urban informal economy were the principal mechanisms of Guatemalan labor-market adjustment. These mechanisms made employment conditions more insecure, as is clearest with respect to work paying less than the legal minimum wage. Such work burgeoned in nonwage arenas of employment in general, but especially in agriculture and commerce. It primarily employed indigenous groups, women, the least-educated, and non-heads of households.

Not to be forgotten, however, is that this pattern unfolded in the context of a redefinition of Guatemala's relationship to the global division of labor. The most successful aspect of structural adjustment in Guatemala has been the substantial growth of export-platform manufacturing. Such production promises to become a chief axis of the country's new, transnationalized model of accumulation. Comparative research on export-platform manufacturing documents its tendency to employ predominantly young, female labor with low levels of education, as well as to use a labor process characterized by high worker turnover, long hours, and low pay (González 1991; Pérez Sáinz 1996; Pérez Sáinz and Castellanos de Ponciano 1991; Monzón 1992; Petersen 1992; see the chapters on the Dominican Republic [2], Costa Rica [4], and Mexico [8]).

Camus (1994) poses a series of questions on the comparative employment consequences of this new pattern of industrialization for underdeveloped countries. Camus finds that export-platform manufacturing is not as open to the gamut of low-skilled workers as it may appear. Due to management's hiring policies, this sector tends to employ young female workers who rank above the norm in years of schooling, have never belonged to labor unions, and are capable of withstanding an exceedingly intense factory regime. Furthermore, learning and training tend to result from the initiative of workers rather than the policies of management. Traditional, or Taylorist, methods of work organization prevail, although in isolated cases the innovative methods of flexible specialization are used. The rapid growth of export-platform production is part of a transnational strategy by manufacturing firms to take advantage of national and subnational labor markets in crisis, such as Guatemala's, in which households are compelled to send as many members as possible into the workforce. As a result, the industry's workers tend not to identify with the culture and interests of the firms, but rather with the subsistence needs and dynamics of their own households (see Pérez Sáinz 1994 and 1996).

In Guatemala, the geographic location of export-assembly activities reflects explicit government policy choices. The failure of the Santo Tomás Duty Free Zone, established in 1973, exposed the state's inability to provide adequate infrastructure for export-assembly operations. One of this volume's hypotheses anticipates a territorial dispersion of urban employment, to a large extent because of an apparent trend in the geography of manufacturing production. In Guatemala, however, not the provinces but the capital city and its environs have become a diffuse duty-free zone in which assembly manufacturing is located. This pattern is similar to that of Costa Rica (see Pérez Sáinz 1994 and 1996 and Tardanico and Lungo this volume, Chapter 4) while contrasting with the cases of the Dominican Republic and Mexico (see the chapters by Itzigsohn [2] and by Oliveira and García [8], this volume).

Nevertheless, two spatial phenomena merit attention. Camus (1994) observes that some export-platform firms — especially large Korean firms — are locating in the department of Chimaltenango, some 30 miles west of Guatemala City on the Pan-American Highway. They seek to take advantage of an abundant supply of indigenous and campesino labor, thereby avoiding both employment competition with other firms and the threat of unionization. At the same time, many of Guatemala's locally owned assembly operations have subcontracted production to smaller establishments. As a consequence, some indigenous communities in the highlands have become peripheral economic spaces tied to the transnationalized model of industrialization. In a study of one such community, San Pedro Sacatepéquez, in the department of Guatemala, Pérez Sáinz and Leal (1992) found that subcontracting linkages have generated a surprisingly high degree of local economic prosperity. The study nevertheless emphasizes the top-down structure of subcontracting and the tenuousness of labor's position, which render the community's prosperity extremely vulnerable.

On the whole, export-assembly production may render ambiguous the division between formal and informal employment. For one thing, this new version of manufacturing is indeed much more accessible to low-skilled workers than was its predecessor, import-substitution manufacturing. Conceivably, then, the traditional role of educational attainment in excluding a large share of the workforce from economic participation could diminish. As Camus (1994) stresses, however, new barriers may be erected on the basis of other attributes, such as gender and age. Insofar as this occurs, employment will not be as open to the array of low-skilled workers as expected. Furthermore, new practices of industrial organization and associated state policies seem to be worsening the conditions of formal employment itself while boosting the relative attractiveness of informal employment.

Three possibilities with significant overlap emerge. First, informality could become synonymous with the economics of poverty. As such, informality generally could represent the means of subsistence for a majority of the population in underdeveloped countries such as Guatemala that are excluded from the prosperity of globalization. Second, subcontracting could generate informal employment by giving increased business to informal firms. These firms would confront the dilemma of either remaining subordinate — and hence easily displaced — within a vertical chain of subcontracting or else scrambling to achieve a degree of autonomy, which only a few might attain. And finally, agglomerations of small firms, enmeshed within a dense socioterritorial web of social capital and economic linkages, may manage to partake in globalized accumulation. The latter scenario centers on the basic challenge of combining competition — premised on innovation, not imitation — with cooperation oriented toward not mere survival but growth (Pérez Sáinz 1994).

The consolidation of the new model of globalized accumulation points toward labor-market transformations that will challenge radically the present frameworks of analysis. This reconfiguration extends from the dominant zones of the world economy to the highly subordinate and vulnerable periphery, such as Guatemala.

Notes

1.   We must not lose sight of the sheer horror of these years of violence. Jonas (1991, 149) estimates that some 440 hamlets were destroyed, more than 100,000 people were assassinated or "disappeared," and more than one million people fled their homes. A significant percentage were forced into exile, especially in Mexico.

2.   The plan pursued exchange-rate unification, inflation control through the contraction of credit, and, of course, reduction of the public deficit through increases in public service fees, as well as the elimination of price subsidies on certain basic products. To offset the resulting price increases, the government implemented moderate pay hikes in the public sector and requested the private sector to do the same.

3.   The only nationwide data available are provided by the 1981 national census and the 1986-1987 and 1989 sociodemographic and employment surveys. Fortunately, the timing of these studies matches the periodization used in the chapter's preceding section.

4.   The methodological problem of underrepresentation always surfaces when considering female labor-force participation. It may be that part of women's reported increase reflects improved care in data collection due to enhanced sensitivity to the presence of women in the labor pool. It should be mentioned that the rate of female participation estimated from the National Survey of Family Incomes and Expenditures, carried out in 1979 and 1981, is 19 percent, which is higher than the census estimate (García and Gomáriz 1989, 197).

5.   The same pattern and virtually the same dimensions of change hold even when eliminating the "unknown" data that are included for 1981 but eliminated thereafter.

6.   In 1989, wage workers accounted for 48.6 percent and unpaid family workers for 16.5 percent of total national employment (see Table 4).

7.   Negreros (1989a) emphasizes this pattern. Between 1981 and 1989, women's share of total employment in each occupational category increased: employers, from 12.2 to 19.1 percent; public sector employees, from 23.2 to 30.1 percent; private sector wage employees, from 20 to 25.9 percent; self-employed, from 7.9 to 25.3 percent; and unpaid family employees, from 7.6 to 21.5 percent (see Table 4).

8.   Combining data for females and males, we find that self-employment and unpaid family employment rose only slightly as a portion of total employment, from 47.7 to 49.9 percent.

9.   For both years, however, the sum of the industry percentages of total employment do not equal 100 percent due to the presence of a residual category, "other activities."

10. Seemingly consistent with the broader evidence on the acute growth of precarious and informal employment among women is that, strictly speaking, between 1986-1987 and 1989 female jobs grew fastest not in manufacturing (37.1 percent) but in the residual industry category of "other activities" (89.4 percent).

11. In fact, Guatemala's index of urban primacy, one of the highest in Latin America, began to decline toward the end of the 1970s (Pérez Sáinz 1992).

12. This occurred, of course, as over the entire decade women's employment not only grew most rapidly in agriculture, manufacturing, and commerce but grew more rapidly than men's employment in each of these industries (see Table 4). Women's employment, then, did not become more tertiarized, but rather became more concentrated in agriculture and manufacturing. Between 1981 and 1989, women's reported shares of industry sector jobs increased from 2.4 to 8.1 percent in agriculture; 23.9 to 42.9 percent in manufacturing; and, as noted above, from 33.5 to 54.9 percent in commerce and from 47.4 to 50.5 percent in services.

13. To repeat, from 1981 to 1989, men's but not women's employment became more tertiarized (Table 4).

14. With respect to Table 6, the operational definitions of "formal" and "informal" sector need to be explained. The formal sector is made up of three occupational categories: entrepreneurs, public employees, and wage earners in private sector firms. The informal sector is made up of four categories: micro-entrepreneurs, wage earners working in micro-enterprises, the self-employed, and unpaid family workers. The relative weight of the formal and informal sector in total employment was 60.1 and 33 percent, respectively (Pérez Sáinz 1991, 48). In accordance with PREALC's definition, a formal firm is an establishment employing five or more paid workers. Three other clarifications are necessary: Domestic employment is excluded from the informal sector; independent professionals are not included in the formal sector; and the informal sector includes agricultural employment (which, if excluded, drops the magnitude of informality by roughly one-half a percentage point).

15. On gender differences within the informal sector in the metropolitan area of Guatemala City, see the work of Bastos and Camus 1993. On the presence of women in this sector at the national level, see Barrios 1993.

16. Labor stability is greater in the informal than the formal sector due to the greater labor tenure of micro-entrepreneurs and self-employed workers.

17. Funkhouser's (1993) study on labor income in the department of Guatemala shows that aspects of human capital, such as education and job experience, are higher in the formal than informal sector. Nevertheless, the study indicates that the formal sector's average earnings returns on human capital tended to decline at the end of the 1980s.

References

Barrios, Silvia. 1993. "El sector informal urbano en Guatemala: eje de articulación de la marginalidad económica y cultural." In *Del trabajo no remunerado al trabajo "productivo."* San José, Costa Rica: Fundación Arias.

Bastos, Santiago, and Manuela Camus. 1993. "Establecimientos informales y hogares populares en Ciudad de Guatemala: un enfoque de género." In *Ni héroes ni villanas: género e informalidad urbana en Centroamérica,* eds. R. Menjívar and J.P. Pérez Sáinz. San José, Costa Rica: FLACSO.

Baumeister, Eduardo. 1991. "La agricultura centroamericana en los 80." *Polémica* (14-15): 53-79.

Bulmer-Thomas, Victor. 1989. *La economía política de Centroamérica desde 1920.* San José, Costa Rica: Banco Centroamericano de Integración Económica.

Camus, Manuela. 1994. "La maquila en Guatemala: un acercamiento a las relaciones laborales." In *Globalización y fuerza laboral en Centroamérica,* ed. J.P. Pérez Sáinz. San José, Costa Rica: FLACSO.

ECLAC (Economic Commission for Latin America and the Caribbean). 1995a. *Economic Survey of Latin America and the Caribbean 1994-1995.* Santiago, Chile: ECLAC.

ECLAC. 1995b. *Social Panorama of Latin America 1995.* Santiago, Chile: ECLAC.

FLACSO/SEGEPLAN/UNICEF. 1992. "Estudio de las políticas de estabilización y ajuste estructural y sus efectos en la población vulnerable - informe de investigación." Mimeo.

Funkhouser, Edward. 1993. "Wage Structure in Guatemala." Mimeo.

Gálvez Borrell, Víctor. 1991. "Transición y régimen político en Guatemala, 1982-1988." *Cuadernos de Ciencias Sociales - FLACSO* 44.

García, Ana Isabel, and Enrique Gomáriz. 1989. *Mujeres centroamericanas.* San José, Costa Rica: FLACSO/Universidad para la Paz/CSUCA.

González, Mario Aníbal. 1991. "El desarrollo de la industria maquila en Guatemala. Estudio de casos de la ocupación de la mano de obra femenina - informe de investigación." Mimeo.

INE (Instituto Nacional de Estadística). 1985. *IX Censo de Población.* Guatemala.

INE. 1987. *Encuesta Nacional Socio-demográfica 1986-1987. Empleo. Total República.* Vol. 2. Guatemala.

INE. 1990. *Encuesta Nacional Socio-demográfica 1989. Empleo. Total República.* Vol. 2. Guatemala.

INE. 1991. *El perfil de la pobreza en Guatemala.* Guatemala.

Jonas, Susanne. 1991. *The Battle for Guatemala: Rebels, Death Squads and U.S. Power.* Boulder, Colo.: Westview Press.

Monzón, Silvia. 1992. "Condiciones de vida de la mujer asalariada en las plantas maquiladoras de confección. Area Metropolitana de Guatemala." B.A. thesis. Guatemala: Escuela de Ciencias Políticas, Universidad San Carlos.

Negreros, Silvia. 1989a. "Características básicas del empleo femenino en Guatemala." Guatemala: PNUD/Ministerio de Trabajo y Previsión Social. Mimeo.

Negreros, Silvia. 1989b. "Estacionalidad agrícola, salarios y empleo temporal en Guatemala." *Cuadernos de Ciencias Sociales-FLACSO* 23.

Orellana, René, and R. Avila. 1989. "Poverty and Labour Market Access in Guatemala City." In *Urban Poverty and the Labour Market: Access to Jobs and Incomes in Asian and Latin American Cities,* ed. G. Rodgers. Geneva: International Labour Organization (ILO).

Pérez Sáinz, Juan Pablo. 1991. "Informalidad urbana en Guatemala." In *Informalidad Urbana en Centroamérica. Entre la Acumulación y la Subsistencia,* eds. J.P. Pérez Sáinz and R. Menjívar. Caracas: FLACSO/Nueva Sociedad.

Pérez Sáinz, Juan Pablo. 1992. "Ciudad de Guatemala en la década de los ochenta: crisis y urbanización." In *Urbanización en Centroamérica,* eds. A. Portes and M. Lungo. San José, Costa Rica: FLACSO.

Pérez Sáinz, Juan Pablo. 1994. *El dilema del Nahual: globalización, exclusión y trabajo en Centroamérica.* San José, Costa Rica: FLACSO.

Pérez Sáinz, Juan Pablo, ed. 1994. *Globalización y fuerza laboral en Centroamérica.* San José, Costa Rica: FLACSO.

Pérez Sáinz, Juan Pablo. 1996. *De la finca a la maquila: modernización capitalista y trabajo en Centroamérica.* San José, Costa Rica: FLACSO.

Pérez Sáinz, Juan Pablo, Manuela Camus, and Santiago Bastos. 1992. *...Todito, todito es trabajo. Indígenas y empleo en Ciudad de Guatemala.* Guatemala: FLACSO.

Pérez Sáinz, Juan Pablo, and E. Castellanos de Ponciano. 1991. *Mujeres y empleo en Ciudad de Guatemala.* Guatemala: FLACSO.

Pérez Sáinz, Juan Pablo, and A. Leal. 1992. "Pequeña empresa, capital social y etnicidad: el caso de San Pedro de Sacatepéquez." *Debate* 17.

Petersen, Kurt. 1992. "The Maquiladora Revolution in Guatemala." *Occasional Paper Series* 2. New Haven, Conn.: Orville H. Schell Jr. Center for International Human Rights, School of Law, Yale University.

PREALC (Programa Regional del Empleo para América Latina y el Caribe). 1986. *Cambio y polarización ocupacional en Centroamérica.* San José, Costa Rica: Editorial Universitario Centroamericano.

Rivera Urrutia, E., and Ana Sojo. 1986. "El perfil de la política económica en Centroamérica: la década de los ochenta." In *Centroamérica. Política económica y crisis,* eds. E. Rivera Urrutia et al. San José, Costa Rica: DEI.

Ruíz, Carlos. 1990. "La situación de la pobreza en Guatemala en la década de los ochenta." Guatemala: FLACSO. Mimeo.

Chapter 4

Continuities and Discontinuities in Costa Rican Urban Employment[1]

Richard Tardanico and Mario Lungo

The exceptionality of Costa Rica is a basic theme of comparative Central American studies. Historically, Costa Rica has not departed from the Central American norm of linkage with the world economy through a narrow band of agricultural exports. Costa Rica has departed from the isthmian norm, however, with regard to the sociopolitical underpinnings and development consequences of such international linkage. This is particularly true for the period from the early 1950s through the 1970s, when under the impetus of the National Liberation Party (Partido Liberación Nacional — PLN) the state's leadership orchestrated a modernizing agenda of political reform and national development. These policies strengthened the economy's infrastructure, extended the social and political rights of citizenship, elevated the living standards of the population at large, and erected a stable democratic regime (Bulmer-Thomas 1987; Dunkerley 1988; Kincaid 1989; Rovira Mas 1987; Torres Rivas 1993).

To what extent has such exceptionality survived the subsequent years of economic crisis and structural adjustment? This question stands at the core of debate over Costa Rica's transition from state-centered programs of import-substitution development and social welfare to neoliberal programs of fiscal austerity and reorganization, nontraditional exports, and international tourism, under which the country has experienced by far the most rapid macroeconomic recovery in Central America (Céspedes and Jiménez 1995a; Clark 1995; ECLAC 1983-1995a; Franco and Sojo 1992; Rovira Mas 1987). The question is all the more pressing in view of the striking divergence during the mid-1990s between the presidential campaign oratory of social-democratic reform by José María Figueres, the PLN candidate, and the post-election realities of neoliberal policy under his administration (CCAR 1996; EIU 1996; Johnson 1995; *La Nación* 1996; McPhaul 1996a and 1996b; *Mesoamerica* 1996a, 1996b, 1996c, and 1996d;

Richard Tardanico is associate professor of sociology at Florida International University. Mario Lungo is professor of architecture and urban studies at the Universidad Centroamericana José Simeón Cañas in El Salvador and teaches urban studies at FLACSO - Costa Rica.

Samara 1997). This divergence underscores the national complexities of Costa Rica's parliamentary democracy and the domestic impact of both neoliberal and globalizing trends in the world economy.

In spite of these pressures, the vastness of Costa Rica's sociopolitical and infrastructural advantages may keep it ahead of the rest of Central America in the quest to obtain the upper end of those economic activities that in the future may relocate from the more advanced zones of the world economy to its periphery, as in the case of the recent decision by Intel, the U.S.-based microchip leader, to build a large-scale plant to produce microchips in Costa Rica[2] (see EIU 1996; Gereffi and Korzeniewicz 1994; SAPG 1994). Anchored in the state-centered programs of the pre-crisis era, these advantages stand to minimize the socioeconomic losses that result from Costa Rica's increased vulnerability in the world economic and geopolitical order. Still, the array of international and national forces that underlie Costa Rica's growing emphasis on neoliberal reforms render the country more subordinate to external decisions and trends and portend over the long run a reduction in living standards for segments of its middle and lower classes (see Bodson, Cordero, and Pérez Sáinz 1995; Castro Valverde 1995; Clark 1995; *Inforpress Centroamericana* 1996a; Mesa-Lago 1995; *Mesomerica* 1996c and 1996d; Pérez Sáinz 1994 and 1996; and Vega 1996).

This chapter addresses continuity and discontinuity in urban Costa Rican employment and social inequality under economic crisis and structural adjustment from 1980 to 1991.[3] It indicates that employment conditions became somewhat more heterogeneous and unequal within, and in some respects more unequal across, the sectors, occupations, and social groups of urban Costa Rica. The principal characteristic of such change was not increased unemployment but a modest worsening of employment composition. The merely incremental thrust of change reflects the social-democratic and organizational features of the state, the conflict-diffusing interplay of class structure and national identity, and the country's privileged access to foreign aid in a setting of Central American strife and U.S. intervention. Change appears relatively abrupt, though, in certain economic, social, and spatial arenas of the labor market.

Much of the worsened pattern that is documented represents a short-term interruption of post-crisis recovery in macroeconomic and socioeconomic conditions during the early 1990s, which was followed by several years of sharp improvement but then yet another period of some extent of deterioration (Castro Valverde 1995; CCAR 1996; Céspedes and Jiménez 1995a and 1995b; ECLAC 1983-1995a and 1996; Johnson 1995; *Mesoamerica* 1996d; Morley 1995, Chapter 5; Samara 1997; Trejos 1995; Vega 1996; see also this volume Chapter 1, Table 2). A fundamental question is whether Costa Rica's fiscal and economic imbalances and policy responses of the mid-1990s represent a passing downturn or the onset of deep-seated problems that, in the post-Cold War era of geopolitical realignment and intensified global market competition, reflect the diminishing returns or exhaustion of the neoliberal model as well as the particular vulnerabilities of a very small country on the periphery (see, for example, Díaz 1997 and Wallerstein 1995). To be sure, Intel's decision to undertake major microchip production operations in Costa Rica promises to catalyze a strategic upgrading of Costa Rica's position in the global commodity chains of production and employment in both manufacturing and complementary services. Intel's operations will be conducted under free trade zone arrangements, the financial and political terms of which are as yet unknown.[4] The impact on Costa Rica's labor market and social inequality will unfold at the intersection of state, market, and society under not only economic globalization and the post-Cold War order but also the country's evolving variant of neoliberal policy. An optimistic scenario is that these circumstances will establish a new, high-tech variant of Costa Rican exceptionalism. This would instigate economic dynamism akin to Chile's yet in sharp contrast to Chile's glaring polarities of wealth and power (see Díaz this volume, Chapter 6), minimize the erosion of Costa Rican standards of social, political, and economic equity. A pessimistic scenario is that, even if the circumstances do yield significant growth and linkages in economy and employment, turn-of-the-century global and national politico-economic conditions will restrict the sectoral, fiscal, social, and locational benefits. This would accelerate the erosion of Costa Rican exceptionalism by widening as well as qualitatively redefining the socioeconomic and political gap between the haves and have-nots.

Overview: Contemporary Transitions in the Political Economy of Costa Rica

Following the civil war of 1948, the PLN's campaign of state and nation building involved a "peculiar combination of anti-oligarchic modernism and anti-communist populism" (Dunkerley 1988, 596). From the early 1950s through the 1970s, the PLN's leadership managed to institutionalize a far-reaching agenda of political reform, economic development, and social welfare, even as competing parties often held the reins of the presidency. Facilitated by the abolition of the standing army, an expansionary world economy, and national export prosperity, the agenda included the strengthening of the state's hand in the economy, the modernization of the economy's infrastructure, and the construction of a broad network of state-provided social services (Bulmer-Thomas 1987; Dunkerley 1988; Kincaid 1989; Paige 1987; Rovira Mas 1987; Torres Rivas 1993).

What emerged was a political regime that, in accountability and stability, remains without peer in Central America. By no means did the post-1948 path of state and nation building free Costa Rica from the fundamental problems of capital, technology, infrasructure, and market that plague very small countries on the periphery of the world economy. Among the surviving problems is a national distribution of wealth and income that, while equitable by Central American and Latin American standards, is inequitable by worldwide standards (UNDP 1995, 178, 203). Even so, throughout the 1970s the country registered dramatic gains in per capita wealth and overall living standards. Such gains solidified the bases of Costa Rica's political democracy and stability while widening its development advantages over the rest of Central America and much of Latin America in general (Bulmer-Thomas 1987; Dunkerley 1988; Kincaid 1989; Rovira Mas 1987).

Against a Central American background of sociopolitical and economic crisis, however, Costa Rica's plunge in per capita income between 1980 and 1983 was Central America's second most severe, behind that of El Salvador (ECLAC 1983-1985). This occurred because undergirding much of Costa Rica's continued progress in economic development and social welfare during the 1970s were foreign loans, which, given a steep rise in interest rates and fall in the terms of trade, the state could no longer repay (Dunkerley 1988; Rovira Mas 1987). By 1983 the economy already was responding to the stabilization plan of President Luis Alberto Monge (1982-1986), as U.S. and multilateral aid leaped with Costa Rica's emergence as a bulwark against regional threats to U.S. interests. Monge implemented "shock treatment" measures to reduce the fiscal deficit, tighten the currency exchange market, and encourage international loan agreements.[5] At the same time, though, checks and balances within the state as well as leadership's PLN roots and its geopolitical leverage with foreign lenders enabled Monge to retain continuity with pre-crisis policy in key spheres. This continuity included selective measures to cushion the social and market impact of austerity. For example, the administration provided food aid and temporary jobs to the poorest families and controlled the prices of key groceries. The stabilization plan gave way under Monge to a gradualist policy of heterodox structural adjustment, including the raising of the legal minimum wage relative to the average wage. Such action set the policy tone for the subsequent presidency of the PLN's Oscar Arias (1986-1990), whose principal addition to social policy was a massive program of public housing. Reinforcing such gradualism were the politics of presidential elections in 1985-1986 and 1989-1990 (Dunkerley 1988; García-Huidobro et al. 1990; McPhaul 1994; Nelson 1989; Rovira Mas 1987).

Yet, while organizational reforms enhanced the efficiency of government social services, social expenditures and subsidies began a long-range per capita decline. Moreover, state leadership thus fostered the expansion of nontraditional exports (such as ornamental plants, tropical fruits, assembled apparel and electronics) by shifting the state's resources away from not only most segments of the lower and middle classes in town and country but also those segments of manufacturing and agriculture — large and small — whose production was oriented to the domestic market. Leadership began a long-range process of dismantling state enterprises and more decisively of reducing trade protection and subsidies for Costa Rica's producers of food for the local market, as well as for its producers of manufactured goods for the local and Central American markets. Organized labor, which never was strong in the non-state sector of urban Costa Rica, lost ground to a state-sponsored alternative movement, *solidarismo*, which eschews collective bargaining in favor of capital/labor harmony. Between

1987 and 1992, real urban minimum wages and average real wages bounced around a line of stagnation or decline, as state policy appears to have sought competitiveness in nontraditional exports by keeping mean wage increases below the rate of inflation (CEPAS 1992 and 1993; Céspedes and Jiménez 1995a and 1995b; Clark 1995; ECLAC 1986-1994; Edelman and Monge Oveido 1993; Franco and Sojo 1992; García-Huidobro et al. 1990; Gindling and Berry 1992; Levitsky and Lapp 1992; Pérez Sáinz 1996; Samara 1997).

Some popular protest did occur. Among the instances were urban demonstrations in 1983 against a dramatic hike in electricity rates, an urban movement for low-income public housing, and rural demonstrations in the mid-1980s against cutbacks in subsidies for food producers. On the whole, though, protest was minimal. The reasons include the political fragmentation of social groups, selective state programs of welfare and small business subsidy, electoral democracy, nationalism and anticommunism in the face of Central American conflicts, generous U.S. and multilateral aid, and macroeconomic recovery[6] (Dunkerley 1988; Edelman 1991; Franco and Sojo 1992; Kincaid 1989; Nelson 1989).

With the election of the United Social Christian Party (Partido Unidad Social Cristiano — PUSC) candidate Rafael Calderón to the presidency (1990-1994), the gradualism of PLN adjustment policy gave way to a more orthodox approach. To be sure, the country's political structure precluded the elimination of welfare programs as well as impeded the application of strict orthodox measures in other spheres. Still, the state's managers confronted a steep slide in U.S. concessionary aid, the heavy — if diminished — weight of foreign debt obligations, and new negotiations over multilateral aid. Given the ideological bent of the Calderón team, it responded by more vigorously pursuing fiscal austerity and market liberalization, with macroeconomic and socioeconomic indicators falling abruptly in the early 1990s. The gap between political oratory and practice, however, was substantial. To a considerable degree, this gap reflected vociferous resistance to austerity policies based in the public universities and the public bureaucracy. More generally, it reflected the politics of Costa Rica's electoral cycle: As the tightened belt of austerity measures was loosened, macroeconomic conditions recovered sharply, and wage levels leaped (Castro Valverde 1995, 28; CEPAS 1993; ECLAC 1994-1995a; McPhaul 1994; Mesa-Lago 1995; Samara 1997; Trejos 1995).

This upswing notwithstanding, the PLN returned to the presidency in 1994 with the election of José María Figueres, who pledged to renew the state's commitment to social welfare and subsidies for small and medium-sized producers. The most basic mandates of neoliberalism, though, have become entrenched in both the PLN and the PUSC, and by no means did Figueres's pledges amount to a wholesale abandonment of neoliberal objectives. As of 1995-1996, the administration's policies demonstrated that the ideological climate of neoliberalism, the PUSC's majority in Congress, and the country's heightened external vulnerabilities in the post-Cold War climate of economic transnationalization and slashed foreign subsidies make unlikely substantial departures from neoliberal guidelines.[7] Indeed, the Pacto Calderón-Figueres, signed in June 1995, laid the political groundwork for a bipartisan march toward more orthodox neoliberal policies, and, even as a distinctively Costa Rican approach to issues such as privatization seems likely to endure, the accord pushes social discontent and oppositional currents to the margins of the bipartisan channels of electoral democracy. The *Pacto* therefore represents a troubling deviation from the structure of Costa Rican politics and society as established after the civil war of 1948 (CCAR 1996; EIU 1996; ECLAC 1996; *Inforpress Centroamericana* 1996; Johnson 1995; *La Nación* 1995; McPhaul 1996a; *Mesoamerica* 1996a, 1996b, and 1996c; Samara 1997).

Essential to this chapter's focus on employment restructuring are six aspects of the changes that have been discussed: First, the PLN and PUSC administrations since the early 1980s have followed the same basic path of neoliberal-inspired reform, which veered toward greater orthodoxy in the 1990s; second, the impact of Costa Rican and U.S. neoliberal policy on production, exports, and tourism gathered steam from the late 1980s onward; third, economic and social conditions that transcend the short-range dynamics of adjustment may have given economic and social restructuring a head start in agriculture rather than manufacturing and services (Clark 1995; Edelman 1991; Edelman and Monge Oveido 1993; Franco and Sojo 1992; Morley 1995, Chapter 5; Pelupessy 1991; Rojas and Román 1993); fourth, the state's organizational structure, social and nationalist underpinnings, access to foreign aid, and policy flexibility have muted popular discontent; fifth, no other Central American economy has approximated Costa Rica's success in altering its linkages to a restructuring world market; and sixth, the challenge of sustaining a healthy pace of economic growth, a high standard of social welfare, and state responsiveness to mass social discontent and political demands is formidable in a post-Cold War context of shrinking external aid and intensifying global competition.[8]

Urban Employment, 1980-1991

Sectoral Recomposition

In Costa Rica, as elsewhere in Latin America, the rapid growth of public sector employment in the mid-twentieth century was essential to the expansion and consolidation of state authority, as well as to the modernization of the national economy. Thus, it was tightly bound up with the undertakings of state leadership to develop socioeconomic infrastructure, markets, and industries. As import-substitution development proved unable to generate adequate employment for an urbanizing population, the growth of public sector jobs enabled state leadership not only to continue consolidating its political authority but also to stabilize and upgrade employment. In doing so, it provided a substantial part of the urban working classes and the poor with decent jobs and benefits as well as an avenue of upward mobility (see Castro Valverde 1995; Dunkerley 1988; Valverde, Trejos, and Salas 1993).

Between 1980 and 1991, the state's austerity measures caused employment to decline in urban Costa Rica's public sector, which, particularly for unskilled and semiskilled workers, likely would have contributed to growth in the labor market's proportion of precarious and informal jobs. If both aspects of this process occurred appreciably, then policies of austerity and privatization have represented a critical point in the unraveling of Costa Rica's social-democratic nexus of state, employment, and social welfare.

Contrary to expectations, the data indicate that public sector employment in urban Costa Rica did not decline but rather increased (Table 1; see Castro Valverde 1995). The increase in public sector employment was based on the interrelation of the social-democratic structure of the Costa Rican state with the politics of electoral patronage and, in the setting of Central America's regional conflicts of the 1980s, the massive inflow of U.S.-based concessionary aid. Under the administrations of the PLN's Monge (1982-1986) and Arias (1986-1990), adjustment in public sector employment took the principal form not of net job elimination but of diminished job growth along with wage austerity. Not until the PUSC's more orthodox neoliberal Calderón took office, however, were measures to shrink public sector

Table 1.
Employment by Institutional Sector

	% Net Growth	% Total Emp[a]		% Female[b]	
	1980-1991	1980	1991	1980	1991
Public Sector					
Male	3.6	25.8	22.0		
Female	14.7	33.8	25.9		
Total	**7.8**	**28.3**	**23.4**	**37.7**	**40.1**
Private Sector					
Male	27.9	74.2	78.0		
Female	67.3	66.2	74.1		
Total	**39.4**	**71.7**	**76.6**	**29.1**	**34.9**

Source: Calculations based on DGPTE (July 1980, July 1991) for urban Costa Rica.
a = Sectoral percentages of total male, total female, and grand total of employment.
b = Female percentage of total employment in each institutional sector.

employment implemented in earnest; and even then, the political leverage of government employees and the politics of an upcoming presidential election arrested such shrinkage. They also increased average pay in the public sector relative to that in the private sector, as had begun during the electoral cycle toward the end of the Arias administration.[9] Between the early 1980s and early 1990s, though, the average pay of the public sector's professional, administrative, and technical personnel fell in relation to that of the economy's less-skilled labor, as policy tended to be most protective of minimum wage earners (Castro Valverde 1995, 19-33, Tables 2-5; Céspedes and Jiménez 1995a, 62, 64, 87-88, 90, 141-144; García-Huidobro, Hintermeister, Ponce, and Pollack 1990; Gindling and Berry 1992).

Thus, employment in the public sector increased, but at a much slower rate than did employment in the private sector. Compared with the pre-crisis era, then, there occurred a noticeable but certainly not extreme shift in the percentage of total employment from the public to the private sector.[10]

Data on employment and educational attainment indicate, however, that this shift was far from evenly distributed across the various strata of the labor force (Table 2). In spite of some growth in urban Costa Rica's employed workers with primary education or less, jobs for this stratum appear to have contracted precipitously in the public sector while rising in the private sector. In contrast, for tertiary-educated workers employment surged in the public and private sectors alike, as less pronounced job growth occurred in both arenas for workers with a maximum of secondary education. It appears, in short, that net retrenchment of public sector employment corresponded to unskilled and semiskilled workers only (see Castro Valverde 1995, 41; Valverde, Trejos, and Salas 1993). The comparatively fast job growth in the public sector for tertiary-educated workers may in part reflect the momentum of neoliberal policy toward not a reduction of the state's role in the economy but a reorientation of its role toward transnationalized accumulation[11] (Castro Valverde 1995, 41-42; Clark 1995; Franco and Sojo 1992; see Smith, Acuña, and Gamarra 1994).

Despite the Calderón administration's plan, as of 1992 the overwhelming share of exiting public sector workers had not received government subsidies to ease their economic transition. The administration subsequently opted for a more piecemeal tactic of public sector job reduction (Castro Valverde, 47-48; Valverde, Trejos, and Salas 1993). For these and later cutbacks, research needs to examine the processes of public sector job elimination (for example, retirement, privatization, resignation, and layoffs, with and without government subsidies to exiting workers) as well as the occupational pattern by state organizational sector, geography, age, and gender. It then needs to relate the processes to subsequent changes in employment composition and in socioeconomic welfare and inequality.

On the whole, therefore, the shrinkage of public sector employment took place in a relative rather than absolute sense. Yet for low-skilled workers the process seems to have involved a net retrenchment of public sector jobs.

Table 2.
Employment by Institutional Sector and
Educational Attainment

	% Net Growth	% Total Emp[a]	
	1980-1991	1980	1991
Public Sector			
Primary education or less	-31.8	27.8	17.7
Secondary education	8.5	36.4	36.8
Tertiary education	36.2	35.8	45.5
		100.0	100.0
Private Sector			
Primary education or less	13.6	55.8	46.0
Secondary education	58.0	35.9	41.1
Tertiary education	114.8	8.3	12.9
		100.0	100.0
Total			
Primary education or less	5.1	48.1	39.3
Secondary education	43.8	35.8	40.1
Tertiary education	65.5	16.1	20.6
		100.0	100.0

Source: Calculations based on DGPTE (July 1980, July 1991) for urban Costa Rica.
a = Percentages of total employment within each institutional sector and for aggregate of
   employed labor force.

How did change in the distribution of employment between the public and private sectors cross paths with the reconfiguration of employment by industry? Contrary to the first of the three hypotheses on this question presented in Chapter 1, the tertiary economy's share of total employment (as measured by the sum of commerce and service jobs) did not rise but rather dropped slightly (Table 3), as its rate of unemployment increased (from 3.9 percent to 5.6 percent). The industry whose employment did rise proportionately was manufacturing, based on its comparatively fast pace of growth, even as its rate of unemployment climbed the most steeply of any sector (from 5.2 percent to 7.2 percent).[12] The data do

Table 3.
Employment by Industry

	% Net Growth	% Total Emp[a]		% Female[b]	
	1980-1991	1980	1991	1980	1991
Manufacturing					
Male	32.8	21.5	23.7		
Female	94.8	20.4	26.5		
Total	**52.4**	**21.4**	**24.7**	**31.5**	**40.3**
Construction					
Male	-2.3	12.5	10.2		
Female	55.9	0.4	0.4		
Total	**-1.4**	**8.5**	**6.5**	**0.6**	**2.4**
Commerce					
Male	19.2	21.3	21.0		
Female	34.1	22.2	19.9		
Total	**24.2**	**21.5**	**20.6**	**33.6**	**36.3**
Services					
Male	21.8	44.7	45.1		
Female	40.1	57.0	53.2		
Total	**28.8**	**48.6**	**48.2**	**38.2**	**41.6**

Source: Calculations based on DGPTE (July 1980, July 1991) for urban Costa Rica.
a = Sectoral percentages of total male, total female, and grand total of nonagricultural
employment.
b = Female percentage of total employment in each industry.

not report the subsectoral composition of employment in manufacturing or other industries. Other evidence suggests that, as the second hypothesis predicts, jobs in export production grew notably as a share of all employment in manufacturing, apparently most rapidly during the early 1990s (Bodson, Cordero, and Pérez Sáinz 1995; Céspedes and Jiménez 1995a, 99-103; Schoepfle and Pérez-López 1993, 133-135; see Clark 1995; Itzigsohn 1996; Pérez Sáinz 1994, 25). The largest percentage of Costa Rica's export manufacturing firms has been in apparel assembly, followed distantly by electronics assembly. Between 1990 and 1995, however, the number of apparel/textile firms dropped by one-third as a result of foreign competition (EIU 1996 [3rd quarter], 28). In this setting, the national balance of manufacturing production and employment is shifting toward more technology- and skill-intensive electronics- and manufacturing-parts assembly (see EIU [4th quarter] 1996).

In view of the third hypothesis on sectoral recomposition, there should be a rise in less-skilled, low-wage labor as a portion of total employment in manufacturing. Using primary schooling or less as a proxy for less-skilled labor, it emerges that, inconsistent with the hypothesis, manufacturing jobs for workers with secondary education or more grew faster than did the sector's jobs for less-educated workers (Table 4). Some part of this finding is bound to reflect Costa Rica's secular rise in the educational attainment of workers (Céspedes and Jiménez 1995a, 103) rather than change in the characteristics of manufacturing jobs themselves. In any case, jobs for workers with secondary schooling or more grew faster in manufacturing than in any other sector (Table 4). These unexpected findings may reflect some upgrading of job skills, pay, and conditions in certain subsectors of manufacturing relative to others both within and outside manufacturing. At the same time, though, jobs for workers with no more than primary schooling grew faster in manufacturing than in the rest of the urban economy (Table 4). Together with the industry's trajectory for more educated workers, this trend suggests a distinctive pattern of occupational diversification and dispersion in manufacturing relative to other industries (see Bodson, Cordero, and Pérez Sáinz 1995; Céspedes and Jiménez 1995a, 102-114; EIU [4th quarter] 1996; Itzigsohn 1996).

In synthesis, the sectoral recomposition of employment in urban Costa Rica was modest on the whole but evidently abrupt for select groups of unskilled and semiskilled workers. Inconsistent with the most basic prediction is that employment redistribution by institutional sector was based not on a net reduction of public sector jobs but on the faster growth of private sector employment. Apparently, however, net transfer of employment from the public to the private sector did occur in the case of less-skilled workers, for whom the shift seems to have been precipitous. Concerning urban industries, an unexpected finding is that the tertiary economy's share of all employment did not rise but fell somewhat, as jobs increased more rapidly in manufacturing than in commerce and services. Export jobs increased their share of all manufacturing employment, as expected, a shift that may have gained speed in the early 1990s. Employment differentiation

Table 4.
Employment by Industry and Educational Attainment

	% Net Growth	% Total Emp[a]	
	1980-1991	1980	1991
Manufacturing			
Primary education or less	23.6	55.2	45.1
Secondary education	76.8	38.9	45.4
Tertiary education	152.0	5.9	9.5
		100.0	100.0
Construction			
Primary education or less	-25.3	72.4	55.7
Secondary education	57.5	22.1	35.9
Tertiary education	48.6	5.5	8.4
		100.0	100.0
Commerce			
Primary education or less	7.0	48.9	42.3
Secondary education	32.4	43.5	46.6
Tertiary education	80.8	7.6	11.1
		100.0	100.0
Services			
Primary education or less	1.6	37.9	30.5
Secondary education	33.4	35.3	36.2
Tertiary education	56.3	26.8	33.3
		100.0	100.0

Source: Calculations based on DGPTE (July 1980, July 1991) for urban Costa Rica.
a = Percentages of total employment within each industry.

within manufacturing may have been more complex than the anticipated trend of downgraded skills, pay, and conditions. Judging on the imperfect basis of the educational composition of workers, a substantial portion of its jobs either held their ground or were upgraded. Still, the finding that job growth for both the more- and the less-educated workers was fastest in manufacturing points to a relatively high degree of socioeconomic divergence in the sector.

What occurred, in sum, is essentially an incremental reorientation of employment from the public sector to the private sector and from tertiary activities to manufacturing, together with a notable job shift in manufacturing to export production. For less-skilled workers in the public sector, job elimination was seemingly marked. The degree to which job elimination in the public sector may have pushed such workers into low-end employment in manufacturing, for export or domestic markets, or in other activities is unknown.

Growth of Precarious and Informal Employment

To what degree did precarious and informal employment expand its share of the urban labor market, as comparative studies predict? Insofar as this occurred, growth in the percentages of total employment in unregistered, nonwage, small-firm, temporary, part-time, and subminimum-wage jobs is expected as is growth in full-time jobs with undeclared income (see the discussions in Rakowski 1994; Roberts 1995; and Standing and Tokman 1991). In the context of some short-term worsening in the rate of unemployment, there is indeed some degree of such growth. Taking into account the longitudinal problems of data comparability, the indicators reflect a consistent pattern of deterioration in employment composition, albeit one that may be modest in wider Latin American perspective and that — under electoral circumstances and as Costa Rica's state and economy were thrust into a world of intensifying competition — was part of a series of pronounced labor-market fluctuations during the 1990s[13] (Tables 5 and 6). As nonwage jobs expanded more rapidly than wage jobs, the fastest growing occupational category of all was self-employment, trailed distantly by unpaid employment (Table 6; see the PREALC data cited in Thomas 1996, 88; Castro Valverde 1995; Céspedes and Jiménez 1995a; Gindling and Berry 1992; Morley 1995, Chapter 5; Tardanico 1996a and 1996b).

PREALC (cited in Thomas 1996, 88) portrays a Costa Rican process of informalization that conforms to the standard prediction for Latin American countries. But the United Nations Economic Commission for Latin America and the Caribbean (ECLAC) (1995b, 133) indicates that professional and technical labor, rather than labor at the low end of the skill spectrum, was the primary component of the proportional growth of nonwage jobs (see also Castro Valverde 1995, 42-44, Table 13). To the extent that it may be empirically valid, the ECLAC profile could reflect several overlapping shifts of long- or short-term duration: the rebalancing of public and private sector

Table 5.
Employment Categories[a]

	% Net Growth	% Total Emp[b]		% Female[c]	
	1980-1991	1980	1991	1980	1991
Nonwage					
Male	46.7				
Female	150.7				
Total	**70.3**	**20.1**	**26.1**	**22.7**	**33.5**
Wage					
Male	14.3				
Female	32.6				
Total	**20.5**	**79.9**	**73.9**	**33.7**	**37.1**
Part-time					
Male	44.9				
Female	162.6				
Total	**103.0**	**9.7**	**15.2**	**56.0**	**67.8**
Full-time					
Male	14.0				
Female	14.6				
Total	**14.2**	**61.7**	**53.3**	**27.7**	**27.8**
Small-firm					
Male	42.7				
Female	92.5				
Total	**59.5**	**32.1**	**38.5**	**33.7**	**40.7**

Continued on next page

Table 5—Continued

	% Net Growth	% Total Emp[b]		% Female[c]	
	1980-1991	1980	1991	1980	1991
Large-firm					
Male	14.1				
Female	28.7				
Total	**18.7**	**60.2**	**53.7**	**31.5**	**34.2**
Full-time subminimum-wage					
Male	72.4				
Female	15.6				
Total	**42.8**	**17.6**	**25.6**	**52.1**	**42.2**
Full-time minimum-wage+					
Male	-14.3				
Female	-0.8				
Total	**-11.3**	**82.4**	**74.4**	**22.1**	**24.7**
Full-time with undeclared income					
Male	196.6				
Female	99.6				
Total	**167.6**	**9.4**	**22.1**	**30.6**	**22.8**
Full-time with declared income					
Male	-4.2				
Female	4.7				
Total	**-1.8**	**90.6**	**77.9**	**27.4**	**29.2**

Source: Calculations based on DGPTE (July 1980, July 1991) for urban Costa Rica.

a = Part-time refers to less than 30 hours per week, full-time to more than 46 hours per week; small-firm to less than five employees, large-firm to more than nine employees. Data on subminimum-wage and minimum-wage+ earners refer only to principal jobs of employed labor force working more than 46 hours per week and with declared income. The legal minimum wage increased relative to the average real wage between 1980 and 1991 (ECLAC 1983-1994).

b = Only nonwage/wage, subminimum-wage/minimum-wage+, and full-time with undeclared income/declared income are comprehensive and thus sum to 100 percent of employment in each paired category for each year. Nonwage includes unpaid family workers and self-employed non-professional/non-technical workers, as well as employers and self-employed professional/technical workers.

c = Female percentage of total employment within each category.

Table 6.
Employment by Occupational Category

	% Net Growth	% Total Emp[a]	
	1980-1991	1980	1991
Employer			
Male	-0.2	7.8	6.4
Female	89.2	2.0	2.5
Total	**9.0**	**6.0**	**5.0**
Self-employed			
Male	72.6	13.5	19.2
Female	202.0	9.2	18.6
Total	**103.5**	**12.2**	**19.0**
Unpaid employed			
Male	58.6	1.2	1.6
Female	41.6	3.2	3.1
Total	**49.6**	**1.9**	**2.1**
Wage employed			
Male	14.3	77.5	72.8
Female	32.6	85.6	75.8
Total	**20.5**	**79.9**	**73.9**

Source: Calculations based on DGPTE (July 1980, July 1991) for urban Costa Rica.
a = Percentages of total male, total female, and grand total of employment. Self-employed
    includes professional/technical and non-professional/non-technical workers.

employment, the growth of professional and technical self-employment in subcontracted activities, and the particularly harsh circumstances for firms and workers in 1991. This ostensible pattern implies that inasmuch as the profile and degree of change are not artifacts of methodological revisions in the employment survey, then they substantially represent not worsened job conditions in the strict sense but a reconfiguration of income-earning opportunities for professional and technical labor. Yet not to be overlooked is the fact that a major dimension of worldwide restructuring is indeed greater insecurity for professional and technical labor, as the restructuring of job markets tends to generate a mix of considerable gains and losses within these occupational strata (Roberts and Tardanico 1997; Sassen 1994; Tilly 1996; see especially the chapters in this volume on Argentina [7], Chile [6], and Mexico [8]). If this was so in urban Costa Rica, then the situation principally encompassed not informalization per se but an appreciable worsening in the average conditions of professional and technical work.

Compatible with the ECLAC data — but certainly not incompatible with the PREALC data — are various pieces of evidence. For example, T.H. Gindling and Katherine Terrell (1995) document an abrupt increase in 1991 in the percentage of workers with maximums of secondary and tertiary education, as well as with a maximum of primary education, earning less than the legal minimum wage. This increase coincides with a finding presented later in this chapter, which, consistent with ECLAC's (1995b, 136, 141) data, reveals a marked downward redistribution of full-time earners by income level in all occupational, industry, and gender categories. Various analysts conclude that, as a consequence of the Costa Rican state policy's long-range support of the legal minimum wage relative to the average real wage, there occurred a net decrease in urban income inequality, as measured primarily by the Gini coefficient, among households between 1980 and 1989, before 1991's acute drop in average wages[14] (Morley 1995, 30-32, 138), and among the full-time labor force with reported income between 1987 and 1992, when average wages began to recover (Trejos 1995, 8-10; see Castro Valverde 1995, Tables 6.2, 15; Céspedes and Jiménez 1995a, 91-110). Running counter to this conclusion is ECLAC's (1995b, 147-148) evidence on inter-household income inequality, also as measured by the Gini coefficient.[15] This evidence indicates a net increase in urban, but not rural, inter-household inequality between 1981 and 1992, even as Costa Rica remained just behind Uruguay in Latin American urban equitability.

In measuring social inequality, all such data underestimate the total incomes of the rich and the poor, but particularly the former, above all during an age of economic transnationalization and speculative earnings.[16] Even when recognizing this limitation, it should also be remembered that the various measures of income inequality capture some of its facets more than others. Conceivably, for instance, much of the Costa Rican evidence reflects the statistical weight of greater income bunching in the vicinity of the minimum wage while failing to convey a widened range between the very highest echelon of earners and the others (see, for example, the theoretical discussions on measurement and interpretation in Bulmer-

Thomas 1996, 13-19, and Moore 1966, appendix). Longitudinally and comparatively, such speculation can be defended as an exercise not in nit-picking but in seeking to uncover changes in the national fabric of social inequality — such as an emerging combination of greater egalitarianism in some respects and greater polarization in others — with potential ramifications for the character of sociopolitical change.[17] Carlos Castro Valverde (1995, 46) observes that, under long-range circumstances of stagnation or decline in average real wages, the loss in earnings power by the middle-class occupations versus manual labor signifies that Costa Rica's "channels of upward social mobility are much more limited than in the past and that the counterparts to those members of the labor force who have managed to move upward into the middle sectors are the others who have fallen downward from the middle sectors." For both Costa Rica and other national cases, a basic part of the research agenda should be to integrate a wide complement of measures of income inequality with other quantitative and qualitative evidence on the social relations of employment and social class (Bodson, Cordero, and Pérez Sáinz 1995; Bromley and Birkbeck 1988; Bulmer-Thomas 1996; Díaz this volume, Chapter 6; Elson 1995; Gilbert 1994; Menjívar Larín and Pérez Sáinz 1993). In the aftermath of the Cold War and under global economic restructuring, future findings on Costa Rica may reveal more frequent short-term gains and losses in social inequality and social welfare around a long-term trend of erosion.

To recapitulate, the data point to some amount of worsening in employment composition, whose extent of informalization per se is unclear. This worsening appears to have occurred largely in the early 1990s, followed by periods of considerable improvement and of some degree of regression.

Within this framework, Chapter 1 observed that, according to the comparative literature on tertiarization, job growth in manufacturing fosters an upgrading, while job growth in commerce and services fosters a downgrading, in the composition of employment. It also observed that, in contrast, the comparative literature on restructuring asserts that the relationship of manufacturing to employment composition has changed since the 1960s or so, when job inequalities in manufacturing began to be reorganized and widened on a world scale (Amsden and van der Hoever 1996; Gereffi 1994).

The data presented in Table 7 largely support the restructuring argument for urban Costa Rica, as nonwage, small-firm, part-time, and subminimum-wage jobs apparently increased as portions of aggregate employment in manufacturing, along with full-time jobs with undeclared income. How, though, does manufacturing compare to the other sectors? As research on the tertiarization of employment predicts, the growth rates in wage, large-firm, and full-time jobs and in full-time jobs with undeclared income were highest in manufacturing[18] (Table 7). Yet, consistent with studies on restructuring, precarious and informal employment was the category of fastest growth in every industry, including manufacturing.[19] In

Table 7.
Employment Categories by Industry[a]

	% Net Growth	% Total Emp[b]	
	1980-1991	1980	1991
Manufacturing			
Nonwage	118.9	20.9	30.0
Wage	34.9	79.1	70.0
Part-time	198.2	7.5	14.7
Full-time	32.9	67.4	58.8
Small-firm	100.4	27.5	34.9
Large-firm	40.0	66.0	58.5
Full-time subminimum-wage	73.9	19.2	28.6
Full-time minimum-wage+	3.3	80.8	71.4
Full-time with undeclared income	218.8	7.9	19.0
Full-time with declared income	16.9	92.1	81.0
Construction			
Nonwage	108.3	18.5	29.2
Wage	-26.4	81.5	70.8
Part-time	77.9	3.9	7.0
Full-time	9.0	76.0	69.6
Small-firm	103.4	29.2	52.4
Large-firm	-38.7	69.8	37.7
Full-time subminimum-wage	57.3	9.1	20.1
Full-time minimum-wage+	-37.1	90.9	79.9
Full-time with undeclared income	269.7	6.5	26.5
Full-time with declared income	-28.4	93.5	73.5
Commerce			
Nonwage	24.7	36.7	36.9
Wage	23.9	63.3	63.1
Part-time	83.5	9.7	14.4
Full-time	16.6	69.2	65.8

Continued on next page

Table 7—*Continued*

	% Net Growth	% Total Emp[b]	
	1980-1991	**1980**	**1991**
Commerce—continued			
Small-firm	29.3	51.0	51.7
Large-firm	24.2	36.5	35.5
Full-time subminimum-wage	42.7	21.6	30.2
Full-time minimum-wage+	-9.2	78.4	69.8
Full-time with undeclared income	121.7	12.2	23.2
Full-time with declared income	-2.0	87.8	76.8
Services			
Nonwage	116.8	10.3	17.4
Wage	18.6	89.7	82.6
Part-time	91.4	11.6	17.4
Full-time	6.0	54.0	44.7
Small-firm	62.8	26.0	32.6
Large-firm	16.9	69.1	62.2
Full-time subminimum-wage	11.0	16.2	20.0
Full-time minimum-wage+	-14.7	83.8	80.0
Full-time with undeclared income	212.2	7.2	21.3
Full-time with declared income	-10.1	92.8	78.7

Source: Calculations based on DGPTE (July 1980, July 1991) for urban Costa Rica.

a = Part-time refers to less than 30 hours per week, full-time to more than 46 hours per week, small-firm to less than five employees, large-firm to more than nine employees. Data on subminimum-wage and minimum-wage+ earners refer only to principal jobs of employed labor force working more than 46 hours per week and with declared income. The legal minimum wage increased relative to the average real wage between 1980 and 1991 (ECLAC 1983-1994).

b = Only nonwage/wage, subminimum-wage/minimum-wage+, and full-time with undeclared income/declared income are comprehensive and thus sum to 100 percent of employment in each paired category for each year. Nonwage includes unpaid family workers and self-employed non-professional/non-technical workers, as well as employers and self-employed professional/technical workers.

fact, by these measures manufacturing generally headed the urban economy in the growth rate of not just legally regulated and relatively well-paying jobs but also precarious and informal jobs. This evidence of a comparatively marked bifurcation of employment conditions in manufacturing complements that presented earlier on the widening of educational inequality among the sector's workers (Table 4). To repeat, research needs to examine the subindustry, territorial, and temporal dimensions of such change.

The next question concerns the consequences of the increase in the economy's share of precarious and perhaps informal employment for occupational inequality. This volume's hypotheses predict not only that the average earnings of employers in urban Costa Rica exceeded those of wage workers and the self-employed but also that the earnings gap between employers and the other groups became more unequal under conditions of restructuring. The evidence for the full-time employed supports the first prediction; it does not, however, support the second (Tables 8 and 9).[20]

Table 8.
Gender Trends in Average Real Earnings by Industry
and Occupational Category, San José[a]

	% Net Growth		Female % of Male Earnings	
	Male 1980-1991	Female 1980-1991	1980	1991
Occupational Category				
Employer	-29.9	-42.3	55.3	45.6
Self-employed	-3.3	1.1	74.6	78.0
Wage employed	2.2	9.9	74.8	80.4
Industry				
Manufacturing	-1.4	14.4	59.9	69.5
Construction[b]	-2.4	NR	NR	NR
Commerce	-5.5	10.2	63.9	74.5
Services	-1.2	11.1	70.2	78.9
Aggregate				
Average change[c]	-4.2	7.2	69.3	77.5

Source: Calculations based on DGPTE (July 1980, July 1991) for San José.
a = Refers only to principal jobs of employed labor force working more than 46 hours per week and with declared income. Occupational and aggregate figures reflect earnings in agriculture.
b = Due to the paucity of female employment in construction, data on female earnings in that industry are not reported.
c = Weighted average, including male earnings in agriculture and female earnings in agriculture and construction.

Table 9.
Inequality of Average Earnings by Occupational Category,
Industry, and Gender, San José[a]

	Aggregate		Male		Female	
	1980	1991	1980	1991	1980	1991
Occupational Category						
Employer	— (1)	— (1)	— (1)	— (1)	— (1)	88.4 (3)
Self-employed	44.4 (2)	60.5 (3)	44.0 (2)	60.6 (3)	59.5 (2)	91.7 (2)
Wage worker	42.5 (3)	62.7 (2)	44.0 (2)	64.2 (2)	59.5 (2)	— (1)
Industry						
Manufacturing	77.8 (4)	75.7 (4)	78.0 (3)	77.8 (3)	66.6 (3)	68.6 (3)
Construction	87.9 (2)	82.3 (2)	78.0 (3)	77.0 (4)	NR[b]	NR[b]
Commerce	83.0 (3)	79.0 (3)	84.5 (2)	80.8 (2)	76.9 (2)	76.6 (2)
Services	— (1)	— (1)	— (1)	— (1)	— (1)	— (1)

Source: Calculations based on DGPTE (July 1980, July 1991) for San José.
a = Percentages of the average earnings in the highest-ranked occupational category or industry; numbers in parentheses refer to annual rank in the occupational and industry earnings hierarchies. Data cover only principal jobs of employed labor force working more than 46 hours per week and with declared income; data for occupational categories include agriculture. Self-employed includes non-professional/non-technical and professional/technical workers.
b = Due to the paucity of female employment in construction, data on female earnings in that industry are not reported. Female earnings in construction and agriculture are reflected in data on occupational categories, however, as are male earnings in agriculture.

Between 1980 and 1991, the average real earnings of employers plunged, compared with a much less marked fall among the self-employed and some gain among wage workers. Thus, while employers on average maintained their status as the leading earners, this advantage narrowed substantially, probably because ownership of microenterprises expanded as wage jobs became less desirable to persons possessing sufficient economic and social capital to head microenterprises. These circumstances stand to have weakened the aggregate composition of microenterprises and their owners in terms of capital, equipment, skill, and market position, while increasing the competition among them. At the same time, the self-employed dropped below wage workers in the earnings hierarchy, likely for reasons that parallel the case of petty employers (see Bodson, Cordero, and Pérez Sáinz 1995; ECLAC 1995b, 136; Itzigsohn 1996; Lungo 1995; Morley 1995, Chapter 5; Trejos 1991).

A related prediction is that the distribution of earners shifted toward the low end within each occupational category. Such a downward redistribution indeed occurred in each occupational category (Table 10; see

Table 10.
Percentage Distributions of Employment by
Occupational Category and Increments of
Official Minimum Wage[a]

	Employers		Self-Employed		Wage Workers	
	1980	1991	1980	1991	1980	1991
<1	6.7	11.1	18.1	33.1	18.3	25.1
1<2	19.4	31.8	46.7	45.2	46.6	52.6
2<3	17.0	27.5	17.4	13.4	19.1	11.9
3<4	18.3	17.2	9.4	3.8	9.1	5.3
4<5	6.5	1.5	3.9	0.7	2.7	1.9
>5	32.1	10.9	4.5	3.8	4.2	3.2
	100.0	100.0	100.0	100.0	100.0	100.0

Source: Calculations based on DGPTE (July 1980, July 1991) for urban Costa Rica.
a = Refers only to principal jobs of employed labor force working more than 46 hours
    per week and with declared income. The legal minimum wage increased relative to
    the average real wage between 1980 and 1991 (ECLAC 1983-1994). Self-employed
    includes professional/technical and non-professional/non-technical workers.

ECLAC 1995b, 136; Gindling and Terrell 1995). Across the categories, the data reveal a decrease in the percentage of full-time earners at the high end, cases of proportional decrease and increase in the middle levels, and an increase in the percentage of earners at the low end. The relative shift into full-time jobs paying subminimum wages was evidently most pronounced for the self-employed. As with other data on precarious and informal employment, those on the distribution of earners are likely to reflect the acute deterioration of labor-market conditions in 1990-1991 (Gindling and Terrell 1995). This deterioration, again, is part of a series of short-range ups and downs.

To summarize, precarious and possibly informal employment became more prominent features of Costa Rica's urban labor market, as restructuring studies anticipate, although the degree of such change is unclear, and in the setting of electoral politics, it soon gave way to marked improvement. Along with some growth in the rate of unemployment, the clearest trend was a reallocation of full-time earners toward or below the official minimum wage, which was most acute for the self-employed. This downward trend occurred not only in the various occupational categories of nonwage employment, however, but also in wage employment, thereby cautioning against attributing the deterioration of employment conditions solely to informalization. Indeed, the worsening of employment conditions in the formal sector well may have minimized the incentive of ownership and managers in legally regulated firms to informalize their labor arrangements (see Itzigsohn 1996). Consistent with comparative research on restructuring, manufacturing seems to have been the industry of most intense change and greatest complexity in the mix of formal and informal employment.

Research needs to shed light on these matters by documenting the processes and contours of such change as they cut across urban industries and subindustries, social classes and occupations, gender, age, natives and immigrants, the urban spatial hierarchy, and sociospatial nodes of urban/ rural linkage.[21] It likewise needs to relate these contours to the perceived options of household members and to tease out the secular and cyclical components of shifts in formal and informal employment.

Gender Realignment

Studies on gender and economic restructuring lead one to expect a rise in the female portion of urban Costa Rica's employment and unemployment (see Chapter 1). This occurred for employment, if probably to a much lesser degree than reflected in the official data, but not for unemployment[22] (Tables 1, 3, 5, and 6). The proportional rises involved a slump in the male rate of labor-force participation (from 72.1 percent to 70.1 percent) and, even as the female share of the working-age population remained virtually constant, a rise in the female rate (from 30.3 percent to 35.6 percent). The data, however, are likely to exaggerate the extent of the actual female upturn.

On the male side, rates of labor-force participation dropped for every age group, especially for those at the lower and upper reaches of the age continuum, with the exception of an increase for 20- to 29-year-olds (Table 11). For women, rates rose for every age group, especially for those age 30 and older, with the exception of a decrease for 12- to 19-year-olds (Table 11). The female pattern of change points to a reduced influence of marriage and the bearing and raising of children on labor-force participation (see Dierckxsens 1992; Goldenberg 1993). One cannot say whether this gender balance of change represents acceleration, deceleration, or mere continuation of a long-range trajectory, though the sharp increase in participation rates for 30+ year-old women suggests an intensified upturn for that group. As later addressed, this upturn may be substantially linked to demand-side changes in the structure of manufacturing production and employment, along with supply-side changes in the composition of households and the sociopolitical standing of women. Women's somewhat reduced percentage of total unemployment is consistent with other evidence on post-1980 employment dislocations of urban Costa Rican men (see Tardanico 1996a).

Comparative studies underline the connections of change in the nexus of gender and labor-force participation with change in the organization of households (Safa 1995; Wolf 1992). For urban Costa Rica, change in gender aspects of labor-force participation unfolded as the average size of house-holds fell slightly (from 4.5 to 4.2 persons), the portion of households headed

Table 11.
Rates of Labor-Force Participation by Gender and Age

	Male		Female	
	1980	1991	1980	1991
Age				
12-14	12.2	9.3	3.7	3.2
15-19	46.9	40.0	23.9	22.3
20-29	87.0	88.8	44.0	48.0
30-39	97.8	96.5	46.9	54.0
40-49	97.5	94.2	33.5	49.0
50-59	91.1	85.3	15.0	28.5
60-69	55.5	51.9	10.1	14.3
70+	26.2	17.3	3.3	4.2
Average[a]	**72.1**	**70.1**	**30.3**	**35.6**

Source: Calculations based on DGPTE (July 1980, July 1991) for urban Costa Rica.
a = Weighted average.

by women rose (from 22.7 percent to 24.9 percent), and the average number of labor-force participants per household did not change at all (staying at 1.6 persons). The latter trend suggests that what grew on average was not the number of labor-force participants in households but the female portion of such participants, who became dispersed across more and smaller domestic units (see ECLAC 1995b, 71-72). The trend underscores the need to examine possible secular and cyclical shifts in the gamut of coping and mobility practices of households and their individual members across social classes. Among such practices are those concerning fertility and other matters of household size, composition, consumption, and activity. Nor should it be forgotten that Costa Rica's state programs of social welfare remain extensive by Latin American standards (see Mesa-Lago 1995; Sojo 1994).

Regarding gender and employment, the public sector has been a strategic channel of women's access to secure, government-regulated jobs in Costa Rica, particularly for professionals (Gindling 1993; Sáenz and Trejos 1993). A key issue, then, is the impact of structural adjustment on the gender composition of employment by institutional sector. As has been seen, as a result of adjustment policies, job growth was more rapid in the private than in the public sector (Table 1). While this was true for men and women alike, in both sectors job growth was fastest for women. The female share of jobs remained higher in the public than in the private sector, though the difference between the two lessened.

For women more than men, however, what net job growth did occur in the public sector was polarized by educational level (Table 2). That is, net growth of male jobs in the public sector occurred for workers with a maximum of secondary or tertiary education; in contrast, the sector's net growth of female jobs occurred only for workers with a maximum of tertiary education. To be sure, job growth by gender and education was also polarized in the private sector, where tertiary-educated workers — led by women — were the educational category of fastest growth (Table 2). Yet the primary issue is that reduction in the public sector's role as a key avenue of access to legally regulated, stable jobs was evidently more pronounced for less-skilled women than less-skilled men; to confirm or reject this notion, one would have to document comparative trends in the quality of the job opportunities for such workers in the public and private sectors. A secondary issue is that, perhaps especially for women, the focus of job opportunities for professionals seems to have shifted from the public to the private sector (see Castro Valverde 1995, 39-48; Céspedes and Jiménez 1995a, 108-114).

As for the consequences of reduced job growth, wage austerity, and organizational change in the public sector for the gender composition of employment by industry, research on economic tertiarization and on global restructuring again leads to contrasting predictions. The former predicts that, despite the slowed expansion of employment opportunities in the public sector, job growth for women will be highest in services and commerce (Infante and Klein 1991). The latter predicts that, in locales where export-assembly production is substantially expanding, job growth for women will be fastest in manufacturing and that job growth in that industry will be faster for women than men (Standing 1989).

The evidence supports the restructuring perspective (Tables 3 and 12). Female employment did increase most rapidly in manufacturing. And, with the exception of the aberrant case of construction — where few women were employed and where male employment shrank — the economy-wide advantage of women over men in the pace of job growth was greatest in manufacturing. This occurred despite the fact that manufacturing was also the site of fastest job growth for men. A result was that manufacturing surpassed commerce and almost caught services in the ranking of industries with the highest percentages of female employment. That is, even as services continued to be the industry employing the highest proportion of the female and the male labor forces alike, manufacturing came just short of equaling services in sectoral percentage of female versus male workers (Tardanico 1996a and 1996b). There are no longer-range data on this shift. Even so, the fact that escalating demand for female labor began during the mid-1980s, in the setting of local policies of structural adjustment and the U.S. government's Caribbean Basin Initiative, suggests that this sectoral pattern represents a sharp break from the past (see Clark 1995; Pérez Sáinz

Table 12.
Probability of Employed Labor-Force Participants Having Principal or Sole Job in Manufacturing by Age[a]

	Male			Female		
	1980	1991	% Change	1980	1991	% Change
Age						
12-19	35.1	31.6	-10.0	28.8	27.5	-4.5
20-29	21.2	25.1	18.4	20.4	26.1	27.9
30-39	11.3	18.5	63.7	20.6	28.0	35.9
40-49	10.1	18.2	80.2	9.7	24.0	147.4
50-59	16.8	19.6	16.7	19.0	20.7	9.0
60-69	14.5	22.7	56.6	22.1	34.2	54.8
70+	6.6	19.2	190.9	35.3	46.8	32.6

Source: Calculations based on DGPTE (July 1980, July 1991) for urban Costa Rica.
a = Percentage of all employed persons (full-time and part-time) in each gender-age category whose principal or sole job is in manufacturing.

1994 and 1996). An important question concerns the degree to which a nascent masculinization of export-assembly jobs may have begun diminishing this trend[23] (see Cordero 1994).

The topics of austerity, privatization, and industry sector transformation raise issues concerning the gender balance of precarious and informal employment. Chapter 1 points out that, according to many writings on gender and restructuring, the growth of precarious and informal employment is largely synonymous with the upturn in women's share of jobs. The argument is that, in a polarizing labor market, women become increasingly concentrated in low-end jobs. For urban Costa Rica, precarious and perhaps informal jobs grew as a portion of the labor market (Table 5). To the extent that such growth was intertwined with the period's rise in women's share of jobs, the data should reveal several trends, as argued in Chapter 1. These anticipated trends are, first, that growth rates for women were highest in precarious and informal jobs; second, that growth rates were higher for women than men in precarious and informal jobs; and third, that growth rates were lower for women than men in formal, relatively stable and desirable jobs.

In the context of a steeper rise in the unemployment rate for men than women, the evidence only partially fits this pattern (Table 5). As hypothesized, the growth rate for women was highest in precarious and informal employment, and across the indicators of such employment, the growth rate was almost exclusively higher for women than men. The sole exceptions,

Table 13.
Percentage Distributions of Aggregate, Male, and Female
Employment by Increments of Official Minimum Wage[a]

	Aggregate		Male		Female	
	1980	1991	1980	1991	1980	1991
<1	17.6	25.6	11.6	20.9	33.5	37.0
1<2	44.9	50.4	46.9	52.5	39.5	45.4
2<3	18.7	12.9	20.0	13.8	15.4	10.4
3<4	9.7	5.8	10.5	6.5	7.7	4.2
4<5	3.1	1.7	3.6	1.7	1.6	1.7
>5	6.0	3.6	7.4	4.6	2.3	1.3
	100.0	100.0	100.0	100.0	100.0	100.0

Source: Calculations based on DGPTE (July 1980, July 1991) for urban Costa Rica.
a = Refers only to principal jobs of employed labor force working more than 46 hours per week and with declared income. The legal minimum wage increased relative to the average real wage between 1980 and 1991 (ECLAC 1983-1994).

however, are telling: greater proportional shifts for men than women into full-time subminimum-wage jobs and full-time jobs with undeclared income (Tables 5 and 13; see Gindling and Terrell 1995, Table A6). These exceptions underscore the eroded position of certain categories of male workers under economic crisis and structural adjustment. Another unexpected finding is that the indicators of formal jobs either increased faster or decreased more slowly for women than men (Table 5).

So, consistent with the restructuring literature, women became even more overrepresented than before in precarious and informal employment. Inconsistent with the literature, women reduced their share of full-time jobs paying less than the legal minimum wage, while increasing their share of formal and better paid employment.

The consequences of employment shifts for earnings inequality between men and women have barely been addressed. According to studies on restructuring, employment is likely to have become more polarized by gender, thereby exacerbating the unequal distribution of income between male and female workers (see Chapter 1). Yet, the average real earnings of full-time workers decreased for men but increased for women, as the gender gap in full-time earnings diminished across industries and most occupational categories (Table 8; see Céspedes and Jiménez 1995a, 107-108). Sectorally, the average real earnings of full-time workers rose most for women in manufacturing, an indicator of its export prosperity and gender realignments, and dropped most for men in commerce and construction, an indicator of the former's high proportion of low-skilled workers and the latter's extreme vulnerability to market fluctuations. Occupationally, average real earnings rose more for women than men among the full-time wage employed and self-employed; though, consistent with research on restructuring, they dropped more for women than men among full-time employers. The occupational pattern suggests that not just formal employment but, to a more limited extent, some kinds of informal employment enabled women to advance or defend their relative earnings positions (see the chapters in this volume by Itzigsohn [2] and Pérez Sáinz [3] and Tardanico 1996a and 1996b).

Thus, the gender distribution of earnings among full-time workers remained biased against women. Unexpectedly, though, the gender gap in full-time earnings decreased not only at large but, disregarding the outlying case of construction, for all industries and for the occupational categories of wage employment and self-employment.

This does not mean that women achieved large-scale gains. Considering the broader data on earnings inequality, there is a general reallocation of female and male full-time workers from the upper and middle tiers to the lower tiers of the distribution of earners (Table 13). The principal difference is that, in terms of proportional reallocation into subminimum wage jobs, the downward shift was more extreme for men, who had the most to lose, than for women, many of whose earnings probably rose as they remained in the labor force for increased stretches of time, worked more overtime hours, and improved their basic skills. Sectorally, the focus of proportional gain by full-time female versus male workers was manufacturing jobs at the one-to-two minimum wage tier (Tardanico 1996a and 1996b). This would seem to reflect the dynamism of export manufacturing, a weakened relative position of import-substitution production, and related gender recomposition in manufacturing employment as a whole. For women and men in manufacturing and other industries, a fundamental issue is the degree to which formal and informal employment each became linked to upward and downward earnings mobility as well as to defense of previous earnings levels (Itzigsohn 1996; Menjívar Larín and Pérez Sáinz 1993; Pérez Sáinz 1994 and 1996; Portes and Schauffler 1993; Roberts 1995).

Hence, the profile of employment change in urban Costa Rica just partially supports the predictions derived from studies on transnational restructuring and gender. As predicted, women's share of employment rose,[24] with, leaving aside the unusual gender case of construction, the upturn being greatest in manufacturing. Nevertheless, women's share of unemployment somewhat decreased; and while the female percentage of the informal labor market generally rose, by the measure of employment in subminimum wage jobs, it fell. Furthermore, women's share increased in not only informal employment but also formal employment. Finally, gender inequality shrunk in the average real earnings of full-time workers.

With respect to earnings, what appears to have occurred are two basic gender patterns of labor-market realignment: a narrowing of income inequalities between full-time employed men and women at the aggregate level and a widening of income inequalities among such men and among such women (on this issue in Asian perspective, see Lantican, Gladwin, and Seale, Jr. 1996). Against the backdrop of a greater upturn in unemployment for men than women, relative employment gains in general by women versus men seem based less on the strength of female ascent — such as through advances in their legal rights, intra-household leverage, schooling attainment, employment experience and continuity, and cultural acceptance in desirable jobs — than on the momentum of male descent. In the absence of data on the dynamics of firms and of employment mobility, one cannot specify how the process of gendered change intersected with the socioeconomic dynamics of industries, occupational and skill differentiation, social class, national origins, household composition and structure, and age. Neither can it be said how the process operated across territorial locales or the extent to which it reflected long-term or short-term features of economy, state policy, and sociodemographic structure.

Territorial Redistribution

Insofar as Costa Rica conforms to what the comparative theoretical literature identifies as a spatial reconfiguration of the world economy, between 1980 and 1991, its urban employment underwent geographic decentralization. This process would be led by a centrifugal push involving the rapid growth of export-assembly manufacturing. Given Costa Rica's concurrent booms in nontraditional agricultural exports and international tourism in provincial areas, geographic decentralization of urban employment in commerce and services is likely to have taken place as well.[25]

The Costa Rican evidence provides only partial support for these predictions. Urban employment and unemployment on the whole became insignificantly less concentrated in the principal city, San José, as officially demarcated. Dropping just minimally were San José's share of Costa Rica's urban employment (from 62.4 percent to 60.8 percent) and urban unemployment (from 55.4 percent to 54.6 percent). The focus of what locational decentralization did occur was employment in the private sector, especially for women. The main feature of such change was that manufacturing, as expected, underwent notable employment redistribution away from San José to elsewhere in urban Costa Rica (Table 14); this redistribution was striking in the case of employment for women, a finding that coincides with comparative predictions. Diverging from this hypothesis, however, urban employment in services became just marginally relocated, and the spatial distribution of urban jobs in commerce did not change. The only industry whose urban employment became even somewhat more centralized in San José was construction (Table 14).

Why was the degree of net urban decentralization insignificant? To the extent that measurement error can be discounted, the geographic distribution of urban employment remained anchored in the heavy concentration of population, infrastructure, government, services, and markets in the city

Table 14.
San José's Percentages of Costa Rican National - Urban
Employment by Gender, Institutional Sector, and Industry

	1980	1991
Aggregate		
Male	62.1	61.1
Female	62.8	60.3
Total	**62.4**	**60.8**
Public Sector		
Male	51.3	53.7
Female	50.7	49.5
Total	**51.1**	**52.0**
Private Sector		
Male	62.2	59.7
Female	68.1	64.0
Total	**63.9**	**61.2**
Manufacturing		
Male	68.3	64.7
Female	83.1	69.7
Total	**73.0**	**66.7**
Construction		
Male	58.1	58.8
Female	38.2	100.0
Total	**57.8**	**59.9**
Commerce		
Male	64.9	64.6
Female	54.9	55.5
Total	**61.5**	**61.3**
Services		
Male	59.0	58.2
Female	58.8	57.1
Total	**58.9**	**57.7**

Source: Calculations based on DGPTE (July 1980, July 1991) for San José and urban
   Costa Rica.

and the wider metropolitan agglomeration of San José, whose national dominance was undiminished (Lungo, Pérez, and Piedra 1992). A prime example is the growth of export manufacturing in general and export-processing zones in particular. Such growth indeed spread across the metropolitan agglomeration, to the provinces and towns of Alajuela, Heredia, and Cartago, as well as beyond the agglomeration to coastal Puntarenas on the west and Limón on the east. Thus, as noted above, urban jobs in manufacturing became spatially decentralized, dramatically so for women. An explicit goal of government policy in this domain has been to promote export-oriented activities as a means of generating employment and development in poor regions. So far, though, the national redistribution of manufacturing jobs — at least in registered firms — has extended barely beyond the metropolitan agglomeration. In 1990, 99.2 percent of Costa Rica's registered export industrial enterprises were located in the greater metropolitan area. While over the previous four years there was a decrease in the national proportion of such enterprises located in San José (from 68.1 percent to 65.7 percent), the metropolitan agglomeration remained far and away the leading site of export-assembly activity (Lungo, Pérez, and Piedra 1992; Pérez Sáinz 1996, Chapters 3 and 4).

Similar national tendencies seem to characterize firms and employment in tourism, commerce and services overall, and construction (Lungo, Pérez, and Piedra 1992). The principal destinations of tourists are provincial, which may mean that much of the associated change in employment appears in the rural rather than the urban data. In any case, however, the location of the international airport and the major services (hotels, tour agencies, car rental agencies) in San José and its contiguous areas has placed much of the expansion of tourism firms and jobs in that zone. This in part is why the geographic distribution of urban employment in commerce did not change, a related factor being San José's wave of expansion in luxury shopping centers, expensive restaurants, and other such facilities. Urban employment in construction became slightly more centralized in San José in the setting of the national government's projects of infrastructural and housing development, together with the growing weight of San José's commercial real estate market. Discerning the spatial configuration of enterprises and jobs in producer services is an important research topic (see Roberts 1995; Sassen 1994).

In short, contrary to prediction, Costa Rica's urban employment in the aggregate did not become appreciably more decentralized. Urban decentralization was significant, though, in manufacturing employment, especially for women. Yet even in this case, the territorial redistribution of jobs away from San José did not substantially extend beyond its metropolitan agglomeration.[26] The evidence leads to the conclusion that, in contrast to expectations based on the restructuring literature, the period's changes in Costa Rica's urban employment did not challenge its long-established sociogeographic mold. Possible shifts in the location of employment within urban districts — including their potential points of intersection with neighborhood-based and home-based jobs — as well as between urban and rural zones are key questions for future research (see Benería and Roldán 1987; Menjívar Larín and Pérez Sáinz 1993).

Conclusion

Comparative studies on Central America underscore the exceptionality of Costa Rica, particularly as national leadership consolidated the state's social-democratic structure and its programs of import-substitution development and social welfare after the civil war of 1948. To what degree has such exceptionality survived the subsequent period of economic crisis and structural adjustment? With this question in mind, this chapter has examined continuities and discontinuities in Costa Rica's urban employment between 1980 and 1991.

The chapter offered speculation that employment discontinuity and deterioration were less abrupt in urban Costa Rica than in the rest of urban Central America and most of urban Latin America as a whole. In addition, the notable swings in urban Costa Rica's employment indicators during the 1990s substantially reflect its more pronounced vulnerabilities in an era of post-Cold War geopoliticsand economic globalization, which suggests comparison with the fluctuations of the post-crisis 1980s.

In general, the reorganization of employment by institutional sector, industry, and geographic location was small in scale. The state's class and organizational features and its geostrategic position minimized austerity-based job cuts in the public sector, while the main industry shift was modest growth in manufacturing's share of employment. Four subsets of change, however, seem to have been marked: first, net job loss for workers in the public sector with no more than primary schooling, compared with net job growth for public sector workers with at least secondary schooling; second, a reorientation of manufacturing jobs toward export production; third, a rise in women's share of manufacturing employment, which may have been greatest at the low end of production for the export and domestic markets alike; and fourth, an increase in the percentage of manufacturing jobs — especially for women — located outside the official boundaries of San José. The latter shift was limited, however, in that the overwhelming share of the jobs relocated not to the more distant, small urban areas of Costa Rica but to areas within San José's metropolitan agglomeration.

Apparently pronounced as well were increases in precarious and perhaps informal jobs and in women's jobs as shares of the labor market. In both cases, though, the data overestimate the extent of change, and it must be remembered that conditions and earnings of informality can be superior to those of formality. It nevertheless appears that the distribution of full-time earners shifted downward toward and below the legal minimum wage. Although this change appears greatest for nonwage workers, particularly the self-employed, it also encompassed wage workers, who remained by far the largest part of the labor force. This means that the period's economic transformations eroded the standing of some portion of workers in both the formal and informal economies, with the extent of earnings decline in the formal economy perhaps keeping informalization from being even more extensive. The gender data suggest, however, that some members of the labor force in nonwage and wage employment alike made earnings gains or at least maintained their relative positions on the earnings ladder.

The increase in women's share of jobs was greatest in manufacturing. Yet growth in the female share of employment in general was not simply a matter of informalization. Women's percentage of jobs rose in both the formal and informal economies, while men's percentages rose in full-time jobs paying subminimum wage and full-time jobs with undeclared income. Lastly, gender inequality in the average earnings of full-time workers did not grow but shrunk, the explanation seeming to lie at least as much in men's losses as women's gains. Overall, though, what occurred in the gender arena coincides with the larger complex of change: some amount of reorganized or worsened inequality within every sectoral and social category of the labor market. Identifying the gender, age, class, occupational, and sectoral processes of authentic female gains is important to the agenda of understanding the complexity of social realignments connected with restructuring. So too is recognition of the apparent trend of skilled young men, as they confront narrowed economic options, increasingly seeking jobs in the more skilled parts of export-assembly manufacturing.

Subsequent research needs to disentangle the dimensions of cyclical and secular change and to connect the range of development options to points of potential improvement or deterioration in employment conditions.[27] Among other things, it needs to explore myriad aspects of shifts in the interplay of state organization and policy, economic sectors and subsectors, social class, gender, age, national origins, and geography. This chapter's analysis has not touched upon pertinent matters such as change in the insertion of other Central Americans in the local labor market, in national flows of migration, and in urban-rural and inter-urban labor circuits. Neither has it addressed change in the embeddedness of employment in the organization, perceptions, and activities of households and communities. And the chapter has not examined shifts in the socioeconomic processes of occupational mobility and their consequences for household, community, class, and politics.

One possible reason for urban employment's strength of continuity with pre-crisis conditions is that, as a very small peripheral country for which agricultural exports have been the main linkage to the world economy, the attachments of Costa Rica's urban zones to global circuits of accumulation may be comparatively weak in worldwide perspective (see Roberts 1995). A consequence may be that rural rather than urban Costa Rica has been the first-order conduit for receiving and transmitting the local ramifications of global restructuring (see Céspedes and Jiménez 1995a; Clark 1995; Edelman 1991; Morley 1995, Chapter 5; Rojas and Román 1993; Tardanico 1996b). Such restructuring may be increasing the complexity of ties between the rural and urban economies. Insofar as agricultural exports have been the first-order conduit, then the role of state policy in mediating the patterns of this rural/urban flow merits attention.

This external explanation for continuity needs to be assessed from the vantage point of other very small countries in Latin America and the Caribbean (see this volume's chapters on the Dominican Republic by Itzigsohn [2] and Guatemala by Pérez Sáinz [3]; discussions on the wider Caribbean Basin in Pérez Sáinz 1994 and Portes, Itzigsohn, and Dore-Cabral 1994; and discussions on Uruguay in Lombardi and Veiga 1988, Lustig 1995, and Portes 1989).[28] It may partially tell why, for instance, manufacturing's gain in employment share was modest. The explanation is less satisfactory in recounting why, for example, public sector jobs did not decrease in absolute terms. The fact that there was no net reduction in public sector jobs illustrates the importance of both local institutional features and geopoliticsin mediating the impact of global restructuring — even in a highly vulnerable economy on the periphery.

Yet discontinuities apparently did occur in the social structure of employment. These suggest that, in the aftermath of the Cold War and Central America's turmoil of the 1980s and in light of Costa Rica's fiscal crisis of the mid-1990s, the ability of state leadership to maintain Costa Rica's socioeconomic exceptionality is waning. Inasmuch as a more technology- and skill-intensive segment of economic activities comes to relocate from the more advanced areas of the global division of labor to its periphery, urban Costa Rica's institutional and infrastructural advantages are likely to conserve much of its competitiveness relative to the rest of Central America, as well as to other parts of the worldwide periphery (see EIU [4th quarter] 1996; Gereffi and Korzeniewicz 1994; SAPG 1994; Wallerstein 1995). Even so, the current trajectories of post-Cold War geopolitics, economic global- ization, and national state policy portend long-term socioeconomic losses for significant portions of urban Costa Rica's middle and lower classes.

Notes

1. Our thanks to Professor Juan Diego Trejos of the Universidad de Costa Rica for facilitating access to data and to Mark Samara for sharing insights from his master's thesis research at Florida International University. We alone, however, are responsible for the analysis of the data and for any errors of interpretation.

2. Intel's decision, made in late 1996, came as Costa Rica's manufacturing economy continues to lose low-skill, apparel-assembly operations to low-cost competitors in the Caribbean Basin and beyond. Intel's multiyear investment is estimated at US$300 million to US$500 million (EIU [4th quarter] 34), a massive sum by Costa Rican standards. A more routine example of upgrading in the manufacturing economy is Motorola's recent decision to shift the production of ceramic filters for electronic products from a U.S. plant to a Costa Rican plant. Among the current examples in the service economy are American Express's data-processing operations in Costa Rica, which deal with the company's Latin American billings, and the decision of the Taiwan-based computer company, Acer, to establish operations in Costa Rica to provide long-distance technical service to its customers in the Americas. For a services-oriented vision of Costa Rica's economic future, see SAPG 1994.

3. This chapter is based on data from Costa Rica's national employment survey of households; the data used are for households in what are officially classified as urban areas and thus do not address urban workers who reside in rural locales (DGPTE 1980 and 1991). As with such surveys in general, these data inevitably miss much of the complexity of labor-force participation and employment, such as "hidden" unemployment and employment and simultaneous engagement in multiple income-earning activities. This is particularly so for women, children, and the elderly. A particular shortcoming of the Costa Rican data is that, due to methodological changes in the survey, post-1986 data overestimate some labor-market shifts, prime examples being the reduction in the public sector's share of total employment, the growth of precarious and informal employment, and as a result of the latter, probably the extent of feminization as well (see Céspedes and Jiménez 1995a, 127-140). We compensate for this problem by tempering our interpretations based on the reported magnitude of change in precarious and informal employment.

4. EIU (1996 [4th quarter], 33-34) reports that Intel's facility in Costa Rica "will finish processes initiated in Ireland, Israel and the USA... and could eventually produce up to one-fifth of Intel's worldwide production ... [The activities are] expected to provide over 3,500 jobs and to generate indirect employment established at 20,000 jobs. Additionally, the sheer size of the operation is expected to bring in complementary suppliers... Public- and private -sector organizations have begun to coordinate efforts to facilitate backward and forward linkages."

5. Carmelo Mesa-Lago has suggested that, given Monge's background as a leading Costa Rican trade unionist and given the merely incipient state of neoliberal ascendance in Latin America when he assumed the presidency, Monge's taking the

lead in orchestrating and implementing Costa Rica's stabilization shock treatment and in initiating the longer course of structural adjustment may have signified a more dramatic personal political shift than that of dependency theorist Fernando Henrique Cardoso in the 1990s. Cardoso, of course, successfully campaigned for the Brazilian presidency as a neoliberal and once in office indeed pursued a neoliberal line of action (see Mesa-Lago 1995).

6.   Unlike the rest of Central America and Mexico, increased emigration was not a major response in Costa Rica to the problems of the 1980s. On the contrary, Costa Rica became the site of a swelling population of refugees from the political strife of other Central American countries.

7.   Nevertheless, a public opinion survey conducted in September 1996 indicates that Costa Ricans remain strongly committed ideologically to the state's interventionist role in defending what by Latin American and Central American standards is a high level of social welfare and an egalitarian social distribution of income and wealth (*La Nación* 1996; see Vega 1996).

8.   Mark Samara (1997) amply documents that, contrary to many analyses, the formulation of the austere dimensions of structural adjustment policy in Costa Rica since the early 1980s has been no simple matter of U.S. government agencies and multilateral financial institutions dictating policy. Rather, within the framework of Costa Rica's highly constrained options and the diffusion of neoliberal ideology across the Americas, the country's state managers themselves have commonly proposed adjustment measures that are more extreme than those expected by representatives of the U.S. government, the International Monetary Fund, and the World Bank. The Costa Ricans have done so in anticipation of shifts in the world economy and to influence the terms of international negotiation. Simultaneously, of course, the Costa Rican leadership has been able to negotiate comprises between neoliberal macroeconomics and the domestic exigencies of forestalling social discontent and political instability, if often because of effective constitutional constraints on the policy-making independence of the presidency (see Dunkerley 1988; Franco and Sojo 1992; Nelson 1989; Rovira Mas 1987). At issue in the mid- to late 1990s is state leadership's continued capacity to modulate the forces of neoliberal macroeconomics on behalf of domestic social and political priorities, especially in view of the Pacto Calderón-Figueres.

Whatever the social and political consequences of the Pacto turn out to be, Costa Rica's general course of domestic and international negotiation coincides with a fundamental cross-national conclusion of this volume: that domestic institutions, ideologies, and initiatives must be taken seriously in efforts to understand Latin America's highly variable national patterns of political, economic, and social restructuring during the late twentieth century.

9.   During the 1980s and 1990s, public sector pay either declined slower or rose faster in parastatal agencies, where the wage-setting power of central government authority was comparatively weak and relations of political patronage were less constrained (Castro Valverde 1995, 26; Céspedes and Jiménez 1995a, 62, 87-88, 90).

10.   As a percentage of total employment, nationwide public sector employment apparently remained at roughly its 1991 level in 1992-1993 (Castro Valverde, 23-24; Céspedes and Jiménez 1995a, 100) but, under Figueres, dropped significantly by 1995 (Vega 1996).

Between 1980 and 1991, the slowed growth of jobs in the public versus the private sector took place as the urban economy's aggregate rate of unemployment rose from 4.6 percent to 6.0 percent. Within this span, the rate of unemployment soared between 1980 and 1982, dropped steadily to its lowest level of the decade by 1989, and rose substantially between 1989 and 1991. The rate dropped again between 1991 and 1994, contracting to the low level that typified the late 1980s, and then rose in 1995 (see, for example, ECLAC 1996). Aside from the economic crisis of the early 1980s, over the last 15 years or so, Costa Rica has generally ranked within the stratum of Latin American countries with the lowest rates of unemployment; in 1991 it edged upward into the middle stratum (ECLAC 1980-1994). This chapter argues that not increased unemployment but a modestly worsened composition of employment was the main characteristic of urban labor-market change from 1980 to 1991 (see Bodson, Cordero, and Pérez Sáinz 1995; CEPAS 1993; Vega 1996).

11. Castro Valverde (1995, 41) writes that this trend may reflect a decrease in the state's role in the construction of physical infrastructure as it becomes more specialized in services. In any case, Mylena Vega (1996) observes that by 1995 the percentage of "middle-class" employment located in the public sector had dropped sharply (see Castro Valverde 1995, 47-48).

12. The rate of unemployment in construction remained at 7.2 percent, though the sector lost employment (Table 3).

13. The data do not directly capture temporary jobs or jobs not covered by social security. Charting the trend in temporary jobs is important in view of comparative and Costa Rican evidence suggesting the increased instability of employment (see Bodson, Cordero, and Pérez Sáinz 1995; Roberts 1995). Due to changes introduced in Costa Rica's employment census, the post-1986 data overstate the growth of precarious and informal employment. Another factor is that some share of the growth in nonwage employment stands to have represented a shift by professionals, semi-professionals, and technicians into the occupational categories of self-employed or employer, though research needs to assess the extent to which the overall employment conditions of this part of the labor force improved, stayed the same, or worsened (see Bodson, Cordero, and Pérez Sáinz 1995; Castro Valverde 1995, 41-44; ECLAC 1995, 133; Morley 1995, Chapter 5; Vega 1996). Nevertheless, some share of the growth in wage employment stands to have represented the expansion of not formal labor but informal labor in microenterprises (for example, Bodson, Cordero, and Pérez Sáinz 1995; Trejos 1991; and the PREALC data cited in Thomas 1996, 88).

14. Samuel Morley (1995, 142) writes, however, that the rate of urban poverty fell slowest for informal workers and their families during the 1980s, which implies widened inequality between informal and formal workers.

15. Castro Valverde (1995, Table 15) indicates that between 1990 and 1992 there was an increase in the portion of total income accruing to the upper 20 percent of wage earners and a decrease for each of the other levels of wage earners. Between 1987 and 1992, however, each of the lower three levels registered an increase in portion of total income, which is consistent with Juan Diego Trejos's (1995) analysis.

16. And, of course, they do not address changes in the distribution of wealth — the more fundamental issue from the standpoint of class structure — which tends to be more unequal than income.

17. Some 30 years ago, Barrington Moore, Jr. (1966, appendix, "A Note on Statistics and Conservative Historiography") cautioned against losing sight of the fact that statistical data are among the multiple tools used to get at "qualitative alterations in the relations men [sic] have with one another...[and] changes in the form of social patterns" (520).

18. Services had the least proportional increase in full-time subminimum wage earners, an obvious factor being that a considerable share of service jobs are located in the public sector. We cannot comment on the impact of possible job growth and earnings changes in producer services and up-scale personal services (see Sassen 1994).

19. The fastest growing nonwage occupational categories in manufacturing were self-employment (151.9 percent) and employer (70.1 percent). The growth rate of employers ranked last in every other sector; that of self-employment ranked first in commerce and second, behind the minute category of unpaid employment, in construction and services. As a percentage of total employment, self-employment led the nonwage categories in every industry, though construction came to surpass commerce as its site of greatest relative presence. By the same standard, employers remained most represented in commerce, followed by construction. Unpaid workers also remained most represented in commerce, followed by manufacturing in 1980 but by construction in 1991.

20. Due to data problems on occupational earnings inequality with respect to urban Costa Rica in general, the data cited on occupations refer to San José only. The trends for San José and urban Costa Rica at large, however, are identical, while there is insignificant difference between them regarding full-time employment as a percentage of total employment.

21. Concerning age, data indicate that 12- to 19-year-olds were the full-time workers most likely to earn less than legal minimum pay in 1980 (48.5 percent) and 1991 (51.6 percent). The data also indicate, though, that relative growth in the proportions of each age group of full-time workers at this level was least for 12- to 19-year-olds (6.4 percent) and 70+ year-olds (-10.8 percent), the latter being the group with the second highest percentage of full-time subminimum-wage earners in 1980. The relative increases for the other age groups were as follows: 20- to 29-year-olds, 69.8 percent; 30- to 39-year-olds, 82.9 percent; 40- to 49-year-olds, 78.0 percent; 50- to 59-year-olds, 178.7 percent; and 60- to 69-year-olds, 29.2 percent. The apparent trend is toward faster growth in the share of full-time subminimum-wage earners among groups of intermediate age — that is, prime income-earning age — than for youths and the elderly. By this measure, then, the relative worsening of employment conditions was most extreme for workers of intermediate age.

Not to be overlooked is the need for research on the comparative labor-market roles of Central American refugees and native Costa Ricans in rural and urban settings (see Bodson, Cordero, and Pérez Sáinz 1995; Céspedes and Jiménez 1995a and 1995b; *Inforpress Centroamericana* 1996b).

22. That is, the yearly data for 1980-1991 seem to indicate that a major portion of the reported growth of the female portion of the labor force (from 31.9 percent to 36.4 percent) and employment (from 31.5 percent to 36.2 percent, including the categories of urban-based agriculture and unknown) is a mere artifact of the post-1986 revision of the methodology of Costa Rica's official survey. While women remained overrepresented among the unemployed, their reported portion of

unemployment dropped slightly (from 41.2 percent to 40.4 percent). This occurred as the proportional rise in the male rate of unemployment (from 4.0 percent to 5.6 percent) was greater than that in the female rate (from 5.9 percent to 6.7 percent).

23. Since export-assembly manufacturing accounted for an enlarged part of total manufacturing employment in urban Costa Rica, it could be expected that, in line with international evidence, women under the age of 30 increased their share of all jobs in manufacturing (see, for example, Safa 1995, 23). In fact, the share of manufacturing jobs accounted for by 12- to 29-year-olds fell from 57.6 percent to 36.1 percent among women and from 54.3 percent to 38.9 percent among men. Because this trend conforms to the wider aging of the employed labor force, a stricter assessment requires considering change in the portion of employed females and males under 30 years of age whose principal or sole job was in manufacturing. This portion dropped for 12- to 19-year-old males and, to a lesser degree, for 12- to 19-year-old females, while rising for 20- to 29-year-old males and females as well as for the older groups (Table 12).

For 12- to 19-year-old males, the likelihood of having principal or sole employment in agriculture rose from 5.2 percent to 12.1 percent and in commerce from 24.0 percent to 26.6 percent. For 12- to 19-year-old females, in agriculture it rose from 0.6 percent to 2.3 percent and in commerce from 29.1 percent to 34.2 percent. The general pattern of such change signals an interindustry reordering of job opportunities, incentives, and preferences for adolescent males and females relative to the other gender-age groups. The augmented relative importance of adolescent employment in agriculture — which for all age groups was 1.7 percent of urban Costa Rica's total employment in 1980 and 0.9 percent in 1991 — may reflect the expanded presence of poor immigrants from elsewhere in Central America as well as the expanded role of subsistence activities more broadly. In the setting of both increased economic hardship and transnationalized consumerism, growth in the relative importance of adolescent employment in commerce — above all for females — may in part reflect the proliferation of international-style retail activities (for example, fast-food chains, supermarket chains, up-scale shopping complexes, and tourism; see Díaz this volume, Chapter 6), along with changes in the hiring preferences of employers and the job preferences of teenagers. Likewise, pertinent to shifts in the employment structure of adolescents is the increased practice of combining jobs with school attendance (see Tardanico 1996a).

24. The annual data for 1980-1991 suggest, however, that the results of the post-1986 surveys exaggerate the extent of female proportional gains in the labor force and employment.

25. Prominent aspects of the tourism boom are "ecological tourism" and foreign investment in the construction of resort complexes on the Pacific coast. As of the mid-1990s, there is concern that, especially in the absence of massive infrastructural development, Costa Rica's tourism prosperity has peaked.

Regarding the extent of locational change in Costa Rican employment, we acknowledge that restricting analysis to the urban pattern of such change overlooks the possibility of change in the larger urban/rural pattern of nonagricultural employment.

26. It appears that any notable increase in rural manufacturing employment largely would have been contained within the agriculturally oriented areas of the metropolitan agglomeration. The overwhelming portion of spatially decentralized

manufacturing, however, seems to have been located in export-processing complexes (Lungo, Pérez, and Piedra 1992; Pérez Sáinz 1994 and 1996; Schoepfle and Pérez López 1993).

More generally, the most basic difference between urban and rural Costa Rica in the characteristics of labor-market restructuring during this period may have been, against a baseline of much lower average earnings in rural areas, a higher rate of earnings growth in rural than urban areas. Average full-time rural earnings were 67.7 percent of urban earnings in 1980 and 76.5 percent in 1991 (see Céspedes and Jiménez 1995a, 101, 105-107; Tardanico 1996b).

27. Again, the long-range evidence indicates that the more abrupt changes reported in this chapter surfaced during the deepening of neoliberal reforms and acceleration of economic restructuring in the early 1990s, which gave way to improved employment conditions by 1993-1994 followed by downturn in 1995-1996.

28. Likewise of relevance is the case of Chile, in view of its leading-edge economic and export dynamism among Latin American countries, the fundamental importance of the linkages between its urban and rural economies, its relatively high level of economic and social infrastructural development, its traditionally high standard of living, and, by comparison with Costa Rica and other Latin American countries of the Caribbean Basin, its distant location from the United States. While the contemporary cases of Costa Rica and Chile do not make for symmetrical comparison in the strict sense, they do yield provocative insights into Latin American convergence and divergence in political, economic, and social restructuring (see Díaz this volume, Chapter 6).

References

Amsden, Alice H., and Rolph van der Hoeven. 1996. "Manufacturing Output, Employment and Real Wages in the 1980s: Labour's Loss Until the Century's End." *Journal of Development Studies* 32(4):506-530.

Benería, Lourdes, and Martha Roldán. 1987. *The Crossroads of Class and Gender: Industrial Homework, Subcontracting, and Household Dynamics in Mexico City.* Chicago: University of Chicago Press.

Bodson, Paul, Allen Cordero, and Juan Pablo Pérez Sáinz. 1995. *Las nuevas caras del empleo.* San José, Costa Rica: FLACSO.

Bromley, Ray, and Chris Birkbeck. 1988. "Urban Economy and Employment." In *The Geography of the Third World*, ed. Michael Pacione. London: Routledge.

Bulmer-Thomas, Victor. 1987. *The Political Economy of Central America since 1920.* Cambridge: Cambridge University Press.

Bulmer-Thomas, Victor. 1996. "Introduction." In *The New Economic Model in Latin America and Its Impact on Income Distribution and Poverty*, ed. Victor Bulmer-Thomas. New York: St. Martin's Press.

Castro Valverde, Carlos. 1995. "Estado y sectores medios en Costa Rica: redimensionamiento de un pacto social." *Cuadernos de Ciencias Sociales.* San José, Costa Rica: FLACSO.

CCAR (*Caribbean & Central America Report*). 1996. "Figueres Reshuffles His Cabinet: Private Sector Approves but Public Less Impressed." London. July 25:3.

CEPAS (Centro de Estudios para la Acción Social). 1992. *Costa Rica: balance de la situación.* San José, Costa Rica.

CEPAS. 1993. *Boletín Informativo.* San José, Costa Rica (March).

Céspedes, Víctor Hugo, and Ronulfo Jiménez. 1995a. *Apertura comercial y mercado laboral en Costa Rica.* San José, Costa Rica: Academia de Centroamérica and Centro Internacional para el Desarrollo Económico.

Céspedes, Víctor Hugo, and Ronulfo Jiménez. 1995b. *La pobreza en Costa Rica.* San José, Costa Rica: Academia de Centroamérica.

Clark, Mary A. 1995. "Nontraditional Export Promotion in Costa Rica: Sustaining Export-led Growth." *Journal of Interamerican Studies and World Affairs* 37(2):181-223.

Cordero, Allen. 1994. "¿Hay un nuevo modelo de producción en la industria costarricense?" In *Globalización y fuerza laboral en Centroamérica*, ed. Juan Pablo Pérez Sáinz. San José, Costa Rica: FLACSO.

Díaz, Alvaro. 1997. "New Developments in Social and Economic Restructuring in Latin America." In *Politics, Social Change, and Economic Restructuring in Latin America*, eds. William C. Smith and Roberto Patricio Korzeniewcz. Coral Gables, Fla.: North-South Center Press at the University of Miami.

Dierckxsens, Wim. 1992. "Impacto del ajuste estructural sobre la mujer trabajadora en Costa Rica." *Cuadernos de Política Económica*. Heredia, Costa Rica: Universidad Nacional de Costa Rica.

DGPTE (Dirección General de Planificación del Trabajo y el Empleo). 1980 and 1991. *Encuesta de Hogares: Empleo y Desempleo*. San José, Costa Rica (July).

Dunkerley, James. 1988. *Power in the Isthmus: A Political History of Modern Central America*. London: Verso.

ECLAC (Economic Commission for Latin America and the Caribbean). 1983-1995a. *Economic Survey of Latin America and the Caribbean*. Santiago, Chile: ECLAC.

ECLAC. 1995b. *Social Panorama of Latin America*. Santiago, Chile: ECLAC.

ECLAC. 1996. *Cepal News*. Santiago, Chile: ECLAC.

Edelman, Marc. 1991. "Shifting Legitimacies and Economic Change: The State and Contemporary Costa Rican Peasant Movements." *Peasant Studies* 18(4):221-249.

Edelman, Marc, and Rodolfo Monge Oveido. 1993. "Costa Rica: The Non-Market Roots of Market Success." *NACLA Report on the Americas* 26(4):22-30.

EIU (*The Economist Intelligence Unit*). 1996. *Country Studies: Costa Rica, Panama*, quarterly. London.

Elson, Diane, ed. 1995. *Male Bias in the Development Process*, 2nd ed. Manchester: Manchester University Press.

Franco, Eliana, and Carlos Sojo. 1992. *Gobierno, empresarios y políticas de ajuste*. San José, Costa Rica: FLACSO.

García-Huidobro, Guillermo, Alberto Hintermeister, José Galán Ponce, and Molly Pollack. 1990. *La deuda social en Costa Rica*. Geneva: Organización Internacional de Trabajo/Programa Regional del Empleo para América Latina y el Caribe OIT/PREALC.

Gereffi, Gary. 1994. "Rethinking Development Theory: Insights from East Asia and Latin America." In *Comparative National Development: Society and Economy in the New Global Order*, eds. A. Douglas Kincaid and Alejandro Portes. Chapel Hill: University of North Carolina Press.

Gereffi, Gary, and Miguel Korzeniewicz, eds. 1994. *Commodity Chains and Global Capitalism*. Westport, Conn.: Praeger.

Gilbert, Alan. 1994. "Third World Cities: Poverty, Employment, Gender Roles and the Environment during a Time of Restructuring." *Urban Studies* 31(4-5):605-633.

Gindling, T.H. 1993. "Por qué las mujeres ganan menos que los hombres en Costa Rica." San José, Costa Rica: Universidad de Costa Rica, Instituto de Investigaciones en Ciencias Económicas, no. 164.

Gindling, T.H., and Albert Berry. 1992. "The Performance of the Labor Market during Recession and Structural Adjustment: Costa Rica in the 1980s." *World Development* 20(11):1599-1616.

Gindling, T.H., and Katherine Terrell. 1995. "The Nature of Minimum Wages and Their Effectiveness as a Wage Floor in Costa Rica, 1976-91." *World Development* 23(8):1439-1458.

Goldenberg, Olga. 1993. "Género e informalidad en San José." In *Ni héroes ni villanas: género e informalidad urbana en Centroamérica*, eds. Rafael Menjívar Larín and Juan Pablo Pérez Sáinz. San José, Costa Rica: FLACSO.

Infante, Ricardo, and Emilio Klein. 1991. "The Latin American Labour Market." *CEPAL Review* 45(December):121-135.

Inforpress Centroamericana. 1995. "PLN ¿cambio al neoliberalismo?" Guatemala. June 15:15-16.

Inforpress Centroamericana. 1996a. "Seguridad alimentaria en riesgo." Guatemala. October 24:5-6.

Inforpress Centroamericana.1996b. "Dramática situación de migrantes nicaragüenses en Costa Rica." Guatemala. December 5:11-12.

Itzigsohn, José. 1996. "Globalization, the State, and the Informal Economy: The Articulation of Informal and Formal Economic Activities and the Limits to Proletarianization in the Periphery." In *Latin America in the World-Economy*, eds. Roberto Patricio Korzeniewicz and William C. Smith. Westport, Conn.: Praeger.

Johnson, Tim. 1995. "Big Government Downsizing Hits Costa Rica Hard." *The Miami Herald*, November 16:18a.

Kincaid, A. Douglas. 1989. "Costa Rican Peasants and the Politics of Quiescence." In *The Costa Rica Reader*, eds. Marc Edelman and Joanne Kenen. New York: Grove WeidenFeld.

La Nación. 1995. "Motores tibios contra la pobreza." San José, Costa Rica. May 4(electronic issue).

La Nación. 1996. "Ticos fieles a Estado benefactor." San José, Costa Rica. September 9(electronic issue).

Lantican, Clarita P., Christian A. Gladwin, and James L. Seale, Jr. 1996. "Income and Gender Inequalities in Asia: Testing Alternative Theories." *Economic Development and Cultural Change* 44(2):235-264.

Levitsky, Steve, and Tony Lapp. 1992. "Solidarismo and Organized Labor." *Hemisphere: A Magazine of Latin American and Caribbean Affairs* 4(2):26-31.

Lombardi, Mario, and Danilo Veiga. 1988. "La urbanización en los años de crisis en el Uruguay." *Occasional Papers Series Dialogues*. Miami: Latin American and Caribbean Center, Florida International University.

Lungo, Mario. 1995. "La ciudad y la nación, la organización barrial y el estado: los dilemas de la urbanización en Costa Rica a principios de los años 90." Unpublished paper, Program in Comparative International Development, Department of Sociology, The Johns Hopkins University.

Lungo, Mario, Mariám Pérez, and Nancy Piedra. 1992. "La urbanización en Costa Rica en los años 80." In *Urbanización en Centroamérica*, eds. Alejandro Portes and Mario Lungo. San José, Costa Rica: FLACSO.

Lustig, Nora, ed. 1995. *Coping with Austerity: Poverty and Inequality in Latin America*. Washington, D.C.: The Brookings Institution.

McPhaul, John. 1994. "Costa Rica Restructures Its Debt." *The Miami Herald*. November 4:14A.

McPhaul, John. 1996a. "Costa Rican Alliance Aims at Boosting Economy." *The Miami Herald*. July 8:9A.

McPhaul, John. 1996b. "Deficit's Big Interest Payments Draining Costa Rica's Economy." *The Miami Herald.* October 7:8A.

Menjívar Larín, Rafael, and Juan Pablo Pérez Sáinz, eds. 1993. *Ni héroes ni villanos: género e informalidad urbana en Centroamérica.* San José, Costa Rica: FLACSO.

Mesa-Lago, Carmelo. 1995. *Alternative Models of Development in Latin America: Market, Socialist, and Mixed Approaches.* Unpublished manuscript, Department of Economics, University of Pittsburgh.

Mesoamerica. 1996a. "Costa Rica." San José, Costa Rica. January:6-7.

Mesoamerica. 1996b. "War of Words: A Look Inside Costa Rica's Contentious Privatization Debate." San José, Costa Rica. January:8-9.

Mesoamerica. 1996c. "Costa Rica." San José, Costa Rica. February:9-10.

Mesoamerica. 1996d. "Economic Instability Felt by all Sectors." San José, Costa Rica. October:11.

Moore, Jr., Barrington. 1966. *The Social Origins of Dictatorship and Democracy.* Boston: Beacon.

Morley, Samuel A. 1995. *Poverty and Inequality in Latin America: The Impact of Adjustment and Recovery in the 1980s.* Baltimore: The Johns Hopkins University Press.

Nelson, Joan M. 1989. "Crisis Management, Economic Reform, and Costa Rican Democracy." In *Debt and Democracy in Latin America*, eds. Barbara Stallings and Robert Kaufman. Boulder, Colo.: Westview Press.

Paige, Jeffery M. 1987. "Coffee and Politics in Central America." In *Crises in the Caribbean Basin*, ed. Richard Tardanico. Newbury Park, Calif.: Sage Publications.

Pelupessy, Wim, ed. 1991. *Perspectives on the Agro-Export Economy in Central America.* Pittsburgh, Pa.: University of Pittsburgh Press.

Pérez Sáinz, Juan Pablo, ed. 1994. *Globalización y fuerza laboral en Centroamérica.* Caracas: FLACSO/Nueva Sociedad.

Pérez Sáinz, Juan Pablo. 1996. *De la finca a la maquila: modernización capitalista y trabajo en Centroamérica.* San José, Costa Rica: FLACSO.

Portes, Alejandro. 1989. "Latin American Urbanization during the Years of the Crisis." *Latin American Research Review* 24(3):7-44.

Portes, Alejandro, José Itzigsohn, and Carlos Dore-Cabral. 1994. "Urbanization in the Caribbean Basin: Social Change during the Years of the Crisis." *Latin American Research Review* 29(2):3-37.

Portes, Alejandro, and Richard Schauffler. 1993. "Competing Perspectives on the Latin American Informal Sector." *Population and Development Review* 19(1):33-60.

Rakowski, Cathy A., ed. 1994. *Contrapunto: The Informal Sector Debate in Latin America.* Albany: State University of New York Press.

Roberts, Bryan. 1995. *The Making of Citizens: Cities of Peasants Revisited.* London: Arnold.

Roberts, Bryan, and Richard Tardanico. 1997. "Employment Transformations in U.S. and Mexican Gulf Cities." *LACC Occasional Paper Series.* Miami: Latin American and Caribbean Center, Florida International University.

Rojas, Manuel, and Isabel Román. 1993. "Agricultura de exportación y pequeños productores en Costa Rica." *Cuadernos de Ciencias Sociales* 61. San José, Costa Rica: FLACSO.

Rovira Mas, José. 1987. *Costa Rica en los años '80.* San José, Costa Rica: Editorial Porvenir.

Sáenz, María Inés, and Juan Diego Trejos. 1993. "Las formas de inserción de la mujer al mercado de trabajo en Costa Rica." San José, Costa Rica: Universidad de Costa Rica, Instituto de Investigaciones en Ciencias Económicas, no. 165.

Safa, Helen I. 1995. *The Myth of the Male Breadwinner: Women and Industrialization in the Caribbean.* Boulder, Colo.: Westview Press.

Samara, Mark A. 1997. "State Mediation of Structural Adjustment: The Case of Costa Rica." Unpublished master's thesis. Miami: Graduate Program in International Studies, Florida International University.

SAPG (Social Agenda Policy Group). 1994. "A la búsqueda del siglo XXI: nuevos caminos de desarrollo en Costa Rica." Washington, D.C.: Inter-American Development Bank.

Sassen, Saskia. 1994. *Cities in a World Economy.* Thousand Oaks, Calif.: Pine Forge Press.

Schoepfle, Gregory K., and Jorge F. Pérez-López, eds. 1993. *Work Without Protections: Case Studies of the Informal Sector in Developing Countries.* Washington, D.C.: U.S. Department of Labor, Bureau of International Labor Affairs.

Smith, William C., Carlos Acuña, and Eduardo Gamarra, eds. 1994. *Latin American Political Economy in the Age of Neoliberal Reform.* Coral Gables, Fla.: North-South Center at the University of Miami.

Sojo, Ana. 1994. "Política social en Costa Rica: reformas recientes." *Cuadernos de Ciencias Sociales* 67. San José, Costa Rica: FLASCO.

Standing, Guy. 1989. "Global Feminization through Flexible Labor." *World Development* 17(7):1077-1095.

Standing, Guy, and Victor E. Tokman, eds. 1991. *Towards Social Adjustment: Labour Market Issues in Structural Adjustment.* Geneva: International Labour Organization.

Tardanico, Richard. 1992. "Economic Crisis and Structural Adjustment: The Changing Labor Market of San José, Costa Rica." *Comparative Urban and Community Research* 4:70-104.

Tardanico, Richard. 1996a. "Restructuring, Employment, and Gender: The Case of San José, Costa Rica." *Studies in Comparative International Development* 31(3):85-122.

Tardanico, Richard. 1996b. "From Crisis to Restructuring: The Nexus of Global and National Change in the Costa Rican Labor Market." *Review: Fernand Braudel Center* 19(2):155-196.

Thomas, Jim. 1996. "The New Economic Model and Labour Markets in Latin America." In *The New Economic Model in Latin America and Its Impact on Income Distribution and Poverty,* ed. Victor Bulmer-Thomas. New York: St. Martin's Press.

Tilly, Chris. 1996. *Half a Job: Bad and Good Part-time Jobs in a Changing Labor Market.* Philadelphia, Pa.: Temple University Press.

Torres Rivas, Edelberto. 1993. *History and Society in Central America*. Austin: University of Texas Press.

Trejos, Juan Diego. 1991. "Informalidad y acumulación en el Area Metropolitana de San José, Costa Rica." In *Informalidad urbana en Centroamérica: entre la acumulación y la subsistencia,* eds. Rafael Menjívar Larín and Juan Pablo Pérez Sáinz. Caracas: FLACSO/Nueva Sociedad.

Trejos, Juan Diego. 1995. "Empleo, distribución del ingreso y pobreza durante los inicios del ajuste en Costa Rica 1987-1992." *Documentos de Trabajo*. San José, Costa Rica: Universidad de Costa Rica, Instituto de Investigaciones en Ciencias Económicas, no. 173.

UNDP (United Nations Development Program). 1995. *Human Development Report 1995*. New York: Oxford University Press.

Valverde, José Manuel, María Eugenia Trejos, and Minor Mora Salas. 1993. *La movilidad laboral al descubierto*. San José, Costa Rica: Servicios de Promoción Laboral.

Vega, Mylena. 1996. "La clase media costarricense." *La Nación* (electronic version). May 8. San José, Costa Rica.

Wallerstein, Immanuel. 1995. *After Liberalism*. New York: The New Press.

Wolf, Diane Lauren. 1992. *Factory Daughters: Gender, Household Dynamics, and Rural Industrialization in Java*. Berkeley: University of California Press.

Chapter 5

Economic Crisis, State Policy, and Labor-Market Change: The Case of Urban Venezuela

Víctor Fajardo Cortez and Miguel Lacabana

In Venezuela since the early 1980s, labor's income-earning capacity has fallen dramatically. With an empirical focus on 1987-1992, this chapter examines how economic crisis in Venezuela affected the state's policymaking and the consequent impact on urban employment patterns and social inequality. The analysis indicates that the trend toward diminishing income-earning capacity has encompassed men as well as women, whose share of the labor force has notably expanded.

During the period studied, public sector employment has declined as a portion of total employment, tertiary employment has grown in importance, and employment in export manufacturing has remained marginal. The proportional expansion of informal employment was minuscule during the late 1980s and early 1990s, but the sector's occupational composition changed, as its reported percentage of employers increased. According to survey research in several low-income districts of metropolitan Caracas, the informal sector's percentage of women may have increased as well. Urban employment has become less contained within Caracas, but the territorial redistribution of employment has been to the city's surrounding regional agglomeration rather than to interior cities. The fundamental conclusion is that — from a starting point of a comparatively high standard of state protections and subsidies, employment conditions, and social welfare — Venezuela's urban labor force has undergone a process of large-scale impoverishment, a trajectory that has intensified during the mid-1990s.

Víctor Fajardo Cortez is research professor of economics at the Centro de Estudios del Desarrollo (CENDES), Universidad Central de Venezuela; and graduate professor at the Instituto de Altos Estudios Diplomáticos, Ministry of Foreign Relations, and at the Instituto Venezolano de Planificación, Ministry of Planning. Miguel Lacabana is graduate professor of economics at CENDES, Universidad Central de Venezuela.

Translated by Richard Tardanico and Vanessa Gray.

Economic Crisis and Policy Response

Venezuela's economic crisis is part of a more general crisis of politics and society that revolves around the extreme dependence of the economy, state, and society on revenues generated by petroleum exports (see Karl 1995). The "petro-model" had sustained a high level of government expenditure and subsidy of national businesses and mass living standards, but it began to come apart during the 1970s as the world market price of oil dropped and Venezuela's external debt mounted. A surge in oil revenues in 1979-1981 postponed the model's breakdown. During the 1980s, however, as oil prices and revenues plunged and foreign creditors demanded payment on Venezuela's bloated loan obligations, the model virtually unraveled. Amid the accelerated reorganization of the global political economy, Venezuela's domestic crisis has worsened as its state machinery and business enterprises have proved incapable of meeting the demands of a reconfigured world order. Specifically, the government's policy responses have been hamstrung by the state's organizational inflexibilities, including a rigid state-party structure of political patronage and influence, and the economy has been crippled by a woeful lack of entrepreneurial competitiveness in the international market.

Within this framework, Venezuela failed in its multiple attempts at economic restructuring between 1983 and 1988. Structural adjustment was the overriding objective of government leadership from 1983, the final year of the presidency of Luis Herrera Campíns, of the Christian Democratic party COPEI (Comité de Organización Política y Electoral Independiente), until the end of the subsequent presidency of Jaime Luchinchi, of the social democratic party Acción Democrática, in 1988. Yet executive initiatives were poorly orchestrated, and patchwork efforts were the norm. In 1984-1985, these efforts amounted to a recessive adjustment that, in a setting of high inflation and falling real wages, aimed at squeezing out public sector savings in order to boost the nation's foreign currency reserves to meet payments on the foreign debt. Economic growth resumed in 1986-1988 and inflation was contained, but fiscal, trade, and financial balances deteriorated greatly, and international reserves were liquidated.

In December 1988, the nation's voters elected Acción Democrática candidate Carlos Andrés Pérez to a second term as president (1988-1992) by an overwhelming majority. During the electoral campaign, it was widely acknowledged not only that some form of economic restructuring was inevitable but that, in the context of Venezuela's regime of petroleum-dependent social democracy, all social strata would have to endure significant cuts in living standards (see Tardanico and Lungo on Costa Rica this volume, Chapter 4). The Pérez government formulated an adjustment plan, dubbed the *Gran Viraje*, that was consistent with the neoliberal wave that had already swept across most of Latin America. It included both stabilization measures to achieve macroeconomic equilibrium in the short term and structural adjustment measures with the long-term objective of reorganizing the state and economy. Such reorganization was intended to reduce the state's fiscal and interventionist weight and to enhance its organizational flexibility and efficiency while de-emphasizing the economy's declining traditional exports (oil, minerals, coffee, and cacao) in favor of more competitive nontraditional goods and services.

Over its four-year duration, the *Gran Viraje* failed to achieve the sought-after transformations, and the Venezuelan economy headed in precisely the opposite direction. Moreover, the policy's economic package undermined the quest to tame inflation, even to the point of making stabilization impossible in the medium term (see Cortés this volume on Argentina, Chapter 7). Macroeconomic indicators for 1992 demonstrate that the economy had regressed to its 1988 state of imbalance, and, rather than gearing up for innovation and internationalization, business firms and organized labor simply had maneuvered to protect their flanks within the institutional confines of the pre-crisis era. This maneuvering interlocked with a similar pattern of action within the state's bureaucratic apparatus, whose own varied interests also proved far too addicted to the petro-state's protections and privileges to embark on a new course of institution building (see Karl 1995).

In view of entrenched resistance and myriad policy contradictions that further stymied the adjustment plan, the magnitude of the fiscal deficit was less worrisome than the state's continued heavy dependence on oil revenues. What is more, fiscal reform in 1990 caused the state's non-oil revenues to drop.

Meanwhile, petroleum continued to dominate Venezuelan exports, and the country experienced a surge in imports. New market-liberalizing regulations that ruled out the application of various import controls compounded the economy's vulnerability to imports. On the export side, the Pérez government drastically devalued the currency, established a floating exchange rate, lowered and simplified tariffs, eliminated anti-export regulations, and emphasized the liberalization of foreign capital inflows. Government officials anticipated a quick and favorable response by national and foreign investors.

Official optimism led to plans for state-led, export-oriented megaprojects. Economic realities, however, soon deflated the government's projections for private investment and for nontraditional export earnings. The Pérez administration carried out few of the anticipated petrochemical projects. It suspended plans for the aluminum industry after the bottom fell out of that export market. Moreover, the Cristóbal Colón natural gas project — Venezuela's largest and most ambitious megaproject — is still pending after protracted negotiations. Venezuela's negative trade balance was exacerbated by the lack of new domestic or foreign investment in export-oriented production.

To be sure, the *Gran Viraje* can be credited with removing domestic institutional barriers to international commerce, putting Venezuela in compliance with the new regime of global trade. Progress was also made toward shrinking the state by means of privatization of telecommunications, the national airline, banks, sugar refineries, ports, hotels, and other state-held entities. In this setting, Venezuela's strong growth in gross domestic product — 6.8 percent in 1990, 9.7 percent in 1991, and 5.8 percent in 1992 (ECLAC 1995a, 49) — surpassed official expectations.

The motor driving this growth, however, was the extraordinary petroleum income of 1990, resulting from the Persian Gulf War, and the high volume of state spending financed by huge public deficits in 1991-1992. Contrary to the objectives of the *Gran Viraje*, Venezuela's most dynamic economic activity was in public sector consumption and investment, which between 1988 and 1991 rose as a share of aggregate demand, as private investment and consumption dropped. The period's rapid pace of national economic growth — the world's fastest, President Pérez declared repeatedly — became unsustainable in 1993.

An overview of other sectoral growth rates during the Pérez administration reveals additional undesirable economic trends. Fastest net growth was in domestically oriented nontradables, such as electricity and water (25.5 percent), public administration services (23.5 percent), petroleum-related activities (22.8 percent), and construction (19.9 percent). Manufacturing displayed only modest net growth (13.8 percent), while agriculture slightly contracted (by 1.5 percent). Tradables did not play a leading economic role. Although expanding at a pace similar to nontradables, this meant simply that they remained constant as a share of the nation's economy.

Persistent inflation was another unintended result of the *Gran Viraje*. Policy planners had anticipated large price fluctuations during the first year of implementation as price controls and subsidies were eliminated and the currency devalued. They established relative price stability at the outset with the expectation that by 1990 inflation would begin falling toward rates characteristic of Venezuela's major trading partners. Officials predicted they would rein in inflation by combining fiscal and monetary restrictions with nominal, partially compensatory wage adjustments (Cordiplan 1989). They also thought that a mix of trade policy and exchange-rate policy would neutralize the structural causes of inflation (monopolies, oligopolies, and production rigidities).

Then, completely unexpectedly, the general price index for 1989, the first year of adjustment, jumped by 84.5 percent, triple the projected rate. The rate of inflation began to drop, but by the early 1990s, it settled at more than 30 percent, historically a high level for Venezuela. Inflationary pressures resulted primarily from the massive fiscal deficit of 1991-1992; policymakers utilized currency devaluations to meet the government's financial needs, thereby creating a vicious circle of deficit-inflation-devaluation. This and other sources of inflation compounded a wide range of growth-strangling forces, such as high interest rates and the overarching climate of pronounced sociopolitical uncertainty, which discouraged national and foreign private investment.

High inflation and signs of recession indicated that the Venezuelan economy was headed into a cycle of stagflation — the opposite of the growth-with-inflation scenario that the Pérez government had promised. More basically, the Venezuelan economy had not achieved significant structural change toward diminished reliance on the petro-state's protections, subsidies, and patronage or toward export diversification and competitiveness. Quite the contrary, the results of the *Gran Viraje* were the reverse of the program's avowed objectives (see, for example, Goodman et al. 1995; McCoy et al. 1995).

Labor-Market Change

From 1981 to 1989, Venezuela's gross domestic product (GDP) per capita dropped by an accumulated 23.6 percent. From 1990 to 1992, the mini-oil boom and public deficit spending enabled it to rebound by an accumulated 14.7 percent, before it again contracted in 1993-1994 by 7.5 percent. The downward path has continued into mid-decade (ECLAC 1995a, 50).

Ongoing economic crisis and the succession of erratically implemented adjustment policies profoundly affected Venezuela's urban labor market. Most crucially, they made the task of earning a living much more difficult. After peaking in the mid-1980s, the rate of unemployment declined as parts of the economy underwent short-term recovery. At the same time, however, Venezuelans began to work longer hours, take on supplementary jobs, and send more family members into the labor force.[1] The middle classes did so to minimize or avoid household economic losses; the poor did so in order to survive.

Within a long-term setting of painful aggregate decline, the economy's fluctuations and policy inconsistencies were associated between 1987 and 1992 with growth in Venezuela's officially measured labor force from 56.1 percent of the total population to 60.1 percent.[2] This five-year rise would have been even greater if not for a continued slowing of Venezuela's population growth rate. As hypothesized in Chapter 1, labor-force growth was due largely to the incorporation of women, whose rate of labor-force participation jumped from 31 to 39 percent, while men's remained at 81 percent. As part of a long-term trajectory, women's share of the labor force thus increased from 28 to 32 percent.

In regard to the composition of employment, public sector jobs grew by 17 percent. As hypothesized, though, they declined from 21.7 percent of all wage-earning jobs in 1986 to 19.5 percent in 1992[3] (ECLAC 1995b, 134). Coming on the heels of a much sharper, austerity-based downturn in public sector employment during the early 1980s, this decline was merely incremental and relative, a sign of political resistance to the shrinkage of the state's machinery. In the meantime, the tradables sector's share of total employment dropped from 33 to 29 percent while the nontradables sector rose. Job increases in nontradables were greatest in commerce and services, whose employment share grew from 53 to 57 percent, representing, as anticipated, a continued tertiarization of jobs. With respect to earnings, the portion of workers making less than the legal minimum wage remained higher in the tradables sector (from 37.5 to 49.7 percent) than in the nontradables sector (from 32 to 43.6 percent). The net rate of growth of submininum-wage earners was somewhat greater, however, in nontradables (36.3 percent, versus 32.5 percent in tradables). Taking into account the role of government employment in boosting average earnings in the nontradables sector, this trend suggests that, consistent with another hypothesis, pay in manufacturing may have fallen relative to that in tertiary activities.

Against the background of long-term contraction, the economy's short-term swings of 1987-1992 were associated with the continued expansion of the labor force, particularly for women; modest relative decline in the public sector's share of wage jobs; the continued tertiarization of employment; acute growth in the percentage of subminimum-wage earners; and a decreased rate of unemployment. The most pronounced change was the reallocation of workers to the low end of the earnings distribution, which coincides with the longer-range and broader course of socioeconomic deterioration (see, for example, ECLAC 1995b).

Geographically, metropolitan Caracas's proportion of national employment decreased (from 22.3 percent in 1989 to 18.1 percent in 1993), while employment increased in the urban-regional agglomeration tied to Greater Caracas (from 6.5 to 12 percent of national employment) (see Portes 1989 and the chapters in this volume on Costa Rica [4], Guatemala [3], and Chile [6]).[4] Employment in urban and rural areas in the interior of Venezuela had been hit hard by economic crisis and nascent politico-economic restructuring and showed little growth. This spatial process had several components: geographic decentralization of economic activities in response to high property values and other diseconomies of massive urban scale; rapid growth of residential population, including migration from rural areas, and of associated tertiary activities in response to both urban diseconomies and nearby economic expansion; and the zone's long-standing agricultural production for the Greater Caracas market.

Within these territorial contours, the principal socioeconomic change was that many workers made less than before. Yet this shift was not tantamount to significant informalization. On the contrary, informal employment only grew from 37 to 38 percent of total employment.[5] Hence, the thrust of employment deterioration was neither unemployment nor informalization but an abrupt worsening of average pay. Of course, this worsening could have been confined mostly to the informal economy. To what extent was this true? And to what extent was the process bound up with a broader erosion of labor conditions?

A range of features could be involved in erosion of labor conditions. Without negating the insights derived from the formal/informal dichotomy, the notion of "precarious employment" transcends the dichotomy's inherent conceptual problems in addressing contemporary labor-market inequalities in Latin America. These problems arise from the tendency to attribute worsened conditions globally to the informal economy. The alternative emphasis on precarious employment emphasizes job conditions that violate norms established by the International Labour Organization (ILO), whether the jobs are "formal" or "informal" (see Chapter 1 and Díaz on Chile [6] this volume). Employment is precarious, therefore, when by ILO standards it is unstable and is inadequate in pay and benefits; when labor lacks basic workplace rights, such as the ability to unionize and to appeal management decisions in cases of employment termination, overtime assignments, and hazardous conditions; or when the work itself is illegal. This chapter's analysis is based on a measurement index that permits the assessment of dimensions and degrees of precarious employment (see Pérez Sáinz and Menjívar Larín 1991). The index pays special attention to the purchasing power of job earnings in relation to basic consumption needs. Employment is therefore considered precarious if it does not allow the worker's household access to goods and services deemed essential by mainstream Venezuelan socioeconomic standards. The index also incorporates the number of hours worked and whether or not jobs have social security coverage.[6]

The index allows for interpretation of the findings of surveys conducted among the residents of four low-income districts of metropolitan Caracas in 1987 and 1992.[7] The findings indicate that the share of resident workers in these districts holding precarious employment — whether "extreme" or "relative" (see note 6) — increased from 62 to 67 percent. Of this increase, the category of extremely precarious employment only rose from 20 to 21 percent of the jobs held by the workers sampled. This marginal increase is attributable to Venezuela's still comparatively strong sociopolitical restrictions on the erosion of job conditions. Among this volume's case studies, the institutional-regulatory framework in urban Venezuela invites particular comparison with that of Costa Rica and contrast with those of countries such as the Dominican Republic and Argentina.

As anticipated, employment conditions in the informal sector were worse than in the formal sector. The incidence of precarious jobs among the sampled workers grew from 80 percent in 1987 to 85 percent in 1992 among the informally employed, versus from 52 percent to 55 percent among the formally employed (all of whom were wage workers). The extent of extreme precariousness increased minutely within the two groups, basically remaining at 36 percent among the informally employed versus 11 percent among the formally employed, while both groups experienced substantial increases in relative precariousness. Among the informally employed, the inter-occupational gap in the extent of precarious conditions widened. Thus, precarious conditions came to characterize all of the surveyed domestic-service workers (from 80 to 100 percent) and informal wage workers (from 87 to 100 percent), while increasing just marginally among the informal self-employed (from 78 to 81 percent).

In the formal and informal sectors alike, it appears that precarious employment in urban Venezuela is becoming even more prevalent in the mid-1990s as the economy worsens and as the government's renewed commitment to neoliberal reform leads to the dismantling of labor protections (see Cortés on Argentina [7] and Díaz on Chile [6] this volume).

Formal Employment

Until recently, political patronage financed by oil revenues drove the expansion of public sector employment in Venezuela (Karl 1995). Budgetary constraints and austerity policies increasingly are challenging this pattern. In this context, the privatization of state enterprises, early retirement incentives for government employees, and higher pay in the private sector have triggered a diminution of the public sector's share of the labor force.

Public sector jobs in Venezuela grew by 17 percent between 1987 and 1992, compared with 42 percent growth in the formal private sector.[8] As the former's long-term rate of job growth declined relative to the latter's, the public sector's acute drop in salary levels caused protracted labor conflicts. In this regard, strikes by sanitation workers, teachers and professors, and others intensified the societal climate of crisis and of plummeting public confidence in the ability of the state's managers and bureaucracy to administer the nation's affairs. For public sector workers, the highly insulated union leadership, traditionally entrenched in patronage arrangements with political party and state machinery, has been usurped by alternative, grassroots leadership. Insurgent public sector workers reject the translation of their demands into the politically coopted agenda of the union bureaucracy, causing intra-labor divisiveness. The deepening fiscal crisis has made it unlikely that the state sector labor force will recoup its pre-crisis income levels. Even so, into the early 1990s, the strength of state sector organized labor and its patronage relations slowed the decline of not only jobs but also pay. ECLAC (1995b, 137) reports that average wages in urban Venezuela's state sector fell by 25.4 percent relative to the poverty line between 1986 and 1992, compared with a fall of 28 percent in the private sector, including a significant increase in state sector but not private sector wages in 1992.[9] More generally, however, the contours and intensity of the period's labor conflicts in the state sector reveal a growing contradiction between the demands of accumulation and legitimation: Since the Venezuelan state can no longer distribute petroleum-based income on the massive scale that it previously did, the nation's accumulation is becoming premised increasingly on painful reductions in real wages and government social subsidies[10] (McCoy et al. 1995).

Unexpectedly, the nation's formal employment decreased just slightly (from 63 to 62 percent) relative to informal employment. As already mentioned, the stability of this share during a time of national economic distress largely is a result of the continued strength of Venezuela's regulatory institutions into the early 1990s. Yet it also reflects a sharp drop in the formal private sector's average wages. This drop in wages partly explains the capacity of the formal private sector to generate job growth, and thus to minimize the transfer of job growth to the informal sector, in the face of a severe economic downturn.

The most important compositional changes within the formal private sector were, as noted earlier, an increase in the weight of tertiary employment (from 53 to 57 percent) and a decrease in manufacturing's weight as an employer — including the inability of Venezuela's state-dependent business class to launch a sizable export-manufacturing industry (see Naim and Francés 1995 and Cortés on Argentina this volume, Chapter 7). Of those members of the labor force employed in the nation's urban formal sector in 1992, 92 percent were wage earners. Occupationally, the number of employers fell in formal sector manufacturing and tertiary activities between 1987 and 1992, while that of wage earners rose significantly and that of the self-employed doubled. This configuration of occupational change was anchored in the flight of professionals from relatively low-paying public sector jobs and in the subcontracting of many of the economy's service activities to less expensive providers.

The implementation of innovative, flexible participatory approaches to management-labor relations in Venezuela has been marginal and limited to the segment of the country's relatively few export-oriented manufacturers that must ensure a high quality in order to compete internationally (see Pérez Sáinz 1994 and Roberts 1995). A prime instance of such innovation is the metals-machinery industry, especially in the production of automotive parts. But again, such innovation has been sparse, and within a broader framework of employment polarization, it has served as a new source of labor-market inequality (Alonso et al. 1991).

Informal Employment

Many studies emphasize the heterogeneity of informal employment (Lacabana 1990 and 1992; Portes, Castells, and Benton 1990; Rakowski 1994; Roberts 1995) and indicate that, notwithstanding the structural interconnections between production in the formal and informal econo-mies, most informal economic activities in Latin America represent subsis-tence practices among the poor. That is, informal economic activities are principally coping responses to falling real incomes and to the scarcity of employment opportunities.

From 1987 to 1992, employment in Venezuela's informal economy as a share of total urban employment moved only slightly from 37 to 38 percent. Informal employment was most extensive and fastest growing in commerce.

The proportional increase in urban informal jobs during the period of the study was much less than predicted, but the occupational structure of informal employment changed somewhat. Job growth in the informal economy was distributed by occupational category as follows: employers, 49 percent; nonprofessional self-employed, 37 percent; and wage labor, 19.5 percent (see the chapters this volume on the Dominican Republic [2], Guatemala [3], Costa Rica [4], Argentina [7], and Mexico [8]). The increases for employers and the self-employed must be understood in socioeconomic context. Given the expanding numbers of informal employers and the intensifying competition among them during marked economic downturn in Venezuela, mean earnings are very low. Instability of both production demand and labor supply forces these individuals to shift back and forth constantly between the positions of employer and self-employed. The rapid expansion of petty commerce has integrated informal self-employment into open common income-earning strategies of individuals and households.

Two informal occupational categories, domestic service worker and unpaid family worker, declined as shares of employment and in the latter case in absolute terms as well (see Pérez Sáinz on Guatemala this volume, Chapter 3). There are two reasons for their decline. First, the widespread drop in household income caused a decrease in demand for domestic employees. Second, a growing subsistence practice among the poor is to send as many family members as possible into income-earning activity, which boosts family income but shrinks the number of unpaid family workers.

The survey results suggest that among the informal workers and their families residing in low-income neighborhoods, informality is increasingly a permanent rather than temporary labor-market category and is becoming an entrenched way of life. This preliminary observation points toward a conclusion that has been gaining currency in much of Latin America: Informality is neither transitory nor incidental; instead, it is increasingly an integral feature of emerging economic structures on a transnational scale (Portes, Castells, and Benton 1990; Rakowski 1994; Roberts 1995). If, for most of these workers, informality fails to meet basic needs and to provide an escape from poverty, it still offers hope and an alternative to open unemployment. Nevertheless, Venezuela faces a potential scenario in which many of its citizens are excluded from the mainstream economy and, living in sociospatial isolation in ghettos, turn to chronic violence and organized criminal activity as a means of securing income and social status.

Gender and Employment

Labor-market incorporation of women accounts for much of the growth of Venezuela's labor supply between 1987 and 1992. In continuation of a long-term trend, over the five-year period of the study, women's labor-force participation swelled from roughly 28 to 32 percent of the overall pool. As of 1992, 83 percent of all working Venezuelan women were employed in commerce and services. Women's pace of employment tertiarization during the five-year period was twice as fast as men's.

With regard to age, the growth of female labor was most rapid among women 45 years of age and older. The employment of women between 15 and 44 years of age rose by about 30 percent. Yet the employment of 45- to 64-year-old women doubled, while that of women over 65 leaped by approximately 150 percent.[11] Thus, between the late 1980s and early 1990s, family members becoming employed for the first time tended to be middle-age to older women and to work in the informal economy in jobs located in their homes or neighborhoods. Home and neighborhood have become both social and economic spaces, as the feminization of these spheres converges.

Women's jobs tend to be more precarious than men's. Nationally, 48.5 percent of wage-earning women and 62 percent of self-employed women made less than the official minimum wage in 1992, compared with 34 percent and 24 percent for men. In the low-income districts of metropolitan Caracas surveyed, the proportion of precarious jobs among the men sampled held constant (53 percent) between 1987 and 1992, but among the women it increased from 68 to 72 percent. This trend appears in the formal sector, too, where women's precarious employment climbed from 52 to 62 percent of all jobs held by women.

Most certainly, a discussion of the feminization of the labor market and precarious employment in Venezuela must include the intensification of socioeconomic pressures on the male labor force, particularly its less-skilled members. For example, the relative constancy of measured levels of precarious employment among men in the low-income urban zones conceals widening inequalities between the more-skilled and less-skilled men within both the formal and informal economies (see ECLAC 1995b, 170). Indeed, employers reportedly are expanding their practice of substituting young female for older male workers as a cost-cutting measure in the tertiary economy. On balance, though, preliminary evidence from a handful of low-income residential districts in Caracas suggests a hypothesis: Among Venezuela's urban poor, the labor-market costs of economic crisis — not to mention the social and psychological costs of simultaneously grappling with the nonmarket and market spheres of daily life — have fallen disproportionately on the shoulders of women.

Conclusions

Venezuela entered the 1980s with a standard of both labor and living conditions that ranked among Latin America's highest, anchored in the state-centered distribution of revenues derived principally from petroleum exports. With the exception of a brief upturn in petroleum prosperity and an expansion of state deficit spending during the early 1990s, the Latin American and global conditions documented throughout this volume buffetted this state-centered petro-model of national development. On the one hand, Venezuela's national leadership could not rescue the country's petro-model in the face of powerful countervailing forces in the world political economy. On the other, neither did national leadership manage to extricate itself from the model's domestic thicket of patronage-based sociopolitical alliances in order to implement a coherent version of neoliberal reform. Stuck with an economic model mired in patronage, the institutional underpinnings of Venezuelan politics, economy, and society teetered on the precipice of collapse.

The overriding socioeconomic consequence of the petro-model's crisis was a plunge in labor's average earnings and the country's level of social welfare, as poverty's reach rapidly extended and income inequality greatly widened. After falling sharply during the early 1980s, the public sector's portion of total employment eroded only slightly between the late 1980s and early 1990s, as resurgent oil prices and a last-ditch infusion of government expenditure staved off acute cuts. Nevertheless, neither production nor employment in export manufacturing met the new global challenges. Hence, as unemployment descended from the high peak it had reached during the 1980s, tertiary activities anchored job growth in a labor market characterized socially by decreasing average income and geographically by the relatively rapid expansion in the fringes of the Caracas regional agglomeration. Participation in the labor force grew considerably faster for women than men, especially for middle-aged and older women, whose numbers are disproportionately high in the informal economy. Between the late 1980s and early 1990s, informal employment gained only marginal ground in the labor market as a whole, which reflects the long-standing regulatory features of Venezuelan state and economy. Informal employment underwent gendered demographic and occupational change, but so did formal employment. The overarching labor-market trend has been toward wrenching deterioration of average job earnings in the informal and formal economies alike.

With the addition of resurgent unemployment, job earnings have continued to drop in urban Venezuela during the mid-1990s. As the state's executives have declared a renewed campaign of neoliberal reform, the social contours of continued labor-market transformation are of critical importance to the future of Venezuelan democracy and development. Even if this renewed campaign does reignite and sustain significant economic growth, trends in Venezuela and elsewhere in Latin America suggest that it either will fail to mend or will worsen the social wounds inflicted over the last decade. The same trends indicate, however, that a return to the statist, "petro" programs and structures of Venezuela's past is by no means a viable alternative under turn-of-the century world conditions. The search for an alternative strategy, then, is crucial to the prospects of Venezuela, as well as to those of Latin America at large.

Notes

1.   The rate of unemployment rose from 6.6 percent in 1980 to 14.3 percent in 1985, then dropped to 11 percent in 1990. During the mini-economic recovery of 1990 to 1992, unemployment fell to 8 percent. This took place, however, as average real wages experienced a net decline of 1.3 percent during the mini-recovery, encompassing both an abrupt drop of 10.5 percent in 1990-1991 and an abrupt rise of 9.2 percent in 1991-1992 (ECLAC 1988, 62; 1995a, 52-53). Keeping the broader picture in mind, between 1985 and 1992, average real wages plunged by a net 46.5 percent and then dropped by another 20 percent in 1993 (as unemployment decreased from 8 to 6.3 percent) (ECLAC 1988, 62; 1995a, 12, 53). ECLAC (1995b, 146) reports that the rate of household poverty in urban Venezuela jumped from 18 percent in 1981 to 32 percent in 1992, as the inter-household distribution of income became strikingly more unequal (from a Gini coefficient of 0.306 to 0.380).

2.   Unless otherwise noted, data are based on OCEI 1987, 1992.

3.   ECLAC (1995b, 134) reports that the public sector accounted for 24.8 percent of Venezuela's wage-earning jobs in 1981.

4.   As of 1990, the largest metropolitan areas and their shares of the national population were as follows: Caracas, 15.4 percent; Maracaibo, 7.5 percent; Valencia, 5.7 percent; Maracay, 4.4 percent; and Barquisimeto, 4.1 percent. Since the 1980s, rural-urban migration has been oriented not to metropolitan Caracas but to its regional agglomeration and to urban areas of the Venezuelan interior (see Portes 1989; Roberts 1995). In 1992 the Caracas metropolitan area accounted for 16 percent of the national population, 20 percent of employment, 35 percent of the workforce with incomes worth more than five times the official minimum wage, and 29 percent of the workforce with incomes worth more than 10 times the official minimum wage.

5.   We define "informal employment" as consisting of wage and nonwage workers in firms of fewer than five workers, the nonprofessional self-employed, and wage-earning domestic employees. This definition is consistent with that of PREALC (Programa Regional del Empleo para América Latina y el Caribe). While in many respects we prefer alternative definitions (see Portes, Castells, and Benton 1990; Rakowski 1994), the one we have selected enables us to analyze the Venezuelan government's labor-market data (see Lacabana 1990 and 1992).

6.   See Lacabana (1992, 56) for a detailed discussion of this index, which is based on the work of Juan Pablo Pérez Sáinz (see Pérez Sáinz and Menjívar Larín 1991) elsewhere in Latin America. Our index assigns scores on the basis of a job's income level, length of work week, and presence or absence of social security coverage. For any given job, the assigned score may range from zero to 100, that is, from most precarious to nonprecarious. The scoring is categorized as follows: zero to 24, "extreme precariousness"; 25 to 50, "relative precariousness"; 51 to 100, "nonprecarious."

7.   For a description of the survey methodology, see Cariola et al. 1992.

8.   Recall that resurgent oil revenues in 1990 delayed the full brunt of economic crisis.

9.   According to ECLAC (1995b, 137), between 1981 and 1992 average wages in relation to the poverty line dropped by 50 percent in the public sector and 52.1 percent in the private sector.

10. Although the state's petroleum revenues swelled in 1996, the windfall is earmarked to make payment on the external debt, in accordance with an agreement reached in 1996 with the International Monetary Fund.

11.   Employed women 65 years of age or older represented some 2 percent of total female employment in 1992. Employed women between 45 and 64 years of age represented about 18 percent of the female total.

References

Alonso, Oswaldo, Marisa Fermín, Manuel Guevara, and Miguel Lacabana. 1991. *Nuevas demandas de recursos humanos en tres sectores industriales.* Caracas: Instituto Latinoamericano de Investigaciones Sociales de la Fundación Friedrich Ebert (ILDIS).

Cariola, Cecilia, Luisa Bethencourt, José Darwich, Beatriz Fernández, Ana Gutiérrez, and Miguel Lacabana, eds. 1992. *Sobrevivir en la pobreza: el fin de la ilusión.* Caracas: Editorial Nueva Sociedad.

Cordiplan. 1989. *Crecimiento sin inflación en la decada de los noventa. Programa macroeconómica del Gobierno de Venezuela.* Caracas.

ECLAC (Economic Commission on Latin America and the Caribbean). 1988. *Economic Survey of Latin America and the Caribbean 1988.* Santiago, Chile: ECLAC.

ECLAC. 1995a. "Balance preliminar de la economía de América Latina y el Caribe 1995." *Notas sobre la economía y el desarrollo,* no. 585/586 (December). Santiago, Chile: ECLAC.

ECLAC. 1995b. *Panorama social de América Latina 1995.* Santiago, Chile: ECLAC.

Goodman, Louis W., Johanna Mendelson Forman, Moisés Naim, Joseph S. Tulchin, and Gary Bland, eds. 1995. *Lessons of the Venezuelan Experience.* Washington, D.C.: The Woodrow Wilson Center Press; Baltimore: The Johns Hopkins University Press.

Karl, Terry. 1995. "The Venezuelan Petro-State and the Crisis of 'Its' Democracy." In *Venezuelan Democracy under Stress,* eds. Jennifer McCoy, Andrés Serbín, William C. Smith, and Andrés Stambouli. Coral Gables, Fla.: North-South Center at the University of Miami.

Lacabana, Miguel. 1990. "Informalidad y desarrollo: algunas consideraciones." *Revista Cuadernos del CENDES* 12.

Lacabana, Miguel. 1992. "Trabajo y pobreza: la precariedad laboral en el mercado de trabajo urbano." In *Sobrevivir en la pobreza: el fin de la ilusión,* eds. Cecilia Cariola, Luisa Bethencourt, José Darwich, Beatriz Fernández, Ana Gutiérrez, and Miguel Lacabana. Caracas: Editorial Nueva Sociedad.

Lacabana, Miguel. 1993. "La calle como puesto de trabajo: reflexiones sobre la relación estado-sector informal." *Revista Cuadernos del CENDES* 22.

McCoy, Jennifer, Andrés Serbín, William C. Smith, and Andrés Stambouli, eds. 1995. *Venezuelan Democracy under Stress.* Coral Gables, Fla.: North-South Center at the University of Miami.

Naim, Moisés, and Antonio Francés. 1995. "The Venezuelan Private Sector: From Courting the State to Courting the Market." In *Lessons of the Venezuelan Experience,* eds. Louis W. Goodman, Johanna Mendelson Forman, Moisés Naim, Joseph S. Tulchin, and Gary Bland. Washington, D.C.: The Woodrow Wilson Center Press; Baltimore: The Johns Hopkins University Press.

OCEI (Oficina Central de Estadística e Informática). 1987, 1992. *Indicadores de la fuerza de trabajo.* Caracas.

Pérez Sáinz, Juan Pablo, ed. 1994. *Globalización y fuerza laboral.* San José, Costa Rica: FLACSO.

Pérez Sáinz, Juan Pablo, and Rafael Menjívar Larín, eds. 1991. *Informalidad urbana en Centroamérica: entre la acumulación y la subsistencia.* Caracas: FLACSO/ Nueva Sociedad.

Portes, Alejandro. 1989. "Urbanization during the Years of the Crisis." *Latin American Research Review* 24(3):7-44.

Portes, Alejandro, Manuel Castells, and Lauren E. Benton, eds. 1990. *La economía informal. Estudios en países avanzados y menos desarrollados.* Buenos Aires: Editorial Planeta.

Primera Carta de Intención. 1989. Caracas: Gobierno de Venezuela.

Rakowski, Cathy A., ed. 1994. *Contrapunto: The Informal Sector Debate in Latin America.* Albany: State University of New York Press.

Roberts, Bryan. 1995. *The Making of Citizens: Cities of Peasants Revisited.* London: Arnold.

Chapter 6

Chile: Neoliberal Policy, Socioeconomic Reorganization, and Urban Labor Market

Alvaro Díaz

Profound changes have characterized Chile's urban labor market since the 1970s, especially under the military dictatorship of General Augusto Pinochet (1973-1990) and the post-dictatorship, civilian administrations of Patricio Aylwin (1990-1994) and Eduardo Frei (1994-present). After decades of slow growth (1952-1973) and stagnation (1973-1983), the Chilean economy entered a period of vigorous expansion that has continued into the mid-1990s. Between 1985 and 1995, average yearly growth of the gross domestic product (GDP) was 7 percent, driven by exports that climbed from 28 to 37 percent of GDP. After a painful economic downswing in 1981-1983, Chile's state and business class mobilized important economic resources: From 1985 to 1995, capital investment multiplied threefold, and employment grew by almost 40 percent. In an age of markedly diminishing worldwide returns for natural resource industries and exports (see Thurow 1996; Weeks 1996), much of the economy's expansion has indeed been premised on its huge comparative advantages in natural resources, such as marine biomass, copper, industrial and native forestry, and soils and climate for fruit production.

According to the standard explanation, Chile's economic transformation since the 1970s is a result of the free-market reforms imposed by Augusto Pinochet's military authoritarian government. This explanation is in part true. Between 1973 and 1990, the technocratic elite supported by the military and the business sector effected a far-reaching set of neoliberal programs that opened the economy, privatized more than 1,500 state-owned enterprises, and dismantled state controls of the market. These reforms became embedded in a new constitution and regulatory regime.

Yet, the free-market explanation leaves out a good part of the story. To begin with, these reforms did not weaken the state (Martínez and Díaz 1996; see Sassen 1996 and Smith et al. 1994). The public sector was grossly

Alvaro Díaz is director of the Division of Productive Development in Chile's Ministry of Economy.

Translated by Richard Tardanico.

reduced in size, and the state's traditional industrial policy was dismantled. Nonetheless, the state's macroeconomic regulatory and strategic price-setting capacities were strengthened, including the formation of a key program to subsidize nontraditional exports. Moreover, the technocratic leadership overcame the state's fiscal crisis not only by implementing more efficient tax schemes and reducing public spending, but also by strikingly diverging from market-based principles through protection of the state-owned copper company, CODELCO, whose near total earnings in 1984 were transferred to the public sector, representing 15 percent of total public sector income. Furthermore, by redistributing property rights to wealthier groups, the technocrats greatly strengthened the upper strata of private business. Hence, by no means is Chile governed exclusively by the "invisible hand" of the market. The market power of large private corporations has become vastly greater than in the past: Fifty private conglomerates exercise horizontally diversified control over large segments of the economy. These conglomerates are "price-takers" in the world markets but "price-makers" in the local markets (Martínez and Díaz 1996). They are quite tangible manifestations of the "visible hand" that also governs the Chilean economy.

In sum, a more precise interpretation of Chile's macroeconomic transformation must account not only for the country's market success but also for both the institutional success of state sector management and the state-engendered, organizational success of private conglomerates. Compared with the rest of Latin America, Chile's economy is now more formidably organized and its state institutions more capable of economic governance.[1]

The decade of 1985-1995 must be separated into two segments: 1985-1990, the final years of the Pinochet dictatorship, and 1990-1995, the first years of the democratic governments of Patricio Aylwin and Eduardo Frei of the Concertación Democrática (Democratic Alliance), a coalition of center-left political parties. The final years of the Pinochet dictatorship encompassed vigorous economic recovery from the downturn of the early 1980s. There was no recovery in social terms, however. As of the late 1980s, approximately 45 percent of the population lived below the poverty line, income inequality had not diminished, more than 10 percent of the workforce was unemployed, average wages were still below the 1981 level, and human rights violations were rampant. These conditions explain the defeat of the authoritarian regime in both the 1988 plebiscite and the 1990 presidential election. The aftermath of the dictatorship has been character-ized by a mix of political transition to democracy and sustained economic momentum that so far has preserved the fundamental institutions of the neoliberal model.

As the economy's upswing has continued during the post-dictatorship era, the country's financial standing has improved as well, including more favorable savings and investment ratios, reduction in the relative weight of the external debt, and the establishment of single-digit annual inflation. The impact of sustained, high levels of economic growth on social and employment indicators also has been positive, standing in stark contrast to the situation during the Pinochet dictatorship. Unemployment has fallen to less than 6 percent and poverty from 44.6 to 28.5 percent of the population. Average real wages have jumped by 23.3 percent, and the government's real social spending has swelled by 30 percent. More generally, Chile's social indicators have remained on a par with those of Argentina, Uruguay, and Costa Rica — the highest in Latin America (see Bengoa 1994; CEPAL 1995a and 1995b).

Chile's post-dictatorship administrations, moreover, have emerged with a major policy advantage relative to their post-dictatorship counterparts in the other Southern Cone countries of Argentina, Uruguay, and Brazil (see Cortés this volume, Chapter 7): The Chilean administrations have not had to impose neoliberal reforms, whose deleterious social consequences are widely documented. In Chile, neoliberal reforms — fiscal cutbacks, economic denationalization, privatization, the dismantling of the import-substitution regulatory system, and labor flexibilization — were imposed not by civilian government but by the military dictatorship. Thus, Chile's neoliberal transformation had a decade's head start on the rest of the Southern Cone, as well as on Latin America at large.[2] Chile's civilian administrations, therefore, have escaped the sociopolitical backlash associated with the imposition of neoliberal plans. Moreover, they also have benefited politically from the economy's rapid upturn, which has attenuated the tensions and conflicts attached to the country's still pronounced socioeconomic inequalities.

Not only is the Chilean economy in the midst of considerable growth, it also has entered into a second phase of export development (Díaz 1995a). Contrary to the "curse" theory of abundant natural resources in less-developed countries (Auty and Evans 1994), Chile has experienced an impressive diversification of exports within the framework of value-added upgrading. Over the next decade, to be sure, natural resources will remain at the core of the nation's export economy, which thus faces the threat not only of world-market gluts but also "Dutch disease" that could damage the prospects of the country's manufacturing sector (Díaz 1995a; Weeks 1996). Nevertheless, over the past decade, a new set of "clusters" has emerged from the economy's primary sector (mining, forestry, fishery, and agriculture) with forward and backward linkages to manufacturing and services. Between 1985 and 1995, the overall impact on the export structure of goods and services was as follows: Non-processed natural resource products dropped from 69.5 to 40 percent of total exports; processed natural resource products (refined copper, cellulose, fish meal, fish oil, and processed fruits and seafood) rose from 17 to 26 percent; manufactured exports, whether or not based on local natural resources (food, textile and apparel, plastic products, paper, printed products, household furniture, and some capital goods), rose from 1.5 to 14 percent; and service exports (tourism, production services, and software exports) rose from 12 to 20 percent.

Another component of the second export phase is the expansion of Chilean investments in neighboring countries. Almost nonexistent before 1990, such investments have soared to US$4.3 billion a year and are anchored in the privatization policies of neighboring governments and in energy, paper, steel, and commerce.

Nonetheless, Chile continues to suffer a highly skewed distribution of income as well as the potential long-term problems of an economy centered on the export and processing of natural resources. Despite notable socioeconomic gains since the late 1980s, no more than halting progress has been made in reducing the social concentration of income, which remains greater than in the late 1960s. Among Latin American countries, only Brazil has a worse record of income concentration (CEPAL 1995b).

Chile's highly skewed income inequality stems from two sets of conditions. First are the economy's structural problems. For instance, some 6,000 firms in the public and private sectors produce for export, but 60 percent of Chilean exports are generated by only 18 firms. Most of the leading export firms have a high capital-labor ratio and thus employ relatively few workers. Only by broadening Chile's profile of exporters to incorporate a much larger portion of medium and small firms will the structure of the economy promote an appreciable social redistribution of income.

Second and even more fundamental are the political and social inequalities embedded in the state's neoliberal regulatory institutions, among the most important of which are the state's weak mechanisms for regulating markets and producer conglomerates. This weakness leads to an unfavorable price structure, including the transfer of the costs of externalities and investment risks to consumers, small firms, and workers.[3] Although the tax system is efficient by many criteria, it has not proved capable of redressing such inequalities. Indeed, those who pay taxes in the highest income brackets represent only about 0.3 percent of all taxpayers — which, practically speaking, could be considerably higher.

Chile's marked social inequalities not only reflect past conditions. There is mounting evidence that continued high economic growth during the late 1990s will foster not more but less socially and territorially inclusive prosperity. Alongside vigorously expanding sectors, such as forestry, agroindustry, chemicals and plastics production, metallurgy, and modern services, there are other sectors that are struggling to adjust (such as textiles and apparel) and still others that are clearly being marginalized (such as coal mining). The territorial winner seems to be the Santiago metropolitan agglomeration, including its rural zones; the territorial losers seem to be the extreme north and south (Arica and Punta Arenas) and other urban and rural zones located in the south in general. Chile's incorporation into the Southern Cone Common Market (MERCOSUR) and its possible eventual incorporation into the North American Free Trade Agreement (NAFTA) (or, at least, a bilateral trade agreement with the United States) will exacerbate such territorial and sectoral inequalities. These formal measures of internationalization probably will inflict the harshest losses on traditional agriculture (wheat, rice, and meat) but open up new possibilities in manufacturing, commerce, and services.

Such creative and destructive forces are galvanizing sociopolitical pressures for change, the ultimate direction of which is unclear. In this setting, two institutional features may either open up or close off the paths to a more advanced Chilean export economy. One is the current democratic transition, which, although far from complete, is led currently by center-left forces with the potential to carve out the political space necessary for progressive socioeconomic change. The other involves the inequalities and rigidities of the inherited neoliberal institutional order, which lacks the capacity to cope with the formidable new challenges to Chilean development, such as market and environmental regulation, social and economic infrastructure, and the administration of multilateral treaties.

Chile has begun a transition to a post-neoliberal regime. While pragmatic in its politics, the current center-left government under Eduardo Frei is politically sensitive to social pressures. Demands are indeed accumulating around such issues as poverty, market asymmetries, regional development, and a new political agenda that goes beyond the baseline challenge of democratic transition to address the need for a new generation of public goods (such as high-quality education and training, information infrastructure, technology development, and environmental conservation). Matters of politico-economic decentralization are of increasing concern as well. None of these new demands and challenges can be met within the framework of a neoliberal model.

Neoliberalism, however, is still the hegemonic ideology among Chile's political and economic elite, and the anti-democratic features of the state's machinery remain in place. This situation, which stands in the way of the building of a new institutional order, poses the most obvious danger: the governments of the democratic transition will be confined largely to the technical role of administering the economy's growth, that is, possessing the leeway to do some compensatory social tinkering but lacking the means to undertake fundamental change. Such an impasse creates serious obstacles to authentic democratization as well as to the long-range construction of a new export economy that could embody not only growth but also social equity and environmental sustainability. Even so, there are grounds for optimism. Most important is the possibility that Chile's democratic transition will accelerate and deepen, beginning especially in 1997, when Pinochet, who still commands the armed forces, enters the final stage of his withdrawal from the political arena (see Garretón 1994; Vergara 1994).

How have such politico-economic and social dynamics intersected with changes in the urban labor market? This chapter will demonstrate that since the 1970s employment conditions have become much more unequal and precarious, yet that, even as the public sector's share of total jobs has dropped since the early 1980s, urban employment has become not more but less informal. Employment has become more tertiarized over the long run and more geared to exports since the early 1980s, while manufacturing since then has regained some of its previously lost share of urban jobs. Primary production has significantly increased its share of urban jobs as well. Against this backdrop, women's percentage of jobs has risen sharply, a trend that has been more pronounced in tertiary activities than in manufacturing and in the lower than upper reaches of occupations and earnings. Finally, Chile's export-based growth and transformation have not weakened but strengthened the interurban economic and labor-market hegemony of the Santiago metropolitan agglomeration.

The Urban Labor Market

Sectoral Transformations

Chilean society has been urban for decades. As early as 1940, more than one-half of Chile's population lived in cities, and by the 1960s, it had become a "hyper-urbanized peripheral country" (Friedman and Lackington 1967). Urbanization continued between the mid-1960s and mid-1990s, as the urban share of the country's population grew from 72.5 to 86.4 percent (Table 1).

Since the 1970s, the sectoral structure of urban employment has not displayed a linear trend but instead has passed through two phases of large-scale change. The first phase encompassed the initial decade of military-authoritarianism (1973-1984), when the Pinochet government applied an extreme brand of neoliberalism via accelerated trade liberalization, massive privatization, the brutal political repression of organized labor, and the tearing down of the import-substitution industrialization (ISI) era's scaffolding of labor-market regulation. Chile's economic downturns (1974-1975 and 1982-1983) were more acute during this phase than during the depression of the 1930s; their political and economic impact "destructured" the ISI pattern of urban employment. This can be seen by comparing the first two columns of Table 2, which show the averages for 1966-1970 and 1980-1984 (see also Figures 1 and 2). The most basic indicators of destructuring are the

Table 1.
Trends in Urban Employment

Categories	1966	1994
Total population (thousands)	8,761	13,994
Population over 15 years old (thousands)	5,271	9,857
Urban population/total population (%)	72.5%	86.4%
Urban workforce/total workforce	74.9%	87.1%
Urban employment/total employment	74.3%	86.6%
Female urban employment/total employment	24.6%	33.7%
Workforce over 15 years old/total	43.3%	37.3%
Workforce's average years of schooling	5.0	10.5

Source: INE 1995.

Table 2.
Social Destructuring, 1966-1970
versus 1980–1984 and 1990–1994

Labor-market indicators (as a % of workforce)	Destructuring of the ISI model[a]	Emergence of an open and export-based economy	
	1966-1970 (Average)	1980-1984 (Average)	1990-1994 (Average)
Unemployment	4.0%	19.6%	4.4%
Wage employment	60.2%	39.2%	60.4%
Emergency employment	0.0%	11.0%	0.0%
Public sector employment	8.5%	8.0%	6.5%
Agricultural and fishing employment	16.0%	19.4%	17.2%
Manufacturing employment	23.5%	10.4%	16.3%
Services employment	46.8%	61.8%	51.5%

a = The ISI model refers to import-substitution industrialization.
Source: INE 1995.

Figure 1.
Tertiary Sector: Output and Employment
% of GDP and National Employment

Sources: INE, Central Bank of Chile.

Figure 2.
Informal Urban Employment, 1976-1994

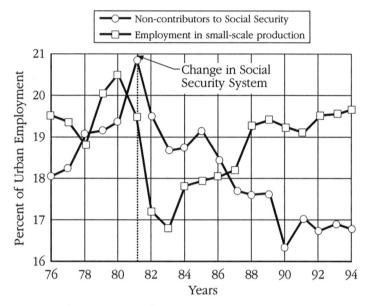

Sources: INE and AFP Superintendency.

surge in unemployment and overexpansion of tertiary employment, along with the contraction of public sector, manufacturing, and wage employment. The expansion of unemployment and informal employment would have been even greater if not for a massive government program of emergency employment (Programa de Empleo de Emergencia — PEE), which in 1982 gave jobs to more than one-half million people. Even so, real wages plunged, urban and rural poverty soared, and income became more concentrated in the upper social classes.

The second phase of large-scale change is charted in the last two columns of Table 2, which present the averages for 1980-1984 and 1990-1994. As partially captured in the data for 1990-1994, the second phase is characterized by an initial stage of economic recovery until 1989 and accelerated expansion from 1990 onward. As previously mentioned, the 1990s have witnessed the emergence of a reorganized, faster-growing export economy. Even as the labor force grew rapidly between 1984 and 1994, unemployment dropped sharply. The percentage of the workforce engaged in tertiary activities did not rise, as anticipated by one of this volume's hypotheses, but diminished. Labor was mainly absorbed not into the public sector or — as anticipated by another hypothesis — into the informal sector, but into urbanized primary employment, construction, manufacturing, and the producer-services segment of the tertiary economy. Even as the proportion of employment in manufacturing expanded, however, it fell considerably short of its pre-1973 level (see Díaz 1996).

The economy's shift from downswing to upswing reconfigured urban employment in ways that are both similar to and different from the rest of Latin America. Table 3 summarizes Chile's sectoral reconfiguration in 25-year perspective.

According to Table 3, over the long run, the relative weights of employment in the public sector and manufacturing fell in Chile[4] as they did in most of Latin America. Since 1983, though, Chile's portion of jobs in manufacturing has risen as exports have climbed (in contrast to the case of Mexico, as described by Oliveira and García this volume, Chapter 8). Again, over the long run, Chile's proportion of urban employment in agriculture,

Table 3. Structure of Urban Employment

	1970	1978	1986	1994
Categories	%	%	%	%
Agriculture	1.6	3.3	6.6	4.8
Fishing	0.5	1.0	1.5	2.0
Mines and quarries	2.1	2.7	2.3	1.9
Total primary employment	**4.2**	**7.0**	**10.4**	**8.7**
Manufacturing	29.6	19.0	15.6	18.2
Construction	7.4	4.4	5.5	8.0
Utilities	0.8	1.0	0.7	0.8
Total secondary employment	**37.8**	**24.4**	**21.8**	**27.0**
Commerce	17.6	20.1	19.5	21.0
Transport and storage	8.3	8.1	6.9	8.3
Financial services	2.4	3.7	4.8	6.8
Public sector employment	12.0	12.0	9.3	6.1
Other private services	17.0	20.0	21.3	22.2
Emergency employment program	0.0	4.7	6.0	0.0
Total tertiary employment	**57.3**	**68.6**	**67.8**	**64.4**
Unemployment rate	**6.1**	**15.6**	**10.0**	**6.4**

Source: INE, National Employment Survey (1976-1994), 4th Quarter.

forestry, fishing, and mining more than doubled, as primary employment became more urbanized. This shift also has occurred in countries such as Brazil, Ecuador, and Colombia.[5] Moreover, as in Latin America in general, Chilean employment became more tertiarized over the long run, a trend especially involving commerce and finance.[6] Particularly in the 1990s, producer services and modern consumer services (supermarkets, shopping malls, fast-food restaurants) have grown as percentages of all tertiary employment.[7] Yet, unlike most of Latin America, tertiary employment has dropped as a percentage of total employment since at least the early 1980s, due to the contraction of public employment and the reduction of emergency programs as well as to the urbanization of primary employment and the export-manufacturing boom.

The possibility of urbanization of primary employment, especially in intermediate cities, is not taken into account in this volume's set of hypotheses (but see Roberts 1995). Underlying the urbanization of primary employment in Chile was the modernizing agrarian reform undertaken by the Frei and Allende governments between 1964 and 1973, which ended the country's traditional tenancy system. Consequently, there emerged a seasonal labor force that is concentrated in agriculture in the central valley and in forestry in the south[8] and that resides in intermediate and small urban areas such as Rancagua, Talca, Curicó, Temuco, and Osorno. This pattern is likely to sharpen as economic globalization proceeds. In mining and fishing, the latter of which has gained in job share, the concentration of production in large firms has not generated new satellite towns, as had happened in the past. Instead, mining and fishing activities and jobs expanded upon previously built urban and port infrastructure.

Between 1973 and 1983, Chile experienced deindustrialization, which primarily damaged the metals-machinery and textile industries geared to the home market. Thereafter came a sharp recovery in manufacturing production for the home market and, beginning in 1988, for neighboring Latin American markets as well. Beginning in 1983, the proportion of employment in manufacturing rose, though, to repeat, it did not recoup its pre-1973 level. Manufacturing's employment growth in the 1980s and 1990s has involved the differentiation of production into two major branches: first, batch import-substitution industrial production destined for the domestic market and, increasingly since the late 1980s, for Latin American markets as well; and second, large-scale natural resource-based industrial production destined for the world market. The latter represents a key underpinning of Chile's economic boom.

Chile does not and probably will not produce massive quantities of motor vehicles or very low-wage footwear and clothing. Yet Chile has managed to increase its exports of more quality-based and niche manufacturing products (such as medium-priced footwear and textile goods, machinery, plastics, and furniture), especially to South America. This increase probably will accelerate as a result of Chile's joining MERCOSUR, although major currency devaluations in other Latin American countries would jeopardize the tendency.

Much more dynamic and globalized is export manufacturing based on local mining, fishing, forestry, and agricultural resources. Despite its trend toward capital-intensive technology, such large-scale, natural resource-based industrial production has been an important component of urban job growth. In addition, it has established clusters with increasing upstream and downstream linkages with domestic production in metals-machinery, chemicals, and packaging industries, as well as with a broad range of producer services (Díaz 1995a). This aspect of the Chilean experience is thus comparable to that of Brazil, whose manufacturing upturn in the 1990s has also been partially anchored in natural resource-based industry. A basic socioeconomic problem, however, is that such agroindustrial production combines large organizational scale and modern technology with top-down, neo-Taylorist labor-management relations and low-skilled, cheap labor, including the substantial exploitation of female workers.

Since 1970, the structure and importance of tertiary employment has undergone immense transformations (see Table 3). In 1970, public sector jobs represented more than 20 percent of urban tertiary employment, while the rest of the period's tertiary jobs were located mostly in traditional services. In 1994, however, public sector jobs represented less than 10 percent of tertiary employment as the share of modern service employment increased greatly. During the 1990s, employment has advanced rapidly in producer services, above all financial services, followed by modernized personal services. Thus, tertiary employment has become not less but more formalized and more oriented to wage labor.

Chile's recent transformations in the manufacturing and service industries have occurred in the context of the local consolidation of internationalized practices of business management for more than a decade (Díaz 1994). The new management culture emphasizes the reduction of company payrolls through organizational decentralization and labor flexibility, which involve expanded subcontracting of production processes and services. Basic change in production arrangements has reduced the share of direct employment in manufacturing firms and increased its share in firms providing inputs, including service inputs. While this structure is spreading throughout Latin America, it appears most deeply entrenched in Chile, where the systematic implementation of the globalized management culture began in the 1970s and disseminated through the economic system in the 1980s (Díaz 1994). The consequences for the persistence of Chile's acute class inequalities is a theme that runs throughout this chapter.

Regulatory Transformations

The literature on global restructuring tends to undervalue the role of national political and social institutions in shaping endogenous patterns of labor-market change (see Tardanico this volume, Chapter 1). In the case of Chile, the importance of such institutions is obvious because, unlike the rest of Latin America, the structural changes of the 1980s were preceded by neoliberal reforms that in the 1970s reorganized the regulatory framework governing the logic of firms and labor markets (Garretón 1994; Vergara

1994; on this matter in comparative-historical perspective, see Granovetter and Tilly 1988 and Tilly and Tilly 1994). Table 4 provides an overview of the long-term political construction of Chile's "flexible labor" regime.

In 1979-1981 the Pinochet dictatorship dismantled labor-market regulatory mechanisms and the social security system associated with the import-substitution era, with the exception of selected enclaves (the central bank and the state mining company, CODELCO). The government's actions both legalized the flexible use of labor and injected a huge mass of capital — held in pension fund contributions — into the financial system. The impact of the new, neoliberal framework of labor regulation became apparent after the economic crisis of 1982-1983. Based on the cumulative effects of state-led economic reforms under Frei, Allende, and Pinochet, as well as the latter's wider military-authoritarian interventions, Chile underwent both rapid economic growth and reorganized social polarization during the period of intense change in world division of labor. By 1990 — when the civilian Aylwin administration took office — the neoliberal transformations had been consolidated.

Yet the labor market's institutional transformation is far from over. The neoliberal framework involves deeply entrenched laws that are cemented in the power of large business and of the political right in general. This framework and its laws are impeding efforts to strengthen the state's legitimacy in the post-dictatorship era. In this setting, social and political pressures are mounted to redress not only the harsh inequalities but also the structural weaknesses of the neoliberal regulatory mode in terms of the economy's long-range productivity and growth. An important aspect of this campaign is the broadened leeway that state leadership has accorded labor unions to rebuild their membership base in the 1990s. After plunging from 45 percent of wage earners in 1970 to 11 percent in 1986, union membership rose to 30 percent of wage earners in 1994.

The structural and political obstacles to unionization remain formidable, however. The economy's stark contrast between robust growth and acute inequality has broadened political support for labor reforms. Proposed reforms would bolster the state's enforcement of labor regulations in firms, expand the scope of collective bargaining, and make unemployment insurance, social security, and health care programs more responsive to the instabilities inherent in economic globalization and restructuring.

In short, Chile's political climate has grown more favorable to reforms of the neoliberal-authoritarian regime of labor-market regulation, although the old regime continues to have powerful defenders. By no means, then, are the political outcomes of current struggles over such reforms a foregone conclusion. The outcomes promise to be more decisive than any likely changes in world markets in determining the future prospects of Chile's "economic miracle."

Table 4.
Structural Reforms of Labor-Market Regulation

Basic Reforms	1972-1973	1973-1989	1990-1994
1. Labor-Market Regime	*1966-1973: The rate of unionization advanced from 20.1 to 31.3% of wage earners. *Company unions and other labor organizations are strong, and many sectors negotiate in groups of firms. *Close coordination between parties and unions. *Importance of public-sector unions. *No-dismissal law. *Labor tribunals. *Obligatory wage adjustments.	*Union repression *Suspension of collective bargaining and the right to strike (1973-1979). *Wage indexation in formal sector up to 1981. Between 1982-1989 increases in minimum wage below average wages. *Virtual disappearance of collective contracts (1974-1979). **New Labor-Market Institutional Framework** *From 1979: More than one union allowed per firm; collective bargaining only at firm level and twice yearly; voluntary union membership; right to strike for a maximum of 60 days and elimination of labor tribunal. *Unionism in public sector prohibited. *Expansion of emergency employment programs (until 1988).	*Labor legislation enacted in 1979 remains in force, with minor reforms of no consequence for collective bargaining. *Between 1986-1989: Rate of unionization grows from 14.2 to 18.9% of wage earners. *1990-1994: Unionization rises only to 19.1%. *Unionism in public sector prohibited. There is growth, however, without attaining the level of the 1960s. *Increases in minimum wage exceed those of average wage.
2. Social Security Regime	*Mixed system based on employer and employee contributions, together with a fiscal subsidy for the poorest one-third employees. *High nonwage costs (40% of wages).	*Reforms to the social security system (1981). *Workers pay into private sector pension funds with individual accounts. *Inactive workers to be financed by the state.	*In 1991 there were 900 thousand pensioners in the old system and less than 90 thousand in private sector pension funds. By 1994, membership in such pension funds rises to 3.7 million. *Low non-wage costs (3% of wages).

Source: Meller 1990.

Precarious and Informal Employment

To what extent has urban employment in Chile become more precarious and informal? The case of Chile between 1984 and 1994 does not confirm the hypothesis of expanded informality as a share of total employment. Yet, consistent with the hypothesis is that, even as the rate of unemployment has dropped and average real wages have risen, the share of precarious employment has not diminished but grown.

"Informal" employment refers to labor activity that falls outside the reach of legal regulation and thus is not covered by certain basic worker protections (such as labor contracts or access to social security coverage). "Precarious" employment refers to labor activity that is unstable and that involves, according to some combination of local and international acceptability, unjust workplace conditions or a high degree of variable income. From this perspective, informal employment tends to be precarious, but by no means is all formal employment equitable, stable, and secure. Not only the levels of informal and precarious employment but also their extent of convergence with or divergence from each other are prime indicators of a society's local state/class structure and relation to the international division of labor (see Portes 1995; Roberts 1995).

Figure 2 addresses the growth pattern of informal employment in Chile during the period 1976-1994. It does so according to two definitions: informal employment, measured as the percentage of workers who are not affiliated with the pension system; and the urban informal sector (UIS), which is more or less equivalent to small-scale urban production (as conceptualized by PREALC, Programa Regional del Empleo para América Latina).[9]

Both measures agree that the percentage of informal employment peaked in 1980-1981, then diminished in the early 1980s. They disagree in that the social security measure charts a continued net decline in the percentage of informal employment in the 1980s, albeit involving some increase in the 1990s, while the PREALC measure charts a sustained pro-cyclical increase since the early 1980s. On balance, however, they both say that between 1976 and 1994, the percentage of informality either declined or remained constant; that is, neither measure demonstrates long-range net gain in informal employment's share of the labor market.

The same conclusion emerges from data on change in the balance between wage and nonwage employment, the latter being a rough indicator of informal employment (see Tables 2 and 5). The proportion of nonwage employment rose from 27.5 percent of all urban employment in 1972 to 44 percent in 1982, based overwhelmingly on job loss by public sector and manufacturing workers and on the consequent need of such workers and members of their households to engage in informal income-earning activities. During the economy's post-crisis upswing, however, this process was reversed as nonwage jobs decreased to 34.7 percent of all urban jobs in 1994, virtually the same level as in the pre-Pinochet years.[10]

Table 5.
Patterns of Wage Employment

	1966	1972	1982	1988	1994
Wage employment as % of total employment in rural and urban areas					
Urban	65.5	72.5	56.0	64.2	65.3
Rural	56.8	44.1	41.0	48.7	48.8
Gender % of total wage employment					
Female	16	n.a.	26	25	29
Male	84	n.a.	74	75	71
Wage earners/employer ratio (excluding public sector)					
Primary sector	45	33	22	16	19
Secondary sector	55	n.a.	25	25	21
Tertiary sector	26	n.a.	23	13	12

Source: INE (1966-1972), 2nd quarters; (1976-1992), 4th quarters.

Four elements appear responsible for the absence of net informalization over the long run. First, since 1984, rapid economic growth has boosted the demand of firms for workers, thereby improving labor's chances of obtaining work in medium and large firms or with contracts that include social security benefits. Second, the privatization of the social security and health systems has created a market of some 20 pension fund managers competing to attract worker-affiliates who pay individual monthly contributions. This arrangement imposes no obligation on employers and thus gives them no incentive to bypass the channels of legality. Third, the labor reforms of the early 1980s made hiring and firing more flexible by encouraging individual contracts over collective contracts. That is, firms could now issue formal labor contracts without being bound by the legal rigidities of the previous era. Fourth, the state has come to exercise a greater "formalizing" influence in Chile than in most of Latin America, stemming not from its effective capacity to regulate the labor market — which is weak — but from its post-1983 effectiveness in fiscal regulation. Therefore, firms now have a financial incentive to operate formally, a practice that has extended organizationally into their employment practices as well. Reinforcing this practice is the strengthening of labor unions since 1990.

Together, these elements have favored the growth of formal over informal employment since the early 1980s, without substantially reducing management's discretion in hiring and firing workers. As Figure 2 shows, however, the formalization of employment has been halted since 1990. This pattern suggests the following hypothesis: Given the institutional arrangements established under the Pinochet dictatorship, Chile's economy has reached the upper limit of its capacity to generate formal jobs. Indeed, associated with the economy's high degree of openness is the intensification of competitive pressures that push firms to rely on flexible labor in order to minimize production costs and maximize adaptability.

Against this backdrop there appears evidence not only that employment formalization has reached its upper limit but also that precarious conditions have come to characterize a widened fraction of formal employment. For instance, in spite of the re-waging that has occurred since 1983, the share of wages in national income has remained stagnant at around 38 percent, as the significant productivity gains of workers have well surpassed their gains in real hourly pay. This trend involves loss of the public sector's leadership in wage determination (Mizala and Romaguera 1991), the expanded share of wage jobs in small firms (Table 6), and the virtual doubling of women's share of wage jobs since the mid-1960s. In this context, 70 percent of wage earners are not unionized, nor do they have access to collective bargaining. Twenty percent of wage earners in firms with more than 10 employees and 64 percent of wage earners in firms with fewer employees do not have employment contracts (PET-MIDEPLAN 1993), a situation that pertains disproportionately to women, youths, and those 50 and older. Moreover, a high proportion of pension fund members only pay contributions sporadically.

Perhaps most disturbing is what amounts to a "re-waging of poverty" (Díaz 1994). This process — which may be occurring, to one degree or another, in much of urban Latin America — is challenging the supposition that poverty is exclusively a function of unemployment and informal

Table 6.
Female Shares of Employment by Industry

Industries	1976	1994	% Change
Agriculture and livestock (%)	4.4	11.1	152
Mining (%)	2.5	4.0	60
Manufacturing (%)	26.0	27.3	5
Utilities (%)	4.7	8.9	89
Construction (%)	0.9	2.8	211
Commerce (%)	35.0	43.7	25
Transport and communication (%)	7.5	11.6	55
Financial services (%)	24.5	35.5	45
Communal, social, and personal services (%)	45.1	57.2	27

Source: INE 1976, 1994, 4th quarters.

employment. Of the poorest 40 percent of Chile's employed population in 1990, 33.6 percent were wage workers, and 25.2 percent were self-employed; in 1993, 36.2 percent were wage workers, and 20 percent were self-employed. This pattern implies proportional growth in wage employment that is legally regulated, or "formal," but that is precarious not only in remuneration but commonly in other respects as well.

Summing up, between 1984 and 1994, Chile's urban workers raised their average real incomes and became more continuously employed, and over the long run employment became not more but less informalized. Yet, such an improvement has not meant a corresponding reduction in the precariousness of employment. The Chilean state's regulatory mechanisms do not protect workers — especially the less skilled — from the job impact of recessionary cycles and industrial reorganization. Nor do they provide substantial labor rights in the face of the authoritarian management practices that persist in the majority of firms. To be sure, employment conditions have improved for skilled workers, technicians, and professionals, whose leverage derives from their strategic importance to a robust, internationalizing economy and whose share of total employment increased. What is seen, though, is that associated with Chile's export-based prosperity, there is a pronounced degree of heterogeneity and polarization in employment conditions, whose driving forces are likely to create an expanded layer of informal workers in the near future.

Gendered Inequality

Not until 1975 was there a significant increase in Chile's rate of female labor-force participation, which has picked up especially since 1985. From 1976 to 1994, the portion of women over 15 years of age participating in the labor force rose from 25.2 to 35.2 percent, as the female share of the total labor force grew from 20 to 32 percent.[11] Nonetheless, the labor force remains significantly less feminized in Chile than in other Latin American countries such as Mexico, Brazil, and Colombia (see CEPAL 1995b; Henríquez and Pérez 1994; Oliveira and García this volume, Chapter 8).

All industries except manufacturing have displayed notable gains in women's share of employment since 1976 (Table 6). The most appreciable relative gains have been in construction and in agriculture and livestock, which employ only small percentages of women. More important, on balance, are the gains in tertiary employment, where approximately 80 percent of women workers are concentrated. Women's portion of jobs increased across the spectrum of tertiary activities, from traditional and informal services to modern and formal ones. The female portion of total wage jobs climbed from 16 percent in 1966 to 26 percent during the economic crisis of the early 1980s. After falling to 25 percent in 1988, it rose to 29 percent in the 1990s as the economy's restructuring accelerated (Table 5). Given that formal employment's share of the labor market expanded after 1983, this trend implies that women's recent job growth more than men's has revolved around the formal sector.

The minimal increase in the female percentage of Chilean manufacturing employment stands in sharp contrast to most of the other countries addressed in this volume with the exception of Argentina. Consistent with these and other Latin American cases, however, is the fact that women's share grew in light industries such as garment and goods manufacturing but declined relatively in various other sectors (electronics and metals-machinery production) due to a strong expansion of male employment (Abramo 1993). Thus, inasmuch as Chile's post-1983 upswing in manufacturing prosperity is not based on low-skill, light industrial production, the feminization of its employment in manufacturing has not approximated the scale witnessed especially in Mexico and parts of the Caribbean Basin.

Women's average real wages, like men's, increased between 1984 and 1994. Moreover, between 1990 and 1993, average female income increased from 64 to 69 percent of men's, and in the case of wages, the ratio increased from 73 to 78 percent. What is striking, though, is that earnings discrimination against women is much greater at the upper than the lower end of the ladder. In 1992, the average pay for women with no more than primary schooling was 82 percent of what equivalent men earned; for women with university degrees, it was just 52 percent of the male standard (INE 1992). By the same token, the male/female income gap was widest within the uppermost income decile of the population. It was also widest among 35- to 54-year-olds and in services. Interestingly, gendered income inequality was less extreme among the self-employed and informal workers than among wage workers (INE 1992).

So, between 1976 and 1994, the feminization of the Chilean labor force was considerable. Women remained overwhelmingly employed in services, whose portion of female workers rose across the gamut of formal and informal activities. While women's share of manufacturing jobs remained considerable, it did not increase appreciably. This finding reflects the composition growth in Chilean manufacturing. The female share of manufacturing jobs did increase in the low-end apparel and food industries but not in the mid-range industries that are the focus of the country's expanded employment in manufacturing. Gendered income inequality diminished, as women's income rose faster than men's. Women's relative gains, though, were concentrated in the less-skilled portions of the labor market.

Geographic Distribution

The next question is whether the transition to a denationalized, export-based economy has fostered the geographic decentralization of employment. Except for the country's extreme north (Arica) and extreme south (Punta Arenas), the internationalization of civil society in Chile has lagged far behind that of the movement of capital and goods, given the vast distances and minimal transportation integration between Chile's urban centers — which are powerfully dominated by Santiago — as well as between them and other cities of South America. In the near future, transportation links with the rest of the Southern Cone and the Americas at large are bound to increase as economies become more integrated. So far, however, Chile's extent of societal internationalization has been curtailed sharply, as it is virtually an insular country, bordered by the Andes Mountains, the Atacama desert, the Pacific Ocean, and the Antarctic.

While the entire length of Chile has port access to the Pacific Ocean, it lacks economically important interior zones compared to such countries as Mexico, Colombia, Brazil, and Argentina. Nor does Chile have zones with significant differences in their comparative spatial advantages such as northern Mexico due to its contiguity with the United States. Thus, the spatial differentiation of the country's urban production and employment stems from two conditions: geographic discontinuity in natural resource endowments[12] and the extreme locational concentration of capital, infrastructure, the state's machinery, and population in the capital city of Santiago, which is located in the heart of Chile. Since colonial times, Santiago has been Chile's territorial anchor of power and wealth as well as the country's sole territorial point of integration with the world economy.

Chile's import-substitution economy of the mid-twentieth century reinforced the concentration of productive capacity in the Santiago metropolitan region.[13] During that era, Santiago's principal importance was as a service and commercial center. The era's state-sponsored relocation of some manufacturing activity to cities such as Concepción (in the south) and Arica (in the north) did not undo the spatial pattern of economic as well as demographic concentration.[14] It did, on the other hand, enhance the economic diversity of the country's urban areas.

Yet, during the subsequent era of neoliberal political and economic reorganization, Greater Santiago's share of national employment did not fall, as studies on global restructuring would lead one to expect, but rather increased from 34 percent in 1966 to 43 percent in 1994. This increase was based on a gain in the city's share of national tertiary employment, as its share of national manufacturing employment remained at 56 percent. Within this framework, Greater Santiago's portion of national manufacturing jobs fell in years of economic downturn (1975-1976 and 1982-1983) but rose in years of upturn (1976-1980, 1986-1994) (de Mattos 1995; on change in the composition of the metropolitan region's employment, see Table 7).

The territorial concentration of jobs in the metropolitan area between 1986 and 1994 has been much greater for women (48.6 and 49.4 percent) than men (34.9 and 37.6 percent), although the rate of increase has been greater for men. The continued, much higher territorial concentration of female rather than male jobs would seem to reflect the reinforcement of Santiago's fundamental role as a service and commercial node, together with Chile's slight growth in women's portion of manufacturing jobs. In fact, Santiago's portion of female manufacturing jobs has decreased somewhat since the early 1980s (from 63.1 to 61 percent). Nevertheless, as the national momentum of global restructuring has intensified in the 1990s, this trend is being somewhat reversed, as some amount of geographic reconcentration of manufacturing jobs is under way (de Mattos 1995).

Table 7.
Structure of Employment in the Santiago Metropolitan Region
percentage

Industry	1967	1994
Agriculture, hunting and fishing	6.5	4.2
Mining	0.4	0.3
Manufacturing	30.8	21.8
Construction	5.2	6.9
Utilities	0.9	0.8
Commerce	20.4	21.6
Transport and communication	5.1	6.9
Services	30.1	37.5

Sources: INE 1994 (author's estimates); ODEPLAN 1971.

This chapter has discussed the urbanization of employment in primary activities, a process that focuses on intermediate cities, such as Los Angeles, Rancagua, and Temuco, and that stands to accelerate. In view of both this trend and the unchallenged hegemony of metropolitan Santiago, to what extent have provincial urban areas been winners or losers in Chile's economic transformation? Even as Santiago's share of population over 15 years rose from 37.2 percent in 1980 to 39.6 percent in 1994, there has been sharp net growth in the population of provincial cities as a result of the export boom. This phenomenon was quite generalized in the 1980s, but significant interurban inequalities are surfacing in the 1990s. Alongside provincial cities of continued rapid growth and modernization are other cities that are now losing ground. Those provincial cities that are prospering in the 1990s are connected with the export boom (Iquique, customs-free area; Los Angeles, forestry; Temuco, agroindustry). Those that are falling behind are connected with the market displacement of activities, such as electronics assembly (Arica in the north), coal mining (Lota-Schwager in the south), and customs-free imports (Punta Arenas in the extreme south).

So, employment in Chile has become not less but more concentrated in the Santiago metropolitan agglomeration, a trend that coincides with the long-range trajectory of Chilean history. The recent trend has been more pronounced for female than male labor, as the former is overwhelmingly employed in tertiary activities, the focus of Santiago's past and present dominance in the urban hierarchy. Provincial cities have tended to share in the nation's export-oriented dynamism. Nonetheless, the deepening of internationalization in the 1990s is giving shape to an interurban pattern characterized by greater differentiation and inequality — precisely the emerging contour of the Chilean labor market as a whole.

Conclusions

The Chilean economy's "free-market" boom since the early 1980s is, in fact, grounded in large-scale state intervention, both before and during the military dictatorship of Augusto Pinochet. While divergent in their sociopolitical foundations and economic objectives, two commonalities marked the policy actions of the democratic Frei and Allende administrations of the 1960s and early 1970s, on the one hand, and the Pinochet dictatorship on the other hand. First, they were driven not by external forces, such as the market logic of exports or the mandates of multilateral financial agencies, but by domestic state/class forces. Second, the state-centered reforms of the Frei and Allende governments laid the institutional and infrastructural underpinnings that, in the context of the unanticipated, eventual sweep of economic globalization, permitted the Pinochet team's authoritarian-neoliberal interventions to score a dramatic macroeconomic success after 1983.

Chile's prospects for authentic democratization hinge partly on the extension of the long-term chain of ironies in that the consolidation of a neoliberal regulatory order under Pinochet's dictatorship freed the post-dictatorship, civilian governments of Aylwin and Frei from having to implement measures of austerity and market deregulation during the 1990s. The continuation of the economy's rapid growth and transformation, then, has facilitated the post-military political transition. At the same time, however, the state's deeply entrenched, neoliberal framework entails political, economic, and social rigidities that pose severe obstacles to the achievement of a more equitable income distribution and strengthened democratic institutions—and even to the durability of economic prosperity.

Against this backdrop, Chile's urban labor market has undergone profound reorganization and social polarization since the 1970s. The relative weight of public sector employment has dropped, and, since the 1980s, the labor market has become not more but less tertiarized. The latter has occurred as post-1983, export-based prosperity has boosted the shares of employment in urbanized primary activities, construction, and — in the aftermath of previous severe losses — manufacturing. The share of employment in financial services has grown as well, while jobs in personal services have become more numerous in supermarkets, shopping malls, restaurant chains, and so on. Urban employment in general has become more focused on internationalized activities. This is particularly true of jobs in urbanized primary activities such as copper refining and fruit processing, agroindustrial and mid-range manufacturing, and financial services, which, along with agricultural exports, represent the economic core of the Chilean boom. Despite its post-1983 surge, the portion of employment in manufacturing remains below its peak level of previous decades. More relevant, however, is the fact that manufacturing production and employment have become divided into two principal branches: mid-range, import-substitution activities geared not only to the domestic market but, since the late 1980s, to Latin American markets as well; and large-scale, technology-intensive agroindustrial production geared to the world market. The former branch's long-term prospects are not favorable. The latter branch, so far, has gone unchallenged, but the absence of a significant push into more advanced forms of manufacturing has created an Achilles' heel (see Weeks 1996). Nevertheless, agroindustrial production represents a strategic bridge between the economy's rural and urban dynamism, while simultaneously forging important production and job linkages with urban import-substitution manufacturing and producer services.

Chile's configuration of sectoral change faces possible modification as the globalization of the national economy accelerates. The possibilities are inextricably bound up with the country's ongoing political challenges and struggles. The same is true for the labor market's contours of social inequality.

What, then, have been the ramifications of sectoral change for social inequality? The point of departure for answering this question is the highly repressive, antilabor campaign undertaken by the Pinochet dictatorship, which razed the import-substitution era's edifice of labor rights, replacing it with a new regulatory structure of "flexible labor." Within this political framework, the average real wages of Chilean workers have risen considerably under vigorous economic growth since 1983, but no progress has been made in redressing what remains among the most unequal distributions of income in Latin America. The portion of urban informal employment expanded greatly in the 1970s and early 1980s but has since contracted to its pre-Pinochet level. Its sharp contraction reflects not only the rapid growth of business demand for labor but also various aspects of the new labor regime that reduce the incentive of firms to seek informal workers, largely by giving employers much greater leeway to hire and fire and by placing the burden of social security payments on the workers themselves. It appears, nonetheless, that formalization of urban employment has reached its peak under the present structural economic conditions and the labor regime and that intensified globalization is generating a new upswing in informal employment.

Yet, even as informal employment and unemployment receded during the 1980s and average real wages turned upward, labor-market conditions remained highly precarious. Most basically, labor's rights are still minimal in the face of the authoritarian management practices that continue to typify Chilean firms, a problem compounded by a historical decline in union membership and the widespread use of the internationalized management approach of flexible specialization. Notwithstanding the re-waging of employment and substantial productivity gains during the economic boom, the wage share of national income has remained low and stagnant. What is most telling, however, is the "re-waging of poverty," which has begun to challenge the notion that poverty is solely a problem of informal employment and unemployment.

In this setting, women's percentage of the labor force climbed more steeply than ever, though it has yet to reach the levels of such countries as Brazil and Mexico. Women's employment continued to be highly concentrated in tertiary activities. While the female share of manufacturing jobs remained significant, its net growth was minute between the mid-1960s and mid-1990s, as capital-intensive manufacturing became a leader in the economy's export-based expansion. Women's average earnings rose faster than men's after 1983, especially in the early 1990s. The pattern of male/ female earnings inequality indicates that discrimination against women is greatest in the upper rungs of the occupational ladder.

The clearest territorial winner in the restructuring of the Chilean economy and labor market is the Santiago metropolitan agglomeration. In this regard, contemporary restructuring has reinforced the most basic historical feature of urban-regional hierarchy in Chile. The reinforcement of Santiago's hegemony is anchored in its role as a center for advanced services and as the nation's internationalized metropolis. Yet, by no means have provincial urban areas been excluded from the impressive prosperity of the period since the economic crisis of 1982- 1983. This was particularly the case during the 1980s, as export-led recovery spread gains quite widely across the national territory. Even so, during the 1990s, the economy's entry into a new phase of export-led transformation — based on diversification and expansion of scale in primary exports, advances in agroindustrial production, growth in intermediate-level manufacturing exports, developments in producer services, and investment in neighboring countries — is drawing harsher lines between the geographic winners and losers. As in the labor market at large, then, the spatial trend is toward greater differentiation and inequality.

Chile's macroeconomic gains of the last decade or so are impressive against Latin America's regional backdrop of tenuous, uneven recovery from the economic downswing of the early 1980s. Nevertheless, without denying the dramatic fall in the incidence of officially demarcated poverty over the last several years, the social features of Chile's economy and labor market remain trapped under the state and class debris of the Pinochet dictatorship. The overriding question is whether enough of this debris can be cleared away during the current political transition to expand Chile's "miracle" to incorporate equity, sustainability, and authentic democratization.

The regulatory regime of neoliberalism is clearly incapable of addressing the wide array of formidable new economic, environmental, and sociopolitical challenges. Chile now confronts the challenge of establishing politico-constitutional alternatives to its current neoliberal and authoritarian framework, which poses a greater threat to the future of the economy's prosperity than do any conceivable changes in the organization of world markets.

Notes

1. The neoliberal success also has to do with historical underpinnings that were constructed before the military coup of 1973 by the governments of Eduardo Frei Montalva (1964-1970, the father of the current president) and Salvador Allende (1970-1973), whose policies radically contrasted with the subsequent neoliberalism. These two governments undertook at least three massive reforms that — quite ironically — would prove crucial to Chile's post-1973 neoliberal success. The agrarian reform of 1964-1973 affected more than one-half of the country's arable land, dissolving the inefficient traditional *latifundio* and facilitating the post-1973 emergence of a new class of dynamic agrarian entrepreneurs. The nationalization of the copper industry in 1971 eventually permitted Pinochet's government to capture massive rents in dollars, thereby playing a key role in overcoming its acute fiscal crisis. Finally, the expansion of a vast segment of state-owned companies under Frei and Allende became critical to the success of the military dictatorship's aggressive wave of privatization and thus to the emergence of a successful class of domestic, internationally oriented entrepreneurs.

These reforms could hardly have been carried out by the military government since — again ironically — they would have demanded that it directly confront its sociopolitical bases of support. Thus, the radical reforms undertaken by Frei and Allende during the 1960s and 1970s paved the way for the neoliberal reforms after 1973. That is, the Frei and Allende reforms dissolved the sociopolitical brick and mortar of the traditional oligarchic status quo and even of the import-substitution regime that had been built since the 1930s but that had come to stagger under the weight of structural inefficiencies.

Under Pinochet, the state's market capacity was not driven by market dynamics nor by the mandates of multilateral financial agencies. It was driven, rather, by the initiatives of national state leadership within the logic of changing state-class relations (see Garretón 1994;Vergara 1994).

2. Chilean trade liberalization began in 1975. After signing on to the World Trade Organization in 1994, the Chilean government agreed to enter the Southern Cone Common Market (Mercado Común del Cono Sur — MERCOSUR). The government is currently negotiating its entry into the North American Free Trade Agreement (NAFTA), or at least, as a possible interim stage, a bilateral trade agreement with the United States.

Privatizations took place throughout 1973-1990, signifying the transfer from the public to private sector of 3,700 farms as well as 470 companies and banks. Two more public sector firms were privatized between 1990 and 1994, and the privatization of firms supplying drinking water and a medium-sized hydroelectric firm is under discussion. Some 30 public sector companies remain, the most important of which is CODELCO — a mega-company in the copper industry — which will not be privatized during the 1990s, if ever.

3.   For example, while the pension system has been successful with respect to the mobilization of capital, it has been unsuccessful with respect to the average level of pensions it pays to retirees, some 900,000 of whom receive pensioned incomes of less than US$150 per month.

4.   Between 1970 and 1986, public sector employment declined from 21 to 11 percent of tertiary employment. Not to be overlooked, though, is the importance of the Pinochet government's emergency jobs program (Programa de Empleo de Emergencia — PEE) of the early 1980s. Arguably, PEE generated precarious "semi-public sector" employment, which together with the period's high rate of unemployment, maintained a "reserve army" of workers that facilitated the labor force's rapid expansion under conditions of rising economic demand after 1983.

5.   The downward trend in the percentage of urban primary employment between 1986 and 1994 is related to the reduction of urban unemployment and the high growth of manufacturing and construction employment.

6.   Chile, Argentina, and Uruguay have been highly urbanized and tertiarized societies since the 1960s — well before the rest of Latin America (see Allen 1993).

7.   Research needs to examine Chile's subsectoral employment trends within services. For this chapter, I have been able to tease out the subtrend for financial services but not for distributive, social, producer, and personal services (see Browning and Singelman 1978).

8.   Employment in mining declined due to the disappearance of coal mines in the south and the displacement of small-scale copper mining by large-scale mining that utilizes advanced technology.

9.   For Figure 2, the urban informal sector (UIS), as defined by PREALC's original formulations, is equivalent to self-employed workers, plus non-remunerated family members, minus professionals and technicians located in the previous categories. In contrast, informal employment is equal to the volume of employment, minus the annual stock of active taxpayers who pay at least one monthly pension payment during the year. This indicator is a minimum proxy. Its pattern of change will not be substantially different from that of others based, for example, on individual contracts or on health system contributions. I have estimated both UIS and informal employment as proportions of the total urban workforce.

10.   Between 1966 and 1994, there were three phases in the trajectory of wage employment in Chile. The first phase (1966-1973) involved an increase in the share of urban wage employment due to growth in public sector and manufacturing jobs, although agrarian reform caused dewaging in the countryside. The second phase (1973-1982) involved urban and rural dewaging due to the impact of structural adjustment on public sector, manufacturing, and agricultural employment. The third phase (1983-1994) has involved urban re-waging due to the rapid growth of the export-based economy, although it has not encompassed rural re-waging. In the third phase, urban re-waging has centered on the private sector, since the public sector's fraction of all employment has shrunk.

11.   As is typical of such data, these underestimate the level of female labor-market participation (Henríquez and Pérez 1994).

12.   Mining is concentrated in the extreme northern desert, agriculture in the central region, forestry in the south, and fishing principally in the coastal north and south.

13. Apart from the capital city itself, the metropolitan agglomeration includes Chile's main ports (Valparaíso and San Antonio) and intermediate cities such as Viña del Mar and Rancagua. Taking the intermediate cities into account, Santiago's metropolitan agglomeration constitutes a territorial network of urban and agricultural wealth that centers on the capital city.

14. Import-substitution development was initiated during a period when almost one-half of the nation's population lived in urban areas. Given long-run agricultural stagnation, a result was the acceleration of migration from the countryside to urban areas, especially to the Santiago metropolitan region (see Friedman and Lackington 1967).

References

Abramo, L. 1993. "Reconversión productiva, cambio tecnológico y empleo femenino en América Latina." In *Repercusiones de la reconversión productiva y del cambio tecnológico sobre el empleo y las condiciones de trabajo de la mujer.* Santiago, Chile: International Labour Organization (ILO).

Arango, L.G. 1991. *Mujer, religión e industria fabricato 1923-1982.* Medellín: Editorial Universidad de Antioquia.

Allen, J. 1993. "¿Hacia una economía posindustrial?" *Zona Abierta* no. 65/66:47-102. Madrid, Spain.

Auty, R., and D. Evans. 1994. "Industrial Policy Reform in Six Large Newly Industrializing Countries: The Resource Curse Theory." *World Development* 22 (1):11-26.

Bengoa, J. 1994. *La distribución de los ingresos y los derechos económicos, sociales y culturales.* Santiago, Chile: Centro de Estudios Sociales, SUR (mimeo).

Browning, H. L., and J. Singelman. 1978. "Transformation of the U.S. Labour Force: The Interaction of Industry and Occupation." *Politics and Society* 8 (3-4): 481-509.

CEPAL. 1995a. *Situación de la pobreza en Chile: encuesta CASEN 1994. Cuadro de Resultados.* Santiago, Chile: División Estadística y de Proyecciones, CEPAL (mimeo).

CEPAL. 1995b. *Panorama social en América Latina 1995.* Santiago, Chile: CEPAL.

De Mattos, Carlos. 1995. "Reestructuración, globalización, nuevo poder económico y territorio en el Chile de los noventa." Working paper. Santiago, Chile: Pontificia Universidad Católica de Chile, Instituto de Estudios Urbanos.

Díaz, A. 1993. "PYMEs y subcontratación en Chile." *Revista Proposiciones* 24 (November). Santiago, Chile: Centro de Estudios Sociales, SUR.

Díaz, A. 1994. "Restructuring and the New Working Classes in Chile: Trends in Waged Employment, Informality and Poverty 1973-1990." Geneva: UNRISD discussion paper 1239, December.

Díaz, A. 1995a. "La segunda fase del desarrollo exportador: dilemas y desafíos para una nueva estrategia de desarrollo." *Economía y Estadística* 10. Santiago, Chile: INE.

Díaz, A. 1995b. *Tendencias de la reestructuración económica y social en Latinoamérica.* College Park: University of Maryland, Department of Sociology.

Díaz, A. 1996. "La industria chilena entre 1970-1994: de la sustitución de importaciones a la 2ª fase exportadora." In *Estabilización macroeconómica, reforma estructural y comportamiento industrial.* Buenos Aires, Argentina: Alianza Editorial.

Friedman, J., and T. Lackington. 1967. "La hiperurbanización y el desarrollo nacional en Chile." In *Estructura social en Chile*, ed. Hernán Godoy. Santiago, Chile: Editorial Universitaria.

Gálvez and Bravo. 1994. "Siete décadas de registro de trabajo femenino 1854-1920." *Estadística y Economía* 7 (July). Santiago, Chile: Instituto Nacional de Estadísticas (INE).

Garretón, M. A. 1994. "The Political Dimensions of Processes of Transformation in Chile." In *Democracy, Markets, and Structural Reform in Latin America*, eds. W. C. Smith, C. H. Acuña, and E. A. Gamarra. Coral Gables, Fla.: North-South Center at the University of Miami.

Granovetter, M., and C. Tilly. 1988. "Inequality and Labor Processes." In *Handbook of Sociology*, ed. N.J. Smelser. Newbury Park, Calif.: Sage.

Guardia, A. 1995. "Empleo, subempleo y crecimiento económico 1986-1995." *Estadística y Economía* 11 (December). Santiago, Chile: Instituto Nacional de Estadísticas (INE).

Henríquez, H., and E. Pérez. 1994. "La subestimación de la participación femenina en las actividades económicas: encuesta suplementaria a mujeres inactivas." *Estadística y Economía* 8. Santiago, Chile: Instituto Nacional de Estadísticas (INE).

INE (Instituto Nacional de Estadísticas). 1995. *Ingresos 1966-1994 de hogares y personas: encuesta suplementaria de ingresos*. Santiago, Chile: INE.

INE. 1992. *Anuario de Estadísticas 1992*. Santiago, Chile: INE.

Martínez, J., and A. Díaz. 1996. *Chile: The Great Transformation*. Washington, D.C.: The Brookings Institution.

Meller, Patricio. 1990. "Revisión del proceso del ajuste chileno de la década del 80." *Colección Estudios CIEPLAN* 30 (December). Santiago, Chile: CIEPLAN.

Mizala, A., and P. Romaguera. 1991. *¿Es el sector público un sector líder en la determinación de los salarios? Evidencia para la economía chilena*. Santiago, Chile: Colección Estudios Cieplan 33 (December).

Oficina de Planificación Nacional del Gobierno de Chile (ODEPLAN). 1971. *Plan Nacional de Desarrollo 1991*. Santiago, Chile: ODEPLAN.

Programa de Economía del Trabajo-Ministerio de Planificación (PET-MIDEPLAN). 1993. *Encuesta Nacional de Hogares*. Santiago, Chile: MIDEPLAN.

Portes, A., M. Castells, and L.A. Benton, eds. 1989. *The Informal Economy: Studies in Advanced and Less Developed Countries*. Baltimore: The Johns Hopkins University Press.

Portes, A. 1995. *Entorno a la informalidad: ensayos sobre teoría y medición de la economía no-regulada*. Mexico, D.F.: Editorial Miguel Angel Porrua/ FLACSO.

Roberts, B. 1995. *The Making of Citizens: Cities of Peasants Revisited*. London: Arnold.

Sassen, S. 1991. *The Global City*. Princeton, N.J. : Princeton University Press.

Sassen, S. 1994. *Cities in a World Economy*. Thousand Oaks, Calif.: Pine Forge Press.

Sassen, S. 1996. *Loss of Control? Sovereignty in an Age of Globalization*. New York: Columbia University Press.

Smith, W.C., C.H. Acuña, and E.A. Gamarra, eds. 1994. *Democracy, Markets, and Structural Reform in Latin America.* Coral Gables, Fla.: North-South Center at the University of Miami.

Thurow, L.C. 1996. *The Future of Capitalism.* New York: Morrow.

Tilly, C., and Tilly, C. 1994. "Capitalist Work and Labor Markets." In *The Handbook of Economic Sociology,* eds. N.J. Smelser and R. Swedberg. Princeton, N.J.: Princeton University Press; New York: Russell Sage Foundation.

Tironi, E., and J. Martínez. 1980. *Clase obrera y modelo económico.* Santiago, Chile: Centro de Estudios Sociales, SUR (mimeo).

Vergara, P. 1994. "Market Economy, Social Welfare, and Democratic Consolidation in Chile." In *Democracy, Markets, and Structural Reform in Latin America,* eds. W. C. Smith, C. H. Acuña, and E. A. Gamarra. Coral Gables, Fla.: North-South Center at the University of Miami.

Weeks, J. 1996. "The Manufacturing Sector in Latin America and the New Economic Model." In *The New Economic Model in Latin America and Its Impact on Income Distribution and Poverty,* ed. V. Bulmer-Thomas. New York: St. Martin's Press.

Chapter 7

Argentina: State Policy and the Urban Labor Market

Rosalía Cortés

In no other Latin American country has the politics of neoliberal transformation been more sweeping than in Argentina. Yet Argentina lags far behind countries such as Chile and Mexico in the translation of neoliberal policies into world-market competitiveness. At the same time, a wide segment of Argentine workers has recently lost socioeconomic ground whether the national economy has grown, stagnated, or declined. Thus, during Argentina's rapid economic upswing in the early 1990s, both open unemployment and precarious employment swelled rather than shrank. The swelling turned massive in 1995-1996 as the regional fallout of Mexico's financial crisis laid bare the speculative underpinnings and extinguished the sparks of Argentine growth. The plight of many of the nation's workers and their families may worsen if, in the face of the remobilized remains of a once-combative labor movement, President Carlos Menem manages to orchestrate a new wave of legal reforms that further deregulates the labor market.

This chapter examines the sweep of change in the urban labor market and social inequality in Argentina from the mid-1970s to the early 1990s. With regard to the volume's comparative hypotheses, the chapter delineates the following changes: 1) notable decline in the labor market's portion of public sector employment, including not only the civilian but also the military branches of government; 2) tertiarization of employment in a setting of pronounced deindustrialization; 3) within the framework of generally poor export performance, ambiguity as to how much of the remaining portions of manufacturing employment — which, contrary to expectation, did not generally become more feminized — were geared to foreign markets; 4) continued feminization of the labor market's tertiary activities, with increasing emphasis on the entry of female income-earners in compensation for the displacement of male earners; 5) sharp expansion of unemployment and precarious and informal employment, with the growth rate of unemployment being led by women but that of informal employ-

Rosalía Cortés is a researcher at the Consejo Nacional de Investigaciones Científicas y Técnicas (Conicet) in Argentina and at FLACSO-Argentina.
Translated by Richard Tardanico.

ment by men; and 6) continued diminution of Greater Buenos Aires's share of urban population, and probably labor market, relative to that of secondary cities, combined with the likelihood of reinforcement of the leading metropolis's strategic hegemony in economy and employment.

Economic and Social Policies

Military-Authoritarian Government, 1976-1983

Adolfo Canitrot observes that the structure of the country's state/society relations is a fundamental cause of Argentina's contemporary crises. Writing on the sweep of national politics since the Second World War, he argues,

> Ideologically conceived as the leader in the process of social and economic transformation, the state, in fact, rarely gained enough autonomy from political forces to be perceived as more than an instrument of power or a prize for the winners of recurrent political struggles. This perception was closely related to traditional authoritarian practices and to the scant legitimacy given to the law and to constitutional rights (Canitrot 1994, 75).

The two leading political protagonists have been Peronism, anchored in working class and lower-middle class support, and the military, anchored in the support of the entrepreneurial classes. While united by nationalism, Catholicism, and anti-Marxism, the Peronists and the military have competed for governing power, generally subordinating economic policy to political exigencies (Canitrot 1994, 75).

As of the early 1970s, the politico-economic outcome of this competition was highly contradictory. On one side stood a massive complex of statist enterprises in basic services and heavy industry, together with a broad but weak sector of light industry and cross-cutting multinational corporations. Entangled in state bureaucracy and captive to particularistic claims by private business and organized labor, this complex failed to build competitive economic momentum. On the other side stood a policy of macroeconomic populism, revolving around wage increases, deficit spending, and industrial protectionism (Canitrot 1994, 77-78). In this setting, the "Second Peronism" of 1973-1976[1] — which had supplanted the military-sponsored authoritarian rule of 1966-1973 — collapsed under the weight of "uncontrollable political polarization, mismanagement of the economy, and severely damaging international economic trends" (Smith 1991, 224). Under economic recession and raging inflation, the military intervened in the form of a second round of authoritarian government (1976-1983).

During the presidency of General Jorge Rafael Videla (1976-1981), economic policymakers attempted to quell hyperinflation by implementing orthodox stabilization measures, while renegotiating the external debt with the International Monetary Fund (IMF), deregulating foreign investment, and selectively dismantling manufacturing protection and subsidies. The latter set of measures was intended to attract foreign capital, reduce the domestic price of manufactured goods, and give impetus to industrial modernization and exports. By no means, however, was deregulation applied uniformly. Indeed, monopolistic business conglomerates — domestic and foreign, old and new — profited from fiscal exemptions and state subsidies that, consistent with the military's post-Second World War vision of import-substitution development, were meant to reinforce the economy's basic infrastructure and heavy manufacturing. In the meantime, the military government unleashed a campaign of state terrorism and repression at its opposition — very widely defined — and took political aim at organized labor. For instance, the collective negotiation of wages was replaced by a top-down arrangement, the minimum wage was frozen, and the right to strike was suppressed. The economic program did not work. As inflation remained beyond control and financial speculation crowded out productive investment, deindustrialization became pronounced and bankruptcies spread. Consequently, unemployment burgeoned, wages contracted, business monopolies were strengthened, and the recession deepened (Azpiazu 1991; Azpiazu, Basualdo, and Khavisse 1986; Feldman and Sommer 1984; Smith 1991, 231-242, 249-255).

The economic and political crises continued after late 1981, when a palace coup replaced President General Roberto Viola (who had been inaugurated at mid-year) with General Leopoldo Fortunato Galtieri. The crises were dramatically compounded by the Malvinas war in mid-1982, when Galtieri was ousted in favor of General Reynaldo Bignone. The humiliated, politically splintered, and internationally isolated armed forces were no match for the groundswell of popular and business anti-military opposition, which itself was disunited. The candidate of the Peronists — who were tainted by a secret labor union-military pact — was not victorious in the presidential election of October 1983; rather, the winner was Raúl Alfonsín, the candidate of the Unión Cívica Radical (the Radical Party). His administration would head the rebuilding of a society that had been bludgeoned by military repression and an economy that — like those of Chile and Uruguay but unlike those of Brazil and Mexico — had for many years been trapped in a paradoxical vise of debt and deindustrialization (Smith 1991, 260; see the chapters this volume by Díaz on Chile [6] and by Oliveira and García on Mexico [8]).[2] There were, of course, urban class realignments as well, most clearly the wrenching dislocations suffered by the industrial working class, public sector bureaucrats, and a wide range of business owners in manufacturing and services, versus the notable gains registered by some segments of the upper bourgeoisie. William C. Smith (1991, 253-254) writes that the primary beneficiaries of the military's policies between 1976 and 1983:

> ... were probably a small number of large nationally owned firms. These firms, taking advantage of state subsidies and/or easy access to foreign loans, were able to diversify their investments in the agribusiness sector, in areas of basic infrastructure, and in the lucrative construction business. Many firms also branched out into the rapidly expanding import business and, above all, into financial activities of all types. These firms not only consolidated their leading positions in their respective original spheres but began to form the core of a new dominant entrepreneurial group.

The Return to Civilian Government:
The Program of the Radical Party, 1983-1989

Alfonsín confronted a fundamental challenge: to consolidate democracy while stabilizing the economy. Given not only the economy's disarray but the surviving leverage of the military hard-liners, the strengthened leverage of the dominant classes, inter-party disharmony, and the determination of labor unions to recoup lost economic and political ground, Alfonsín's challenge was indeed formidable.

Remaining faithful to the Argentine logic of putting politics ahead of economics and acting unilaterally, the Alfonsín government began by defying the IMF, foreign creditors, and transnational business in favor of a program to bolster the domestic economy and redistribute income. The program attempted to do so by combining fiscal austerity with reduced interest rates and increased real wages. By mid-1985, however, it lay victim to galloping inflation, the suspension of new foreign loans, economic decline, and fractious inter-party and government-labor union relations. In its place came the "Austral Plan," which shifted gears by targeting inflation as the principal enemy. The Plan revolved around a new, tightly controlled currency (the Austral), strict wage and price controls, fiscal austerity, and high levies on public services. The short-term results were highly favorable, as inflation plunged, the budget deficit shrank, manufacturing output climbed, and the trade balance improved. Yet, complaining of low prices and high tax burdens, agricultural producers protested and manufacturing firms sent capital abroad and caused major product shortages for consumers and industry alike, while organized labor demanded wage hikes. In response, the government softened the Austral Plan in mid-1986, quickly undoing the early macroeconomic successes. Policy efforts to restore some semblance of macroeconomic order met renewed business and labor opposition, and by early 1988 the administration had no recourse but to agree to a drastic IMF program of fiscal and wage austerity, privatization, deregulation, and debt repayment. The subsequent explosion of hyperinflation led Alfonsín's desperate economic team to apply shock therapy, which did lower inflation but largely to the benefit of leading industrial and financial entrepreneurs and at the expense of agricultural producers and wage workers. Yet another burst of hyperinflation ensured victory by the opposing Peronist Party in the presidential election of May 1989 (Acuña 1994, 32-37; Azpiazu 1991; Canitrot 1994, 81-82; Cortés 1985a, 1985b, 1986; Cortés and Marshall 1993; Marshall 1988; Smith 1991, 269-285).

Peronism's Neoliberal Reincarnation, 1989-Present

During the electoral campaign, Carlos Menem, the Peronist candidate, had espoused the party's traditional platform of statism and populism as the way out of economic crisis, while eschewing policy specifics in favor of a vague calling for a "productive revolution." Upon taking office, however, Menem abruptly turned his back on the Peronist platform, instead carrying out what he called "major surgery without anesthesia" — Latin America's most radical program of neoliberal reform. Carlos H. Acuña (1994, 38) observes that the thrust of the Menem administration's radical policies:

> ... was not the result of a coherent plan or a clear division of labor among the different areas of government. Thus, a trial-and-error style of policymaking and implementation developed and was layered over the existing tension between long-term objectives and conjunctural impera- tives... the implementation of these policies was often erratic, inefficient, contradictory, and plagued by power struggles within the executive branch ....

This absence of coherence reflected the still unresolved conflicts resulting from political realignments not only between the state's executive and legislative branches but also between the state and the various segments of urban and rural capital, political parties, organized labor, and the middle classes. The overriding issue was which social groups would bear the heavy burdens involved in reducing and rebalancing the state's weight in the economy (Acuña 1994, 51-62; Smith 1991, 299).

The course of neoliberal policy was indeed erratic in 1989-1991, as with starts and stops, hyperinflation persisted in spite of budget austerity, recession, falling real wages, and rising unemployment. In April 1991 the Menem administration put into effect the "Convertibility Plan Plan," a policy package that represented a huge gamble. The Convertibility Plan made the Austral freely convertible into dollars. It also prohibited the central bank from printing money without full backing by gold or foreign currencies and through deregulation, trade liberalization, and privatization, more generally attacked the fiscal deficit, prices, and labor costs. According to Acuña (1994, 47), "these measures and the speed of their implementation formed the basis of a veritable neoliberal revolution in the model of accumulation and the structure of social relations in Argentina" (see Azpiazu 1994; Kosacoff 1993).

The Convertibility Plan slashed inflation, stabilized wages, made credit more accessible, and accelerated investment into privatized indus- tries. These conditions underlay a boom in consumer imports and in inflows of foreign currency and capital and a surge in gross domestic product (GDP) per capita by an accumulated 25.7 percent between 1991 and 1994 — the largest in all of Latin America (ECLAC 1995, 17). Beneath the impressive facade, however, lurked myriad problems. The exchange rate became greatly overvalued, contributing to the emergence of a serious balance-of-trade deficit; the rise in prices for nontradables far outstripped that in tradables, and the pace of job creation was minimal, as the rate of unemployment almost doubled (Acuña 1994, 48; ECLAC 1995, 69; Pessino 1995). A common feature of the aggressive privatization program — against a backdrop of rampant corruption — was the undervaluation of public sector companies; a prime consequence of the program was the reinforce- ment of monopolies in the supply of basic services and industrial inputs. Another problem was sectoral and regional inequity in the application of deregulatory measures. For instance, the automotive industry received continued protection in exchange for its agreement to become more export-oriented. Moreover, in order to forestall the loss of political support in the provinces, the government left in place old-style industrial promotion arrangements in Tierra del Fuego, Catamarca, San Juan, La Rioja, and San Luís. In this political and macroeconomic context, the performance of manufacturing firms was favorable in sectors such as chemicals and metals but unfavorable in others such as machinery, electronics, processed food, textiles and apparel, and furniture. Overall, the economy experienced deindustrialization and a widening breach between larger and smaller firms in terms of preferential government treatment, access to credit and inputs, performance, and survival (Azpiazu 1994; Bisang et al. 1995; Kosacoff 1993; LASR 1996, 7).

Within the framework of sociopolitical and economic realignments, social policy came to facilitate government and business control over labor, most basically by flexibilizing wage determination, job contracts, and layoffs and by reorganizing pension programs (see Díaz this volume on Chile [6]). These changes resulted from negotiations among the Menem administration, employer associations, and pro-government labor unions. In place of centrally determined, periodic wage adjustments and wage indexation, wage setting based on productivity criteria and decentralized bargaining was introduced. Reforms in the regulation of work activities led to the intensification of work time and the performance of multiple tasks, especially in manufacturing. New collective agreements cut the indirect labor costs of firms by reducing employer contributions to the much-weakened social security system, while also establishing both public and private systems for the capitalization of pension funds (Cetrángolo 1994).

How did the Menem government manage to implement this array of sweeping reforms in economic and social policy, which represented a fundamental shift in resources from labor and the public sector to portions of the business class? Acuña (1994, 51-62) ventures some explanations. With respect to organized labor, Menem utilized his legitimacy, as a Peronist candidate, to wrest concessions from unions to minimize strikes and protests before the election. Subsequently strengthening Menem's hand were worker support for the newly elected president, the impact of stagflation in diminishing labor's capacity to mobilize against the sudden surge of neoliberal reforms, and the government's carrot-and-stick approach to exploiting union disunity (see Cortés and Marshall 1993). With respect to the portions of the business class (such as in textiles and electronics manufacturing) that stood to lose from the withdrawal of state protections and subsidies, effective opposition was stymied by the political weakness of their industry associations during a time of severe economic losses. Some of the economically and politically stronger business groups that depended on state contracts were placated by privileged access to the acquisition of public sector firms. With respect to political parties, Menem's policy strategy gained considerable support in the rival Radical Party, which became weakened by its divisions in regard to the Menem government. As for the Peronists, Menem carried off the improbable feat not only of dramatically transforming the party from the bulwark of populistic, prolabor programs to that of neoliberal reform but also of retaining its electoral support. He did so by stressing the depth of the economic crisis and the lack of policy alternatives, moving decisively to name his loyalists to the party's leadership slots and to its candidacies for elected office, and gaining additional policy leeway as the economy improved (see Fajardo Cortez and Lacabana this volume, Chapter 5, and McCoy et al. 1995, on the contrasting case of Venezuela's Partido Acción Democrática and attempted neoliberal reforms). These and the other politico-economic dynamics of the Menem administration have unfolded under what has been characterized as "strong leadership and weak institutions" (Manzetti 1995, 5).

Menem's orchestration of a pact with Alfonsín, the head of the rival Radical Party, enabled the president to seek reelection as part of a series of constitutional reforms. In May 1995 Menem won a landslide victory based mainly on the electoral support of the urban poor, whose economic burdens had been mitigated by the quashing of hyperinflation,[3] and of the rich, the principal beneficiaries of the government's corruption-laden and otherwise unevenly applied privatization measures and market reforms. Nonetheless, the financial fallout from Mexico's peso crisis already had reached Argentina. Over the longer run, the economy contracted — largely at the expense of construction, manufacturing, and agriculture and of small and medium, domestically oriented companies — and, as shall be seen, unemployment and precarious employment ballooned. In spite of stirrings of aggregate economic recovery in late 1996, the convergence of austerity policies, employment crisis, and Menem's determination to implement a far-reaching program of labor deregulation undermined his political grip on the Peronist trade unions, triggered a series of major labor strikes, and undercut his standing in public opinion polls (SCR 1996b and 1996c).

Urban Labor Market and Social Inequality

P olitico-economic crisis and restructuring have altered urban Argentina's industry composition of output and employment. Most basically, trade liberalization, privatization, the mix of weakened and redefined state regulatory activity, market changes, and new investment patterns have intensified the long-range shift in production and employment from manufacturing to services. As the share of manufacturing in the gross domestic product was sliced from 31.6 percent in 1974 to 25.4 percent in 1993, the number of manufacturing firms dropped by 13.5 percent between 1974 and 1985 and by 18.5 percent between 1985 and 1994. The volume of employment in manufacturing plunged by 28.8 percent between 1980 and 1990. It continued to fall during the early 1990s, not just in non-monopolistic firms producing principally for the domestic market (textiles, clothing, footwear) but also, as a consequence of labor-saving technological and organizational innovations, in monopolistic, exporting firms[4] (Azpiazu 1994; Bisang et al. 1995; ECLAC 1995, 84, 88; Pessino 1995; see Oliveira and García this volume on Mexico [8]). As for job composition in manufacturing, between the mid-1980s and the early 1990s, the number of the sector's establishments employing more than 100 workers decreased by 27 percent (LASR 1996, 7). During the early 1990s, moreover, state manufacturing enterprises were privatized on a massive scale, shifting much industrial employment from the public to the private sector. It is unclear, though, whether export-oriented jobs have increased since as a percentage of total manufacturing jobs.

Since the years of military dictatorship, plans to reform the organizational structure of the state have involved the objectives of not only reduction but also decentralization. The reduction in civilian public sector employment has focused on the machinery of the central government, including parastatal entities, rather than on that of provincial and municipal governments. The volume of central government employment was decreased during the military dictatorships, rose during the Alfonsín presidency, and under Menem has been cut by an officially reported 42 percent — much of which, however, reflects organizational decentralization rather than the actual elimination of public sector jobs.[5] Employment in the public sector has become more feminized, in no small part because males — particularly male professionals — have predominated among the sector's workers opting to take advantage of retirement incentive packages. Under Menem, privatization has shrunk the central government's workforce by 89,000 through such incentive packages as well as attrition. In contrast to the central government, since the mid-1970s jobs in provincial and municipal governments have increased not only in number but relative to total provincial employment. Such jobs have increased for two reasons: First, the process of decentralization has transferred employment away from the central government to provincial and municipal governments; second, patronage arrangements have remained strong, both between local government officials and their clienteles and between local officials and central government officials who have sought to minimize political disaffection in the provinces (Orlansky 1992). During the early 1990s, such patronage arrangements were curtailed inasmuch as privatization and job cuts became more extensive while net growth in public sector jobs slowed.

Not only many layers of civilians but also the armed forces in general have been losers in the diminution of state sector functions, budgets, and employment. Recognition of the domestic politics of demilitarization in Argentina provides a corrective to reductionist thinking that attributes the downsizing of state machinery in Latin America solely to the economics of debt crisis and globalization. While an assessment of the employment magnitude and contours of demilitarization lies beyond the scope of this chapter, the ramifications of the process for both the economy and social inequality should not be overlooked (see, for example, Acuña and Smith 1995).

Against the background of these transformations, the labor force of Greater Buenos Aires has undergone changes in size and composition[6] (Tables 1 and 2). Under military dictatorship and economic crisis (1976-1983), Argentina's urban labor force contracted for two principal reasons:

Table 1.
Greater Buenos Aires
Rates of Variation in Labor-Force Participation, Unemployment,
and Employment by Gender[a]

	Participation		Unemployment		Employment	
	Males	Females	Males	Females	Males	Females
1976-1983	-5.0	-0.8	0.6	0.4	-5.6	0.4
1984-1989	0.0	6.0	3.7	2.8	-3.7	3.2
1990-1994	2.8	3.9	3.3	19.5	-0.5	-15.6

Source: Calculations based on INDEC, *Encuesta Permanente de Hogares*.
a = Percentage change between extremes for each period.

Table 2.
Greater Buenos Aires
Rates of Variation in Labor-Force Participation,Unemployment,
and Employment for Household Heads and Spouses[a]

	Participation		Unemployment		Employment	
	Heads	Spouses	Heads	Spouses	Heads	Spouses
1976-1983	-6.3	0.6	0.7	0.1	-7.0	0.5
1984-1989	3.1	7.0	3.2	3.9	-0.3	3.1
1990-1994	-0.7	5.3	3.9	7.2	-4.6	-1.9

Source: Calculations based on INDEC, *Encuesta Permanente de Hogares*.
a = Percentage change between extremes for each period.

Demographically, an increase in the population's share of elderly members decreased its share of working-age members; economically, reductions in public and private sector labor demand and in labor's average income prompted migrant workers — from both rural Argentina and neighboring countries — to return home.[7] Still another reason was the rechanneling of the economy's labor demand from manufacturing to services, which in absolute numbers cut mainly into the employment of low-educated male heads of households, but which also slashed female employment in manufacturing. Going in the other direction, though, the employment rate of female spouses rose slightly, as a result of both the job hardships of male heads and continued strong economic demand in female-oriented service occupations, such as domestic service[8] (see Cortés 1985). The same gendered pattern persisted as the economy's woes lingered during the post-military government of Alfonsín (1983-1989), the primary difference being the acceleration of growth in women's employment and unemployment, led again by spouses. Under the Menem administration (1989-present), the gross domestic product turned sharply upward, of course, during 1991-1994. Beginning in mid-1993, however, the rate of unemployment rose sharply as well — above all, for semiskilled and unskilled workers — due to the shedding of jobs in construction, manufacturing, privatized companies, and the public sector[9] (Tables 2 and 7; Pessino 1995). Among men, the rate of unemployment increased most sharply among household heads, but it increased some six times faster among women, especially non-heads of households, than among men, as economic hardship continued to fuel the bulk of women's expanding labor-force participation (Tables 1-6). Women's unemployment climbed relative to men's in the setting of abrupt drops in demand for female labor in commerce, domestic service, and manufacturing. The share of employed women in Buenos Aires with principal jobs in manufacturing dropped from 24.8 percent in 1980 to 18.9 percent in 1991 and 13.1 percent in 1995. This net proportional decline, 47.2 percent, is more extreme than that of men, 32.3 percent[10] (author's calculations from INDEC 1985, 1995), based on the devastation of craft manufacturing and the absence of a significant push toward low-wage, export-platform production. The steeper decline in the female than male percentage of employment in manufacturing is inconsistent with expectations derived from the literature on the worldwide reorganization of manufacturing (see this volume, Chapter 1 and the chapters on Mexico [8], Venezuela [5], and Chile [6]).

Keep in mind that Argentina's labor-market conditions have become downgraded in spite of a long-term upgrading in the workforce's educational composition (IEC 1970, 1981, 1991). A perusal of job advertisements in

Table 3.
Greater Buenos Aires
Rates of Labor-Force Participation by Gender
and Educational Attainment

	Primary Incomplete		Primary Complete to Secondary Incomplete		Secondary Complete to Tertiary Incomplete		Tertiary Complete	
	Males	Females	Males	Females	Males	Females	Males	Females
1974	70.5	23.2	79.8	27.4				
1980	61.6	22.1	78.9	25.8				
1988	73.6	32.8	77.0	28.9	79.90	37.7	89.2	75.7
1990	60.4	24.4	77.8	30.2	82.95	50.3	91.7	77.4
1992	60.8		78.9		83.30		91.0	

Source: Calculations based on INDEC, *Encuesta Permanente de Hogares*.

Table 4.
Greater Buenos Aires
Rates of Labor-Force Participation by Level of
Per Capita Household Income and Gender

	Lowest 30%		Middle 50%		Highest 20%	
	Males	**Females**	**Males**	**Females**	**Males**	**Females**
1974	40.8	13.1	58.5	23.2	74.2	41.1
1980	40.3	10.0	56.8	25.6	66.1	37.4
1988	44.2	17.7	56.6	29.9	69.8	48.0
1990	38.7	12.8	54.9	28.2	70.6	51.7
1992	40.0	13.3	57.7	31.2	71.7	50.2
1993	40.3	17.1	59.1	33.3	72.9	52.5

Source: Calculations based on INDEC, *Encuesta Permanente de Hogares.*

Table 5.
Greater Buenos Aires
Percentage of Females in Total Employment and
Unemployment by Level of Per Capita Household Income

	Lowest 30%		Middle 50%		Highest 20%	
	Em-ployed	**Unem-ployed**	**Em-ployed**	**Unem-ployed**	**Em-ployed**	**Unem-ployed**
1974	25.4	59.6	30.3	46.2	37.8	71.3
1980	21.7	41.0	33.1	48.7	38.5	51.8
1988	29.1	34.1	37.5	43.0	43.9	60.4
1990	26.6	39.3	27.7	49.8	43.2	30.7
1991	24.3	37.5	37.2	32.9	44.3	73.4
1992	25.0	37.5	37.2	32.9	44.3	73.4
1993	27.4	47.4	36.5	55.8	42.8	52.7

Source: Calculations based on INDEC, *Encuesta Permanente de Hogares.*

Table 6.
Argentina
Women as a Percentage of the Total Labor Force

1960	22%
1970	25%
1980	27%
1991	37%

Source: INDEC, *Censo Nacional de Población.*

Buenos Aires newspapers suggests that, as a consequence, secondary school credentials have become a requisite for formal-sector employment in manual occupations. Such credentials, to be sure, have become much more common among the younger than the mature age groups. In view of employment and educational trends, one can anticipate growing displacement of low-educated mature adults from the urban job market (see Pessino 1995, 229, 244).

What has been the long-range impact of such policy, economic, and labor-force trends on the quality of employment? The impact on labor's earnings has been extreme. Average real wages in manufacturing collapsed by roughly one-third between 1975 and 1982, recovering commensurably from 1982 to 1985, but then collapsing anew by roughly one-third between 1985 and 1990, before creeping upward by just 2 percent from 1990 to 1994 (ECLAC 1983, 29; ECLAC 1987, 52; ECLAC 1995, 75). As a portion of total national income, wage income slid from 45 percent in 1974 to 39 percent in 1980 and 32 percent in 1990. In this setting, the incidence of household poverty in Buenos Aires swelled from 5 percent in 1970 to 27 percent in 1990, and urban household income inequality notably worsened (Beccaria 1993). Among the other signs of deterioration is that full-time employment decreased as a portion of the labor market, from 60 percent in 1986 to 54.5 percent in 1995, as that of over-time, full-time employment increased from 16.6 percent to 41.4 percent, probably as employers sought to avoid new hires and thus the constraint of new employee contracts (author's calculations from INDEC 1985, 1995).

Although the longitudinal data present problems of comparability, they suggest notable growth in Buenos Aires's percentage of informal employment[11] (Tables 7-9). Quite interestingly, however, the evidence reveals decidedly faster growth in informal employment for men than women, a trend that contradicts the hypothesis presented in Chapter 1. It therefore appears that the proportional expansion of informal employment in Buenos Aires has been primarily based on the labor-market dislocations of men. Put differently, women's employment grew at a slower pace than men's in the informal economy, but women displaced men — if at typically lower occupational and pay rungs — in the formal economy's public and private sector tertiary activities[12] (see the chapters this volume on Mexico [8], Venezuela [5], and Chile [6]).

Table 7. Argentina
Labor-Force Profile of Household Heads by Educational Attainment[a]

	Total		No Schooling to Primary Incomplete		Primary Complete to Second Incomplete		Secondary Complete to Tertiary Incomplete		Tertiary Complete	
	1980	1991	1980	1991	1980	1991	1980	1991	1980	1991
Percentage of Total Population[b]			40.0	27.7	43.5	48.2	12.2	17.1	4.4	6.9
Percentage of Total Labor Force			34.6	22.9	46.3	50.0	13.7	18.8	5.4	8.3
Occupational Categories as Percentages of Total Labor Force										
Wage	64.7	60.7	35.1	21.3	45.9	50.8	14.1	19.6	4.9	8.3
Self-employed	24.7	26.9	33.1	26.8	48.9	51.3	12.3	14.5	5.7	6.7
Employer	8.6	10.0	18.1	12.6	50.2	45.8	22.7	27.2	9.0	13.9
Family worker	1.8	2.3	62.3	46.0	32.0	43.0	4.8	9.0	0.7	1.9

Source: INDEC, *Censo Nacional de Población*.
a = For each year, figures for columns (total for 1980 and 1991) and rows (all other categories) may not equal 100 percent due to rounding.
b = Refers to the total population's percentage distribution of household heads, whether or not active in the labor force.

Table 8. Greater Buenos Aires
Structure of Total, Male, and Female Employment by Sector

	1974	1980	1988	1990	1992	1993
Informal[a]	20.1	21.2	23.4	24.9	26.0	27.0
Formal[b]	72.3	71.2	66.8	63.9	63.7	64.7
Domestic service	7.5	7.3	9.8	11.3	10.3	8.7
Male: informal	18.0	19.7	23.5	26.2	28.8	28.0
Male: formal	80.6	78.8	73.5	70.5	70.1	70.4
Male: domestic service	1.4	1.6	3.0	3.3	1.1	1.6
Female: informal	24.8	24.3	23.2	22.6	23.6	25.1
Female: formal	55.3	56.4	55.5	53.3	55.5	54.4
Female: domestic service	19.9	19.0	21.3	24.1	20.9	20.5

Source: Calculations based on INDEC, *Encuesta Permanente de Hogares*.
a = Includes employers and wage workers in firms of no more than five employees, the self-employed with income in the lowest 40%, and family workers.
b = Includes the remainder of employers, wage workers, and the self-employed.

Table 9.
Greater Buenos Aires
Percentage Distribution of Employment by Gender
and Occupational Category

	1974		1980		1988		1990		1993	
	Male	Female	Male	Female	Male	Female	Male	Female	Male	Female
Informal[a]	59.7	40.3	61.9	38.1	63.2	36.8	65.4	34.6	65.4	34.6
Formal[a]	74.8	25.2	73.6	26.4	69.1	30.9	68.2	31.8	68.4	31.6
Domestic service[a]	12.8	87.2	14.5	85.5	19.1	80.9	18.3	81.7	12.1	87.9
Total employed	67.1	32.9	66.7	33.3	62.9	37.1	61.9	38.1	62.7	37.3

Source: Calculations based on INDEC, *Encuesta Permanente de Hogares.*
a = See definitions in Table 8.

The noteworthy growth in the relative weight of precarious and informal employment is due substantially to changes in the labor market's regulatory regime (see Díaz this volume on Chile [6]). During the 1980s, there emerged a de facto business practice of flexible utilization of labor, which was by no means restricted to microenterprises; there is evidence, for instance, that large firms increasingly hired workers through employment agencies in order to dodge the state's employment regulations. And since 1991, the state's policy of labor-contract regulation has legitimized the ever more common business practice of partial or total evasion of social security obligations. In this context, another indicator of employment degradation is that the fraction of workers lacking social security coverage and/or other extra-wage benefits rose from 23.6 percent of wage earners in 1989 to 26.6 percent in 1995.[13]

What, finally, have been the consequences of politico-economic crisis and restructuring for the geography of urban employment? Between 1980 and 1991, net international migration into Argentina fell by one-half, while Buenos Aires's drop in labor demand reduced its attraction to foreign workers (Maguid 1995). In the meantime, the establishment of "industrial protection" districts in provinces such as Tierra del Fuego fostered some centrifugal flow of domestic migrants. Yet, during an era of fiscal crisis, these districts did not emerge as regional development poles, and they failed to generate an internationally competitive sector of export-assembly production. The national population share of intermediate urban agglomerations such as Córdoba, Rosario, and Mendoza rose from 27.9 percent in 1980 to 33.6 percent in 1991 — representing continuity with a longer-range trend — even as Greater Buenos Aires's share barely dipped, from 35.1 percent to 34.7 percent[14] (Vapnarksky 1995, 229). This relational inter-urban demographic change, and the virtual absence of change in Buenos Aires's relation to the wider nation, is likely to have encompassed employment as well (see Vapnarsky 1995, 243-47). To some degree or another, the dimension of inter-urban change is undoubtably linked to the growing diseconomies of Greater Buenos Aires's massive scale and to the dynamics of politico-economic restructuring (see Portes 1989; Roberts 1995). Within that framework, both private and public sector dynamics — such as the geographic dispersion of a significant share of public sector jobs under Menem — as well as household options and decisions stand to have contributed to such inter-urban change. What they have involved in terms of geographic reconfigurations of employment structure and social inequality and to what degree and in what forms they will persist are important research questions. For the time being, merely note that the focus of long-range urban economic prosperity on internationalized finance, high-end services, and manufacturing ensures basic continuity in Buenos Aires's *strategic* hegemony in the national (including national urban) economy and labor market. That is, Buenos Aires is functionally as much or more important than ever as a node of national coordination and control (see Sassen 1994; Roberts 1995; and Oliveira and García this volume on Mexico [8]).

Conclusions

How do this chapter's findings pertain to the volume's series of comparative hypotheses? Even considering that much of the reported job reduction in the central government apparatus involves not actual cuts but organizational decentralization, Menem has orchestrated one of Latin America's most pronounced transfers of employment from the public to private sector (see Díaz this volume on Chile [6]). The longer-range transfer is all the more striking when conceptualized as extending to demilitarization as well. This transfer is embedded within an even longer-range process of painful deindustrialization of the labor market, together with the acceleration of growth in its tertiary portion. Argentina's manufactured exports remain uncompetitive in the world market, although the Southern Cone Common Market's (MERCOSUR) market demand and the Menem government's striking deviations from neoliberal policy have recently boosted the country's industrial exports, led by vehicles and vehicle parts, into neighboring Latin American countries (principally Brazil). Yet, in a setting of pronounced net shrinkage of manufacturing jobs in both the monopolistic and non-monopolistic tiers, it is unclear how much of the sector's surviving jobs have become oriented to export production.

So far, then, the evidence is basically consistent with the predicted course of change. Likewise consistent with the predictions is the feminization of the labor market, a process that began in the 1960s. A key change, however, is that there emerged a countercyclical household emphasis on the entry of female income-earners into the lower rungs of the labor market in response to the mounting employment problems of male household heads. Unexpectedly, the feminization of employment did not extend to manufacturing, which has not developed a significant share of export-platform production. And even though, as hypothesized, labor-market conditions became considerably more precarious and, it would seem, more informal, the trend of informalization did not, as hypothesized, revolve around female workers. On the contrary, the growth rate of informal employment appears to have been faster among males, for whom displacement from decently paid, formal employment was more the norm. Women were more likely to enter the ranks of the economy's newly defined, formal — if generally low-paid — employment (see Oliveira and García on Mexico since the late 1980s this volume, Chapter 8). Still, women came to represent an enlarged percentage of the country's expanded numbers of unemployed workers in the 1990s.

As for the geography of change, it seems that, as anticipated, secondary cities gained in share of the nation's urban employment relative to Greater Buenos Aires. Nevertheless, compared with other Latin American countries, national population and employment in Argentina remained highly concentrated in the capital city's metropolitan agglomeration. Moreover, relative both to secondary cities and to the country at large, Buenos Aires did not lose at all — and quite possibly even advanced — as a strategic site of coordination and control for an internationalizing national economy.

As of late 1996, it appears that the Argentine economy is emerging from the acute downturn that ramified from Mexico's financial and economic crisis of mid-decade. At the same time, though, Menem's neoliberal austerity programs remain in full force, and his determination to subordinate the nation's workers further to the exigencies of transnationalized accumulation has galvanized active labor-union opposition and more generally cut into his bases of political support. In comparative Latin American and world perspective, a fundamental question for Argentina in the late 1990s and beyond is this: Will a large share of workers and their families continue to lose socioeconomic ground, no matter what the nation's macroeconomic performance?

Notes

1. The earlier phase of Peronist government was between 1945 and 1955.

2. That is, as Smith points out, the bloated foreign debts of Brazil and Mexico had been associated with large-scale industrialization during the 1970s.

3. Yet by 1993-1994 the short-term economic gains of low-income urban groups — as reflected in growth in the real minimum wage and a decline in the rate of officially measured poverty during Menem's initial round in office — were already being undercut as the rate of unemployment picked up.

4. Manufacturing rose from 23 percent of total national exports in 1980 to 29 percent in 1990, remaining at no more than that level until spurting to 33 percent in 1994, led by vehicle and vehicle-parts exports to neighboring countries (above all Brazil) in the context of both MERCOSUR and the Argentine government's preferential treatment of the automobile industry. In the same context, Argentina's intra-Latin American exports rose from 19 percent of total national exports in 1985 to 45 percent in 1994 (ECLAC 1995, 84, 88; ECLAC 1996, 111, 156). The country remains extremely weak as an extra-regional exporter of manufactured goods.

5. PREALC (cited in Thomas 1995, 88) reports that the public sector's portion of non-agricultural employment in Argentina increased from 18.9 percent in 1980 to 19.3 percent in 1990 and then dropped to 17.7 percent in 1992. Given painful fiscal austerity, provincial and municipal public sector workers — whose ranks include proportionately fewer professional workers than in the central government — have faced severe deterioration in earnings and job conditions.

6. The data presented in most of the tables refer to Greater Buenos Aires rather than to urban Argentina at large.

7. Domestic and foreign migrants had played a significant role in the growth of Argentina's urban labor force during the period of import-substitution industrialization.

8. Keeping the larger picture in mind, women's labor-force participation in Argentina began to increase in the 1960s (Table 6).

9. The rate of unemployment jumped to 18.6 percent in 1995 — 20.2 percent in Buenos Aires — as the economy contracted. Since the early 1990s, unemployment has been highest in construction, followed by manufacturing (Pessino 1995, 225, 228).

10. The share of employed men with principal jobs in manufacturing dropped from 35.3 percent in 1980 to 29.3 percent in 1991 and 23.9 percent in 1995.

11. The data on urban informal employment include employers, wage workers in microenterprises (consisting of no more than five workers), the non-professional self-employed, and family workers. Of course, if the data included domestic service workers — which quite arguably they should — the labor market's

proportion of informal employment, but not necessarily its rate of growth (see Table 8), would be greater.

12. Recall that women's job losses in manufacturing have been proportionately greater than men's.

13. In 1980, just 12.1 percent of wage earners lacked social security coverage and/or other extra-wage benefits.

14. Greater Buenos Aires's share had increased in 1960-1970 but remained unchanged in 1970-1980 (Vapnarsky 1995, 229). Its share of nationwide population remains among Latin America's highest.

References

Acuña, Carlos H. 1994. "Politics and Economics in the Argentina of the Nineties (Or, Why the Future No Longer Is What It Used to Be)." In *Democracy, Markets, and Structural Reform in Latin America*, eds. William C. Smith, Carlos H. Acuña, and Eduardo A. Gamarra. Coral Gables, Fla.: North-South Center at the University of Miami.

Acuña, C.H., and William C. Smith. 1995. "Política y economía militar en el Cono Sur: democracia, producción de armamentos y carrera armamentista en la Argentina, Brasil y Chile." *Desarrollo Económico* 34(October-December):343-378.

Azpiazu, Daniel. 1991. "Programa de ajuste en la Argentina de los años ochenta: década perdida o decenio regresivo." Buenos Aires: FLACSO, mimeo.

Azpiazu, Daniel. 1994. "La industria argentina ante la privatización, la desregulación y la apertura asimétricas de la economía. La creciente polarización del poder económico." Buenos Aires: FLACSO, mimeo.

Azpiazu, Daniel, Eduardo Basualdo, and M. Khavisse. 1986. *El nuevo poder económico de la Argentina en los años 80.* Buenos Aires: Legasa.

Basualdo, Eduardo. 1992. *Formación de capital y distribución del ingreso durante la desindustrialización.* Buenos Aires: IDEP/ATE.

Beccaria, Luis. 1993. "Reestructuración, empleo y salarios en la Argentina." In *El desafío de la competividad. La industria argentina en transformación*, ed. Bernardo Kosacoff. Buenos Aires: CEPAL/Alianza Editorial.

Bissang, R., C. Bonvecchi, B. Kosacoff, and A. Ramos. 1995. "La transformación industrial en los noventa. Un proceso con final abierto." *Desarrollo Económico* 36(Summer):187-216.

Canitrot, Adolfo. 1994. "Crisis and Transformation of the Argentine State (1978-1992)." In *Democracy, Markets, and Structural Reform in Latin America*, eds. William C. Smith, Carlos H. Acuña, and Eduardo A. Gamarra. Coral Gables, Fla.: North-South Center at the University of Miami.

Cetrángolo, Oscar. 1994. "El nuevo sistema previsional." *Estudios de Trabajo* 7:211-243.

Cortés, Rosalía. 1985a. "Cambios en el mercado de trabajo urbano argentino: 1976-1983." *Serie Documentos e Informes de Investigación.* Buenos Aires: FLACSO.

Cortés, Rosalía. 1985b. "La seguridad social en la Argentina: las obras sociales." *Serie Documentos e Informes de Investigación.* Buenos Aires: FLACSO.

Cortés, Rosalía. 1986. "La seguridad social en la Argentina: el sistema provisional." *Documentos e Informes de Investigación.* Buenos Aires: FLACSO.

Cortés, Rosalía, and Adriana Marshall. 1993. "State Social Intervention and Labour Regulation: The Case of Argentina." *Cambridge Journal of Economics* 14(4):391-408.

ECLAC (Economic Commission for Latin America and the Caribbean). 1983. *Economic Survey of Latin America and the Caribbean.* Santiago, Chile: ECLAC.

ECLAC. 1987. *Economic Survey of Latin America and the Caribbean.* Santiago, Chile: ECLAC.

ECLAC. 1995. *Economic Survey of Latin America and the Caribbean 1994-1995.* Santiago, Chile: ECLAC.

ECLAC. 1996. *Statistical Yearbook for Latin America and the Caribbean 1995.* Santiago, Chile: ECLAC.

Feldman, Ernesto, and Juan Sommer. 1984. *Crisis financiera y endeudamiento externo en la Argentina.* Buenos Aires: Centro Editor de América Latina.

INDEC (Instituto de Estadística y Censos). 1970, 1981, 1991. *Censo nacional de población.* Buenos Aires: INDEC.

INDEC. 1974-1995. *Encuesta permanente de hogares.* Buenos Aires: INDEC

Kosacoff, Bernardo. 1993. *El desafío de la competividad. La industria argentina en transformación.* Buenos Aires: CEPAL/Alianza Editorial.

LASR (*Latin American Special Reports*). 1996. "Latin American Industry: Coping with Open Markets." June. London.

Maquid, Alicia. 1995. "L'inmigration des pays limitrophes dan l'Argentine des annes 90, mythes et realites." *Revue Europeene de Migrations Internationales* 11(2):1-21.

Manzetti, Luis. 1995. "Argentina: Market Reforms and Old-Style Politics." *North-South Focus* 4(3). Coral Gables, Fla.: North-South Center at the University of Miami.

Marshall, Adriana. 1988. *Políticas sociales: el modelo neoliberal.* Buenos Aires: Legasa.

McCoy, Jennifer, Andrés Serbín, William C. Smith, and Andrés Stambouli, eds. 1995. *Venezuelan Democracy under Stress.* Coral Gables, Fla.: North-South Center at the University of Miami.

Orlansky, Dora. 1989. "Empleo público y condiciones de trabajo, 1960-1986." *Desarrollo Económico* 113:63-86.

Orlansky, Dora. 1992. "Empleo público y condiciones de trabajo, 1960-1986." *Desarrollo Económico* 113(29):63-86.

Pessino, C. 1995. "La anatomía del desempleo." *Desarrollo Económico* 36(Summer):223-262.

Portes, Alejandro. 1989. "Urbanization during the Years of the Crisis." *Latin American Research Review* 24(3):7-44.

Roberts, Bryan. 1995. *The Making of Citizens: Cities of Peasants Revisited.* London: Arnold.

Sassen, Saskia. 1994. *Cities in a World Economy.* Thousand Oaks, Calif.: Pine Forge Press.

SCR (*Southern Cone Report*). 1996a. "Menem Squares Up to Peronist Unions." October 17:2. London.

SCR. 1996b. "Argentina's New Labour Squeeze." October 17:4-5. London.

SCR. 1996c. "Argentina's Reactivation Prospects: Upswing Has Begun, but Social & Political Questions Remain." December 27:4-5. London.

Smith, William C. 1991. *Authoritarianism and the Crisis of the Argentine Political Economy.* Stanford, Calif.: Stanford University Press, paperback ed.

Thomas, Jim. 1995. "The New Economic Model and Labour Markets in Latin America." In *The New Economic Model in Latin America and Its Impact on Income Distribution and Poverty,* ed. Victor Bulmer-Thomas. New York: St. Martin's Press.

Vapnarsky, C.A. 1995. "Primacia y macrocefalia en la Argentina: la transformación del sistema de asentamiento humano desde 1950." *Desarrollo Económico* 35(July-September):227-254.

Chapter 8

Socioeconomic Transformation and Labor Markets in Urban Mexico

Orlandina de Oliveira and Brígida García

Two overlapping transformations are exerting a powerful impact on Latin America's urban labor markets. The first is the heightened geographic mobility of capital — made possible by new technologies of communication, transportation, and production — that permits investment to flow to those geographic areas where production costs are lower and myriad other conditions are more favorable to firms (for example, government stability, regulations, and subsidies; economic infrastructure, labor supply and relations; and market access). The second transformation is a profound national and supranational realignment of capital-labor relations, including state policies of labor deregulation and the sociodemographic reorganization of workforces (for example, higher proportions of female and contingent labor), which has rendered workforces more docile and cheaper (Carrillo 1993; Marshall 1987 and 1988; Portes and Benton 1984; Rakowski 1994; Roberts 1995; Sassen 1994; Tokman 1991).

The impact of these transformations on Mexico's urban labor market has intensified since the onset of the economic crisis in 1982. Between 1982 and 1988, Mexico's gross domestic product (GDP) per capita and average real wages dropped precipitously (Chapter 1 this volume, Table 2), as the currency was devalued some 40 times and inflation came to exceed 100 percent (see Casar and Ros 1987; Lustig 1992; Tello 1987). Following its implementation of harsh stabilization measures, the government of Miguel de la Madrid (1982-1988) began more definitively to dismantle Mexico's model of statist, import-substitution industrialization in favor of a new, internationalized alternative (Cook, Middlebrook, and Horcasitas 1994; Fernando Cortés and Rubalcava 1993; Orozco Orozco 1992; Orozco and Lozano 1992; Ruíz Durán 1992; Sánchez Daza 1992). The government's course of action was facilitated by the highly centralized organization of the civilian-authoritarian state, which — in a sociopolitical context of impoverishment, fragmentation, and large-scale migration to the United States — enabled the de la Madrid administration to counteract mounting oppositional currents in city and countryside.

Orlandina de Oliveira and Brígida García are professors of sociology at El Colegio de México.

Translated by Richard Tardanico and Vanessa Gray.

Partial macroeconomic recovery ensued during the subsequent government of Carlos Salinas de Gortari (1988-1994), under which policies of neoliberal reform and transnationalization gained momentum, culminating in a constitutional reform that permits the commercialization of *ejidos* (communal landholdings) and in the North American Free Trade Agreement (NAFTA). In 1994-1995, however, the top-down orchestration of restructuring, the economic upturn, the official projections of NAFTA-led modernization and prosperity, and the Salinas group's declarations of neoliberal triumph were met with a series of crushing blows: the Zapatista guerrilla uprising in the southern periphery of Chiapas; the assassination of Salinas' officially appointed presidential successor, Luis Donaldo Colosio; and the "peso crisis," which exposed the speculative, tottering pillars of the economy's apparent rebound. In 1995, Mexico's GDP per capita dropped by 6.9 percent, inflation climbed to some 54 percent, open unemployment reached an unprecedented 7.6 percent, nearly 18,000 companies stopped making contributions to the social security system, and some 800,000 formal sector jobs were lost. These and other dimensions of hardship, turmoil, and uncertainty continue to define Mexico's fundamental realities and challenges (*La Jornada* 1995-1996; *Reforma* 1995-1996).

Within this framework, the first section of this analysis of labor markets and social inequality in urban Mexico describes the tertiarization of employment between 1982 and 1992. In this regard, Mexico's manufacturing sector — ranked second to Brazil's as Latin America's largest and most advanced — has been acutely reconfigured by economic crises, privatization, and transnationalization. Since the early 1980s, Mexico's volume of manufactured exports has leaped, due principally to the vigorous expansion of low-wage, export-assembly production along the northern border. Yet, manufacturing's share of total employment has not experienced growth, but rather a substantial decline, as a redefined sectoral and occupational grid of service activity has led the way in job growth.

The second section examines the proportional growth of nonwage employment and the deepened insecurity of labor conditions. It documents the link between the redefined grid of tertiary employment and the proliferation of precarious income-earning activities, underscoring the degraded position of most workers in the formal and informal economies.

The third section contrasts a surge in the labor-force participation of Mexican women with a modest rise among men. In doing so, it charts the relationship of this gendered pattern with the reorganization of tertiary employment and the growth of nonwage and precarious employment. The section also discusses the nexus between the expansion of export-assembly production and feminization of manufacturing employment.

In view of Mexico's history of profound geographic differences and inequalities, this analysis identifies the most basic labor-market changes that have emerged in the country's principal cities, which are located in the northern, central, and southeastern regions.[1] The employment structures of central, nonborder northern, and southeastern Mexico — the zones where import-substitution industrialization was anchored — have been hit hard by economic crisis and restructuring, which simultaneously have speeded up the transformations and bolstered the importance within manufacturing of export-platform production and employment on the northern frontier (Guirette López et al. 1993). Thus, even as the nation's domestic product has become no less concentrated in Mexico City, its employment has become more dispersed toward the transnational production complexes of the north (Cordera and González 1991; Garza 1991; Garza and Rivera 1994; Pérez Cadena 1993; Romo 1993; see Roberts 1995 and Sassen 1994). Nevertheless, not to be overlooked is that the nation's employment became considerably more oriented to tertiary activities rather than manufacturing.

Tertiarization of Employment

Tertiary employment is quite heterogenous (Browning 1972; Roberts 1995). Recognition of the distinctions between and within producer services (such as finance and business services), social services (education, health care, and government), distributive services (commerce and transportation), and personal services (such as leisure, restaurants, and hotels) is essential to understanding the recomposition of Mexico's urban labor markets under economic crisis and structural adjustment.

The country's nonagricultural labor force traditionally has been concentrated in the tertiary economy. There is little evidence for the commonplace notion, however, that unskilled employment in petty commerce and the like was principally responsible for the expansion of Mexico's urban labor force during the post-Second World War era of import-substitution industrialization. Diverse studies demonstrate precisely the opposite: that manufacturing, producer services, and social services — the very activities that defined urban-industrial and occupational upgrading cross-nationally during that era — were the leading sources of employment growth (García 1975 and 1988; Muñoz 1985; Muñoz and Oliveira 1976).

In 1980 — before the onset of economic crisis — 46 percent of urban Mexican employment was generated by manufacturing and, within the tertiary economy, 31 percent by commerce and 23 percent by producer, transportation, social, and personal services. By 1989, though, just 37 percent of urban employment was in manufacturing, while employment in commerce had risen to 33 percent and services to 30 percent (Garza 1991). The decade's surge in the proportion of tertiary employment was faster for men than women. Between 1979 and 1991, the portion of the male labor force in the tertiary economy rose from 34 to 41 percent, as that of the female labor force remained near 70 percent [2] (ECSO 1979; ENE 1991).

As emphasized in Chapter 1, the long-range dynamics of tertiarization in Latin America cannot be understood without reference to the importance of public sector employment in the growth and upgrading of the region's urban workforces and in the extension of the rights and loyalties of citizenship during the import-substitution era. The creation of public sector employment on a large scale was indeed vital to Mexico's political, economic, and social transformations during the mid-twentieth century (Blanco 1995; Oliveira and Roberts 1994; Roberts 1995). In the setting of the subsequent dramatic reversal of import-substitution policies and the application of severe austerity measures, it is surprising that the share of the public sector in total employment remained at approximately 17.5 percent between 1982 and 1992. This absence of net change, however, encompassed both an upswing and a downswing. The portion of national employment in the public sector rose from 17.5 to 22.5 percent during the de la Madrid administration (1982-1988) but then dropped to 17.5 percent under Salinas de Gortari (1988-1994) as neoliberal reorganization accelerated. Yet, notwithstanding the absence of net change in the fraction of public sector jobs, the composition of such employment was altered, as policies of austerity and privatization slashed the share of its jobs in state-owned enterprises from 23.3 percent in 1988 to 10.8 percent in 1993. At the same time, public sector employment underwent a striking process of organizational and geographic decentralization, as provincial government's share of such jobs soared from 14.5 to 43.7 percent (INEGI 1988 and 1994; see Blanco 1995).

Bearing in mind the national contraction of manufacturing employment since the early 1980s, the more rapid expansion of tertiary employment for men than women, and the net stagnation but reorganization of public sector employment, this chapter now turns to urban Mexico's regional pattern of employment tertiarization.

Between 1982 and 1992, proportional shifts into manufacturing employment took place only in those cities where, as real wages tumbled and structural adjustment policies facilitated economic transnationalization, export-platform output played a leading or rapidly expanding role. The percentage of male and female jobs in manufacturing dropped in most cities in central Mexico (such as Mexico City and Guadalajara), the nonborder north (such as Monterrey), and the southeast (such as Veracruz), which had been the focal points of import-substitution industrialization and where males had accounted for a comparatively high portion of local employment[3] (Oliveira 1989a; Table 1). For example, in Mexico City an average of 750 manufacturing firms closed annually during the 1980s (Garza 1991). In Monterrey, more manufacturing firms opened than closed, but the new firms tended to be smaller than the older firms, while the survivors among the older firms replaced large numbers of workers with labor-saving technologies (Garza 1994; Garza and Rivera 1994). In Veracruz, which had been the principal supplier of pipelines and ships for the government-owned petroleum company PEMEX (Petróleos de México), there probably began a decoupling between the oil industry and local manufacturing.

In contrast to the deindustrialization of employment in the central, nonborder northern, and southeastern zones was the increase in the percentage of male and female employment in manufacturing in the northern frontier, where such employment was feminized the most. The relative increase occurred mainly in Nuevo Laredo and secondarily in Matamoros, upstart sites of export-platform production where garment- and electronics-assembly predominated,[4] rather than in the long-established sites of Ciudad Juárez and Tijuana, where export activities are more diversified (Table 1). Nonetheless, among the northern border cities, manufacturing's share of employment was highest in Ciudad Juárez, where it represented about 33 percent of the male and 40 percent of the female labor force (Table 1). More specific information for the export-platform industry (*maquiladoras*) indicates a sustained proportional increase in the number of blue-collar workers, along with an expansion of the male percentage of blue-collar workers in all border cities (INEGI 1990-1995).

Tertiarization of female and male employment was greatest, of course, in central, nonborder northern, and southeastern Mexico, where deindustrialization of employment was most drastic. For men and women, tertiarization was concentrated not in producer and social services, but in distributive and personal services (Oliveira and García 1993; see Roberts 1995 and Sassen 1994). As discussed in the next section, this reflects the deterioration of labor-market conditions in general, and, for women, tightened pressure to combine income-earning initiatives with household responsibilities.

Nonwage and Precarious Employment

Informal employment is typically defined as consisting of some combination of the following: nonprofessional nonwage workers, wage workers in microenterprises and low-productivity services, and unpaid family workers; workers not covered by social security or protected by labor regulations; or simply poor workers in general (Klein and Tokman 1988; Portes and Benton 1984; PREALC 1983; Rakowski 1994; Roberts 1995). Some studies operationalize informal employment in terms of the characteristics of firms, others in terms of the characteristics of workers, and still others in terms of regimes of labor regulation (García 1988; Oliveira and Roberts 1993; Rendón and Salas 1992; see Díaz this volume, Chapter 6). Given this diversity, this section charts patterns of nonwage employment — a commonly used proxy for unregulated, low-skill employment — that allow analysis of the data collected by Mexico's official employment surveys (García 1988; see note 2). It is not assumed, however, that nonwage employment is synonymous with the lowest earnings and the worst conditions. Research on Mexico and elsewhere indicates, on the contrary, that, under circumstances of economic crisis and restructuring, nonwage employment is often more remunerative and otherwise more desirable than wage employment (Pacheco Gómez Muñoz 1994; Rakowski 1994; Roberts 1995; see Chapter 1 this volume). In any case, nonwage employment is expected to rise as a percentage of overall employment not only because of the worsened economic hardships of households but also the reconfiguration of income-earning opportunities under longer-range social and economic restructuring, including the redefinition of gender relations within households (see García and Oliveira 1994).

Nonwage jobs rose from 33.7 percent of national employment in 1979 to 38.3 percent in 1995. This increase is important, but by no means abrupt[5] (ECSO 1979; ENE 1995; see Oliveira and García 1993; Rendón and Salas 1992). Yet during the crisis years of 1982 to 1987, the increase was marked

Table 1.
Percentages of Male and Female Employment in
Manufacturing and Tertiary Activities

	Male				Female			
Cities	Manufac-turing		Tertiary		Manufac-turing		Tertiary	
	1986	1992	1986	1992	1986	1992	1986	1992
Northern Border								
Ciudad Juárez	32.9	33.3	55.3	56.3	46.8	41.7	52.7	57.6
Matamoros	23.5	26.4	58.9	57.3	43.6	48.6	55.3	50.0
Nuevo Laredo	12.9	22.1	68.7	65.7	15.8	25.9	84.2	72.7
Tijuana	22.2	23.7	64.0	65.2	34.1	24.5	64.9	74.6
Northern-Nonborder								
Chihuahua	22.0	20.2	60.9	62.4	26.1	25.5	72.4	72.6
Monterrey	33.0	28.7	53.1	58.5	19.4	20.3	79.6	78.4
Tampico	12.6	20.9	54.9	63.1	7.1	12.0	85.8	86.8
Torreón	19.9	20.0	61.4	62.9	18.2	19.1	79.6	78.4
Central								
Mexico City	27.6	24.2	64.9	69.4	20.2	17.5	77.8	81.6
Guadalajara	33.3	28.0	54.8	63.1	25.9	21.2	72.5	77.6
León	50.9	46.2	42.6	45.9	34.6	31.4	64.6	66.9
Puebla	30.4	28.3	56.1	59.1	16.5	17.0	79.2	80.4
San Luis Potosí	24.0	23.5	62.0	63.1	17.3	16.8	80.9	81.5
Southeastern								
Mérida	20.1	18.5	64.0	68.4	18.9	11.7	79.6	85.6
Orizaba	29.9	28.4	49.2	48.6	14.9	12.6	82.4	84.5
Veracruz	18.5	13.4	66.7	73.5	8.9	7.6	88.1	89.7

* Tertiary includes distributive services (commerce, communications, and transportation), social services (education, health care, and government), producer services (finance, real estate, and professional services), and personal services (recreational services, restaurants, hotels, and others).
Source: Encuesta Nacional de Empleo Urbano (ENEU), second trimester of 1986, 1992.

Table 2.
Percentages of Male and Female Employment in Wage and Nonwage Activities
(1986-1992)

Cities	Male				Female			
	Wage		Nonwage		Wage		Nonwage	
	1986	1992	1986	1992	1986	1992	1986	1992
Northern Border								
Ciudad Juárez	66.7	70.0	29.2	24.9	85.1	80.1	14.4	18.7
Matamoros	66.3	64.1	25.1	25.7	81.0	85.5	17.4	13.1
Nuevo Laredo	66.3	69.3	24.1	25.2	77.1	80.5	21.1	18.1
Tijuana	62.4	65.2	28.8	29.1	79.2	76.9	18.7	21.7
Northern-Nonborder								
Chihuahua	69.4	66.4	24.5	23.1	80.5	83.6	18.5	14.4
Monterrey	76.8	72.8	18.1	21.0	80.8	75.8	18.4	22.7
Tampico	69.7	64.4	26.0	30.2	76.0	64.0	23.2	34.8
Torreón	66.8	65.2	26.2	26.7	71.1	72.0	27.9	27.1
Central								
Mexico City	73.0	69.4	22.1	25.5	73.3	71.9	25.7	26.6
Guadalajara	65.4	63.8	27.9	29.2	73.6	67.3	24.7	31.0
León	69.3	66.7	22.7	26.5	77.2	73.3	20.8	25.5
Puebla	65.8	63.6	27.8	31.3	65.8	66.0	32.9	32.6
San Luis Potosí	72.8	69.1	19.6	22.7	75.9	78.0	22.6	20.3
Southeastern								
Mérida	67.6	69.3	25.2	23.1	66.3	76.4	31.6	22.2
Orizaba	61.8	63.5	32.0	30.1	55.6	59.9	42.0	38.1
Veracruz	70.6	65.7	21.3	26.0	67.7	66.4	29.8	29.9

Source: Encuesta Nacional de Empleo Urbano (ENEU), second trimester of 1986, 1992.

for 20- to 49-year-old women, whose share of nonwage employment jumped from 7.6 to 18.5 percent. A sign of the role of economic hardship in driving this expansion is that nonwage employment rose mostly among women with children, whose fraction of such employment doubled. Signs that nonwage work spread most among poor households are that the fastest growth was among women with no more than primary schooling and that the number of street vendors nearly doubled (García and Oliveira 1994). During the crisis years, the net growth of nonwage employment was restricted to central and southeastern cities, many of them (Mexico City, Puebla, San Luís Potosí, and Veracruz) areas where the import-substitution development model was based (Oliveira 1989a).

Macroeconomic improvement beginning in 1986 altered this distribution of growth in nonwage employment from the standpoints of both gender and geography. Nonwage employment grew faster for men than for women, and for both groups its reach extended to the more educated layers of the workforce. The geographic focus of such growth for men was the cities of central Mexico. For women the geographic focus shifted to Ciudad Juárez and Tijuana, the leading sites of export-assembly manufacturing on the northern border, as well as to Monterrey, Guadalajara, León, and Tampico, cities of nonborder northern and central Mexico that had escaped the previous net expansion of female nonwage jobs.

Can it therefore be concluded that for men and women the growth of nonwage jobs became linked less to the subsistence responses of households than to the revamping of manufacturing production, as the larger firms began to rely more on the subcontracting of production to smaller firms and to households in the informal sector (see Alonso 1984; Arias 1988; Benería and Roldán 1987; Escobar 1986; González de la Rocha 1986; Marshall 1987; Portes and Benton 1984; Roberts 1995)? The evidence for such a shift is sparse, quite possibly reflecting the fundamental problem of documenting changes in the prevalence of underground economic activities. As far as can be gauged, nonwage jobs grew as a fraction of manufacturing employment not nationally but in urban areas of less than 100,000 inhabitants (ENE 1991; García and Oliveira 1994). This implies that nonwage work became more prevalent only in the marginal, craft segments of manufacturing — probably geared to local and regional markets — that were struggling to survive in the face of intensified competition. The inadequacy of the data and the acceleration of restructuring since the implementation of NAFTA and the onset of the peso crisis in 1994-1995 point to the need for additional research on this topic.

The concept of precarious employment is broader in scope than that of informal employment. It encompasses the gamut of jobs within and beyond the reach of state regulation that falls short of standards established during the import-substitution era, such as social security coverage, affiliation with labor unions, and amount and regularity of workhours and pay. A basic argument of neoliberal theory is that such standards represent distortions in market efficiency and thus should be diluted or eliminated in order to raise labor's productivity. Therefore, a rise is anticipated in the incidence of precarious employment as the state's neoliberal policies reverse labor's political, economic, and social gains of the pre-crisis years (Carrillo 1993; De la Garza 1993; Marshall 1987; Pries 1993; Roberts 1995; see Cortez and Lacabana on Venezuela [5], Díaz on Chile [6], and Cortés on Argentina [7] this volume). This hypothesis is examined by first evaluating data on changes in the access of male and female wage workers to extra-wage job benefits (Christmas bonuses, profit-sharing arrangements, paid vacations, housing loans, health insurance, and social security) between 1986 and 1992, as the labor market was deregulated (Table 3). Then male and female data on the average earnings of wage and nonwage workers in 1992 are evaluated, anticipating that wage workers — who are more likely to have access to extra-wage benefits — earn more than nonwage workers (Table 4).

The percentage of male workers not receiving the above benefits indeed rose in some two-thirds of the cities surveyed, most consistently in some of the import-substitution cities of central, nonborder northern, and southeastern Mexico (Table 3). The corresponding percentage of female workers rose in fewer than one-half of the cities. Where male access to such benefits became not less but more common was in some of the north's nonborder and border cities — specifically, Torreón, Matamoros, and Nuevo Laredo — perhaps as the latest wave of transnationalized restructuring drew a notable swath of male workers from small to larger enterprises in manufacturing and services. The cases of expanded female access occurred on a wider geographic scale. In this regard, studies suggest that men have tended to shift to less protected but more remunerative jobs, while women have tended to give priority to more protected but less remunerative jobs because they provide family access to extra-wage benefits (Oliveira and García 1994).

As for earnings, men, not surprisingly, make more than women on average in both wage and nonwage occupations (Table 4). More pertinent to the hypothesis is that, as expected, wage earnings are higher than nonwage earnings for women in virtually every city, but, unexpectedly, for men in no more than about one-third of the cities. That is, the inter-city tendency involves higher earnings among women in wage jobs than among men in nonwage jobs. There is no longitudinal data on this gender pattern, and hence it cannot be confirmed whether the profile represents continuity or discontinuity with the past. Regarding 1992, however, the male pattern of higher earnings in nonwage rather than wage jobs appears most consistent in the central and nonborder-northern regions, whose cities were pre-crisis bulwarks of import-substitution manufacturing, but it also characterizes Ciudad Juárez and Tijuana, the most industrially advanced of the northern border cities. The male pattern is most common in commerce and least in manufacturing; the female pattern is more consistent across economic sectors.

In short, as female and male employment became more tertiarized, nonwage work generally became a source of higher earnings than wage work for men but not women. How this configuration of occupational earnings unfolded, and continues to unfold, is an intriguing question from the perspective of the territorial, class, and gendered restructuring of Mexican urban employment (Table 4 and Oliveira and García 1993).

Table 3.
Percentages of Employed Males and Females Not Receiving
Extra-Wage Job Benefits

Cities	Males		Females	
	1986	1992	1986	1992
Northern Border				
Ciudad Juárez	18.5	19.5	12.6	11.4
Matamoros	23.5	19.8	11.9	11.3
Nuevo Laredo	33.6	28.2	27.9	23.9
Tijuana	22.3	31.4	13.1	18.1
Northern-Nonborder				
Chihuahua	12.3	17.1	8.0	12.0
Monterrey	13.9	16.1	17.3	17.7
Tampico	14.4	16.8	15.6	15.9
Torreón	20.5	18.1	18.4	13.8
Central				
Mexico City	21.3	25.0	19.3	16.8
Guadalajara	22.2	31.9	18.3	23.4
León	32.6	31.9	34.6	28.1
Puebla	22.2	29.2	23.6	27.9
San Luis Potosí	17.7	22.5	20.3	22.7
Southeastern				
Mérida	23.6	22.1	21.2	13.5
Orizaba	29.5	32.7	32.8	22.2
Veracruz	17.7	22.9	23.2	20.3

Source: Encuesta Nacional de Empleo Urbano (ENEU), second trimester of 1986, 1992.

Table 4.
Percentages of Employed Males and Females in
Low-Income Wage and Nonwage Jobs*
(1992)

Cities	Males		Females	
	Wage	Nonwage	Wage	Nonwage
Northern Border				
Ciudad Juárez	48.2	33.2	61.8	62.4
Matamoros	29.0	48.0	24.5	79.9
Nuevo Laredo	51.8	51.7	60.6	63.9
Tijuana	24.5	12.8	35.5	44.5
Northern-Nonborder				
Chihuahua	39.8	19.9	53.1	47.5
Monterrey	41.4	38.9	49.4	60.8
Tampico	44.4	60.6	65.0	88.4
Torreón	52.5	53.0	60.2	73.7
Central				
Mexico City	55.4	54.8	60.7	81.6
Guadalajara	45.5	36.5	62.6	71.9
León	27.4	16.5	51.1	53.5
Puebla	44.3	46.8	59.6	78.0
San Luis Potosí	45.6	45.0	59.2	77.0
Southeastern				
Mérida	54.7	55.5	60.9	84.6
Orizaba	62.1	56.7	67.0	87.2
Veracruz	43.6	54.4	54.1	79.9

* Low-income refers to less than twice the minimum wage.
  Source: Encuesta Nacional de Empleo Urbano (ENEU), second trimester of 1986, 1992.

Gendered Labor-Force Participation

Consistent with the volume's other case studies, urban Mexico's labor force became more feminized between 1979 and 1995. As the rate of female labor-force participation climbed from 21.5 to 34.5 percent, that of male participation rose to a lesser degree, from 71 to 78.2 percent (ENE 1995; Oliveira and García 1993).

The upturns in women's and men's participation were concentrated during the economic contraction of the early to mid-1980s, which, as elsewhere in Latin America, pressured households into sending more members into the job market (Fernando Cortés 1988; González de la Rocha 1989; Selva 1985). During that period, young single, childless women with intermediate to high levels of education maintained the augmented rates of participation that they had attained during the 1970s, as integral to state-centered, import-substitution development was vigorous, waged employment growth in modern services — including the public sector (Oliveira 1989b; Oliveira and García 1990; Pedrero and Rendón 1982; Rendón 1990). Joining their ranks in the 1980s, however, were older, married women with children and with less schooling (Oliveira and García 1993; see Cortés on Argentina this volume, Chapter 7). The countercyclical surge in women's labor-force participation was oriented to nonwage activities in distributive and personal services in most of urban Mexico but to wage jobs in export-platform manufacturing on the northern border. The rise in men's participation remained predominately within the confines of wage employment — albeit at much reduced average pay — but shifted more abruptly than women's into tertiary employment (Cruz and Zenteno 1989; Oliveira 1989a; Oliveira and García 1990; Pacheco Gómez Muñoz 1988; Pedrero 1990).

As the economy picked up after the mid-1980s, no marked changes occurred in the national rates of female and male labor-force participation. There were sizable increases, though, in the female and male participation rates in the largest metropolitan areas, Mexico City and Guadalajara, and in the cities of the nonborder north, such as the heavy-industry city of Monterrey. These increases were linked to employment tertiarization (Table 5). In the nonborder north, the upswing in women's participation was mostly from a lower baseline than in the other zones surveyed. On the northern border, the female and male rates of participation rose only in Nuevo Laredo, due to its rapid growth of export-assembly manufacturing (Table 5).

Homogenization was the trend for women's labor-force participation rates, even as the continuation of long-term growth in the percentage of female professional and technical employment fostered occupational differentiation and inequality among women (Oliveira and García 1993). In this respect, the participation rates of older, married women with children and with lesser schooling converged upward toward those of their younger, single, childless, and more educated counterparts. For males, in contrast, young single men with at least high school diplomas clearly headed the post-1982 increase in labor-force participation (Oliveira and García 1993).

Table 5.
Male and Female Rates of Labor-Force Participation*

	Male		Female	
Cities	**1986**	**1992**	**1986**	**1992**
Northern Border	72.1	73.9	32.7	33.9
Matamoros	74.3	73.2	36.9	37.6
Nuevo Laredo	69.3	74.5	24.3	30.5
Tijuana	71.3	72.2	28.3	31.1
Northern-Nonborder				
Chihuahua	67.4	72.1	29.7	33.1
Monterrey	67.5	75.5	25.2	34.1
Tampico	69.8	72.6	26.9	36.1
Torreón	68.4	72.2	30.6	33.4
Central				
Mexico City	70.6	74.1	35.9	38.1
Guadalajara	74.0	78.4	32.1	41.1
León	76.0	75.8	27.2	28.1
Puebla	67.7	69.9	30.1	32.9
San Luis Potosí	65.6	67.0	29.2	29.0
Southeastern				
Mérida	70.0	69.4	34.6	31.8
Orizaba	71.0	67.6	32.7	28.2
Veracruz	73.1	73.3	34.0	35.9

* Twelve years of age and older
Source: Encuesta Nacional de Empleo Urbano (ENEU), second trimester of 1986, 1992.

Therefore, women are entering more the low-skill, low-wage tier of an urban economy that is affording few job alternatives, the ramifications of which are profound for the class and gender structures of Mexican society.

Conclusions

To encapsulate these findings from the viewpoint of the cross-national hypotheses presented in Chapter 1, public sector employment did not, as hypothesized, contract absolutely or relatively. As a percentage of overall employment, however, it peaked in the late 1980s and shrunk by the early 1990s to its level of a decade earlier. Consistent with the other hypotheses on sectoral change is that manufacturing employment became notably more oriented to export and low-wage production, whose growth has accelerated since the inauguration of NAFTA and the massive devaluation of the peso in 1994-1995. Nonetheless, manufacturing decreased as a portion of total employment, as tertiarization intensified. While this decrease in manufacturing's share of jobs coincides with the cross-national prediction, it may come as a surprise to many observers in light of Mexico's boom in export-platform production.

Precarious and nonwage employment became more prevalent during the period, as anticipated, although the nonwage component of change appears less pronounced than often portrayed. For men, average earnings were commonly higher in nonwage than wage jobs. Nonwage employment remained most prevalent in commerce. More intriguing is the tentative finding that, contrary to much discussion in the literature on Latin American restructuring, nonwage employment did not grow significantly as a share of jobs in Mexican manufacturing, although it seemingly did become more common in craft production, at least in small cities. To reiterate, however, this finding may reflect the notorious deficiency of large-scale surveys in uncovering irregular forms of employment.

Consistent with a longer-term trend, the Mexican workforce, as predicted, became more feminized, as women's rate of participation rose faster than men's. While greater differentiation and inequality characterized both female and male employment, change in the demographic composition of the workforce differed among women and men. Older, married women with children and with lower levels of schooling became more common in the female workforce, a shift that occurred during the economic crisis of the early 1980s and persisted throughout the subsequent years of moderate recovery. Conversely, young men with higher levels of schooling enlarged their share of the male workforce. The degree of recomposition of the female workforce largely represented the response of households to the intensification of economic hardship, as less experienced, less-skilled women sought employment to mitigate the loss of family income. The recomposition of the male workforce essentially represented both the squeezing of many men from low-skill employment and the reorientation of alternative employment to skilled workers, leaving low-skilled, older men increasingly marginalized economically (see Cortés on Argentina [7] this volume).

A striking feature of the reorganization of Mexico's urban labor market since the early 1980s is the pronounced geographic differentiation of sectoral, occupational, and gender changes. The most basic spatial tendency represents a sharp departure from that of the import-substitution period: Even as Mexico City has maintained its hegemony in the financial market, advanced services, and government decisionmaking, its hegemony as a source of employment has considerably diminished, as job growth has accelerated the most in northern Mexico's transnationalized zones of manufacturing and services (see Garza and Rivera 1994). Attention to the spatial decentralization of employment has focused on the feminization of manufacturing jobs. Receiving insufficient attention has been the decentralization of male jobs in manufacturing and of female jobs in the tertiary sector. The gender pattern of dispersion of public sector jobs from central to provincial government is another topic that merits research.

This chapter began by emphasizing the impact of the transnationalized mobility of capital and the reconfiguration of capital-labor relations on Latin America's labor markets. In this setting, Mexico arguably joins Chile as the region's major economies that have undergone the most thorough overhauls from import-substitution to export production. Mexico appears to stand alone, however, in the degree to which such overhaul has involved not only functional but geographic realignment. This combination represents the national manifestation of a worldwide process whose social and territorial losers in Mexico have far outnumbered its winners.

Notes

1. For our purposes, the central region includes the states of Aguascalientes, Colima, the Federal District (of which Mexico City is a part), Mexico, Guanajuato, Hidalgo, Jalisco, Michoacán, Morelos, Puebla, Querétaro, San Luis Potosí, Tlaxcala, and Zacatecas. The northern region includes Baja California, Baja California Sur, Chihuahua, Coahuila, Durango, Nayarit, Nuevo León, Sinaloa, Sonora, and Tamaulipas. The southeastern region includes Campeche, Chiapas, Guerrero, Oaxaca, Quintana Roo, Tabasco, Veracruz, and Yucatán.

2. For the chapter in general, the data are derived mostly from national and urban occupational surveys, which are more comparable longitudinally than the employment data derived from the population censuses of 1980 and 1990.

3. The data on regional employment change between 1982 and 1986 are reported in Oliveira 1989a.

4. The apparent increase in male employment in manufacturing in the Gulf city of Tampico seems to be an artifact of statistical reclassification.

5. Nonwage employment largely consists of self-employment (rather than employers and unpaid workers) for men and women, but particularly for men.

References

Alonso, José A. 1984. "Mujer y trabajo en México." In *El obrero mexicano*, Vol. 2, 214-274. Mexico, D.F.: Siglo XXI/Instituto de Investigaciones Sociales de la Universidad Autónoma de México.

Arias, Patricia. 1988. "La pequeña empresa en el occidente rural." *Estudios Sociológicos* 6:405-436.

Benería, Lourdes, and Martha Roldán. 1987. *The Crossroads of Class and Gender: Industrial Homework, Subcontracting and Household Dynamics in Mexico City*. Chicago: University of Chicago Press.

Blanco, Mercedes. 1995. *Empleo público en la administración central mexicana. Evolución y tendencias (1920-1988)*. Mexico, D.F.: Centro de Investigaciones y Estudios Superiores en Antropología Social.

Browning, Harley. 1972. "Some Problematics of the Tertiarization Process." Paper delivered at the Congress of Americanists, Rome.

Carrillo Viveros, Jorge, (coord.). 1993. *Condiciones de empleo y capacitación en las maquiladoras de exportación en México*. Mexico, D.F.: El Colegio de la Frontera Norte/Secretaría del Trabajo y Previsión Social.

Carrillo Viveros, Jorge, and Alberto Hernández. 1985. *Mujeres fronterizas de la industria maquiladora*. Mexico, D.F.: Secretaría de Educación Pública.

Casar, José, and Jaime Ros. 1987. "Empleo, desempleo y distribución del ingreso." In *México: informe sobre la crisis 1982-1986*, coord. Carlos Tello. Mexico, D.F.: Universidad Nacional Autónoma de México.

Cook, María Lorena, Kevin J. Middlebrook, and Juan Molinar Horcasitas, eds. 1994. *The Politics of Economic Restructuring: State-Society Relations and Regime Change in Mexico*. La Jolla, Calif.: Center for U.S.-Mexican Studies, University of California at San Diego.

Cordera, Rolando, and Enrique González. 1991. "Crisis and Transition in the Mexican Economy." In *Social Responses to Mexico's Economic Crisis of the 1980's*, eds. Mercedes González de la Rocha and Agustín Escobar. La Jolla, Calif.: Center for U.S.-Mexican Studies, University of California at San Diego.

Cortés, Fernando. 1988. "El mercado de trabajo urbano y la sociodemografía mexicana en la mitad de la década de los ochenta: algunas consideraciones metodológicas." Paper delivered at the III National Conference on Demographic Research in Mexico, Sociedad Mexicana de Demografía, Mexico, D.F.

Cortés, Fernando, and Rosa María Rubalcava. 1993. "La distribución del ingreso familiar en México, 1977-1989: sus marcos económico y social." Paper delivered at the workshop on The Social Framework of Mexico and Southeastern Asia, El Colegio de México, Mexico, D.F.

Cruz, Rodolfo, and René Zenteno. 1989. "Algunas características sociodemográficas de la población económicamente activa femenina en Tijuana." In *Fuerza de trabajo femenina urbana en México*. Vol. I, eds. Jennifer Cooper et al. Mexico, D.F.: Coordinación de Humanidades de la Universidad Nacional Autónoma de México/Miguel Angel Porrúa.

De la Garza, Enrique. 1993. "Prologue." In *La flexibilidad laboral en Sonora*, ed. Alejandro Covarrubias. Mexico, D.F.: El Colegio de Sonora/Fundación Friedrich Ebert.

(ECSO) *Encuesta continua de ocupación*. 1979. Mexico, D.F.: Dirección General de Estadística, Secretaría de Programación y Presupuesto, 1st Trimester.

(END) *Encuesta nacional demográfica*. 1982. Mexico, D.F.: Consejo Nacional de Población.

(ENE) *Encuesta nacional de empleo*. 1988, 1991, 1995. Mexico, D.F.: Instituto Nacional de Estadística, Geografía e Informática (INEGI)/Secretaría del Trabajo y Previsión Social (STPS), Dirección General de Empleo.

(ENEU) *Encuesta nacional de empleo urbano*. 1986, 1992. Mexico, D.F.: Instituto Nacional de Estadística, Geografía e Informática (INEGI).

(ENFES) *Encuesta nacional de fecundidad y salud*. 1987. *Memoria de la reunión celebrada el 30 de septiembre de 1988*. Mexico, D.F.: Dirección General de Planificación Familiar, Secretaría de Salud.

Encuesta nacional de ingresos y gastos de los hogares. 1989. Mexico, D.F.: Instituto Nacional de Estadística, Geografía e Informática (INEGI), 4th Trimester.

Escobar Latapí, Agustín. 1986. *Desarrollo económico y absorción de fuerza de trabajo en México: 1950-1980*. Mexico, D.F.: El Colegio de México.

García, Brígida. 1975. "La participación de la población en la actividad económica." *Demografía y Economía* 9 (1):1-31.

García, Brígida. 1988. *Desarrollo económico y absorción de fuerza de trabajo en México: 1950-1980*. México, D.F.: El Colegio de México.

García, Brígida, and Orlandina de Oliveira. 1994. *Trabajo y vida familiar en México*. Mexico, D.F.: El Colegio de México.

Garza, Gustavo. 1994. "Crisis industrial." In *Atlas de Monterrey*. Mexico, D.F.: Instituto de Estudios Urbanos de Nuevo León (INSEUR-Nuevo León)/ Universidad Autónoma de Nuevo León (UANL)/El Colegio de México.

Garza, Gustavo. 1991. "Dinámica industrial en la ciudad de México, 1940-1988." *Estudios Demográficos y Urbanos* 6(1):209-214.

Garza, Gustavo, and Salvador Rivera. 1994. *Dinámica macroeconómica de las ciudades en México*. Mexico, D.F.: Instituto de Investigaciones Sociales de la Universidad Nacional Autónoma de México (IISUNAM)/Instituto Nacional de Estadística, Geografía e Informática (INEGI), Serie Monografías Censales de México (MOCEMEX).

González de la Rocha, Mercedes. 1986. *Los recursos de la pobreza. Familias de bajos ingresos en Guadalajara*. Mexico, D.F.: El Colegio de Jalisco/Centro de Investigación y Estudios Superiores en Antropología Social (CIESAS)/ Secretaría de Programación y Presupuesto (SPP).

González de la Rocha, Mercedes. 1989. "Crisis, economía doméstica y trabajo femenino en Guadalajara." In *Trabajo, poder y sexualidad*, ed. Orlandina de Oliveira. Mexico, D.F.: Programa Interdisciplinario de Estudios de la Mujer, El Colegio de México (PIEM).

Guirette López, Roberto, et al. 1993. "Concentración industrial y distribución del ingreso en México (1985-1988)." In *Memoria XIII Encuentro de la Red Nacional de Investigaciones Urbanas*. Vol. 3. Mexico, D.F.: Instituto Nacional de Estadística, Geografía e Informática/Red Nacional de Investigación Urbana.

Infante, Ricardo, and Emilio Klein. 1991. "Mercado latinoamericano del trabajo en 1950-1990." *Revista de la CEPAL* 45:129-144.

(INEGI) Instituto Nacional de Estadística, Geografía e Informática. 1990-1995. *Estadística de la industria maquiladora de exportación*. México, D.F.

(INEGI) Instituto Nacional de Estadística, Geografía e Informática. 1988. *Sistema de cuentas nacionales de México. Cuentas de producción del sector público 1980-1986*. Mexico, D.F.

(INEGI) Instituto Nacional de Estadística, Geografía e Informática. 1993. *Avance de información económica*. Mexico, D.F.

(INEGI) Instituto Nacional de Estadística, Geografía e Informática. 1994. *Sistema de cuentas nacionales de México. Cuentas de producción del sector público 1987-1994*. Mexico, D.F.

Klein, Emilio, and Victor Tokman. 1988 "Sector informal: una forma de utilizar el trabajo como consecuencia de la manera de producir y no viceversa. A propósito del artículo de Portes y Benton." *Estudios Sociológicos* 6:205-212.

La Jornada. 1995-1996. Mexico, D.F.

Lustig, Nora. 1992. *Mexico: The Remaking of an Economy*. Washington, D.C.: The Brookings Institution.

Marshall, Adriana. 1987. *Non-Standard Employment Practices in Latin America*. Geneva: International Labour Organization.

Marshall, Adriana. 1988. *The Sequel of Unemployment: The Changing Role of Part-Time and Temporary Employment in Western Europe*. Geneva: International Labour Organization.

Muñoz, Humberto. 1985. "Algunas contribuciones empíricas y reflexiones sobre el estudio del sector terciario." *Ciencia* 36(1):17-28.

Muñoz, Humberto, and Orlandina de Oliveira. 1976. "Migración, oportunidades de empleo y diferenciales de ingreso en la Ciudad de México." *Revista Mexicana de Sociología* 38(1):51-84.

Muñoz, Humberto, and Orlandina de Oliveira. 1979. "Algunas Controversias sobre la fuerza de trabajo en América Latina." In *Fuerza de trabajo y movimientos laborales en América Latina*, eds. Ruben Katzman and José Luis Reyna. Mexico, D.F.: El Colegio de México.

Oliveira, Orlandina de. 1989a. "Empleo femenino en México en tiempos de recesión económica: tendencias recientes." In *Fuerza de trabajo femenina urbana en México*, eds. Jennifer Cooper et al. Mexico, D.F.: Universidad Nacional Autónoma de México (UNAM)/Porrúa.

Oliveira, Orlandina de. 1989b. "La participación femenina en los mercados de trabajo urbanos: México 1970-1980." *Estudios Demográficos y Urbanos* 4(3):465-493.

Oliveira, Orlandina de, and Brígida García. 1990. "Expansión del trabajo femenino y transformación social en México: 1950-1987." In *México en el umbral del milenio.* Mexico, D.F.: Centro de Estudios Sociológicos, El Colegio de México.

Oliveira, Orlandina de, and Brígida García. 1993. *Cambios socioeconómicos y dinámica de los mercados de trabajo en México: 1950-1992.* Mexico, D.F.: El Colegio de México.

Oliveira, Orlandina de, and Brígida García. 1994. "Cambios en la fuerza de trabajo industrial: México 1986-1992." Paper delivered at the XIII World Congress of Sociology, International Association of Sociology, Bielefeld, Germany. July.

Oliveira, Orlandina de, and Bryan Roberts. 1993. "La informalidad urbana en años de expansión, crisis y reestructuración económica." *Estudios Sociológicos* 9:33-58.

Oliveira, Orlandina de, and Bryan Roberts. 1994. "Urban Growth and Urban Social Structure in Latin America, 1930-1990." In *The Cambridge History of Latin America: 1930 to the Present,* ed. Leslie Bethell. Vol. VI. New York: Cambridge University Press.

Orozco Orozco, Miguel. 1992. "1989-1991: se reactiva la acumulación de capital." *Economía Informa* 202:13-18.

Orozco, Miguel, and Luis Lozano. 1992. "Salario y política económica en México." *Economía Informa* 207: 13-17.

Pacheco Gómez Muñoz, María Edith. 1994. "Heterogeneidad laboral en la ciudad de México a fines de los ochenta." Ph.D. dissertation. Mexico, D.F.: Centro de Estudios Demográficos y de Desarrollo Urbano, El Colegio de México.

Pacheco Gómez Muñoz, María Edith. 1988. "Población económicamente activa femenina en algunas áreas urbanas de México en 1986." M.A. thesis. Mexico, D.F.: Centro de Estudios Demográficos y de Desarrollo Urbano, El Colegio de México.

Pedrero Nieto, Mercedes. 1990. "Evolución de la participación económica femenina en los ochenta." *Revista Mexicana de Sociología* 52(1):133-149.

Pedrero Nieto, Mercedes, and Teresa Rendón. 1982. "El trabajo de la mujer en México en los setentas." In *Estudios sobre la mujer: empleo y la mujer. Bases teóricas, metodología y evidencia empírica.* Mexico, D.F.: Instituto Nacional de Estadística, Geografía e Informatica (INEGI)/Secretaría de Programación y Presupuesto (SPP), Serie Lecturas III.

Pérez Cadena, Susana. 1993. "Relocalización geográfica de la industria manufacturera, según los censos económicos." In *Memoria XIII Encuentro de la Red Nacional de Investigaciones Urbanas,* Vol. 3. Mexico, D.F.: Instituto Nacional de Estadística, Geografía e Informática (INEGI)/Red Nacional de Investigación Urbana.

Portes, Alejandro, and Lauren Benton. 1984. "Industrial Development and Labor Absorption: A Reinterpretation." *Population and Development Review* 10(4):589-611.

PREALC (Programa Regional del Empleo para América Latina y el Caribe). 1983. *Empleo y salarios.* Santiago de Chile: Organización Internacional del Trabajo.

Pries, Ludger. 1993. "El reto de la flexibilidad y las relaciones obrero-patronales en México." In *Trabajo industrial en la transición: experiencias de América Latina y Europa,* eds. Ludger Pries and Rainer Dombois. Mexico, D.F.: El Colegio de Puebla/Fundación Friedrich Ebert.

Rakowski, Cathy A., ed. 1994. *Contrapunto: The Informal Sector Debate in Latin America.* Albany: State University of New York Press.

Reforma. 1995-1996. Mexico, D.F.

Roberts, Bryan. 1995. *The Making of Citizens: Cities of Peasants Re-visited.* London: Arnold.

Romo, Arnoldo. 1993. "Cambio de modelo y reestructuración territorial de la industria en México (1980-1988)." *Notas censales,* 6:10-21. Mexico, D.F.: Instituto Nacional de Estadística, Geografía e Informatica (INEGI),

Rendón, Teresa. 1990. "Trabajo femenino renumerado en el siglo veinte. Cambios, tendencias y perspectivas." In *Trabajo femenino y crisis en México. Tendencias y transformaciones actuales,* eds. Elia Ramírez Bautista and Hilda R. Dávila Ibáñez. Mexico, D.F.: Universidad Autónoma Metropolitana-Xochimilco.

Rendón, Teresa, and Carlos Salas. 1987. "Evolución del empleo en México: 1895-1970." *Estudios Demográficos y Urbanos* 2(2):189-230.

Rendón, Teresa, and Carlos Salas. 1990. "Sobre el llamado sector informal. Propuesta de redefinición y formas de medición de sus componentes." Mexico, D.F.: Facultad de Economía, Universidad Nacional Autonóma de México.

Rendón, Teresa, and Carlos Salas. 1992. "El mercado de trabajo no agrícola en México. Tendencias y cambios recientes." In *Ajuste estructural, mercados laborales y Tratado de Libre Comercio.* Mexico, D.F.: Centro de Estudios Sociológicos, El Colegio de México/Fundación Friedrich Ebert/El Colegio de la Frontera Norte.

Roberts, Bryan. 1993. "Enterprise and Labor Markets: The Border and the Metropolitan Areas." *Frontera Norte* 9(5):33-65.

Ruiz Durán, Clemente. 1992. "Fortaleza y debilidades de la recuperación." *Economía Informa* 202:10-12.

Sánchez Daza, Alfredo. 1992. "Alcances y límites de la estrategia de estabilización en México (Una revisión del enfoque adoptado y sus resultados)." *Análisis Económico* 10:61-87.

Sassen, Saskia. 1994. *Cities in a World Economy.* Thousand Oaks, Calif.: Pine Forge Press.

Selva, Beatriz. 1985. "Modalidades de trabajo femenino en San Felipe del Agua." M.A. thesis. Mexico, D.F.: FLACSO.

Souza, Paulo Renato Costa. 1980. "A determinacão dos sálarios e do emprego nas economias atrasadas." Ph.D. dissertation. Campinas, Brazil: Universidad de Campinas.

Tello, Carlos. 1987. "Introducción." In *México: informe sobre la crisis 1982-1986,* coords. Carlos Tello and Enrique González Tiburcio. Mexico, D.F.: Universidad Nacional Autónoma de México.

Tokman, Victor. 1987. "El sector informal: quince años después." *El Trimestre Económico.* 215:513-536.

Tokman, Victor. 1991. "Políticas de empleo para la adaptación productiva en América Latina." *Estudios del Trabajo* 1:3-19.

Zapata, Francisco. 1992. "La crisis del control sindical sobre la dinámica del mercado de trabajo en México." In *Ajuste estructural, mercados laborales y el TLC.* Mexico, D.F.: El Colegio de México/Fundación Friedrich Ebert/El Colegio de la Frontera Norte.

Chapter 9

Restructuring, Employment, and Social Inequality: Comparative Urban Latin American Patterns[1]

Richard Tardanico and Rafael Menjívar Larín

This volume's contributors have explored the contemporary interrelations of local-urban and global restructuring in seven Latin American countries, with emphasis on employment and social inequality. This chapter shall now attempt to make comparative sense of the national findings from the standpoint of the series of hypotheses that informs the case studies. Recall that problems of data quality and comparability restrict the analysis of cross-national change to no more than rough approximations. Problems in distinguishing cyclical from secular change represent another limitation. The following, then, is an exercise not only in testing hypotheses but also in generating hypotheses for future research.[2]

Sectoral Transformations

The study hypothesized, first, that employment in the public sector would drop as a portion of total employment in each country; second, that employment in tertiary activities would rise as a portion of total employment; and third, that employment in export activities would rise as a portion of total employment in manufacturing.[3]

From Public to Private Sector

The rapid growth of public sector employment as a percentage of total employment was crucial to Latin American state-building, import-substitution development, and urbanization during the mid-twentieth century. The degree to which this process has been reversed since the 1980s is vital, therefore, to the reshaping of the region's politics, economies, and societies (Gilbert 1994; Infante and Klein 1991; Mesa-Lago 1994 and 1995; Portes 1989; Roberts 1995 and 1996; Smith, Acuña, and Gamarra 1994a and 1994b).

Richard Tardanico is associate professor of sociology at Florida International University. Rafael Menjívar Larín is director of FLACSO-Costa Rica.

Within the sample of very small, peripheral economies, public sector employment assumed a more significant role in the labor markets of Costa Rica and the Dominican Republic than Guatemala during the 1960s and 1970s. Reflecting Guatemala's history of extremely polarized and repressive societal conditions was the comparative weakness of its state programs of economic and social development during the post-Second World War era, as the non-military portion of the state's machinery remained relatively stunted in size and resources. On the opposite side of the spectrum stood Costa Rica, with a bare-bones public security apparatus that was subordinated unequivocally to a government bureaucracy geared to economic and social intervention. Situated between these polar cases was the Dominican Republic, whose state organization contained both a notable military component and a bloated civil bureaucracy (Aguilera Peralta 1994; Betances 1995; Nelson 1990; Paige 1987; Rovira Mas 1987; Trudeau 1993).

Public sector employment took on major proportions in each of the larger, semiperipheral economies in the sample. The clear outlier was Mexico, where the military occupied a marginal position in the state edifice. The military's political and economic share — including in the form of the armaments segment of import-substitution manufacturing — was greatest in Argentina, followed by Chile, though its small size in Venezuela belied its high level of funding and significant political clout (Acuña and Smith 1995; Burggraaff and Millett 1995; Centeno 1994; Levine and Crisp 1995; Smith, Acuña, and Gamarra 1994a and 1994b).

Such arrangements took shape before and after the Second World War as both instruments and consequences of state actions to consolidate political authority and engineer economic development. Research providing more systematic, cross-national attention to not only the civil-military distributions of resources and employment but also their distributions across the civilian branches of government (including parastatal organizations) would strengthen the assessment of subsequent comparative transformations of labor markets and citizenship rights (see Mesa-Lago 1994 and 1995; Portes 1985; Roberts 1995 and 1996).

The volume's data on the anticipated fall in the public sector's share of the job market since the early 1980s are sparse. They indicate that the number of public sector jobs fell slightly in the Dominican Republic but fell merely in rate of growth relative to private sector jobs in Costa Rica and Guatemala.[4] Neither these nor other known data present a long-range, comparative profile of change in public versus private sector pay in these countries (ECLAC 1995a, 136-137).

José Itzigsohn observes that government leadership in the Dominican Republic justified public sector pay cuts by acknowledging the role of corruption in cushioning the incomes of many state employees. Remember that, following a wave of violent popular protest, austerity measures in the Dominican Republic during the early 1980s gave way to expansionary fiscal measures until the 1990s; that, according to Juan Pablo Pérez Sáinz, Guatemala's post-military, Christian-Democratic administration proved unable to steer a coherent course of adjustment policy; and that, according to Richard Tardanico and Mario Lungo, Costa Rica's initial dose of harsh stabilization policies was followed by gradual adjustment until the next decade. In light of events in the mid-1990s, this comparative pattern suggests that major employment reductions in the public sector are contingent on the intensification of economic and fiscal pressures, as well as on the advent of sociopolitical alignments and state leaderships that are less beholden to traditional patronage and civil/military arrangements (CACR 1996a and 1996b; Castro 1996; *Inforpress Centroamericana* 1995-1996; *Panorama Centroamericano* 1995).

Against this backdrop, three features of the Costa Rican situation take on special relevance: first, between 1980 and 1991, net public sector job loss for workers with no more than primary schooling but significant job growth for those with tertiary education; second, the relative effectiveness of state policy in streamlining public sector programs and bureaucracies without losing sight of pre-crisis social welfare objectives (see Mesa-Lago 1995); and third, recent consideration of eliminating jobs in some government sectors while — potentially financed by privatization measures — increasing jobs in the government sectors of education, health, and security. Tempered by the still weighty role of social welfare politics in Costa Rica, these features are consistent with the notion that neoliberal reforms serve less to weaken state capacities of regulation per se than to refocus them on the exigencies of transnational accumulation (Acuña and Smith 1994; Sassen 1996, 25-30), including the recent incorporation of "human resource development" into this policy equation (Walters 1996, 210-213). The Costa Rican features are also consistent with the rising preoccupation of Latin American governments with the challenges to their authority posed by narcotrafficking, other kinds of contraband and crime, such as that connected to the illegal destruction of natural habitats, and public disorder in general (Aguilera Peralta 1994; Kincaid and Gamarra 1996; see Walters 1996, 209-210). Juxtaposed with the cases of Guatemala and the Dominican Republic, Costa Rica's much greater effectiveness in modifying its state programs and organization suggests wide divergence between the capacities of small-country states on the periphery to negotiate their relations with the new global order. In an age of escalated ethno-territorial conflict in Latin America and beyond, of compelling interest are the ramifications of Guatemala's domestic peace accords for the capacity of its state managers to follow Costa Rica's lead.

Turning to the larger economies, Argentina and Chile would appear to stand apart, within this subsample as well as the volume's entire sample of countries, in the severity of the absolute and relative contraction of their public sector employment. In Argentina, this contraction gathered steam as part of the transition from military to civilian government in the 1980s, when the Alfonsín administration slashed the military's budget, salaries, and personnel. The Argentine military has fared no better under the Menem administration in the 1990s, including an ongoing massive reduction in employment in the country's significant arms-production industry, which spans the military and civilian branches of employment[5] (Acuña and Smith 1995, 132-135, 151; see SCR 1996c). But, as Rosalía Cortés discusses, job and pay contraction already had gained ground in the mainstream of the public sector's civilian machinery, as the Menem government turned Argentina's neoliberal initiatives into the most radical in Latin America[6] (see Acuña 1994; Artana et al.1995; Ellison 1996). The variable dimensions of state sector employment restructuring emerge at the core of Cortés's discussion. In contrast to the military, Argentina's central administration grew, if slowly, in personnel during the 1980s. Faster job growth took place in provincial and municipal government, as a result of the tenacity of both local and central/local patronage alliances. Under the Menem team, however, employment has been reduced aggressively in the central government and parastatal entities as well as in the military, although the organizational decentralization of jobs rather than their elimination per se accounts for much of the central government's reported employment loss. During Menem's first term in office, public sector job growth merely slowed in the provinces and municipalities, to which, in part as a political counterweight to the local damage inflicted by Menem's policies, the decentralized jobs were transferred.

In Chile, the stronger institutional moorings of military power have defended the armed forces from the fate of their Argentine counterparts, including during the shift to civilian government in the 1990s. So far, the Chilean military's substantial share of public sector resources and employment remains unchallenged. This share extends to a state-protected enclave in a highly privatized economy, the arms-production industry, which receives financing through the military's legally guaranteed access to revenues from yet another such enclave, the state-owned copper industry (SCR 1996c). Under the Pinochet dictatorship, technocrats orchestrated the massive decentralization and shedding of public sector functions and employment at most levels — sandwiched around an abrupt reversal of policy course as the state took over numerous financial institutions during the economic downswing of the early 1980s (Velasco 1994; Vergara 1994; Yañez and Letelier 1995). Alvaro Díaz reports that public sector jobs dropped markedly as a percentage of Chile's tertiary employment, with the quite visible hand of military-authoritarianism ensuring that organized labor would not impede the "invisible hand" of the market. Díaz argues that this acute drop in public employment contributed to the swelling of unemployment into the early 1980s and precarious employment into the 1990s.

Orlandina de Oliveira and Brígida García point out that Mexico's percentage of total jobs located in the public sector remained constant between 1982 and 1992, growing until the mid-1980s, but then undergoing blunt reversal. Blanca Heredia (1994, 276-279) observes that, in spite of collapsing real wages, the expansion of public sector employment into the mid-1980s combined with the structure of both state-union relations and public sector opportunities for private gain to obtain labor quiescence within the government apparatus. By the late 1980s, the Salinas administration greatly accelerated the privatization of state enterprises and their workforces that had begun under de la Madrid. In doing so, the Salinas group added the contraction of central-government personnel and the reorganization of surviving state enterprises, such as PEMEX (the state-owned petroleum company), to the politico-economic formula. Increasingly, the state's executives wielded its long-established arsenal of hard-line, cooptive, and divide-and-rule weapons against the fragmented labor unions in the public and private sectors alike. They now did so, however, as part of a neoliberal redefinition of the state's coalitional underpinnings. In Mexico this process was unencumbered, of course, by the civil-military tensions that typify most of the other cases (Centeno 1994, 47-51). Economic crisis reduced the ability of the Mexican state's managers to coopt their actual and potential opponents. Still, the managers had at their disposal new variants of weapons to control and defeat labor: decentralization, bankruptcy, and privatization. They also had the advantage of the nation's growing socioeconomic and territorial differentiation, which, in the context of heightened employment instability and insecurity, further muddied the footing of labor unions (Erfani 1995, 160-163; Middlebrook 1995, Chapter 7; Morris 1995, 56-62; Weiss 1996, 66-68). Oliveira and García write that by the 1990s three features of change in Mexican public sector employment had become evident: shrinkage relative to its peak volume in the mid-1980s, reduction in its component of state-enterprise jobs, and organizational decentralization[7] (see Aitken et al. 1996; Ellison 1996).

Víctor Fajardo Cortez and Miguel Lacabana note that as real wages plunged and underemployment ballooned, public sector jobs increased in Venezuela between the 1980s and early 1990s but decreased as a portion of the labor market. In the setting of economic crisis, such minimal state sector change reflects the failure of government policies to challenge effectively the institutional organization of the oil-anchored political economy, which, based on massive patronage and subsidies, had undergirded one of Latin America's highest standards of living. This failure left Venezuela's political, economic, and social arenas as oriented as ever to rent-seeking claims on petroleum revenues — or, more correctly, on optimistically projected levels of revenue. As Terry Karl (1995, 33-34) argues, Venezuela's state apparatus is a "petro-state" that has relied "on the continued flow of petrodollars for its stability." Karl goes on to say that this reliance has created "strong incentives to 'freeze' existing political arrangements in place" instead of building "capacities to diversify the fiscal base or direct a new agenda ..." (34). Pertinent to the topic of state employment is the almost doubling of the military's personnel in the 1980s, "as the economy worsened and the military offered one of the few employment options for many poor Venezuelans" (Naim 1995, 55). By the early 1990s, the Carlos Andrés Pérez administration, whose first announcement of a harsh austerity package had provoked massive popular violence as well as military rebellion, announced a second package that included layoffs and salary freezes in the public sector and the privatization of state firms. Consistent with similar attempts over the previous decade, implementation fell considerably short of plan, in this case particularly as charges of corruption forced Pérez from office (Karl 1995; Levine and Crisp 1995; Naim 1995). After years of continued policy chaos and macroeconomic degradation, in 1996 the Venezuelan government, under Rafael Caldera, officially committed itself to a renewal of neoliberalism. In light of recent history, the extent to which the new policy blueprint will be implemented is as yet unknown. Within the blueprint are provisions for major reductions in public sector employment and pay and for wide-ranging privatization (Lewis 1996).

Venezuela illustrates the most basic structural and policy dilemma of Latin American countries in the late twentieth century. On the one hand, statist-nationalist approaches are no longer viable, given the current constellation of power and ideology in the world political economy. On the other hand, although neoliberal policies exacerbate the domestic social inequalities and the international economic and political vulnerabilities of the world's less-developed countries, even more damaging may be the failure to orchestrate some version of neoliberal reform that proves acceptable to transnational business interests, Northern governments, and multilateral agencies. It is at this juncture of the dilemma that the comparative political, social, and economic prospects of Latin American countries are being defined (see Acuña and Smith 1994; Bresser Pereira, Maravall, and Przeworski 1994; Roberts 1996).

So, among the larger economies, the hypothesis of cuts in public sector employment as a percentage of total employment receives just partial support from cross-national evidence. Such cuts began earliest and seemingly have been steepest in Argentina, in both the military and civilian branches of government, and in Chile, essentially in the civilian branch only. In Mexico, severe cuts, which have been based most of all on the privatization of state enterprises, were later in coming, while the military's organizational resources and presence in hitherto civilian law-enforcement positions recently have grown. In Venezuela, a coherent policy of public sector job cuts may only now be taking shape. Average pay in the public sectors of these countries has fallen, but its extent of decline relative to the private sector is unclear (ECLAC 1995a, 136-137).

This study's preliminary findings of national variation among the smaller and larger economies underline the importance of domestic institutional structures in mediating world-scale trends. Demilitarization in Argentina demonstrates that contemporary cuts in state sector employment are not always reducible to pressures of debt crisis and global economic restructuring. Epitomizing the contradictions and complexities of neoliberal policy regimes are Chilean copper and Mexican petroleum, which remain under state ownership but have faced internal realignments of organization and labor force.

Post-Cold War economic globalization is intensifying the external pressures for national restructuring (Díaz 1997). Nevertheless, the timing and forms of local policy response — including the identities of the sectors and subsectors of the state's machinery and labor force that bear the brunt of the adjustment burdens — vary considerably. A key comparative question, for example, is how the organizational and employment implications of the new conceptions of public security become negotiated domestically and internationally under conditions of austerity and restructuring. No less important is recognition of the levels at which the conceptual distinction between "public" and "private" sector obfuscates the functioning of fundamental processes of political economy. In this respect, how the state's roles as financier, consumer, producer, distributor, and employer overlap with the grid of commodity chains and labor markets should not be overlooked (Arrighi 1994; Evans 1995; Gereffi and Korzeniewicz 1994; Markusen 1992; Sayer and Walker 1992; Wallerstein 1979 and 1995).

Tertiarization and Export Manufacturing

Given evidence on change in the balance between employment in the public and private sectors, what was found concerning change in the industry composition of employment and the share of export employment in manufacturing?[8] Within the group of smaller economies, tertiary activities continued their pre-crisis trajectory of expansion as a share of total urban and national employment in the Dominican Republic and Guatemala. They seem to have lost ground to manufacturing, however, in urban Costa Rica (while more or less keeping up with it at the national level [Tardanico 1996a]). Moreover, tertiary and secondary employment alike became less connected to public sector employment in all three countries, as summarized above. In the Dominican Republic, decreased employment in import-substitution manufacturing and construction and among both rural and urban-based agricultural workforces more than counterbalanced a surge in export-assembly jobs. In the tertiary sector, there was significant job growth in tourism, which, along with assembly-manufacturing (not to mention the longer-standing role of migration and remittances), is an integral component of the economy's internationalization. Yet most of the tertiary expansion occurred in low-skill, low-wage jobs that were mainly linked to an impoverished domestic market.

So, while manufacturing and tourism became more internationalized in the Dominican Republic, the worsening of the country's employment composition was acute. This was likewise so in Guatemala, even though by the late 1980s manufacturing had become its sphere of most rapid job growth. According to Pérez Sáinz, perhaps most intriguing about Guatemala's pattern is that San Pedro Sacatepéquez, an indigenous community located not far from Guatemala City, appears to have parlayed subcontracting relations with the metropolitan area's export-platform firms into an improved local capacity for accumulation. This possibility underscores the role of the sociocultural fabric of localities in mediating the territorial impact of globalization (Kyle 1995; Lawson 1995; Palat 1996; Pérez Sáinz 1996; Portes, Dore, and Landolt 1997; Roberts 1995; Spener 1996; Wilson 1995). In Costa Rica, meanwhile, the democratic regime-structure of the national state intersected with its stability, efficacy, and highly developed socioeconomic infrastructure relative to small and larger economies in Latin America and the Caribbean to make the country a prime beneficiary of the Caribbean Basin Initiative. According to Tardanico and Lungo, among the consequences revolving around export-platform activities is that manufacturing rose as a percentage of total urban employment. This took place even as Costa Rica's urban and rural economies underwent a boom in international tourism, which became an important job-maker. Some subsectors of Costa Rica's import-substitution manufacturing seem to have remained prosperous, while the expansion of modern services has been substantial (Céspedes and Jiménez 1995, 97; ECLAC 1995b, 184-185; Morley 1995, 185-188). The consequences for change in industry patterns of social inequality in the workforce merit study, particularly in light of Intel's upcoming large investment in microchip production in Costa Rica and its potential economic spin-offs (EIU 1996 [4th quarter], 33-34).

For Costa Rica, the Dominican Republic, and Guatemala, the durability and compositional limitations of job gains in export manufacturing and international tourism are a major worry. Infrastructural advantages alone make Costa Rica by a large margin the best positioned of the three countries to attract new jobs based on the accelerating transfer of high-tech manufacturing (as in the case of the anticipated Intel plant) and knowledge-based service activities (perhaps eventually related to high-tech manufacturing) from the advanced zones to the less-developed zones of the world economy (see Arrighi 1996; EIU 1996; ECLAC 1997, 78, 84; Gereffi and Korzeniewicz 1994). Here too, however, international competition is intensifying, and thus a crucial issue is by how much and under what terms the Costa Rican state can overcome the impact of austerity by increasing its long-range spending on human and physical infrastructure. Even if such spending were substantially increased, a major concern is the social and geographic equity of employment creation in the more advanced manufacturing and service activities.

As for the larger economies, only post-1983 Chile diverges from the hypothesis of continued employment tertiarization (see FitzGerald 1996, 44). According to Díaz, the percentage of Chilean employment in manufacturing remains below that of the early 1970s. Still, the country's post-1983 trend of faster job growth in manufacturing than tertiary activities is striking, given the rapid pace of concurrent growth in advanced-service production and jobs, which are strategic both as local inputs for the economy's export-based surge and as exports to other Latin American countries. The prosperity of the construction industry and the urbanization of primary employment have been significant aspects of Chile's urban-sectoral trajectory. Also significant, though, has been the prosperity of certain segments of Chilean manufacturing itself since the final years of the 1980s. Comparative distance from the U.S. market and notable wage growth are reasons why export-assembly manufacturing has not been a significant part of the economy's upswing. Yet two segments of Chilean manufacturing have been prosperous: those surviving categories of import-substitution production that have taken advantage of expanding demand in the national market or the Latin American export market (for example, medium-priced footwear and textiles, furniture, appliances, chemicals, metals-machinery, cartons and containers, printing) and, more crucially, a new generation of production for the world market based on the industrial processing of the country's abundant supply of natural resources (for example, refined copper, wood chips, paper, fruit and seafood products)[9] (Collins and Lear 1995, Chapters 13 and 14; ECLAC 1997, 72; FitzGerald 1996; Weeks 1996, 280-282, 284-289).

A considerable part of Chile's recent stabilization of employment levels in the import-substitution segment of manufacturing is connected to the export-led economy's flourishing demand for domestic industrial inputs. Even so, the economy's long-term prospects are diminished not only by its high dependence on the export and industrial processing of primary commodities but, as Díaz stresses, by the neoliberal political order's inherent inadequacies in fomenting progress in such areas as social welfare and human capital, research and development, and environmental conservation (see Collins and Lear 1995, Chapters 12 to 15).

Díaz considers as less than accurate the sweeping interpretation of Chile's post-1983 upswing as a direct result of some carefully laid out and orchestrated strategy of market enhancement under the Pinochet government. He claims that the upswing more fully represents a far-from-finalized, substantially accidental outcome of shifting state-class relations since at least the 1960s; of varied and contradictory forms of state intervention in economy and society over that period, including during the Pinochet years; and of serendipitous changes in the world economy. With respect to social welfare and inequality, Díaz aims trenchant criticism at the political and class structures that have undergirded Chile's labor-market transformations since the Pinochet era. Notwithstanding strong increases in average real wages during the 1990s, he argues that these structures — including the concentration of export prosperity in relatively few firms — have exacerbated social inequalities and created a rigid, exclusionary institutional edifice (see Collins and Lear 1995, Chapter 7). He asserts that such consequences pose the most basic threat to the future of Chile's so-called "miracle."

The surprise may be that Mexico does not rank with Chile as an exception to the trend of continued labor-market tertiarization. Oliveira and García delineate two currents of change in Mexico's pronounced economic and employment regionalization since the early 1980s: first, a revamping of organizational structure and technology and a shrinkage of job volume in import-substitution manufacturing, especially in central Mexico and the northern industrial city of Monterrey; and second, the uninterrupted growth, as well as diversification, of export-platform output and jobs along the northern frontier and their diffusion into parts of the country's interior (see FitzGerald 1996; Heredia 1996; Shaiken 1990; Weeks 1996; Wilson 1992). As Mexico's manufacturing employment at large has become more geared to exports, this pattern has yielded a net drop in the relative contribution of manufacturing to national employment. Not to be over-looked is that this net drop extends to the largest, most mature of the northern frontier's manufacturing cities, Ciudad Juárez and Tijuana, where, as the assembly of apparel, electronics, and other such products has spread to new locations along the border, in the interior, and in the Caribbean Basin and beyond, the assembly of such products as auto parts and furniture has taken hold. Oliveira and García assert that manufacturing's portion of national jobs fell not just during the years of economic crisis but during the ensuing years of recovery and accelerated internationalization as well, among the reasons being that just 2.7 percent of Mexico's firms have come to account for some 80 percent of its non-oil exports (Heredia 1996, 36; see Díaz on Chile this volume, Chapter 6). One consequence of the net deindustrialization of employment has been a reallocation of labor into low-wage, locally oriented tertiary activities. Another consequence has been a reallocation of labor into modern services — ranging from the high to low ends of the occupational ladder — much of which is bound up with the economy's transnationalization. In the secondary and tertiary industries alike, crisis and restructuring have caused a painful widening of income inequality (see ECLAC 1997, 26; Heredia 1996; Pánuco-Laguette and Székely 1996; Roberts and Tardanico 1997; see Ferreira and Litchfield 1996 and Lavinas and Nabuco 1995 on Brazil).

The tertiarization of employment also continued in Argentina and Venezuela. Neither of these countries, moreover, contains territorial excep-tions to this trend that approximate the manufacturing dynamism of Mexico's northern frontier. According to Cortés, the sharp outflow of capital from import-substitution manufacturing in Argentina since the 1970s generally has been rechanneled not into export manufacturing but into financial speculation (at home and abroad) and into the privatization of services. Given Argentina's corporatist brand of state-class structure, such disincentives as the high cost of strategic services and industrial inputs, obsolete equipment, monetary instability, the slowness of tariff reform, erratic swings in politics and economy on the whole, and comparative distance from the U.S. market have impeded the shift into export manufac-turing. As for Venezuela, Fajardo Cortez and Lacabana stress the weakness of a local manufacturing class that, in spite of the export opportunities presented by the country's proximity to the United States, has remained tightly bonded to the protectionism and subsidies of the nation's petro-state. Not unlike Argentina, they also stress an erratic course of government policy and economy that has made corruption, capital flight, and speculation incomparably more attractive than domestic industrial investment. While the long-range evidence for Argentina is particularly ambiguous, export activities appear to have augmented their share of total manufacturing jobs in Argentina and Venezuela during the 1990s (ECLAC 1996, 84, 88, and 1997, 32, 34-35, 62, 104; FitzGerald 1996, 39-41; Naim and Francés 1995, 184, 186-191; Weeks 1996, 279-282). In Argentina, MERCOSUR has fostered such an increase, as have state protections and subsidies that diverge markedly from the reigning ideology and practice of market deregulation.[10] According to

Cortés, the automobile industry is most responsible for the recent expansion in Argentina's manufactured exports to MERCOSUR countries (especially Brazil); the increase seems to be extending as well to a smattering of other industries at various levels of technology and scale. In Venezuela, petro-chemicals, aluminum, and steel remain the predominant manufactured exports, which still rank among Latin America's lowest as a portion of national export earnings. Neither country shows any semblance of world-market competitiveness in manufacturing (ECLAC 1995b, 329-332, and 1997, 62, 104; FitzGerald 1996; LASR 1996, 7-9; Naim 1995; Naim and Francés 1995; Weeks 1996).

To summarize, the evidence on the industry composition of employ-ment and on export activity as a portion of overall manufacturing employment provides another instance of ample variation in urban-national change across the spectrum of smaller and larger economies. Although much more precise data are needed, it would seem that, of the entire set of countries, Mexico stands at the high end and Argentina or Venezuela at the low end of a general increase in the fraction of manufacturing jobs linked to export production.[11] The component of organizationally and technologi-cally advanced manufacturing in this increase, including upper-level knowledge inputs into product design and production process, appears largest by far in Mexico — particularly sub-border northern and central Mexico — which continues to follow Brazil at the high end in all measures of Latin American manufacturing (ECLAC 1997, 32, 34-35, 62, 72, 90, 104; FitzGerald 1996; Shaiken 1990; Weeks 1996).

Only in urban Costa Rica and post-1983 Chile does employment seem to have become less concentrated in the tertiary sector. Guatemala may have begun moving in this direction as well. Yet these apparent deviations are not extreme, and their potential durability is unclear. Mindful of subindustry variations, it could be that the shares of manufacturing employment in Costa Rica and Chile have peaked. The less innovative branches of their manufacturing economies already face stiffened foreign competition, such as from other Central American countries and Mexico in the case of Costa Rica and China in the case of Chile. Meanwhile, the more innovative branches stand to absorb fewer workers per unit of output. An important question is how vulnerable Chile's natural resource-based industrial production may be from the standpoints of local environmental sustainability and global market trends. Employment growth in producer services seemingly has been more rapid in Chile than in any of the other countries. Indeed, Chile's export gains in this tertiary subsector are poised to accelerate as it enters MERCOSUR and as the bloc's national economies become more regionally integrated. Much of Costa Rica's long-term development planning revolves around upgraded manufacturing and services as well as tropical resources. Besides the obvious potential connected with the building of Intel's microchip operations in Costa Rica, these include the potential establishment of economic bridges that would link its impressive diversity of natural resources to pharmaceutical research and manufacturing. As mentioned earlier, however, the key question is whether even an exceptional country of the periphery like Costa Rica can maneuver around current trends in world and national political economy that are far from propitious to the state-led advances in economic and social infrastructure required to carry out such development on a major scale.

Returning to Latin America at large, the increasing importance of advanced services leads to two questions. First, how do emerging social inequalities in the labor market of advanced services compare to those in other layers of services as well as in the various layers of manufacturing and agriculture? And second, within the framework of today's constraints on the regulatory powers of the region's states, how can the expanding economic share of advanced services in many localities be translated into decent employment for an increased percentage of the workforce (see Lavinas and Nabuco 1995; Roberts 1995; Sassen 1994)?

Precarious and Informal Employment

The next set of hypotheses pertains to the consequences of change in the public sector and industry shares of urban employment for precarious and informal employment — a proportional increase in which the most basic labor-market trend is anticipated by the literature on global economic restructuring (Amsden and van der Hoeven 1996; Dicken 1992; Gilbert 1994; ILO 1996; Portes, Castells, and Benton 1989; Sassen 1994; Sayer and Walker 1992; Standing and Tokman 1991; Walters 1996). Chapter 1 defined as "precarious" employment that has become less remunerative, less regulated by government, and otherwise less subject to collective and individual control by workers relative to the standards established during the era of state-led, import-substitution development. The chapter defined as "informal" the segment of employment that has escaped state regulation. Not all precarious employment, then, is informal. Indeed, employment can become downgraded exclusively or principally through the mechanisms of the formal economy. Moreover, employment in the formal and informal economies alike is quite heterogeneous. This means that for reasons of pay, autonomy, and flexibility, the holders of various occupations may prefer to work in the informal economy. Further, a worker or household of workers may be engaged simultaneously in formal and informal activities, and they may become more or less engaged in each of these over the life course. In this setting, under certain structural conditions, informality may be conducive to economic gains for some firms, social groups, and locales (Portes, Dore, and Landolt 1997; Pérez Sáinz 1996; Pérez Sáinz and Menjívar Larín 1991; Roberts 1995).

Chapter 1 noted that during import-substitution development, the expansion of not only the organizational apparatus of the state but also manufacturing production was linked to growth in the portion of urban employment that was legally regulated and relatively stable and secure. Thus, it was hypothesized that, since the 1980s, reduced percentages of urban employment in the public sector and in manufacturing have fostered growth in the fraction of jobs that are precarious and informal. Recent research also emphasizes that, in the age of global restructuring, jobs in manufacturing are becoming increasingly precarious and informal. This raises the additional question of whether there has been a decrease in manufacturing's advantage over the non-public sector tertiary economy in the generation of legally regulated, stable, and secure employment (Amsden and van der Hoeven 1996; Benería and Roldán 1987; Boris and Prugl 1996; Córdova 1996; Roberts 1995; Standing and Tokman 1991; Weeks 1996).

At the core of Chapter 2 by Itzigsohn on the Dominican Republic and Chapter 3 by Pérez Sáinz on Guatemala is the argument that employment conditions in each of these countries — which before the economic crisis of the 1980s ranked among Latin America's worst — have become substantially degraded. Such degradation in the Dominican Republic predated the 1980s, as, during the previous decade, the state's managers and some segments of the business class responded to a serious slowdown of the country's import-substitution economy by reorienting it toward international tourism, export-platform manufacturing, nontraditional agricultural exports, and labor emigration and remittances. This reorientation has built upon the government policy of low wages, unenforcement of labor regulations, and flimsy social safety net that reigned during the import-substitution period. It, therefore, has also built upon the policy of promoting or taking advantage of large flows of Haitian migrant labor to the Dominican countryside and Dominican migrants from countryside to city, which have been integral to conserving the urban economy's extensive pool of "reserve" workers. Since the 1970s, average real wages in the Dominican Republic have plummeted, especially as the currency has been devalued since the early 1980s. This trend typifies the economy's internationalized sectors, including manufacturing employment based in the Dominican Republic's extensive network of export-processing zones. In a context of still high unemployment, pay is often lower and other conditions may often be worse in the locally oriented sectors, including the public sector. Employment has become not only more precarious but more informal as well. Informalization has occurred in the international and non-international sectors, but primarily in self-employment in locally geared commerce and services, which have expanded as a percentage of urban jobs. Informal employment, however, is commonly more remunerative than, and otherwise preferred over, its formal counterpart. This reflects much less the significance of informal employment as a channel of accumulation than the declining conditions of formal employment (see Bromley 1994; Gilbert 1994). Itzigsohn emphasizes that as poverty has become deeper and more widespread in the Dominican Republic, economic restructuring is dissolving much of the boundary between its formal and informal economies.

Poverty is more crushing on the whole in Guatemala and the Dominican Republic than in any of the other national cases (ECLAC 1997, 23-26; UNDP 1995). The chapters by Itzigsohn and Pérez Sáinz indicate, though, some noteworthy differences between the two countries in their patterns of labor-market deterioration since the 1980s. To begin with, recent agrarian economic and social transformations have restrained migration from rural to urban areas in Guatemala, while, in conjunction with the urban bias of state policy in the Dominican Republic, they have done more to maintain that country's rural-urban flow. Open unemployment, moreover, seems to have remained much lower in Guatemala than in the Dominican Republic, while Guatemala's percentage of informal employment — which at the outset was probably the highest in the entire sample — may not have grown as fast. The composition of informal employment in Guatemala changed markedly, as there occurred a large drop in the percentage of self-employment but a roughly commensurate rise in the percentage of unpaid household workers (who even before such growth had represented a sizable group in cross-national perspective). In the meantime, a sharp rise in self-employment led the way in the Dominican Republic, although the rate of growth of unpaid household workers, who were a minute part of the labor force, may have been even faster. The steep increase in unpaid household workers in Guatemala and their appreciable increase in the Dominican Republic are a sign of the comparative economic backwardness and social polarization of these two countries.[12]

As in the Dominican Republic, local commerce was urban Guatemala's economic sector of most extensive informality, and, similar to the former country's thrust of informalization, it was probably Guatemala's sector of most intense growth of unpaid family labor. In apparent contrast to the Dominican Republic, however, is that subcontracting linkages with Guatemala City's expanding export-assembly firms seem to have led to unexpected gains in one indigenous community's prosperity in a nearby area. Pérez Sáinz stresses, nonetheless, that the top-down structure of subcontracting relations and the weakness of the community's economic leverage make such prosperity quite fragile. Like Itzigsohn in the case of the Dominican Republic, Pérez Sáinz remarks that the social organization of export-assembly production in Guatemala is among the factors that are blurring the line between the formal and informal economies.

Costa Rica, of course, entered the period of economic crisis and adjustment at a much higher baseline of employment and living standards than did the Dominican Republic and Guatemala (ECLAC 1995a; UNDP 1995). Assessments of how much and in what ways Costa Rica's standards may have fallen tend to vary according to the indicators analyzed and whether the final year of any data set falls within a short-term period of macroeconomic downturn or upturn. What is not contested is that, relative to the net loses suffered in most of Latin America over the last decade and a half, Costa Rica remains within the region's upper echelon by measures of employment and living standards (ECLAC 1997, 18-19, 23-26; UNDP 1995).

Among the lingering effects of Central American political and economic instability is some amount of regional labor migration to Costa Rica, mainly in low-wage jobs in agriculture, petty commerce, and construction. Yet, notwithstanding significant inequalities between its subnational zones, the comparative reach of Costa Rica's nationwide socioeconomic infrastructure and its labor-intensive surge in nontraditional agricultural and manufacturing exports, foreign tourism, and related activities continued to restrict both rural-urban migration and national unemployment. It seems that, after degenerating badly in 1981-1982, the urban labor market's overall conditions improved markedly until turning downward in the early 1990s, then improved considerably in 1993-1994 before encountering another downturn. Over this period, the impact of electoral cycles on Costa Rica's employment conditions appears significant.

A question is whether labor-market swings in the 1990s may be amounting to a long-term trend of erosion in socioeconomic conditions and departure from the country's post-Second World War, social-democratic regime as — in the post-Cold War age of slashed foreign aid and intensifying world-market competition — state leadership in a very small, peripheral economy becomes less capable of defending many workers and their families from the vicissitudes of global restructuring (see Díaz 1997). The political terms and development ramifications of Intel's major manufacturing investment may prove crucial in pushing change in one direction or another.

The watershed for Costa Rica's development model could be the onset of serious cutbacks in middle-class public sector jobs during the mid-1990s (Vega 1996). Tardanico and Lungo suggest that between 1980 and 1991 precarious employment grew as a percentage of total employment in every industry, including manufacturing, the site of fastest net job growth. Given that much of this deterioration may have encompassed middle-class occupations, the authors are less clear about how much of this growth took shape as informalization per se. According to their measures, informality was most extensive in non-public sector tertiary activities, but its net growth may have been fastest in manufacturing (see Itzigsohn 1996). The authors additionally report that, measured at other points in time, the relative weight of urban informal employment did not rise above that of the pre-crisis years, but that the gap in average earnings between formal and informal workers did widen. Even if the portion of informal employment remained unchanged or decreased, a question is whether the Costa Rican economy's capacity to generate formal jobs from the mid-1990s onward can compensate for the ongoing reduction in public sector jobs (see Díaz on Chile this volume, Chapter 6). Another question is whether standard measures have overlooked emerging dimensions of precarious employment. These could involve changes that are unfavorable to labor in, for example, arrangements of work authority, autonomy, and control; the intensity and hazards of work activity; the length and consistency of weekly job schedules; job tenure, earnings stability, and fringe benefits; and social-relational features of earnings inequality[13] (Bodson, Cordero, and Pérez Sáinz 1995; Bromley and Birkbeck 1989; Bulmer-Thomas 1996; Córdova 1996; Díaz 1997; Lawson 1990; Portes 1985; Walters 1996). Such dimensions of precariousness may have become significant within Costa Rica's post-Second World War institutional setting of strong state regulation of economy and society but weak — and, since the early 1980s, weakening — labor unions. As part of a larger contemporary state policy of labor flexibility, the weakness of Costa Rican labor unions may have restricted the incentive of firms to employ informal labor (but see Itzigsohn [1996] on informal subcontracted manufacturing and Gindling and Terrell [1995] on problems in the enforcement of minimum-wage regulation).

Fajardo Cortez and Lacabana report the intensification of a long-range worsening of labor-market conditions in Venezuela as its petro-political economy sprung massive structural leaks. The agricultural impact of such leaks contributed to an increase in rural-urban migration, which, however, remained less weighty than inter-urban population shifts, as employment growth was fastest in the outlying bands of Caracas's urban-regional agglomeration. Against this background, from the late 1980s to early 1990s, informal employment's percentage of the labor market hardly grew, and open unemployment, after leaping during the previous decade, fell back toward its pre-crisis level. The principal characteristic of labor-market deterioration, Fajardo Cortez and Lacabana argue, was a collapse in average real earnings and in other terms of formal and informal employment (see Lander 1996). Together with such deterioration came some change in the occupational composition of the informal economy, as its job growth apparently became fastest for employers. This pattern diverges from those in the Dominican Republic, Costa Rica, Argentina, and Mexico, where the share of self-employment rose, and from that in Guatemala, where the share of unpaid family labor rose. Nevertheless, Fajardo Cortez and Lacabana underscore the low-income workforce's back-and-forth fluidity between the statuses of employer and self-employed, a point that pertains to cross-national discussions of employment categories. The authors imply that stagnant manufacturing production and the tertiarization of the urban labor force reinforced commerce's position as the industry of most informalized employment. They make clear, in any event, that Venezuela's labor-market conditions have taken a distressing turn for the worse during the mid-1990s, including an acute upturn in unemployment (see ECLAC 1997, 18-19, 24, 26).

Chile's first round of restructuring, from the early 1970s to early 1980s, involved surges in unemployment and informal employment, along with a steep, more general decline in employment conditions and earnings. Between 1979 and 1981, it also involved the dismantling of the import-substitution systems of labor-market regulation and social security, as the Pinochet dictatorship emerged at Latin America's neoliberal forefront in exchanging labor protections for labor "flexibility" (see Collins and Lear 1995, Chapter 7). Chile and Argentina stand out among the case studies, then, for the early onset of dramatic decline in employment conditions and for the fact that this transpired under military dictatorship. Díaz emphasizes, however, that the Pinochet government stood apart in the early timing of its success in institutionalizing a comprehensive agenda of neoliberal labor policy. He writes that Chile may nonetheless have experienced Latin America's sharpest net drop in informal employment as a fraction of total employment since the regional economic recovery began in the late 1980s.

According to Díaz, four elements have reduced the proportional weight of informal employment in Chile. First, rapid economic growth and transformation have improved labor's chances of obtaining work in medium-sized and large firms or with contracts that include social security coverage (albeit under terms that are significantly less favorable than before the neoliberal reforms). Second, the privatized social security and health systems impose no charge on employers and thus give them no incentive to bypass the channels of employment legality. Third, the state's armature of labor flexibility has freed firms from the previous legal constraints on hiring and firing. And fourth, the machinery of the state has come to exercise a greater "formalizing" influence in Chile's economy than in most Latin American economies, based primarily on its effectiveness at fiscal regulation. As a result, firms have gained a financial incentive to operate formally, a practice that has extended organizationally to their employment practices as well. Reinforcing this practice has been some recouping of labor-union strength during the post-military transition.

Díaz stresses, though, that while unemployment has been low, informal employment either stable or shrinking, average real wages on a pronounced upswing, and poverty decreasing,[14] Chile's income distribution — second to Brazil's as Latin America's most skewed — has not become significantly more equitable. He also stresses that outside the ranks of those professional, technical, and skilled workers who occupy strategic market slots in the country's expanding and internationalizing economy, labor's sociopolitical leverage is dramatically weaker than before the Pinochet era. He argues that as many aspects of labor conditions in legally regulated, large-firm, and full-time jobs have been degraded, the formal/informal dichotomy and the standard measurement proxies for better/worse employment conditions have become quite unsatisfactory and even misleading as guides to the social structure of Chile's labor market (see Bodson, Cordero, and Pérez Sáinz 1995; Bromley and Birkbeck 1989; Scott 1996; Tilly 1996; Walters 1996). Yet Díaz is not about to jettison the concept of informal economy, pointing out that informal labor in Chile has regained some growth momentum in the 1990s. This signals that, under current politico-institutional and class arrangements and given near-term threats to the less competitive subsectors in agriculture and manufacturing, the economy has possibly reached its upper limit in the reformalization of employment.

In comparative perspective, what may be most salient about Argentina's labor market is that rapid per capita economic growth during the early 1990s did little or nothing to mitigate the country's swelling unemployment and precarious employment. Between 1980 and 1995, average real wages in Argentina contracted by some one-third, while during the mid-1990s, "hyperunemployment" has broken out. From 1991 to 1994 — when Argentina's average yearly growth in domestic product per capita was Latin America's highest — its rate of unemployment climbed as average real wages did no more than inch above their long-range depressed level. Unemployment then ballooned during the economic downswing of 1995-1996, and informal employment remains extensive as the domestic product has dropped and the Menem government has refused to back away from its neoliberal slashing (ECLAC 1997, 18-19, 23, 25; Ellison and O'Donnell 1996; LAWR 1996; SCR 1996a and 1996b).

It was Argentina's civilian government leadership that eventually turned the military dictatorship's nascent market-oriented reforms of the 1970s into Latin America's most radical version of neoliberalism. Under this policy campaign, fueling the country's surge in unemployment and degraded employment has been the elimination of public sector jobs, manufacturing's extreme lack of competitiveness relative to foreign produc-tion in the deregulated domestic market and in export markets and relative to the lure of financial speculation and investment in privatized services, and instability in the construction industry. Cortés indicates that as the population's mean level of education has continued to rise, neoliberal policies and economic restructuring are reinforcing a widened split between the occupational standing of the workforce's more and less educated strata. Good pay and conditions are attached increasingly to professional jobs in the advanced services, while decent formal-sector manual employment in Buenos Aires is becoming restricted to workers who have completed secondary schooling. Cortés remarks that in an intensely competitive, de-industrializing job market, the employability of low-educated adults is in rapid decline (see Gilbert 1994, 613-616; LAWR 1996).

According to Oliveira and García, the growth of precarious employ-ment in both the formal and informal economies has been the fulcrum of labor-market downgrading in urban Mexico, although, linked to the financial crisis of the mid-1990s, the country's unemployment has recently leaped well above its typically low reported rate. From 1980 to 1988, average real wages in Mexico dropped by more than one-third; from 1988 to 1994, steady recovery lifted them slightly above their 1980 level, until they plunged anew in 1995 (Chapter 1, Table 2; see ECLAC 1997, 18-19, 23, 26; Pánuco-Laguette and Székely 1996). Mexico's labor-market configurations unfolded as employment became more dispersed territorially and as labor emigration to and remittances from the United States remained a crucial part of economy, society, and politics. For the crisis years of 1982-1986, Oliveira and García note that nonwage employment was anchored in the subsis-tence activities of poor households, and most of all involved street vending and other tertiary initiatives by low-educated women in Mexico's central and southeastern cities, which generally were major sites of import-substitution manufacturing. The authors write that during the partial macroeconomic recovery of 1986-1992, the proportional growth of nonwage employment encompassed men, primarily in central and northern Mexico's cities of import-substitution manufacturing, as well as women, both in such central and northern cities and in cities on the Mexico-U.S. border. They report that, contrary to much of the theoretical literature, recovery-linked nonwage employment appears to have made no more than small inroads into manufacturing production. Thus, it appears not to have been a substantial force in that sector's reorganization, but instead to have been most important in economically marginal kinds of manufacturing production in small towns. In any case, for men but not women, pay in many cities is higher in nonwage than wage work, a pattern that holds both in the various categories of services and in manufacturing. While the authors do not report longitudinal data on this pattern, they surmise that it has been an aspect of male employment restructuring since the mid-1980s. Nevertheless, the degree of overall growth in nonwage jobs that they document may be less than commonly assumed. This would imply that income losses and other components of employment downgrading were more significant than the growth of informal jobs per se in Mexico's labor-market realignments over the last decade and a half.

Summing up, the chapters stress that urban labor-market conditions have indeed become more insecure, although, without losing grasp of the problems of data reliability and comparability, the degree of change seems more accentuated in some countries than others. The extent to which the broad trend involves heightened open unemployment and/or informalization seems quite variable.[15] Open unemployment skyrocketed in Argentina in the mid-1990s, while also bloating to high levels in Venezuela and Mexico, and it reportedly remained very high in the Dominican Republic as well.[16] This problem calls attention to the cross-national roles of nontraditional export production, the informal economy, and migration in dampening or failing to dampen rises in unemployment (Cerrutti 1997; Gilbert 1994; Humphrey 1994; Portes 1989; Roberts 1996; Sklair 1993; Tiano 1987). The labor markets of two of the small economies, Guatemala and the Dominican Republic, appear to have remained the most informalized. Informal employment's growth as a share of the labor market, however, may have been greatest in Argentina, where such employment, as well as unemployment, had been minimal at the outset. At the other end of the spectrum, both open unemployment and informal employment appear to have shrunk most in Chile. Yet, in the setting of Chile's energetic and generalized income growth, the labor-market insecurities of the Pinochet era persisted as the income distribution remained comparatively unequal and the post-military governments failed to restore labor protections. Very small Costa Rica — with its mixture of neoliberal deregulation, extensive foreign aid, substantial macroeconomic recovery, and notable continuities with pre-crisis social (if not labor) protections — stands out for having minimized the deterioration of employment conditions at large and maintained comparative income equity. Hence, the case of Costa Rica raises questions concerning the consequences of degrees of labor and social protection for the balance between domestic economic competitiveness and social welfare under globalization (see Freeman 1994; ILO 1996; Marshall 1994; Stewart 1995), as well as for the politics of citizenship and democratization (see Mesa-Lago 1995; Portes, Dore-Cabral, and Landolt 1997; Roberts 1995 and 1996; Smith, Acuña, and Gamarra 1994a and 1994b). Across national cases, the composition of employment seems to have remained better in manufacturing than in non-public sector tertiary activities on the whole, but the former's advantage would seem to have eroded. The same relational trend is evidently true of labor-market conditions in the formal versus the informal economy. In this regard, a common theme of the chapters is that the division between the two sectors has become more ambiguous and that, as conditions of formal employment have profoundly declined, the terms of informal employment have become more preferable for an expanded portion of the workforce.

To reiterate, research needs to clarify the cyclical versus transformative aspects of such patterns. It likewise needs to clarify the political, economic, sociocultural, and spatial circumstances in which the informal sector's activities become conjoined with the formal sector production of goods and services, mitigate increases in unemployment, and become more than subsistence redoubts.

In any event, not to be lost in this volume's details is the apparent finding that as important or more important than the expansion of informal employment has been the worsening of formal sector employment conditions. Hence, the insights derived from the concept of informality should not detract attention from the most fundamental problem: a redefinition of the social and political relations of labor, which, for the lower and middle classes, has made earning a living more tenuous in legally regulated as well as unregulated employment.

Gender Recomposition

To what extent have gender realignments been a feature of the comparative labor-market pattern of sectoral changes and reconfigured and widened inequalities? This volume most basically predicted an accelerated increase in women's portion of the officially measured urban labor force, above all in the lower skilled, more unstable, legally unregulated, and lower paid jobs that are attached mainly to the tertiary economy but also to export-assembly manufacturing. The sources of such change are likely to vary from the secular (such as developments in technology, progress in women's rights and educational attainment, decreases in fertility, shifts in the structure of households, intensified consumerism) to the cyclical (such as economic fluctuations, short-range consequences of state policies) (Benería and Feldman 1993; Elson 1995; Menjívar Larín and Pérez Sáinz 1993; Safa 1995; Standing and Tokman 1991; Tiano 1994; K. Ward 1990; *World Development* 1995).

The feminization of labor forces began long before the economic downturn of the 1980s. The chapters tend not to address the question of whether the velocity of this secular trend accelerated, remained the same, or decelerated during the 1980s and beyond. They say no more than the very minimum about the gendered reorganization of households as a social force in labor-market change or, with the principal exception of Oliveira and García's chapter on Mexico, about change in the demographic traits of female workers. The data are more detailed about changes in the composition of women's and men's employment and their significance for gendered inequality.

In the Dominican Republic, the rate of labor-force participation rose for women but fell for men during the 1960s and 1970s, which was the trend for Latin America in general. For the 1980s, Itzigsohn documents a continued upswing in the female rate while, at a much flatter pace, the male rate turned upward anew. He also documents that the most rapid growth in the participation rate was among the population situated between middle adolescence and middle age, as was clearest in the case of females, whose rate contracted for those 45 and older. The net result was a vigorous, continued feminization of the labor force, together with, especially for women, a steeper tilt toward the age-bracket extending from middle adolescence to young adulthood.

Yet feminization appears to have been more extensive in the labor force per se than in employment. That is, most of the decade's female entrants into the Dominican Republic's labor force were officially classified as unemployed, as women's reported rate of open unemployment leaped above men's. Hence, unemployment became considerably more feminized and more inclined to first-time job seekers (see Sklair [1993, 169-180] and Tiano [1987 and 1994] for comparison with northern Mexico). As part of the population's severe impoverishment during the 1980s and 1990s, this apparent trend reflects a much stronger push of hardship than pull of opportunity in expanding the female labor force. It is, therefore, no surprise that the growth of female employment was concentrated at the low end of the occupational structure. The main questions concern the emerging patterns of employment differentiation and inequality among and between females and males.

Notwithstanding the Dominican Republic's boom in export-platform manufacturing during the 1980s, women's jobs grew more rapidly in low-end tertiary activities. Such growth seems to have been anchored in the informal economy, whose organization tends to be most compatible with the burden of women's intensified mix of intra- and extra-household responsibilities, and where women were not only wage workers and self-employed but may have become the owners of a disproportionate fraction of small firms. Women's percentage of jobs in export manufacturing indeed rose, apparently fastest in the low-wage stratum, where they continued to be the majority of workers. Nevertheless, as women took strides in the educational arena, there was an abrupt gain in their percentage of professional and technical jobs, which, alongside the possibly expanded female ownership of informal firms, is a sign of widened occupational divergence within the female workforce. Itzigsohn's data chart neither such trends for men's jobs nor possible changes in male/female earnings inequality. Thus, although women's measured rate of open unemployment became even higher than men's, it cannot be determined whether, for example, men's occupational composition became more dispersed as did women's, or whether the female/male earnings gap widened or shrank. According to Itzigsohn, however, "A high proportion of the labor force involved in informal activities is male and in its mature years... [who] choose to work in the informal economy because of its higher pay and/or better work conditions. This preference ... is connected to the declining formal sector wages and increasingly precarious formal sector labor conditions."

In Guatemala, as in the Dominican Republic, women were most responsible for the labor force's marked expansion. Pérez Sáinz remarks that during the 1980s women's rate of participation doubled, while men's rose modestly. Similar to the Dominican Republic, adolescents and young adults were the age groups that anchored the labor force's growth. As in the Dominican Republic, women's rate of open unemployment in Guatemala came to exceed men's, although the reported levels of female and male unemployment in Guatemala remained minuscule. Restricting attention to the urban economy, the feminization of employment was most intense in manufacturing, as export-assembly manufacturing took off, followed by commerce, where the urban economy's proliferating subsistence-oriented activities were most common.[17] The former trend occurred even as by the second half of the 1980s manufacturing surfaced as the industry of most rapid job growth for men as well as women.

Against this gendered industry background, Guatemalan change in the occupational composition of women's employment was dramatic: surges in the percentages of female jobs in the nonwage categories of self-employment and, particularly, unpaid family employment. Perhaps both components of this female surge, but certainly the latter one, were more extreme than in any other of the national cases. As in the Dominican Republic, then, these indicators of subsistence-based informalization underscore the role of hardship, rather than opportunity, in galvanizing the rapid growth of Guatemala's female labor force during the 1980s. Such indicators, however, were not restricted to women. While the percentage of men holding wage jobs increased marginally and that of self-employed men fell abruptly, the percentage of men working as unpaid family labor swelled. As of 1989, moreover, full-time male workers were more likely than full-time female workers to earn less than the legal minimum wage. Occupational complexity and inequality increased not just in the informal economy but also in the formal economy, as may be most apparent for women. Despite the bloating of employment at the lower layers of the occupational structure, some fraction of Guatemalan women reportedly parlayed educational achievement into technical and professional jobs. There is no evidence on whether and by how much gendered income inequality may have widened or narrowed at the various occupational rungs in the formal and informal economies.

Thus, urban female employment in Guatemala became more weighted toward manufacturing as well as informal and subsistence endeavors. Urban male employment become more tertiarized and slightly more formalized. Within the informal sphere, though, men's employment became decidedly more geared to subsistence activities. Remember that Guatemala's class structure has historically been among Latin America's most exploitive and polarized, and its laminations of backward, subsistence labor among the region's deepest. In both Guatemala and the Dominican Republic, economic hardship emerges as much more important than new economic opportunities in shaping gendered changes in the labor force. Much more needs to be found out, nonetheless, about the social and geographic correlates of the balance between hardship and opportunity in these and other national cases, and, as mediated by state, class, ethnicity, and age, the implications for possible changes in gendered paths of occupational mobility across industries and urban-regional localities and for gendered latitudes of action in households and communities (see, for example, Cerrutti 1997; Humphrey 1996; Jelin 1997; Menjívar Larín and Pérez Sáinz 1993; Portes, Dore, and Landolt 1997; Roberts 1996; Safa 1995; Wolf 1992).

In the Dominican Republic and Guatemala, net growth in the rate of labor-force participation from the early 1980s onward was much greater for women than men. In urban Costa Rica, such growth was restricted to women, as men's aggregate rate of participation decreased. Among urban Costa Rican women, moreover, such growth was not fastest among adolescents and young adults, as it seems to have been in the Dominican Republic and Guatemala; instead, it contracted among adolescents and was fastest among those over 40. For urban Costa Rican men, the net decrease in participation rates was most abrupt at the top and the bottom of the age spectrum, but, with the exception of the modest increase for 20- to 29-year-old men, was otherwise fairly even in age distribution. So, according to Tardanico and Lungo, feminization continued in Costa Rica, as it did in the two other small, peripheral economies, but it involved a pronounced aging of the female labor force along with a net drop in the male rate of participation (see Goldenberg 1993).

Evidence presented elsewhere (Tardanico 1996b) indicates that the fall in Costa Rican men's rate of participation was based on a sharp contraction for unskilled male workers, as measured by years of schooling, whose rate tumbled from the highest to the lowest among the skill strata of the male population. Skilled female workers led a generalized upswing among Costa Rican women and thus led expansion of the labor force as a whole. Without disentangling the influences of age and household dynamics, this evidence suggests a reorganization of employment inequalities between low-skilled and skilled men, between low-skilled and skilled women, and between low-skilled men and women. Low-skilled men, then, would seem to have been undergoing marginalization from the labor market. In contrast to the Dominican Republic and Guatemala, men's share of unemployment expanded in urban Costa Rica, although the rate of unemployment is highest among workers not with a maximum of primary schooling but with some secondary schooling (ECLAC 1995a, 184). Meanwhile, women's share of the labor market rose most in the lower tier but also considerably in the middle and upper tiers. Tardanico and Lungo document that the age and skill distributions of change in gender participation took shape as the average size of households fell somewhat, the portion of female-headed households increased, and the average number of labor-force members per household stayed the same. On balance, therefore, not more household members but more women — including, as in the

Dominican Republic and Guatemala, more women with technical and professional qualifications — entered the labor market. Particularly in view of the trend for unskilled men and the enduring strength of the Costa Rican state's programs of social welfare, this evidence points toward comparative research on cyclical and secular shifts in the gendered coping and mobility practices of households and their individual members (marriage/divorce, family structure, fertility, housing, schooling, income-earning, consumption, migration, decisionmaking), as mediated by characteristics of class, culture, territory, and state (see Benería and Feldman 1993; Cerrutti 1997; Chant 1991; Elson 1995; González de la Rocha 1994; Menjívar Larín and Pérez Sáinz 1993; Roberts 1995; Safa 1995; Tiano 1994; Wolf 1992).

Employment in urban Costa Rica's public and private sectors became more feminized, but female and male jobs alike grew faster in the private than public sector. Evidently the shift toward the private sector was most accentuated for unskilled and semiskilled women, who, along with unskilled men, underwent net job loss in the public sector. The consequent degree of loss or gain in job conditions for such women, as well as men, is uncertain. At the least, however, the pattern signifies that the deemphasis on public sector employment was sharpest for women in middle and lower tier occupations. Urban Costa Rica's social distribution of job contraction in the public sector raises comparative questions about the gender, occupational, class, and territorial impacts of technological innovation and task subcontracting in the privatization of employment.

Recall that employment became more oriented to the tertiary sector for men and women in the urban Dominican Republic and for men but not women in urban Guatemala. In urban Costa Rica, neither female nor male employment shifted in this direction, as for both groups manufacturing was the industry of most rapid job growth. This was especially so for women, as linked to Costa Rica's leap in export-assembly production, manufacturing surpassed commerce and almost caught services as the industry with the highest intrasectoral percentage of female workers. Of comparative interest is the finding that the percentage of urban Costa Rica's labor force employed in manufacturing rose for females and males of all age groups except teenagers, among whom employment instead became more common in commerce and, on a much smaller scale, agriculture. Tardanico and Lungo surmise that this finding implies age-graded shifts on both the demand and supply sides of the labor market, given the spread of international-style commercial activities and consumerism, and perhaps the arrival of poor Central American migrants and the increased prevalence of mixing part-time schooling with employment.

Consistent with both the Dominican Republic and Guatemala, employment change in Costa Rica left women with an enlarged share of precarious and informal jobs. Yet such change left Costa Rican women with an enlarged share of formal and better-paid jobs as well, a trend whose extent of correspondence with the other two cases is uncertain. The Costa Rican data indicate that for men and women hardship was crucial to the labor market's gender realignments. They also suggest that, particularly for women, opportunity was more important in Costa Rica than in the Dominican Republic and Guatemala. In urban Costa Rica, women's average earnings gains were greatest in manufacturing and in wage and self-employment; men's average earnings losses were greatest in commerce and construction and among employers. The gender gap in average earnings did not widen but narrowed, due more to men's losses than to women's gains, while labor-market inequalities on balance appear to have widened both among women and among men.

With regard to the larger economies, change in Venezuela coincides with the cross-national trajectory of labor-force feminization described so far, based on a striking five-year upswing in the participation rate of women as that of men remained constant. According to Fajardo Cortez and Lacabana, the growth rate of female labor-force participants over the brief period of 1987-1992 was highest for older women: an astounding 150 percent for those over 56, diminishing to a still considerable 30 percent for 15- to 44-year-olds. As noted earlier, the predominant changes in Venezuela's labor market were a collapse in average earnings in the formal and informal economies, tertiarization, minimal informalization together with some increase in employers as a portion of informal occupations, and other aspects of aggravated insecurity. As export-assembly manufacturing production and employment did not grow appreciably, women's jobs became more concentrated in tertiary activities — seemingly to a greater extent than in the smaller economies. In fact, women's rate of tertiarization in Venezuela was double that of men. The extent of national change in the gender balance of employment in the urban formal and informal economies is not apparent. In the low-income districts of Caracas surveyed by the authors, however, it appears that the informal sector absorbed most of the new middle-aged and older female workers (who still represented a very small portion of the labor force). Fajardo Cortez and Lacabana conclude that, according to their scaled measure of precarious employment, women workers in these districts shouldered a disproportionate brunt of the labor market's deterioration. This has been so, they claim, not only in the informal economy but to a greater extent in the formal economy.

Chile represents yet another example of pronounced growth in the female share of the labor force. Díaz explains that such growth has been strongest since the mid-1980s, as the economy's recovery and transformation have accelerated. On a scale comparable to Venezuela's, women's employment in Chile is overwhelmingly located in commerce and services. In this regard, women's percentage of jobs has risen significantly since the mid-1970s in every industry except manufacturing. This distribution of female job growth is associated with the marginal position of light manufacturing (such as garment production) in Chile's economic upturn. Díaz points out that since the 1980s women's fraction of employment has increased in garment, food, and agroindustrial manufacturing — the latter being part of the natural-resource based production that is a vital cog in national prosperity. Nevertheless, the surviving import-substitution era production that accounts for an enlarged portion of the country's manufacturing employment remains dominated by male labor. Hence, particularly since the economy took off in the 1980s, urban employment in Chile has become more inclined to tertiary activities for women but not men. Finally, as unemployment has plunged, reformalization has been extensive for female and male workers, and as average real wages have climbed, the gender gap in earnings has shrunk. Of cross-national interest is that this gap is narrowest at the bottom rungs of the employment ladder: among the least educated, the self-employed, and the informally employed. Pertinent to the social underpinnings of Chile's ongoing political transition and debates is that — as with the country's still comparatively unequal distribution of income at large — this gender structure of inequality is part of a socioeconomic grid involving vigorous, generalized income growth, rather than, as in most of the countries, income decline.

Argentina's labor market has undergone massive privatization and deindustrialization, rapid tertiarization and informalization, skidding average pay, and ballooning unemployment. Profound deterioration in employment conditions and living standards has been the fundamental cause of a steep upswing in the long-term rise in women's percentage of the workforce. Cortés writes that Argentine men have tended to experience the most sectoral and occupational displacement. For instance, as public sector employment has sharply contracted in size and average pay, its fraction of female workers has markedly grown, as has occurred in modern services in general. Yet women have been proportionately more likely than men to lose jobs in manufacturing, as the contraction of female jobs in craft industries has not been offset by job expansion in export-platform production. Meanwhile, men's job growth has been faster than women's in commerce. This matrix of job loss and growth in Argentina raises comparative questions about gendered industry, occupational, and task patterns of employment change under economic crisis and restructuring (see Cerrutti 1997; Humphrey 1996; Rubery 1988). As the fraction of wage work grew in the tertiary economy but plunged in manufacturing, a striking aspect of Argentina's plight is the seeming feminization of formal employment versus masculinization of informal employment. This divergence goes against the expectations derived from much of the literature on gender and restructuring. An obvious reason for this unexpected finding is the acute worsening of the conditions of formal employment, which, as discussed often in this volume, commonly makes informal employment more preferable (see Ellison 1996).

In Mexico, the secular growth of women's portion of the workforce intensified under economic crisis and structural adjustment as the rate of participation grew faster for females than males. Oliveira and García state that during the crisis of 1982-1986, the size and composition of the female workforce changed with the addition of disproportionate numbers of low educated, middle-aged and older women who often were married and had children. The participation of younger, single, and better educated women — who headed the pre-crisis growth of the female workforce — increased as well. According to Oliveira and García, this demographic pattern stabilized during the economy's partial recuperation of 1986-1992, coming to encompass Monterrey, northern Mexico's major city of heavy industry, where previous gains in women's participation had been minimal.

The percentage of public sector employment in Mexico had entered into abrupt decline in the late 1980s but had yet to fall below its pre-crisis peak. Further, the percentage of jobs in import-substitution manufacturing drastically shrunk, as the surviving firms underwent technological and organizational renovation, while export manufacturing continued to grow, diversify, and spread across the northern frontier and into the national interior. Such restructuring caused tertiary employment to expand as a share of the labor market, based on the growth of low-wage, locally oriented activities and of modern services, whose jobs span from the upper to lower ends of the occupational structure. The period's tertiarization of urban jobs in Mexico was steeper for men than women. With reference to the group of relatively large economies in the sample, this trend in Mexico contrasts with that in Chile, where men have predominated in the vigorous recent growth of manufacturing employment; in Argentina, where women have been disproportionately dislodged from manufacturing jobs; and in Venezuela, where the heavy manufacturing of state-linked import-substitution production and the weakness of export-assembly industry have provided few jobs for a swelling female workforce.

During the crisis of the early to mid-1980s, the male shift into commerce and services was greatest in the country's urban anchors of import-substitution manufacturing, such as Mexico City, Monterrey, and Guadalajara. Men's shift into commerce and services endured even as the economy underwent some recovery between the mid-1980s and early 1990s. Nonetheless, the proportion of male workers in manufacturing did increase in northern border cities and in two northern subborder cities of expanding export output. This reported increase was dramatic in the small border city of Nuevo Laredo. As for women, the economy's improvement brought about some decrease in the percentage of them employed in manufacturing. The decrease was steep in Tijuana and Ciudad Juárez, the principal cities of export-assembly manufacturing, and in central and southeastern cities as diverse as Guadalajara and Mérida. As with men, however, the share of women with manufacturing jobs reportedly soared in Nuevo Laredo and the northern subborder city of Tampico (Roberts and Tardanico 1997).

Oliveira and García observe that the appreciable growth of nonwage employment caused by economic contraction was led by 20- to 49-year-old women with little schooling, although more educated women and both single and married women also accounted for an expanded segment of nonwage jobs. This female-led growth focused on tertiary subsistence employment, such as street vending, and was most pervasive in the cities of central and southeastern Mexico, the focal points of import-substitution manufacturing. Growth remained faster for nonwage than wage jobs during the subsequent economic upturn, with nonwage employment continuing to be largely confined to low-skill, low-paid commerce and service activities and to be no more than marginally involved in manufacturing production. The principal difference during the years of upturn was the addition of men as a sizable portion of nonwage labor, particularly in the cities of central Mexico and the northern industrial city of Monterrey. At the same time, women's nonwage employment extended its geographic momentum from central Mexico to the northern border cities.

Again considering this set of larger national economies, the gender balance of labor informalization in urban Mexico may have been initially similar to the seemingly smaller-scale, female-centered process in Venezuela but may have eventually diverged in that men appear to have entered the informal economy in more significant proportion in Mexico. The case of Mexico contrasts with Chile, where employment for women and men has become reformalized during the phase of economic upswing. It also seems to contrast with Argentina, where employment has reportedly become more formalized to some degree for women but more informalized for men (see Humphrey 1996 on Brazil).

The comparative evidence on gender points to yet another mix of commonalities and divergencies. The feminization of labor forces continued in every instance, but with apparent short- and long-range differences in the gendered balance of hardship and opportunity, the pace of female and male labor-force growth, and the age composition of the new female entrants. For example, considering the cases for which the authors present pertinent data, the new female entrants were evidently younger in the Dominican Republic and Guatemala than in Costa Rica, Venezuela, and Mexico. This pattern would seem to correlate more youthful composition with more pronounced economic underdevelopment and poverty, including flimsier or nonexistent state programs of social protection. Moreover, employment tertiarization under economic crisis and structural adjustment does not appear to have been always stronger for women than men. It reportedly involved only men in Guatemala, faster growth for men than women in urban Mexico, and neither women nor men in urban Costa Rica. The emerging balance between export-assembly and import-substitution manufacturing would seem to be a reason for such variation, since the former is geared to female and the latter to male workers. Within export-assembly manufacturing, the emerging balance between labor- and technology-intensive production and between manual and non-manual occupations may be relevant as well, since female shares of employment appear highest in the most exploitive activities and jobs. In the Dominican Republic, however, the percentage of not only male but also female workers in manufacturing reportedly diminished in spite of flourishing export-assembly production. Sparse data on gender and public sector employment address no more than the cases of Costa Rica and Argentina. They indicate that under austerity and privatization policies that were far more stringent in Argentina, women's share of public sector jobs rose in both countries. The data for Costa Rica show that the only public sector workers to undergo net job contraction, as opposed to merely slowed growth relative to the private sector, were unskilled and semiskilled women and unskilled men. The expansion of government employment during the mid-twentieth century was essential in upgrading labor conditions, especially for women, and in the political and social construction of citizenship. Thus, the topic of gender in the privatization, reduction, and reorganization of public sector employment merits comparative attention.

Concerning gendered change in precarious and informal employment, the most general shifts appear to have been increased differentiation and inequality among men and among women, together with reduced male/female inequality based more on men's losses than women's gains (see ILO 1995 on wages). The chapters nonetheless suggest significant complexity and variation, as epitomized by divergent labor-market patterns attached to painful economic downswings in Guatemala and Argentina versus the pattern attached to a strong upswing in Chile. As unemployment in Guatemala rose yet remained low, its labor market seems to have become much more informalized for women but slightly more formalized for men, with informal employment for women and men becoming characterized by a distressing surge in unpaid family labor. As unemployment soared in Argentina, its labor market seems to have become somewhat more formalized for women but much more informalized for men, based mainly on expanded male self-employment in commerce. Unemployment dropped sharply in Chile, where average real wages climbed for men and women — especially the latter — while employment became substantially more formalized for both groups. For these and the other cases, research needs to advance comparative knowledge about the gendered interconnections of labor markets and households; their overlap with social and cultural transformations of class, ethnicity, community, and territory; and their consequences for the politics of restructuring.

Territorial Redistribution

The final set of anticipated changes pertains to the sociospatial organization of employment. It was hypothesized that such organization has become more decentralized — that is, more inclusive of provincial urban and regional zones at the relative expense of the dominant, metropolitan zones, whose hegemony was consolidated during the era of state-centered, import-substitution development. This decentralizing process would unfold in the contexts of economic globalization and the Latin American debt crisis, as grafted upon the import-substitution era's geographic extension of economic infrastructure and urban population. Along with the transnational and national deregulation of markets and labor, these trends not only intensify economic competition among firms, nations, and subnational localities. They also boost the attractiveness of provincial urban and regional zones in some branches of manufacturing and services on the basis of modernized infrastructure and an ample supply of cheap yet adequately skilled labor. Reinforcing this trend would be the national-regional impact of new global configurations of agriculture and tourism, which make provincial cities more important as sources of services and handicraft products. These various shifts augment local demand in the provinces for the gamut of everyday goods and services as well. The transnationalization of communities, expanded foreign markets for handicraft products, and narcotrafficking are among the complementary reasons for the predicted territorial deconcentration of some sectors of production and employment, even as the most strategic advanced services become more concentrated territorially at the national, international-regional, and world levels (Arrighi 1996; Dicken 1992; Gereffi 1995; Kyle 1995; Palat 1996; Portes 1989; Roberts 1995; Sassen 1994; Spener 1996).

It is predicted, therefore, that Latin America's labor markets have undergone spatial decentralization. The main components of the trend would be the growth of export-oriented manufacturing and the geographic redistribution in commerce and services that accompanies the provincial expansion of nontraditional agricultural exports and tourism, together with new geographic profiles of migration and remittance. It is expected that such decentralizing arrangements foster greater interurban heterogeneity in occupational and class patterns and that, inasmuch as the decentralizing activities tend to employ women, they foster the gender recomposition of urban labor markets as well.

Employment indeed became more dispersed geographically in the Dominican Republic, where export-processing zones and international tourism burgeoned in the vicinity of the secondary cities of Santiago de los Caballeros, La Romana, and San Pedro de Macorís. Itzigsohn emphasizes, though, that decentralized growth has not incorporated the more backward economic areas that were situated at the margins of the interurban structure of the import-substitution era. Thus, these areas are now situated at the margins of the internationalized economy. Further, internationalized economic dispersion has not challenged the economic and demographic primacy of Santo Domingo but merely eroded its share of national employment and population. Neither have export-processing zones and tourism fostered any significant degree of national territorial equity in economic capacity and living standards, which would have occurred through the emergence of transformative local linkages in the provinces as a catalyst to their economic and social development. The new and expanded activities have, in fact, created spin-off local jobs. Such jobs, however, are of the low-skill, low-wage, casual, and informal variety and are primarily for female labor-force entrants. Moreover, the jobs are geared to fulfilling the demand by export-processing and tourism workers — a large percentage of whom are women and who themselves are generally low-skilled, low-wage labor — for cheap goods and services. Internationalized, decentralized economic growth has therefore reinforced the Dominican Republic's fabric of territorial and social inequality.

By comparison, Costa Rica's boom in foreign tourism seems to have created more geographically widespread and socially equitable employment (see Céspedes and Jiménez 1995, 96-114; Morley 1995, 185-188). With some qualification, nonetheless, in neither Costa Rica nor Guatemala has foreign tourism or export-platform manufacturing notably diminished the urban labor-market primacy of the dominant metropolitan zone.

Despite its comparative success in fomenting national job growth, tourism in Costa Rica appears to have reinforced the relative advantages of Greater San José. It did so, according to Tardanico and Lungo, because the international airport and the major tourism services are located in the greater metropolitan area. Against the backdrop of export- and tourism-based prosperity since the economic crisis, a notable amount of geographic deconcentration of urban employment has occurred in Costa Rica. It has primarily occurred, however, not outside but within the territorial confines of Greater San José's expanding regional agglomeration and is most pronounced by far in export-assembly manufacturing and for women (see Pérez Sáinz 1994 and 1996). Otherwise, the locational focus of government administration, economic infrastructure, capital, and markets in Greater San José has ensured that it absorb most of the country's expanded urban employment.

Much the same pattern has characterized Guatemala, as shaped by the vast infrastructural gulf between Guatemala City and the rest of the nation and by the presence of widespread and intense political violence in the countryside. Coffee and cotton exports do seem to have fostered some instances of more significant, service-based provincial urbanization of employment than in Costa Rica. This process, however, has not altered the labor-market dominance of Guatemala City, which itself has spread across a wider regional agglomeration (Portes, Itzigsohn, and Dore-Cabral 1994, 16-17). In this setting, subcontracted export-assembly production and employment have extended to the outskirts of this agglomeration, where the labor pool is large, cheap, and docile. In the instance of the indigenous town of San Pedro Sacatepéquez, subcontracted production appears to have resulted in a surprising degree of local prosperity, which, as previously discussed, underlines the mediating role of local sociocultural arrangements in molding diverse geographic outcomes of globalization. Pérez Sáinz stresses, though, that the town's economy remains highly vulnerable to the whims of decisions made in Guatemala City and the wider world and thus that its apparent gains are far from secure.

Within the array of larger economies, Venezuela ranks toward the low end in degree of employment concentration in the leading metropolitan area. Fajardo Cortez and Lacabana document that Caracas's portion of nationwide employment has declined. Such decline has been relative not to the cities of the interior — whose own economies have also been stymied by the depressed prices of petroleum and other minerals, manufacturing's lack of international competitiveness, and fiscal shortfalls — but to the growing fringes of the principal metropolis. The movement of economic activities, employment, and population to such outer zones has been a consequence of the diseconomies of massive urban scale, as Alejandro

Portes (1989) detects for Latin America at large and as is evident in the cases discussed here (see also Gilbert 1990 and Roberts 1995). In effect, then, Venezuela's economic woes, as sandwiched around a brief and highly uneven recuperative burst, have not lessened the strategic economic and labor-market position of metropolitan Caracas in the national interurban system. More needs to be learned about comparative change in the characteristics of labor markets and social inequality in Venezuela's metropolitan core, its adjacent areas, and the more distant intermediate and smaller cities during a time of economic distress and reorganization.

In regard to the sharply contrasting economy of Chile, Díaz finds that export-led, transformative prosperity has reinforced the already considerable economic and employment hegemony of metropolitan Santiago. Such hegemony is grounded in finance and other services, whose advanced sectors have become dynamic performers in Chile. Santiago's economy and population have experienced their own dispersion into a wider metropolitan agglomeration as a result of not only diseconomies of massive urban scale but also the proximity of economic activities, such as the wine industry, that are integral to the export boom and whose national service inputs originate in the capital city. Bolstering Santiago's national dominance is Chile's transition from interurban economic and employment growth during the mid- to late 1980s to an abrupt shake-out of urban winners and losers during the 1990s. This transition reflects increased local exposure to the opportunities and risks of internationalization, which Díaz recognizes as "precisely the emerging contour of the Chilean labor market as a whole."

Among the large economies, Argentina ranks toward Chile at the upper end, and, notwithstanding the immensity of Mexico City, Mexico ranks toward Venezuela at the lower end in the concentration of national urban population in the principal metropolitan zone (UNDP 1995, 184-185). In Argentina, Greater Buenos Aires maintained its high level of hegemony over the country as a whole while, as part of a long-range trend, losing in share of population, and presumably employment, to secondary cities such as Córdoba and Rosario. As Cortés writes, it is unlikely, given both the heightened importance of internationalized finance and other advanced services in Argentina and the impact of fiscal crisis in the country's urban areas in general, that Buenos Aires's national position has eroded as an economic and labor-market center for strategic activities of finance, coordination, and control. Meanwhile, Buenos Aires represents a long-standing example of economic and employment dispersion to a wider metropolitan agglomeration.

The national decentralization of urban employment has proceeded most rapidly in Mexico. This pattern did not originate in, but rather has been accelerated by, economic crisis and subsequent policies of restructuring. Oliveira and García observe, of course, that crisis and restructuring have slashed Mexico's volume of employment in import-substitution manufacturing, which was greatest in the cities of central Mexico and the northern city of Monterrey, thereby boosting the relative weight of more feminized, export manufacturing along the northern border and increasingly in the interior. They explain that across most of the country's urban nodes, employment became considerably more inclined to commerce and services even during the economy's subsequent upturn, especially for men, whose percentage in tertiary jobs converged upward toward women's. Yet territorial decentralization has not been a uniform outcome of economic transnationalization and neoliberal policies in Mexico. Indeed, its gross domestic product has become no less anchored in Mexico City, the administrative and financial center of not only nationalism in the past but transnationalism in the present (Garza and Rivera 1994; see Sassen 1994 and P. Ward 1990). Apparently, however, other forms of territorial decentralization in Mexico have been among Latin America's most pronounced. Among them are export manufacturing; export primary-commodity production; foreign tourism; government and government-sponsored service activities, such as higher education; Mexico-U.S. border-market agglomerations; routes of national and international migration; and urban-regional economic differentiation. Oliveira and García thus depict an accelerated geographic dispersion and specialization of Mexico's urban labor markets and a recasting of their interlocational inequalities, within a setting of U.S.-oriented, globalized production complexes (see Garza and Rivera 1994; Heredia 1996; Roberts and Tardanico 1997; Shaiken 1990; Sklair 1993; Spener 1996; P. Ward 1990).

As with the other sets of hypotheses, comparative data on urban-territorial change suggest appreciable differences in national employment patterns. Centrifugal forces are indeed at play in every country examined, calling for research on the sectoral and occupational array of continuities and discontinuities with the import-substitution decades. Such forces have reinforced the longer-term transformation of metropolitan labor markets — perhaps especially the dominant ones — into regional agglomerations, while fomenting infrastructural and skill advancement, functional redefinition and specialization, and rapid growth in many smaller cities. Among these cases, though, it seems that only in Mexico have the forces substantially lessened the national labor-market primacy of the dominant metropolitan agglomeration (see Angotti 1995; Portes 1989; Roberts 1995). An intersecting topic, change in the sociospatial organization of employment within urban areas, which has consequences for the interplay of social inequality, political mobilization, and the built environment, has not been explored in this volume (Angotti 1995; Hays-Mitchell 1995; Jelin 1997; Portes 1989; Portes, Dore, and Landolt 1997; Roberts 1995; Sassen 1994; P. Ward 1990). In any event, tentative findings on territorial change coincide with the comparative Latin American perspectives elaborated by such scholars as Alan Gilbert, Alejandro Portes, and Bryan Roberts, who direct attention to contemporary local relations with world-market transformations, as filtered through national matrices of state, society, and geography (Gilbert 1990; Portes 1989; Portes, Itzigsohn, and Dore-Cabral 1994; Roberts 1995).

Conclusion

G lobal restructuring appears to be taking a diversity of local paths with respect to urban employment and social inequality in Latin America. There apparently is not even uniformity in terms of the broadest domestic institutional and geo-economic influences on better or worse national urban conditions. For instance, military-authoritarian government and extreme distance from the United States became attached to booming employment and average earnings in Chile but to bloated underemployment in Argentina, albeit with the commonality of widened gaps between rich and poor. Conversely, electoral democracy and proximity to the United States became attached to significant labor-market recovery and comparative equity in Costa Rica but to deteriorating labor markets and swelling poverty in the Dominican Republic and Venezuela. Increasingly, no national, subnational, industrial, occupational, or gendered case of relative prosperity is immune to the vagaries of globalization and deregulation. It would seem more difficult than ever for social groups or locations seriously lagging in state protections and subsidies, infrastructure, technology, and skill to do more than minimize their socioeconomic losses relative to the emerging new global order.[18]

These tentative conclusions are frankly pessimistic. There is, nonetheless, some room for optimism, most fundamentally in the notorious inability of social scientists to predict the future of societal transformations and in the potential connections of restructuring to innovative, progressive social and political initiatives at the local, national, and transnational levels. As conceptualized within a burgeoning literature, such initiatives run a gamut of emerging approaches that sometimes embrace, sometimes reject, and sometimes simply attempt to cope with the geographically variable consequences of globalization and market-oriented policies (Arrighi 1996; Brecher and Costello 1994; Bresser Pereira, Maravall, and Przeworski 1994; Godio 1993; Grosfoguel 1996; ILO 1996; Jelin 1997; Mittelman 1996). This volume's findings underscore the apparent restrictions and tenuousness of social inclusion in even the most prosperous of contempory Latin America's national, subnational, and sectoral economies. The contributors would, therefore, concur with a premise that tends to unite the otherwise disparate theoreticians and practitioners of the new initiatives: that essential to their viability is the establishment of effective alternatives to the neoliberal discourse that disconnects state from economy, economy from employment, and employment from community.

Notes

1.   We thank Marcela Cerrutti, Bryan Roberts, and David Spener for their help along the way. The chapter's deficiencies are our responsibility alone.

2.   Concerning our sets of hypotheses, see Chapter 1, note 14, for pertinent Latin American national data as conceptualized and collected by PREALC (Programa Regional del Empleo para América Latina y el Caribe).

3.   It was noted in Chapter 1 that the expansion of jobs in internationalized activities as a share of total urban employment could have been hypothesized not only in manufacturing but in tertiary activities as well. It was also noted, however, that pertinent data are scarce. And, of course, a nationwide focus, as opposed to an urban focus, would have extended the hypothesis to agricultural employment.

4.   Itzigsohn's data do not include workers in state-owned enterprises (see Castro 1996). Our comparative data on the state sector are inconsistent in coverage.

5.   Acuña and Smith (1995) report that Brazil, Argentina, and Chile account for virtually all of Latin America's capacity in arms production. They write that "Argentina and Chile ... have the capacity to manufacture and export relatively unsophisticated 'niche' weapons systems," while "Brazil ... is a 'full-service' arms producer manufacturing 'mid-tech' ground, sea, and air combat systems of relatively greater quality and capability ..." (130). On this topic from the vantage point of urban-regional development in the United States during and after the Cold War, see Markusen (1992).

6.   Recall that cutbacks in civilian public sector employment in Argentina actually began under the military dictatorships of 1976-1983.

7.   Mexico's armed forces remain comparatively weak in terms of number of personnel, share of the government's budget, and political influence. During the mid-1990s, however, their budget and influence — including what some analysts describe as the militarization of key sectors of law enforcement — have increased precipitously due to rebellions in the country's southern periphery, the government's campaign against narcotraffickers, and rising street crime (Snow 1996; see Aguilera Peralta 1994 and Kincaid and Gamarra 1996).

8.   Our discussion focuses, of course, on trends in employment composition rather than production composition.

9.   Weeks (1996, 280-282) reports that Chilean manufacturing's share of total national exports ranks just sixth in Latin America — behind Brazil, Mexico, Argentina, Colombia, and Venezuela — even as the share has doubled since the mid-1970s. Weeks emphasizes, moreover, that Chilean manufacturing has not become significantly more geared to capital-goods production, a fundamental point of economic vulnerability.

10. Nonetheless, exemplifying Argentina's deindustrialization is the automotive industry — a prime beneficiary of state protections — whose imports have risen from 10 percent of inputs in the 1970s to 40 percent in the 1990s (LASR 1996, 7).

11. Of course, technological and organizational innovations may minimize job growth or eliminate jobs in manufacturing sectors that are attempting to become more competitive in foreign markets.

12. The fact that, unlike the data for most of the other countries, the Guatemalan data do not distinguish the urban and rural labor markets may be of some relevance to this comparative finding. The percentage of unpaid family employment may have increased marginally over its pre-crisis level in Costa Rica as of 1991, but it had decreased as of 1993-1994; it reportedly increased more substantially over its pre-crisis level in Argentina as of the early 1990s. Elsewhere, it seems to have either decreased or remained unchanged.

13. The latter includes the sociopolitical ramifications, for class, gender, intra-household, and community relations, of the period's decrease in average real earnings relative to the official minimum wage, which rose in real terms. This trend seems to have involved real earnings losses among professional/managerial, technical, and skilled workers relative to those workers who continued to earn the legal minimum wage. Likewise important are the sociopolitical ramifications of the possibility that, while the above trend may have fostered a more equal distribution of earnings within a wide swath of the labor force, in the context of investment and other such earnings, it may have involved a widened gap between the uppermost tier of the class structure and the other tiers (see Bulmer-Thomas 1996; ECLAC 1997, 19, 23, 25; Gindling and Terrell 1995). Two important questions concern, first, the degree to which the gendered and age-graded initiatives of households may have mitigated this apparent change in occupational earnings inequality and, second, the degree to which the apparent change persisted into the mid-1990s (see Bodson, Cordero, and Pérez Sáinz 1995; Céspedes and Jiménez 1995; Vega 1996).

14. As of 1996, average real wages in Chile were about 35 percent higher than in 1980 (Chapter 1, Table 2). Urban poverty fell from 39 percent of households in 1987 to 24 percent in 1994 (ECLAC 1997, 19, 23; see Scott 1996).

15. As is apparent in the chapters and in the divergences between ECLAC and PREALC data, both the inherent ambiguities of the concept "informal employment" and the diverse approaches to measuring it pose frustrating obstacles to comparative analysis. The same can be said for unemployment. See Walters (1996) on the political economy of changing discourse on unemployment and its interrelations with the growing prevalence of "non-standard" employment in advanced national economies.

16. ECLAC detects a tendency toward "inelasticity in unemployment in relation to GDP," which it characterizes as "one of the causes of the unequal distribution of the benefits of growth" (LAWR 1997, 9; see Walters 1996).

17. Nationwide, the fastest rate of feminization of Guatemalan industries during the 1980s was reportedly in agriculture.

18. Exceptional cases such as those documented by David Kyle (1995) in Ecuador and Juan Pablo Pérez Sáinz (this volume and 1994) in Guatemala — which are linked to varieties of both local sociocultural underpinnings and extralocal relations — should not be exaggerated from the standpoints of local capital

accumulation and employment upgrading, as neither author does. Further, it is unclear that such exceptions impart policy lessons that other localities could hope to replicate, aside from the notion that the development initiatives of grassroots and non-governmental organizations, governments, and multilateral agencies should strive to cultivate local-regional grids of socioeconomic linkage and equity. And even if there is some potential for the replication of such heretofore exceptional conditions on a wider scale, it is probable that doing so would render diminishing returns to the gamut of provincial social groups and localities competing against each other over, for example, remittances derived from immigrant petty business and employment in the United States and earnings derived from subcontracting relations with export-assembly firms and foreign-oriented handicraft distributors. Restrictive immigration policies in the United States, foreign market protectionism, and various technological, organizational, and locational innovations in the manufacturing of consumer products intensify intra-Latin American competition by reducing regional access to such transborder sources of local accumulation (see Bromley 1994; Itzigsohn 1995; Kyle 1995; Pérez Sáinz and Menjívar Larín 1991; Roberts 1995; Spener 1996).

References

Acuña, Carlos H. 1994. "Politics and Economics in the Argentina of the Nineties (Or, Why the Future No Longer Is What It Used to Be)." In *Democracy, Markets, and Structural Reform in Latin America*, eds.William C. Smith, Carlos H. Acuña, and Eduardo A. Gamarra. Coral Gables, Fla.: North-South Center at the University of Miami.

Acuña, Carlos H., and William C. Smith. 1994. "The Political Economy of Structural Adjustment: The Logic of Support and Opposition to Neoliberal Reform." In *Latin American Political Economy in the Age of Neoliberal Reform*, eds. William C. Smith, Carlos H. Acuña, and Eduardo A. Gamarra. Coral Gables, Fla.: North-South Center at the University of Miami.

Acuña, Carlos H., and William C. Smith. 1995. "The Politics of 'Military Economics' in the Southern Cone: Comparative Perspectives on Democracy and Arms Production in Argentina, Brazil, and Chile." *Political Power and Social Theory* 9:121-157.

Aguilera Peralta, Gabriel. 1994. *Seguridad, función militar y democracia*. Guatemala: FLACSO/Fundación Freidrich Ebert.

Aitken, Rob, Nikki Craske, Gareth A. Jones, and David E. Stansfield, eds. 1996. *Dismantling the Mexican State?* New York: St. Martin's Press.

Amsden, Alice H., and Rolph van der Hoeven. 1996. "Manufacturing Output, Employment and Real Wages in the 1980s: Labour's Loss Until the Century's End." *Journal of Development Studies* 32(4):506-530.

Angotti, Thomas. 1995. "The Latin American Metropolis and the Growth of Inequality." *NACLA Report on the Americas* 28(4):13-18, 37.

Arrighi, Giovanni. 1994. *The Long Twentieth Century: Money, Power and the Origins of Our Times*. London: Verso.

Arrighi, Giovanni. 1996. "Workers of the World at Century's End." *Review: Fernand Braudel Center* 19(3):335-351.

Artana, Daniel, Oscar Libonatti, Cynthia Moskovits, and Mario Salinardi. 1995. "Argentina." In *Fiscal Decentralization in Latin America*, ed. Ricardo López Murphy. Washington, D.C.: Inter-American Development Bank.

Benería, Lourdes, and Feldman, Shelley, eds. 1993. *Unequal Burden: Economic Crisis, Poverty, and Women's Work*. Boulder, Colo.: Westview Press.

Benería, Lourdes, and Martha Roldán. 1987. *The Crossroads of Class and Gender: Industrial Homework, Subcontracting, and Household Dynamics in Mexico City*. Chicago: University of Chicago Press.

Betances, Emilio. 1995. *State and Society in the Dominican Republic*. Boulder, Colo.: Westview Press.

Bodson, Paul, Allen Cordero, and Juan Pablo Pérez Sáinz. 1995. *Las nuevas caras del empleo*. San José, Costa Rica: FLACSO.

Boris, Eileen, and Elisabeth Prugl, eds. 1996. *Homeworkers in Global Perspective: Invisible No More.* New York: Routledge.

Brecher, Jeremy, and Tim Costello. 1994. *Global Village or Global Pillage: Economic restructuring from the Bottom Up.* Boston: South End Press.

Bresser Pereira, Luiz, José María Maravall, and Adam Przeworski. 1994. "Economic Reforms in New Democracies: A Social-Democratic Approach." In *Latin American Political Economy in the Age of Neoliberal Reform,* eds.William C. Smith, Carlos H. Acuña, and Eduardo A. Gamarra. Coral Gables, Fla.: North-South Center at the University of Miami.

Bromley, Ray. 1994. "Informality, de Soto Style: From Concept to Policy." In *Contrapunto: The Informal Sector Debate in Latin America,* ed. Cathy A. Rakowski. Albany: State University of New York Press.

Bromley, Ray, and Chris Birkbeck. 1989. "Urban Economy and Employment." In *The Geography of the Third World,* ed. Michael Pacione. London: Routledge.

Bulmer-Thomas, Victor, ed. 1996. *The New Economic Model in Latin America and Its Impact on Income Distribution and Poverty.* New York: St. Martin's Press.

Burggraaff, Winfield J., and Richard L. Millett. 1995. "More than Failed Coups: The Crisis in Venezuelan Civil-Military Relations." In *Lessons of the Venezuelan Experience,* eds. Louis W. Goodman, Johanna Mendelson Forman, Moisés Naim, Joseph S. Tulchin, and Gary Bland. Washington, D.C.: The Woodrow Wilson Center Press; Baltimore: Johns Hopkins University Press.

CACR (*Caribbean & Central American Report*). 1996a. "Dominican Republic: Balaguer-Bosch Alliance Triumphs." July 25:6. London.

CACR. 1996b. "Dominican Republic: Fernández Proposes Clean-up and Sell-off." November 7:4-5. London.

Canitrot, Adolfo. 1994. "Crisis and Transformation of the Argentine State (1978-1992)." In *Democracy, Markets, and Structural Reform in Latin America,* eds. William C. Smith, Carlos H. Acuña, and Eduardo A. Gamarra. Coral Gables, Fla.: North-South Center at the University of Miami.

Castro, Max. 1996. "The Long Transition: Dilemmas of Democracy and Development." *North-South Focus: Dominican Republic* 5(2). Coral Gables, Fla.: North-South Center at the University of Miami.

Centeno, Miguel Angel. 1994. *Democracy within Reason: Technocratic Revolution in Mexico.* University Park: Pennsylvania State University Press.

CEPAL (Comisión Económica para América Latina y el Caribe). 1995. "Balance preliminar de la economía de América Latina y el Caribe." *Notas sobre la economía y el desarrollo,* no. 585/586 (December). Santiago, Chile.

Cerrutti, Marcela. 1997. "Coping with Opposing Pressures: A Comparative Analysis of Women's Intermittent Employment in Buenos Aires and Mexico City." Unpublished doctoral dissertation, Department of Sociology, University of Texas at Austin.

Céspedes, Víctor Hugo, and Ronulfo Jiménez . 1995. *Apertura comercial y mercado laboral en Costa Rica.* San José, Costa Rica: Academia de Centroamérica y Centro Internacional para el Desarrollo Económico.

Chant, Sylvia. 1991. *Women and Survival in Mexican Cities: Perspectives on Gender, Labour and Low-Income Households.* Manchester: Manchester University Press.

Collins, Joseph, and John Lear. 1995. *Chile's Free-Market Miracle: A Second Look.* Oakland, Calif.: Food First.

Córdova, Efrén. 1996. "The Challenge of Flexibility in Latin America." *Comparative Labor Law Review* 17(2):314-337.

Díaz, Alvaro. 1997. "New Developments in Social and Economic Restructuring in Latin America." In *Politics, Social Change, and Economic Restructuring in Latin America,* eds. William C. Smith and Roberto Patricio Korzeniewicz. Coral Gables, Fla.: North-South Center Press at the University of Miami.

Dicken, Peter. 1992. *Global Shift.* New York: The Guilford Press.

ECLAC (Economic Commission for Latin America and the Caribbean). 1988. *Economic Survey of Latin America and the Caribbean 1988.* Santiago, Chile: ECLAC.

ECLAC. 1995a. *Social Panorama of Latin America 1995.* Santiago, Chile: ECLAC.

ECLAC. 1995b. *Economic Survey of Latin America and the Caribbean 1994-95.* Santiago, Chile: ECLAC.

ECLAC. 1996. *Economic Survey of Latin America and the Caribbean 1995-96.* Santiago, Chile: ECLAC.

ECLAC. 1997. *Indicadores Económicos.* Santiago, Chile: ECLAC.

EIU (Economic Intelligence Unit). 1996. *Country Report: Costa Rica, Panama.* Quarterly. London: EIU.

Ellison, Katherine. 1996. "Latin Economies Leaner, Also Meaner." *The Miami Herald.* September 15:1A, 18A.

Ellison, Katherine, and Santiago O'Donnell. 1996. "Workers Bring Argentina to Standstill." *The Miami Herald.* August 9:17A.

Elson, Diane, ed. 1995. *Male Bias in the Development Process,* 2nd ed. Manchester: Manchester University Press.

Erfani, Julie A. 1995. *The Paradox of the Mexican State: Rereading Sovereignty from Independence to NAFTA.* Boulder, Colo.: Lynne Rienner Publishers.

Evans, Peter B. 1995. *Embedded Autonomy: States and Industrial Transformations.* Princeton, N.J.: Princeton University Press.

Ferreira, Francisco, and Julie Litchfield. 1996. "Inequality and Poverty in the Lost Decade: Brazilian Income Distribution in the 1980s." In *The New Economic Model in Latin America and Its Impact on Income Distribution and Poverty,* ed. Victor Bulmer-Thomas. New York: St. Martin's Press.

FitzGerald, E.V.K. 1996. "The New Trade Regime, Macroeconomic Behaviour and Income Distribution in Latin America." In *The New Economic Model in Latin America and Its Impact on Income Distribution and Poverty,* ed. Victor Bulmer-Thomas. New York: St. Martin's.

Freeman, Richard B., ed. 1994. *Working under Different Rules.* New York: Russell Sage.

Garza, Gustavo, and Salvador Rivera. 1994. *Dinámica macroeconómica de las ciudades en México.* Mexico, D.F.: Instituto de Investigaciones Sociales de la Universidad Nacional Autónoma de México e Instituto Nacional de Estadística, Geografía e Informática, Serie Monografías Censales de México.

Gereffi, Gary. 1995. "Global Production Systems and Third World Development." In *Global Change, Regional Response: The International Context of Development,* ed. Barbara Stallings. Cambridge: Cambridge University Press.

Gereffi, Gary, and Miguel Korzeniewicz, eds. 1994. *Commodity Chains and Global Capitalism.* Westport, Conn.: Praeger.

Gilbert, Alan. 1990. "Urbanization at the Periphery: Reflections on Changing Dynamics of Housing and Employment in Latin American Cities." In *Economic Growth and Urbanization in Development Areas,* ed. D.W. Drakakis-Smith. London: Routledge.

Gilbert, Alan. 1994. "Third World Cities: Poverty, Employment, Gender Roles and the Environment during a Time of Restructuring." *Urban Studies* 31(4-5):605-633.

Gindling, T.H., and Katherine Terrell. 1995. "The Nature of Minimum Wages and Their Effectiveness as a Wage Floor in Costa Rica, 1976-91." *World Development* 23(8):1439-1458.

Godio, Julio. 1993. *Los sindicatos en las economías de mercado en América Latina.* Bogotá: Fundación Friedrich Ebert de Colombia.

Goldenberg, Olga. 1993. "Género e informalidad en San José." In *Ni héroes ni villanas: género e informalidad urbana en Centroamérica,* eds. Rafael Menjívar Larín and Juan Pablo Pérez Sáinz. San José, Costa Rica: FLACSO.

González de la Rocha, Mercedes. 1994. *The Resources of Poverty: Women and Survival in a Mexican City.* Cambridge, Mass.: Blackwell.

Grosfoguel, Ramón. 1996. "From *Cepalismo* to Neoliberalism: A World-Systems Approach to Conceptual Shifts in Latin America." *Review: Fernand Braudel Center* 19(2):131-154.

Hays-Mitchell, Maureen. 1993. "The Ties that Bind. Informal and Formal Sector Linkages in Street-Vending: The Case of Peru's *Ambulantes.*" *Environment and Planning A* 25:1085-1102.

Hays-Mitchell, Maureen. 1995. "Voices and Vision from the Streets: Gender Interests and Political Participation Among Women Informal Traders in Latin America." *Environment and Planning D: Society and Space* 13(4):445-469.

Heredia, Blanca. 1994. "Making Economic Reform Politically Viable: The Mexican Experience." In *Democracy, Markets, and Structural Reform in Latin America: Argentina, Bolivia, Brazil, and Mexico,* eds. William C. Smith, Carlos H. Acuña, and Eduardo A. Gamarra. Coral Gables, Fla.: North-South Center at the University of Miami.

Heredia, Carlos. 1996. "Downward Mobility: Mexican Workers after NAFTA." *NACLA Report on the Americas* 30(3):34-40, 43.

Humphrey, John. 1994. "Are the Unemployed Part of the Urban Poverty Problem in Latin America?" *Journal of Latin American Studies* 26(3):713-736.

Humphrey, John. 1996. "Responses to Recession and Restructuring: Employment Trends in the São Paulo Metropolitan Region, 1979-1987." *Journal of Development Studies* 33(1):40-62.

Infante, Ricardo, and Emilio Klein. 1991. "The Latin American Labour Market, 1950-1990." *Cepal Review* 45 (December):121-135.

Inforpress Centroamericana. 1995-1996. Guatemala.

ILO (International Labor Office). 1991. "Políticas de empleo en la reestructuración económica en América Latina y el Caribe." Geneva.

ILO. 1995. "Women Earn Less than Men in Comparable Jobs." *ILO Focus* (Fall). Washington, D.C.

ILO. 1996. *World Employment 1996/97: National Policies in a Global Context.* Geneva.

International Labour Review. 1995. Issue on Employment Policy in the Global Economy. 134(4-5).

Itzigsohn, José. 1995. "Migrant Remittances, Labor Markets, and Household Strategies: A Comparative Analysis of Low-Income Household Strategies in the Caribbean Basin." *Social Forces* 74(2):633-655.

Itzigsohn, José. 1996. "Globalization, the State, and the Informal Economy: The Articulations of Informal and Formal Economic Activities and the Limits to Proletarianization in the Periphery." In *Latin America in the World-Economy*, eds. Roberto Patricio Korzeniewicz and William C. Smith. Westport, Conn.: Praeger.

Jelin, Elizabeth. 1997. "Emergent Citizenship or Exclusion? Social Movements and Non-Governmental Organizations in the 1990s." In *Politics, Social Change, and Economic Restructuring in Latin America*, eds. William C. Smith and Roberto Patricio Korzeniewicz. Coral Gables, Fla.: North-South Center Press at the University of Miami.

Johnson, Tim. 1996. "Latin Trade Unions Losing Power as Economic Changes Continue." *The Miami Herald.* September 15:18A.

Karl, Terry. 1995. "The Venezuelan Petro-State and the Crisis of 'Its' Democracy." In *Venezuelan Democracy under Stress*, eds. Jennifer McCoy, Andrés Serbín, Willliam C. Smith, and Andrés Stamouli. Coral Gables, Fla.: North-South Center Press at the University of Miami.

Kincaid, A. Douglas, and Eduardo A. Gamarra. 1996. "Disorderly Democracy: Redefining Public Security in Latin America." In *Latin America in the World Economy*, eds. Roberto Patricio Korzeniewicz and William C. Smith. Westport, Conn.: Praeger.

Korzeniewicz, Roberto Patricio, and William C. Smith, eds. 1996. *Latin America in the World- Economy.* Westport, Conn.: Praeger.

Kyle, David J. 1995. "The Transnational Peasant: The Social Construction of International Economic Migration and Transcommunities from the Ecuadoran Andes." Unpublished Ph.D.dissertation, Department of Sociology, The Johns Hopkins University.

Lander, Edgardo. 1996. "The Impact of Neoliberal Adjustment in Venezuela, 1989-1993." *Latin American Perspectives* 23(3):50-73.

LASR (*Latin American Special Reports*). 1996. "Latin America Industry: Coping with Open Markets." June. London.

LAWR (*Latin American Weekly Reports*). 1996. "Argentina: More than 6m Lack Adequate Jobs." December 18:586. London.

LAWR. 1997. "Back to (Very) Modest Growth." January 1:8-9. London.

Lavinas, Lena, and María Regina Nabuco. 1995. "Economic Crisis and Tertiarization in Brazil's Metropolitan Labour Market." *International Journal of Urban and Regional Research* 19(3):358-368.

Lawson, Victoria. 1990. "Workforce Fragmentation in Latin America and Its Empirical Manifestations in Ecuador." *World Development* 18(5):641-657.

Lawson, Victoria. 1995. "Beyond the Firm: Restructuring Gender Divisions in Quito's Garment Industry under Austerity." *Environment and Planning D: Society and Space* 13(4):415-444.

Levine, Daniel H., and Brian F. Crisp. 1995. "Legitimacy, Governability, and Reform in Venezuela." In *Lessons of the Venezuelan Experience*, eds. Louis W. Goodman, Johanna Mendelson Forman, Moíses Naim, Joseph S. Tulchin, and Gary Bland. Washington, D.C.: The Woodrow Wilson Center Press; Baltimore: Johns Hopkins University Press.

Lewis, Paul. 1996. "Venezuela Gets Big I.M.F. Credit, Backing Market Reforms." *The New York Times*. June 13:3.

Maingot, Anthony P., ed. 1991. *Small Country Development and International Labor Flows*. Boulder, Colo.: Westview Press.

Manzetti, Luigi. 1995. "Argentina: Market Reforms and Old-Style Politics." *North-South Focus: Argentina* 4(3). Coral Gables, Fla.: North-South Center at the University of Miami.

Markusen, Ann R. 1992. *Dismantling the Cold War Economy*. New York: Basic Books.

Marshall, Adriana. 1994. "Economic Consequences of Labour Protection Regimes in Latin America." *International Labour Review* 133(1):55-73.

McMichael, Philip, ed. 1994. *The Global Restructuring of Agro-Food Systems*. Ithaca, N.Y.: Cornell University Press.

Menjívar Larín, Rafael, and Juan Pablo Pérez Sáinz, eds. 1993. *Ni héroes ni villanas: género e informalidad urbana en Centroamérica*. San José, Costa Rica: FLACSO.

Mesa-Lago, Carmelo. 1994. *Changing Social Security in Latin America: Toward Alleviating the Social Costs of Economic Reform*. Boulder, Colo.: Lynne Rienner Publishers.

Mesa-Lago, Carmelo. 1995. *Alternative Models of Development in Latin America: Market, Socialist, and Mixed Approaches*. Unpublished manuscript, Department of Economics, University of Pittsburgh.

Middlebrook, Kevin J. 1995. *The Paradox of Revolution: Labor, the State, and Authoritarianism in Mexico*. Baltimore: Johns Hopkins University Press.

Mittelman, James H., ed. 1996. *Globalization: Critical Reflections*. Boulder, Colo.: Lynne Rienner Publishers.

Morley, Samuel A. 1995. *Poverty and Inequality in Latin America: The Impact of Adjustment and Recovery in the 1980s*. Baltimore: Johns Hopkins University Press.

Morris, Stephen D. 1995. *Political Reformism in Mexico*. Boulder, Colo.: Lynne Rienner Publishers.

Naim, Moisés. 1995. "Economic Liberalization and Political Stability: The Venezuelan Experience." In *Privatization amidst Poverty: Contemporary Challenges in Latin American Political Economy*, ed. Jorge A. Lawton. Coral Gables, Fla.: North-South Center Press at the University of Miami.

Naim, Moisés, and Antonio Francés. 1995. "The Venezuelan Private sector: From Courting the State to Courting the Market." In *Lessons of the Venezuelan*

Experience, eds. Louis W. Goodman, Johanna Mendelson Forman, Moíses Naim, Joseph S. Tulchin, and Gary Bland. Washington, D.C.: The Woodrow Wilson Center Press; Baltimore: Johns Hopkins University Press.

Nelson, Joan M., ed. 1990. *Economic Crisis and Policy Choice: The Politics of Adjustment in the Third World*. Princeton, N.J.: Princeton University Press.

Paige, Jeffery M. 1987. "Coffee and Politics in Central America." In *Crises in the Caribbean Basin*, ed. Richard Tardanico. Newbury Park, Calif.: Sage Publications.

Palat, Ravi Arvind. 1996. "Fragmented Visions: Excavating the Future of Area Studies in a Post-American World." *Review: Fernand Braudel Center* 19(3):269-315.

Panorama Centroamericano: Reporte Político. 1995. "Avances del proceso de privatización en Centroamérica." No.109:1-3. Guatemala.

Pánuco-Laguette, Humberto, and Miguel Székely. 1996. "Income Distribution and Poverty in Mexico." In *The New Economic Model in Latin America and Its Impact on Income Distribution and Poverty*, ed. Victor Bulmer-Thomas. New York: St. Martin's Press.

Pérez Sáinz, Juan Pablo, ed. 1994. *Globalización y fuerza laboral en Centroamérica*. San José, Costa Rica: FLACSO.

Pérez Sáinz, Juan Pablo. 1996. *De la finca a la maquila*. San José, Costa Rica: FLACSO.

Pérez Sáinz, Juan Pablo, and Rafael Menjívar Larín, eds. 1991. *Informalidad urbana en Centroamérica: Entre la acumulación y la subsistencia*. Caracas: FLACSO/Nueva Sociedad.

Portes, Alejandro. 1985. "Latin America's Class Structures: Their Composition and Change during the Last Decades." *Latin American Research Review* 20(3):7-39.

Portes, Alejandro. 1989. "Urbanization during the Years of the Crisis." *Latin American Research Review* 24(3):7-44.

Portes, Alejandro, Manuel Castells, and Lauren A. Benton, eds. 1989. *The Informal Economy: Studies in Advanced and Less Developed Countries*. Baltimore: Johns Hopkins University Press.

Portes, Alejandro, Carlos Dore, and Patricia Landolt, eds. 1997. *Caribbean Cities on the Threshold of a New Century*. Baltimore: Johns Hopkins University Press.

Portes, Alejandro, José Itzigsohn, and Carlos Dore-Cabral. 1994. "Urbanization in the Caribbean Basin: Social Change during the Years of the Crisis." *Latin American Research Review* 29(2):3-37.

Roberts, Bryan. 1995. *The Making of Citizens: Cities of Peasants Revisited*. London: Arnold.

Roberts, Bryan. 1996. "The Social Context of Citizenship in Latin America." *International Journal of Urban and Regional Research* 20(1):38-65.

Roberts, Bryan, and Richard Tardanico. 1997. "Employment Transformations in U.S. and Mexican Gulf Cities." *LACC Occasional Paper Series*. Miami: Latin American and Caribbean Center, Florida International University.

Rovira Mas, Jorge. 1987. *Costa Rica en los años 80*. San José, Costa Rica: Editorial Porvenir.

Rubery, Cheryl, ed. 1988. *Women and Recession*. London: Routledge.

Safa, Helen I. 1995. "Economic Restructuring and Gender Subordination." *Latin American Perspectives* 22(2):32-50.

Sassen, Saskia. 1994. *Cities in a World Economy.* Thousand Oaks, Calif.: Pine Forge Press.

Sassen, Saskia. 1996. *Loss of Control? Sovereignty in an Age of Globalization.* New York: Columbia University Press.

Sayer, Andrew, and Richard Walker. 1992. *The New Social Economy: Reworking the Division of Labor.* Oxford: Blackwell.

Schoepfle, Gregory K., and Jorge F. Pérez-López, eds. 1993. *Work Without Protections: Case Studies of the Informal Sector in Developing Countries.* Washington, D.C.: U.S. Department of Labor, Bureau of International Labor Affairs.

Scott, Christopher. 1996. "The Distributive Impact of the New Economic Model in Chile." In *The New Economic Model in Latin America and Its Impact on Income Distribution and Poverty,* ed. Victor Bulmer-Thomas. New York: St. Martin's Press.

SCR (*Southern Cone Report*). 1996a. "How Argentina's Economy Has Changed." July 4:4-5. London.

SCR. 1996b. "Argentina's New Labour Squeeze." October 17:4-5. London.

SCR. 1996c. "New Look at Military Balance: US Study Shows Up Argentina-Chile Contrast." November 21:5. London.

Shaiken, Harley. 1990. *Mexico and the Global Economy: High Technology and Work Organization in Export Industries.* La Jolla, Calif.: Center for U.S.-Mexican Studies, University of California at San Diego.

Sklair, Leslie. 1993. *Assembling for Development: The Maquila Industry in Mexico and the United States.* La Jolla, Calif.: Center for U.S.-Mexican Studies, University of California at San Diego.

Smith, William C., Carlos H. Acuña, and Eduardo A. Gamarra, eds. 1994a. *Latin American Political Economy in the Age of Neoliberal Reform.* Coral Gables, Fla.: North-South Center at the University of Miami.

Smith, William C., Carlos H. Acuña, and Eduardo A. Gamarra, eds. 1994b. *Democracy, Markets, and Structural Reform in Latin America.* Coral Gables, Fla.: North-South Center at the University of Miami.

Snow, Anita. 1996. "Ejército gana influencia en la sociedad mexicana." *El Nuevo Herald.* October 16:1B-2B. Miami.

Spener, David. 1996. "Small Firms, Commodity Chains, and Free Trade: The Transformation of the Texas-Mexico Border Region." In *Latin America in the World-Economy,* eds. Roberto Patricio Korzeniewicz and William C. Smith. Westport, Conn.: Praeger.

Standing, Guy, and Victor E. Tokman, eds. 1991. *Towards Social Adjustment: Labour Market Issues in Structural Adjustment.* Geneva: International Labour Organization.

Stewart, Frances. 1995. *Adjustment and Poverty: Options and Choices.* New York: Routledge.

Tardanico, Richard. 1996a. "From Crisis to Restructuring: The Nexus of Global and National Change in the Costa Rican Labor Market." *Review: Fernand Braudel Center* 19(2):155-196.

Tardanico, Richard. 1996b. "Restructuring, Employment, and Gender: The Case of San José, Costa Rica." *Studies in Comparative International Development* 31(3):85-122.

Thomas, Jim. 1996. "The New Economic Model and Labor Markets in Latin America." In *The New Economic Model in Latin America and Its Impact on Income Distribution and Poverty*, ed. Victor Bulmer-Thomas. New York: St. Martin's Press.

Tiano, Susan. 1987. "Women's Work and Unemployment in Northern Mexico." In *Women on the U.S.-Mexican Border: Responses to Change*, eds. Vicki Ruíz and Susan Tiano. Boston: Allen and Unwin.

Tiano, Susan. 1994. *Patriarchy on the Line: Labor, Gender, and Ideology in the Mexican Maquila Industry*. Philadelphia: Temple University Press.

Tilly, Chris. 1996. *Half a Job: Bad and Good Part-time Jobs in a Changing Labor Market*. Philadelphia: Temple University Press.

Tilly, Chris, and Charles Tilly. 1994. "Capitalist Work and Labor Markets." In *The Handbook of Economic Sociology*, eds. Neil J. Smelser and Richard Swedberg. Princeton, N.J.: Princeton University Press; New York: Russell Sage Foundation.

Trudeau, Robert H. 1993. *Guatemalan Politics: The Popular Struggle for Democracy*. Boulder, Colo.: Lynne Rienner Publishers.

UNDP (United Nations Development Program). 1995. *Human Development Report 1995*. New York: Oxford University Press.

Vega, Mylena. 1996. "La clase media costarricense." *La Nación*. May 8 (electronic version). San José, Costa Rica.

Velasco, Andrés. 1994. "The State and Economic Policy: Chile 1952-92." In *The Chilean Economy: Policy Lessons and Challenges*, eds., Barry P. Bosworth, Rudiger Dornbusch, and Raúl Labán. Washington, D.C.: The Brookings Institution.

Vergara, Pilar. 1994. "Market Economy, Social Welfare, and Democratic Consolidation in Chile." In *Democracy, Markets, and Structural Reform in Latin America*, eds. William C. Smith, Carlos H. Acuña, and Eduardo A. Gamarra. Coral Gables, Fla.: North-South Center at the University of Miami.

Wallerstein, Immanuel. 1979. *The Capitalist World-Economy*. Cambridge: Cambridge University Press.

Wallerstein, Immanuel. 1995. *After Liberalism*. New York: The New Press.

Walters, William. 1996. "The Demise of Unemployment?" *Politics & Society* 24(3):197-219.

Walton, John, and David Seddon. 1994. *Free Markets and Food Riots*. Oxford: Blackwell.

Ward, Kathryn B., ed. 1990. *Women Workers and Global Restructuring*. Ithaca, N.Y.: ILR Press.

Ward, Peter M. 1990. *Mexico City: The Production and Reproduction of an Urban Environment*. Boston: G.K. Hall.

Weeks, John, ed. 1995. *Structural Adjustment and the Agricultural Sector in Latin America and the Caribbean*. New York: St. Martin's Press.

Weeks, John. 1996. "The Manufacturing Sector in Latin America and the New Economic Model." In *The New Economic Model in Latin America and Its Impact on Income Distribution and Poverty*, ed. Victor Bulmer-Thomas. New York: St. Martin's Press.

Weiss, John. 1996. "Economic Policy Reform in Mexico: The Liberalism Experiment." In *Dismantling the Mexican State?*, eds. Rob Aitken, Nikki Craske, Gareth A. Jones, and David E. Stansfield. New York: St. Martin's Press.

Wilson, Patricia A. 1992. *Exports and Local Development: Mexico's New Maquiladoras*. Austin: University of Texas Press.

Wilson, Patricia A. 1995. "Embracing Locality in Local Economic Development." *Urban Studies* 32(4-5):645-658.

Wolf, Diane L. 1992. *Factory Daughters: Gender, Household Dynamics, and Rural Industrialization in Java*. Berkeley: University of California Press.

World Development. 1995. Issue on gender, adjustment, and macroeconomics. 23(11).

Yañez, José, and Leonardo Letelier. 1995. "Chile." In *Fiscal Decentralization in Latin America*, ed. Ricardo López Murphy. Washington, D.C.: Inter-American Development Bank.

Index